T0323481

# FINANCIALIZATIONS OF DEVELOPMENT

*Financializations of Development* brings together cutting-edge perspectives on socio-political, socio-historical and institutional analyses of the evolving multiple and intertwined financialization processes of developmental institutions, programs and policies.

In recent years, the development landscape has seen a radical transformation in the partaking actors, which have moved beyond just multilateral or bilateral public development banks and aid agencies. The issue of financing for sustainable development is now at the top of the agenda for multilateral development actors. Increasingly, development institutions aim to include private actors and to lever in private money to support development projects. Drawing on case studies conducted in Africa, Asia, Europe and Latin America, this book examines the ways in which these private finance actors are enrolled and associated with the conception and implementation of development policies. Beginning with a focus on global actors and private foundations, this book considers the ways in which development funding is raised, managed and distributed, as well as debates at the center of global forums where financialized policies and solutions for development are conceived or discussed. The book assembles empirical research on development programs and demonstrates the social consequences of the financializations of development to the people on the ground.

Highlighting the plurality of processes and outcomes of modern-day relations, tools, actors and practices in financing development around the world, this book is key reading for advanced students, researchers and practitioners in all areas of finance, development and sustainability.

**Ève Chiapello** is Professor (Directrice d'Études) at EHESS (School for the Advanced Studies in Social Sciences), Paris, where she holds a chair on "the sociology of the transformations of capitalism". Her present work is about the financialization of public policies, on which she has organized a series of international conferences with the University of Hamburg financed by the Anneliese Maier Research Award received in 2016 from the Alexander von Humboldt Foundation. She is a member of CEMS (Centre d'Étude des Mouvements Sociaux – EHESS/CNRS-UMR 8044-INSERM U1276).

**Anita Engels** is Professor of Sociology at the University of Hamburg. She has spent the past two decades working on climate change and social change, and has published extensively on the creation and dynamics of carbon markets, both in the European Union and in China. Her most recent work focuses on companies and their carbon management strategies, and on real-world laboratories. She is in the board of the Cluster of Excellence Climate, Climatic Change, and Society (CLICCS) at the University of Hamburg, Germany.

**Eduardo Gonçalves Gresse** is a Postdoctoral Researcher at the Cluster of Excellence CLICCS at the University of Hamburg, Germany. In his PhD (Sociology), he investigated the sense-making and the social engagement of non-state actors with the 2030 Agenda in Brazil. He is currently a co-editor of the Hamburg Climate Futures Outlook, an annual publication that introduces a new, interdisciplinary methodology to assess the plausibility of climate futures. His research interests include Sustainable Development Governance, Climate Futures and Brazilian studies.

# Routledge Explorations in Development Studies

This Development Studies series features innovative and original research at the regional and global scale. It promotes interdisciplinary scholarly works drawing on a wide spectrum of subject areas, in particular politics, health, economics, rural and urban studies, sociology, environment, anthropology, and conflict studies.

Topics of particular interest are globalization; emerging powers; children and youth; cities; education; media and communication; technology development; and climate change.

In terms of theory and method, rather than basing itself on any orthodoxy, the series draws broadly on the tool kit of the social sciences in general, emphasizing comparison, the analysis of the structure and processes, and the application of qualitative and quantitative methods.

**Global Development in the Arctic**
International Cooperation for the Future
*Edited by Andrey Mineev, Anatoli Bourmistrov and Frode Mellemvik*

**Financializations of Development**
Global Games and Local Experiments
*Edited by Ève Chiapello, Anita Engels and Eduardo Gonçalves Gresse*

**The Rise of Small-Scale Development Organisations**
The Emergence, Positioning and Role of Citizen Aid Actors
*Edited by Haane Haaland, Sara Kinsbergen, Lau Schulpen and Hege Wallevik*

**Banking and Microfinance Institution Partnerships**
A Comparative Analysis of Cambodia and Australia
*Don Chandima Padmaperuma*

For more information about this series, please visit: www.routledge.com/ Routledge-Explorations-in-Development-Studies/book-series/REDS

# FINANCIALIZATIONS OF DEVELOPMENT

## Global Games and Local Experiments

*Edited by*
*Ève Chiapello, Anita Engels and*
*Eduardo Gonçalves Gresse*

LONDON AND NEW YORK

Designed cover image: alexsl

First published 2023
by Routledge
4 Park Square, Milton Park, Abingdon, Oxon OX14 4RN

and by Routledge
605 Third Avenue, New York, NY 10158

*Routledge is an imprint of the Taylor & Francis Group, an informa business*

*British Library Cataloguing-in-Publication Data*
A catalogue record for this book is available from the British Library

*Library of Congress Cataloging-in-Publication Data*
Names: Chiapello, Eve, editor. | Engels, Anita, editor. | Gonçalves
Gresse, Eduardo, editor.
Title: Financializations of development : global games and local
experiments / edited by Ève Chiapello, Anita Engels and Eduardo Gresse.
Description: New York, NY : Routledge, 2023. |
Series: Routledge explorations in development studies | Includes
bibliographical references and index. |
Identifiers: LCCN 2022046279 (print) | LCCN 2022046280 (ebook) |
ISBN 9780367483937 (paperback) | ISBN 9780367483944 (hardback) |
ISBN 9781003039679 (ebook)
Subjects: LCSH: Finance—Developing countries. | Sustainable development—
Developing countries. | Economic development—Finance. | Development
banks—Developing countries. | Development credit corporations—Developing
countries. | Banks and banking—Developing countries.
Classification: LCC HG195 .F5446 2023 (print) | LCC HG195 (ebook) |
DDC 332.1/5309172/4—dc23/eng/20221117
LC record available at https://lccn.loc.gov/2022046279
LC ebook record available at https://lccn.loc.gov/2022046280

ISBN: 978-0-367-48394-4 (hbk)
ISBN: 978-0-367-48393-7 (pbk)
ISBN: 978-1-003-03967-9 (ebk)

DOI: 10.4324/9781003039679

Typeset in Bembo
by codeMantra

# CONTENTS

# FIGURES

# TABLES

# ACKNOWLEDGMENTS

This volume is an output of the third conference of a series of three organized at the Centre for Globalisation and Governance of the University of Hamburg. The first conference *Social Finance, Impact Investing, and the Financialization of the Public Interest* took place in March 2017. It addressed the financialization of public policies and was convened by Ève Chiapello and Lisa Knoll.[1] The second one, *Finance as a response to global environmental crises? Critical analysis of the 'economicization' of carbon emissions and biodiversity*, took place in November 2017 and was organized by Ève Chiapello and Anita Engels.[2] The third conference, *Financialization and development policies: Critical perspectives on new financial circuits for international development projects,* was held in September 2018. The organization of these conferences was made possible by the funding from the Anneliese-Maier-Research Award, granted to Ève Chiapello by the Alexander von Humboldt Foundation.

The third conference on development policies, which has inspired this book, was organized by a committee that comprises Sara Aguiton (CNRS France), Stefan Aykut (Universität Hamburg), Philipp Golka (Universität Hamburg), Isabelle Guérin (IRD, France), Eduardo Gonçalves Gresse (Universität Hamburg) and Océane Ronal (EHESS France). Their involvement in the preparation of the conference, and then for some of them, in the publication of the book, was decisive. This book gathers a selection of papers presented at this conference, which has been enriched with some papers on topics not present at the event but important for the book. The original papers presented by the authors have been refined through several rounds of revision. We are therefore very grateful to all the authors of this book for their excellent work and contributions to the edited collection. We also thank them for their patience and collaboration with the numerous stages of the review process. The preparation of the book also benefited from the meticulous proofreading work of Fernando Preusser de Mattos, who also deserves a special thanks. Our reflections also benefited from discussions with researchers from the INTEERface research project (funded by ADEME, France, and directed by A. Ducastel). The general framing of the work benefited from Ève Chiapello's fellowship at the Wissenschaftskolleg zu Berlin (2020–2021).

Between the preparation of the conference in early 2018, when the call for papers was sent out, and the publication of the book, several years have passed, including two years of disruption due to the COVID-19 pandemic. We thank Rosie Anderson and her colleagues from Routledge UK for their guidance and patience, as well as the teams of the institutions that helped us, in particular Anika Hummel, Maria Görlich at the Universität Hamburg, Germany, and Joëlle Caugnon at EHESS Paris, for their and kindness and excellent work.

## Notes

1 Two special issues were published from this conference: Chiapello, E., Knoll, L. and Warner, M.E. (2020) 'Special Issue: Social Impact Bonds and the Urban Transformation,' *Journal of Urban Affairs*, 42(6), pp. 815–954; and Chiapello, E. and Knoll, L. (eds.) (2020) 'Social Finance, Impact Investing and the Financialisation of the Public Interest,' *Historical Social Research*, 45(3), pp. 7–205.

2 One special issue was published from this conference: Chiapello, E. and Engels, A. (eds.) (2021) 'The Fabrication of Environmental Intangibles,' *Journal of Cultural Economy*, 14(5). https://www.tandfonline.com/toc/rjce20/14/5.

# FOREWORD

*Philip Mader*

**Philip Mader** is a Political Economist and Sociologist with a focus on international development and an interest in financialization, digital finance and social struggles around debt. He is a Research Fellow at the Institute of Development Studies in Brighton (UK). He has authored *The Political Economy of Microfinance: Financializing Poverty* (Palgrave, 2015) and co-edited *The Routledge International Handbook of Financialization* (2020) and *Poverty & Prejudice: Religious Inequality and the Struggle for Sustainable Development* (Bristol University Press, 2023).

The developing world[1] and the world of development have undergone profound changes driven by changes in the world of finance over the last two to three decades. These have often been inscrutable, opaque or hard to unpack for those outside a relatively small circle of specialist scholars and practitioners who work on or in development finance. The achievement of this volume by Ève Chiapello, Anita Engels and Eduardo Gresse is to make those changes visible and comprehensible in a systematic way and, as a result, hopefully more contestable.

Many will be aware that Adam Smith used the metaphor of the "invisible hand" only once in the *Wealth of Nations* and, to boot, in a passage that appears to justify individuals preferring domestic consumption over international trade, instead of the unfettering and purging of markets of social values.[2] Yet, in spite of Smith, the metaphor has proven tenacious, perhaps thanks to its "handy" attribution of economic processes and outcomes to the wisdom or whims of a mysterious, shadowy and omnipotent entity, and perhaps also because it suits political and economic elites (including establishment economists) to have market outcomes appear inevitable, unalterable and unquestionable. Looking closely, as this book does, at how contemporary development is increasingly imbricated and imbued with "financial motives, financial markets, financial actors and financial institutions," to follow Gerald Epstein's (2005, p. 3) formative definition of financialization, however, one can clearly recognize the many smaller purposive hands playing and creating what the editors call "global games and local experiments". While mainstream economists either struggle or do not even attempt to account for finance's power, usually treating it (with sleight of hand) as a mere conduit for "real" economic forces, financialization studies have cracked open the black box of financial power to examine the social, political and economic forces that create and employ this power. "Financialization" is now well established as the watchword for a growing awareness and unease in both social-scientific scholarship (including heterodox economics) and wider society about how finance has become ever more dominant in the workings of the world, as well as for the sense that there is something wrong, or at least questionable, about this dominance (Mader, Mertens and van der Zwan, 2020).

This volume forges and stakes out the distinct terrain of research on the financialization of development, which was relatively slow to constitute itself as a subfield. It gradually came together from initially disconnected observations about how new forms of private finance were penetrating and reshaping development programming and social work across the Global South, since around the beginning of the current millennium, including through the reconfiguration of welfare systems (Lavinas, 2013), the transformation of urban infrastructures into financial investments (Bayliss and Fine, 2008) and the promotion of microfinance (Elyachar, 2005; Fernando, 2004; Muhammad, 2009). Despite a keen interest in particular place-bound manifestations, such scholarship has always also worked to conceptually and empirically connect the changes seen at the local or national level to the workings of global *haute finance* in a causal manner. Each case or area of activity examined in this book proceeds in this way, systematically establishing the links from global capital accumulation processes to tangible changes, either in local economies, societies and everyday life or in how development promotion is envisioned and operationalized. In doing so, the book connects to and enriches other recent efforts to reveal the drivers of contemporary patterns of capital accumulation, including social-scientific "accumulation studies" (Benquet and Bourgeron, 2021; Ponte, 2020) and the revivified field of inequality studies (Francis et al., 2020; Piketty, 2020).

The volume navigates the sweeping terrain of development financializations – the plural denoting the heterogeneity of processes – oriented by two sets of coordinates. The first is Chiapello's (2020) tripartite analytical framework of financialization as constituted by three interconnected "operations": problematization, tangibilization and financial structuring. The framework's cogency can be demonstrated with the case of microfinance which – although in the era of digital financial inclusion it almost appears a historical artifact – several chapters (Introduction; Kamath and Joseph; Guérin) reveal as the "sharp wedge" that pioneered many of the later financializations of development. The initial *problematization*, or the making of (under)development into a financial problem, drew inspiration from the experimenting and proselytizing activities of figures such as Muhammad Yunus and other pioneers whose contribution Yunus' limelight has often obscured (such as Ela Bhatt in India and Fazle Hasan Abed in Bangladesh).

It culminated in Yunus' widely applauded declaration at the first Microcredit Summit in 1997 that "credit is a human right" and microfinance would create "a poverty-free world", which cemented the notion of expanding commercial microfinance as an urgent humanitarian necessity (Bateman, 2010). The subsequent *tangibilization* of microfinance as an object of financial investment was engineered by development finance institutions (DFIs), above all the World Bank, through its arms-length subsidiary, the Consultative Group to Assist the Poor (CGAP). Its actions to control "the truths about microfinance" (Roy, 2010, p. 46) were focused on generating benchmarks, figures, forms of knowledge and valuation that served to reduce microfinance institutions (MFIs) to financial objects whose primary objective was to attract investment. Finally, the *financial structuring* of microfinance since the early 2000s completed this financialization of development with the integration of assets streams originating from low-income finance users into transnational circuits of capital accumulation (Duvendack and Mader, 2017). The asset forms include bonds, MFI share issues, microcredit-based collateralized debt obligations, as well as smallholders' land pledged as collateral (Green and Bylander, 2021). Readers will recognize these three operations recurring across the different financializations of development in this book.

The other set of coordinates is the separation of financializations of development into distinct processes, with changes to how development is financed on the one side, and the promotion of finance as a form of development *in itself* on the other. This distinction, though subtle, reveals finance working as a lever at different scales. Although all levels are affected, what varies is the level at which finance mainly does its "work" of financializing development. One level is the macro-to-meso level of development financing, where transformations take place among the actors and organizations who fund and implement development programming, including traditional DFIs (Ducastel, Bourblanc and Adelle) but also city governments (Grubbauer and Hilbrandt), the European Union (Mah) and different social service providers and NGOs (Alenda-Demoutiez). The other is the micro level, where development-as-finance is inserted directly among the intended beneficiaries of development, namely poor women and men as health service users (Al Dahdah), recipients of welfare payments (Gronbach; Villarreal), users of essential infrastructures (Bayliss and Van Waeyenberge) and debtors (Res).

Especially the chapters focused on the macro-meso level of development financing reveal time and again the fascinating lengths to which the architects of financialized development programming will go in seeking to appease private finance, and how these "solutions" end up making development activities subservient to the demands and expectations of financial actors. No doubt the increasing entry of financial professionals into the development profession (as documented by Ducastel, Bourblanc and Adelle) has played a huge role in this. Particularly striking in the chapters which deal with DIBs (Alenda-Demoutiez), vaccine funding structures (Ehrenstein) and farmer finance (Ducastel, Bourblanc and Adelle) is how public funding is now increasingly the source of private profits earned through development financing. The expertise and ways-of-seeing that blended finance in a "beyond aid" agenda seem to require inevitably lead to this dubious blending of logics (Gabor, 2021; Mawdsley, 2018) whose result is to "blur the lines" (Ronal, p. 50) such that financing development and the development of finance become hard to distinguish. Indeed, some models seem to be so strongly premised on an assumption that the world's current problems stem from a sheer lack of creativity in designing new financial arrangements, and that if only more public funds were channeled to private investors these problems would be solved, that one must wonder how much more good for humanity could be achieved if the same creativity were applied to actually solving those problems more directly.

Although each of the chapters presents a fascinating case study, it is worth highlighting that some chapters shed light on particularly problematically under-researched areas and actors in the financialization of development. These include Langevin's, Brunet-Bélanger's and Lefévre's chapter on the MasterCard Foundation as an enigmatic actor whose work exemplifies philanthrocapitalism's disturbing conflation of philanthropy with market-building, and Ehrenstein's chapter on "market-making" vaccine financing models and their roots in behavioral economics, and the transfer of the sustainable development agenda in Brazil into the hands of financial sector actors (Gresse and Preusser de Mattos). Many chapters also reveal financialization as a process that is contested, incomplete and fragile, and explore the contradictions, ambivalences and discontinuities encountered by communities, international development actors and sometimes development financiers themselves. They also show how just because something has not "worked" as intended or promised – for example, not succeeded at mobilizing investments or generating returns – it does not mean it did not succeed in other ways, such as changing what is measured or considered doable, altering how "beneficiaries" and promoters of development behave or handing greater power over future development agendas to private sector interests. Although capital accumulation and profit extraction through development activities are an important facet and intended outcome of financialized development policies, "failure" is clearly an acceptable part of experimentation at the financial-developmental frontier, as long as the public covers the costs (Appadurai and Alexander, 2020).

For a collection that is evidence-driven and grounded in a deep understanding of the logics of financial development, is attentive to its nuances and portrays development finance as anything but monolithic, the volume could hardly be clearer and more radical in its overall finding. The financialization of development has done "little to improve the living conditions of vulnerable people in the Global South" and "serves mainly the goals of investors rather than the needs of the recipients" (Conclusion). At a conjuncture of so many crises, in particular the climate crisis, where a dominant role for the financial sector once again seems inevitable, to clarify this is paramount. But it is crucial to not stop at critique. We must ask, as the editors do, why alternative pathways are not pursued and investigate how to promote them, even if under current macro-political circumstances many appear hard to pursue in the short term. The submission of development and developing countries to the "rules" of global finance is not inevitable, as demonstrated not least by well-documented historical and contemporary struggles for non-payment of debts (Laskaridis et al., 2020; Ravelli, 2021). There is no determinism to the trajectory of financialized global capitalism. Substantive and hard-fought-for financial alternatives "from below" exist, whether as part of the manifold experiments of the "social and solidarity economy" (Utting, 2015), experiments in "people-centered" fintech (Bateman and Texeira, 2022) or subversive techniques to enable people to move off the financial "grid" altogether and escape exploitation (Mader, 2022).

Yet we cannot reject development finance altogether either. All development and change need some form of up-front investment: the M with which to start the M-C-M' circulation process, to follow Marx's formula. It is the conditions and strings attached to the M, which are determined by its ownership and control, that shape the outcomes of the onward process. Private finance for development predictably produces private financial results, if not exclusively then at least primarily, if indeed it produces any at all. The risk is that, in facing the post-pandemic recession and the climate crisis, both of which demand colossal investments, the hegemony of the financial sector will be reinforced, leading to worsened global inequalities and skyrocketing sovereign and private debt. All the evidence in this book clarifies that this cannot be the way forward and that financing future development successfully and in ways that do not exacerbate underdevelopment, inequality and exploitation require a greater awareness of why social and private returns usually contradict rather than complement each other. It requires an understanding of why most experiments to invent or create developmental attractions for private finance are so unsuccessful, at least developmentally. And it requires bold new visions of how to reclaim development by bringing the control of finance into the visible hands of the many. Making the invisible hand of finance visible is critical to reclaiming development from the hands of the few.

## Notes

1 Or Global South, global periphery, low- and middle-income countries, etc.
2 Thank you, Ha-Joon Chang, for pointing this out to your students at a time when, presumably, one needed to have read Smith's entire book to know it. The chapter of *The Wealth of Nations* (Book 4, Ch. 2) in which Smith uses the metaphor is one that argues against controls on imports, but the specific context is this: "By preferring the support of domestic to that of foreign industry, he intends only his own security; and by directing that industry in such a manner as its produce may be of the greatest value, he intends only his own gain; and he is in this, as in many other cases, led by an invisible hand to promote an end which was no part of his intention".

## References

Appadurai, A. and Alexander, N. (2020) *Failure*. Cambridge: Polity Press.

Bateman, M. (2010) *Why Doesn't Microfinance Work?: The Destructive Rise of Local Neoliberalism.* London: Zed Books.

Bateman, M. and Texeira, F. (2022) *The Promises and Perils of Investor-Driven Fintech: Forging People-Centered Alternatives.* Amsterdam: The Transnational Institute.

Bayliss, K., and Fine, B. (eds.) (2008) *Privatization and Alternative Public Sector Reform in Sub-Saharan Africa: Delivering on Electricity and Water.* Basingstoke: Palgrave.

Benquet, M. and Bourgeron, T. (eds.) (2021) *Accumulating Capital Today: Contemporary Strategies of Profit and Dispossessive Policies.* Abingdon: Routledge.

Chiapello, E. (2020) 'Financialization as a Socio-technical Process,' in Mader, P., Mertens, D. and van der Zwan, N. (eds.), *The Routledge International Handbook of Financialization.* Abingdon: Routledge, pp. 81–91.

Duvendack, M. and Mader, P. (2017) 'Poverty Reduction or the Financialisation of Poverty?,' in Bateman, M. and Maclean, K. (eds.), *Seduced and Betrayed: Exposing the Contemporary Microfinance Phenomenon.* Santa Fe: University of New Mexico Press.

Elyachar, J. (2005) *Markets of Dispossession: NGOs, Economic Development, and the State in Cairo.* Durham: Duke University Press.

Epstein, G. (ed.) (2005) *Financialization and the World Economy.* Cheltenham: Edward Elgar.

Fernando, J. (ed.) (2004) *Microfinance: Perils and Prospects.* London: Routledge.

Francis, D., Webster, E. and Valodia, I. (eds.) (2020) *Inequality Studies from the Global South.* Abingdon: Routledge.

Gabor, D. (2021) 'The Wall Street Consensus,' *Development and Change,* 52(3), pp. 429–459.

Green, W.N. and Bylander, M. (2021) 'The Exclusionary Power of Microfinance: Over-indebtedness and Land Dispossession in Cambodia,' *Sociology of Development,* 7(2), pp. 202–229.

Laskaridis, C., Legrand, N. and Toussaint, E. (2020) 'Historical Perspectives on Current Struggles against Illegitimate Debt,' in Mader, P., Mertens, D. and van der Zwan, N. (eds.), *The Routledge International Handbook of Financialization.* Abingdon: Routledge, pp. 482–493.

Lavinas, L. (2013) '21st Century Welfare,' *New Left Review,* 84(6), pp. 5–40.

Mader, P. (2022) '"We Put God and Drums in the Front": Spirituality as Strategy in an Adivasi Self-Empowerment Movement,' in Tadros, M. (ed.), *'What About Us?': Global Perspectives on Redressing Religious Inequalities.* Brighton: IDS, pp. 115–144.

Mader, P., Mertens, D. and van der Zwan, N. (2020) 'Financialization: An Introduction,' Mader, P., Mertens, D. and van der Zwan, N. (eds.), *The Routledge International Handbook of Financialization.* Abingdon: Routledge, pp. 1–16.

Mawdsley, E. (2018) '"From Billions to Trillions: Financing the SDGs in a World 'Beyond Aid,'" *Dialogues in Human Geography,* 8(2), pp. 191–195.

Muhammad, A. (2009) 'Grameen and Microcredit: A Tale of Corporate Success,' *Economic and Political Weekly,* pp. 35–42.

Piketty, T. (2020) *Capital and Ideology.* Cambridge, MA: Harvard University Press.

Ponte, S. (2020) 'Green Capital Accumulation: Business and Sustainability Management in a World of Global Value Chains,' *New Political Economy,* 25(1), pp. 72–84.

Ravelli, Q. (2021) 'Debt Struggles: How Financial Markets Gave Birth to a Working-Class Movement,' *Socio-Economic Review,* 19(2), pp. 441–468.

Roy, A. (2010). *Poverty Capital: Microfinance and the Making of Development.* New York: Routledge.

Utting, P. (ed.) (2015) *Social and Solidarity Economy: Beyond the Fringe.* London: Zed Books.

# ACRONYMS AND ABBREVIATIONS

| | |
|---|---|
| AAAA | Addis Ababa Action Agenda |
| ACLEDA | Association of Cambodian Local Economic Development Agencies |
| ADB | Asian Development Bank |
| AFD | Agence Française de Développement (French Development Agency) |
| AfDB | African Development Bank |
| AIF | Asia Investment Facility |
| AITF | EU-Africa Infrastructure Trust Fund |
| AKmi | Association for Karnataka Microfinance |
| AMC | Advance Market Commitment |
| AMK | Angkor Mikroheranhvatho Kampuchea |
| ASER | Annual Status of Education Report |
| ATM | Automated Teller Machine |
| AusAID | Australian Aid |
| B3- B3 S.A. | Brasil, Bolsa, Balcão |
| BANSEFI | Banco del Ahorro Nacional y Servicios Financieros/National Savings and Financial Services Bank |
| BFIL | Bharat Financial Inclusion Limited |
| BNDES | Banco Nacional de Desenvolvimento Econômico e Social (Brazilian Development Bank) |
| BoP | Bottom of the Pyramid |
| CAPEX | Capital Expenditure |
| CBIOs | Decarbonization Credits |
| CCI | City Creditworthiness Initiative |
| CCT | Conditional Cash Transfer |
| CDC | Commonwealth Development Corporation |
| CEO | Chief Executive Officer |

| | |
|---|---|
| CGAP | Consultative Group to Assist the Poor |
| CGD | Center for Global Development |
| CIF | Caribbean Investment Facility |
| CMA | Cambodia Microfinance Association |
| CoP-PFSD | Community of Practice on Private Finance for Sustainable Development |
| CPS | Cash Paymaster Services |
| CRAs | Agribusiness receivable certificates |
| CSR | Corporate Social Responsibility |
| CVM | Securities and Exchange Commission/Comissão de Valores Mobiliários |
| CwA | Compact with Africa |
| DAC | (or DAC-OECD) Development Assistance Committee |
| DCF | Discounted cash flow |
| DCI | Development Cooperation Instrument |
| DEG | Deutsche Investitions- und Entwicklungsgesellschaft (German Investment Corporation) |
| DFI | Development Finance Institution |
| DFID | Department for International Development |
| DIB | Development Impact Bond |
| DIB-WG | Development Impact Bond Working Group (2013) |
| DTaP | Diphtheria, Tetanus, Pertussis (vaccine) |
| E&S | Environmental and Social |
| EAG | External Action Guarantee |
| EBITDA | Earnings Before Interest, Taxes, Depreciation and Amortization. |
| EC | European Commission |
| EDF | European Development Fund |
| EEAS | European External Action Service |
| EFSD | European Fund for Sustainable Development |
| EGS | EU Global Strategy |
| EIB | European Investment Bank |
| EIP | EU External Investment Plan |
| EMDEs | Emerging market and developing economies |
| EP | European Parliament |
| ESG | Environmental, Social and Corporate Governance |
| EU | European Union |
| FAO | Food and Agriculture Organization of the United Nations |
| FDI | Foreign Direct Investment |
| FIEG | Financial Inclusion Experts Group |
| FISEA | Fonds d'Investissement et de Soutien aux Entreprises en Afrique (The Investment and support fund for businesses in Africa) |

| | |
|---|---|
| FMO | Nederlandse Financierings-Maatschappij voor Ontwikkelingslanden N.V./Netherlands Development Finance Company |
| FRP | Fund for Rural Prosperity |
| FSP | Financial Service Provider |
| Gavi | Gavi, the Vaccine Alliance (formerly the Global Alliance for Vaccines and Immunization) |
| GIF | Global Infrastructure Facility |
| GIIN | Global Impact Investing Network |
| GIZ | German Development Corporation; Deutsche Gesellschaft für Internationale Zusammenarbeit |
| GPR | Geschäftspolitisches Project Rating (Corporate Policy Project Rating) |
| GRI | Global Reporting Initiative |
| GSK | GlaxoSmithKline |
| HRFASP | High Representative for Foreign Affairs and Security Policy |
| IBWG | Impact Bonds Working Group (2018) |
| IFAD | International Fund for Agricultural Development |
| IFC | International Finance Corporation |
| IFCA | Investment Facility for Central Asia |
| IFP | Investment Facility for the Pacific |
| ILO | International Labour Organization |
| IMF | International Monetary Fund |
| INGOs | International Non-governmental Organizations |
| IPO | Initial public offering |
| ISE B3 | Corporate Sustainability Index/Índice de Sustentabilidade Empresarial |
| JLG | Joint Liability Group |
| KfW | Kreditanstalt für Wiederaufbau |
| LAIF | Latin American Investment Facility |
| LICs | Low-income countries |
| MC | Mastercard Foundation |
| MDBs | Multilateral development banks |
| MDGs | Millennium Development Goals |
| MFD | Maximizing Finance for Development |
| MFI | Microfinance Institution |
| MICs | Middle-income countries |
| MRI | Mission-related investment |
| MSF | Médecins Sans Frontières |
| NASDAQ | National Association of Securities Dealers Automated Quotations |
| NBC | National Bank of Cambodia |
| NDICI | Neighborhood, Development and International Cooperation Instrument |

| | |
|---|---|
| NDPs | National Development Plans |
| NGO | Non-governmental organization |
| NHIF | Kenyan National Hospital Insurance Fund |
| NIF | Neighborhood Investment Facility |
| NPA | Non-Performing Asset |
| OCSD | Organisation Canadienne pour la Solidarité et le Développement |
| ODA | Official Development Assistance |
| OECD | Organisation for Economic Co-operation and Development |
| OPEX | Operational Expenditure |
| OPIC | Overseas Private Investment Corporation |
| OTC | Over the counter |
| OXFAM | Oxford Committee for Famine Relief |
| PPI | Private participation in infrastructure |
| PPIAF | Public Private Infrastructure Advisory Facility |
| PPP | Public–Private Partnerships |
| PRB | Principles for Responsible Banking |
| PRI | Principles for Responsible Investment |
| PRI | Program-related investment |
| PROIIF | Programa Integral de Inclusión Financiera/Integral Program for Financial Inclusion |
| PROPARCO | Society for the promotion and participation (investment) for economic cooperation – Société de Promotion et de Participation pour la Coopération économique |
| PSD | Private Sector Development |
| PSIs | Private Sector Instruments |
| RBI | Reserve Bank of India |
| ROE | Return on equity |
| SASSA | South African Social Security Agency |
| SCT | Social Cash Transfer |
| SDG | Sustainable Development Goal |
| SEC | US Securities and Exchange Commission |
| SFB | Small finance bank |
| SGSY | Swarnajayanti Gram Swarozgar Yojana |
| SHGs | Self-help groups |
| SIB | Social Impact Bond |
| SIF | Sustainable Infrastructure Foundation |
| SKS | Swayam Krishi Sangham |
| SNTA | Subnational Technical Assistance |
| SSA | Sub-Saharan Africa |
| SSC | South-South Cooperation |
| Telcos | Telecommunication Operators |
| TOSSD | Total Official Support for Sustainable Development |
| UHC | Universal Health Coverage |

| | |
|---|---|
| UK | United Kingdom |
| UN | United Nations |
| UNDP | United Nations Development Program |
| UNICEF | United Nations Children's Fund |
| USAID | United States Agency for International Development |
| WB | World Bank |
| WBIF | Western Balkans Investment Framework |
| WC | Washington Consensus |
| WCED | World Commission on Environment and Development |
| WFE | World Federation of Exchanges |
| WHO | World Health Organization |

# CONTRIBUTORS

**Camilla Adelle** is a Senior Researcher in the Department of Political Sciences and the Centre of Excellence for Food Security at the University of Pretoria, South Africa. Her work focuses on stakeholder engagement and the co-production of knowledge for local food governance.

**Marine Al Dahdah** is a CNRS Researcher at the Center for Studies of Social Movements (CEMS-EHESS), and a member of Unit 1276 "Risks, Violence, Reparation" of the French National Health and Medical Research Institute (IN-SERM). She is an Associate Researcher at Paris University (UParis) and at the Center for Human Sciences (CSH) in Delhi (India). Her research focuses on health policies in Asia and Africa, and more particularly on digital healthcare in India, Ghana and Kenya.

**Juliette Alenda-Demoutiez** completed her PhD in France in 2016, and later served as a Postdoctoral Fellow at the University of Amsterdam. She is now an Assistant Professor in the Department of Economics and Business Economics at Radboud University. Her areas of expertise include environmental sustainability, governance, institutions, macroeconomic indicators, welfare and social economy.

**Kate Bayliss** is a Senior Research Fellow at the University of Sussex and a Research Associate at SOAS University of London and the University of Leeds. She has written extensively on privatization and changing paradigms surrounding private sector engagement in meeting basic needs in the UK and the Global South.

**Magalie Bourblanc** is a Political Scientist at CIRAD (French Agricultural Research Centre for Development), UMR G-EAU (joint research unit, "Water Management, Actors & Uses"), at the University of Montpellier (MUSE), France. She is also an extraordinary Lecturer at CEEPA (Centre for Environmental Economics and Policy in Africa), Faculty of Natural and Agricultural Sciences, University of Pretoria, South Africa. Her works focus on public policy instruments and expert knowledge within public policies.

**Andréanne Brunet-Bélanger** is a PhD candidate in Political Science at the Université de Montréal. She specializes in comparative politics and her interests focus on international organizations and actors. She has been working on research projects in philanthropy since 2017 and is particularly interested in the role of social finance and the economic tools of foundations in market mechanisms.

**Antoine Ducastel** is a Sociologist at CIRAD (French Agricultural Research Centre for Development), UMR ART-dev and at the University of Montpellier (MUSE), France. His work focuses on the funding of public policies, particularly development policies and energy transition policies.

**Véra Ehrenstein** is a CNRS Researcher at the *Centre d'étude des mouvements sociaux* (UMR 8044), *École des hautes études en sciences sociales*. She has a PhD in Science and Technology Studies. Her research explores the relations between science, markets and politics in the fields of climate change and global health. Véra recently published with Daniel Neyland and Sveta Milyaeva the book *Can Markets Solve Problems? An Empirical Inquiry into Neoliberalism in Action* (Goldsmiths Press, 2019).

**Lena Gronbach** is a Researcher and PhD Candidate at the Centre for Social Science Research at the University of Cape Town. Her research focuses on payment digitization for social cash transfer programs in sub-Saharan Africa, as well as the impact of COVID-19 on the use of digital technologies in the field of social protection. She holds degrees in International Business and Development Studies from ESB Business School (Germany), the University of South Africa and the University of Pretoria (South Africa), and has worked as an Independent Consultant for the International Policy Centre for Inclusive Growth.

**Monika Grubbauer** is Professor in History and Theory of the City at the HafenCity University Hamburg. She works on urban transformation, socio-economic restructuring and urban politics in different geographical contexts, with a particular focus on the role of architecture, planning and construction. Recent research includes studies of housing microfinance and large-scale construction projects.

**Isabelle Guérin**, PhD, is a Socioeconomist, Senior Research Fellow at the French Institute of Research for Sustainable Development (IRD) and Associate at the French Institute of Pondicherry. She specializes in the role of debt and credit in the dynamics of poverty and inequality. Her work draws most often from her own field-based original data, combines ethnography and statistical analyses and is interdisciplinary and comparative in nature.

**Hanna Hilbrandt** is Assistant Professor of Social and Cultural Geography at the University of Zurich. Her research explores marginality and exclusion in housing and urban development as well as socio-spatial inequalities in the context of global economic restructuring. Focusing predominantly on Mexico City and Berlin, her work pays close attention to the everyday politics of city-making.

**Nithya Joseph** holds a PhD in the Socioeconomics of Development from the École des Hautes Études en Sciences Sociales (EHESS), Paris. She is currently a Postdoctoral Research Fellow at the Institut Français Pondicherry (IFP). Her research has focused on household finance in rural and semi-urban South India, including such subjects as debt-based labor, small-scale enterprise, microcredit provisioning and gold-based borrowing and lending.

**Rajalaxmi Kamath** is an Associate Professor at the Center for Public Policy at the Indian Institute of Management Bangalore (IIMB). Her primary research concerns studying the everyday cash flows of poor households. She teaches "Business, Government and Society" to MBA students at IIMB.

**Marie Langevin** is a Professor at the Université du Québec à Montréal's Department of Strategy and Social and Environmental Responsibility. She holds a PhD in Political Economy. She is currently working on the Fintech sector, financial inclusion and fringe finance. Her research also engages with philanthrocapitalism, especially with regard to the practices of the Mastercard Foundation.

**Luis Mah** is an Assistant Professor in Development Studies at the Department of Political Economy at ISCTE-University Institute of Lisbon. He is currently heading CEsA – Center for African and Development Studies. He holds a PhD in Development Studies from the LSE. His research focuses on the political economy of international development, with a particular interest in the role of the European Union (EU). The author would like to acknowledge the financial support of the Portuguese Foundation for Science and Technology under the Grants nr. PTDC/CPO-ADM/28597/2017.

**Fernando Preusser de Mattos** holds a PhD in Political Science from the University of Hamburg, Germany, and is currently Institutional Relations Coordinator at the Brazilian Center for International Relations (CEBRI). He has written and researched on foreign and security policy think tanks in Europe and Brazil, Brazilian foreign, security and defense policymaking and contemporary EU-Brazil relations.

**Phasy Res** is a third-year Doctoral Student holding an Institut de Recherche pour le Développement (IRD) fellowship (ARTS) in anthropology at Université Paris 1 Panthéon-Sorbonne, France. She is also a Junior Research Fellow at the Center for Khmer Studies, Cambodia. Her PhD research looks at the relationship between microfinance expansion and land security by examining how access to microfinance shapes the meaning of land (in)security. She has conducted research on a wide range of topics, including agricultural mechanization and intensification, anti-malaria drug resistance, labor migration in the Sub-Mekong region and consumer protection and microfinance during the COVID-19 crisis. Her work has been published in *Espace Politique, Malaria Journal, Development Policy Review, Development and Change*, Mekong Migration Network and The Center for Khmer Studies.

**Océane Ronal** is a PhD Candidate at the School of Advanced Studies in the Social Sciences (EHESS – *École des Hautes Études en Sciences Sociales*, Paris) and affiliated with the CEMS research center (*Centre d'étude des mouvements sociaux*) with a multidisciplinary social sciences academic background: graduated in Anthropology (bachelor's degree at *Aix-Marseille Université*), Political Sciences (master's degree at *Sciences Po Grenoble*) and Comparative Development Studies (master's degree at EHESS Paris).

**Sylvain A. Lefèvre** is a Professor at the Université du Québec à Montréal's Department of Strategy and Social and Environmental Responsibility. He holds a PhD in Political Science. He is the Director of the Centre de recherche sur les innovations sociales (CRISES). He is currently working on the field of philanthropy and the role of foundations in social and environmental issues.

**Elisa Van Waeyenberge** is Co-Head of the Economics Department at SOAS University of London. She has long-standing interests in the way in which global economic policy agenda promoted by International Financial Institutions translates locally, in particular in the context of macroeconomic and infrastructure provisioning policies.

**Magdalena Villarreal**, PhD, is Professor and Senior Researcher at the Centre for Advanced Research and Postgraduate Studies in Social Anthropology (CIESAS) in Mexico. She is a member of the Mexican Academy of Science and level three of the National Research System. Her academic interests focus on the anthropology of money and finance, as well as poverty, migration and gender. She has coordinated multiple research projects on these topics. Her publications include *Women, Social Finance and Economic Violence in Marginal Sectors of Guadalajara; The Anthropology of Debt; and Microfinance at the Interstices of Development*.

# INTRODUCTION

## Financializations of development

*Ève Chiapello, Anita Engels and Eduardo Gonçalves Gresse*

Since the 1980s, the global economic system has undergone significant and numerous transformations. Public policies and forms of government in developed countries have evolved in tandem with the reconfiguration of the capitalist system and the changes in North-South relations. This book examines development policies as they interact with one of the important features of the transformation of the capitalist system over the past 40 years: its financialization (Epstein, 2005; van der Zwan, 2014).

We define financialization as "the increasing dominance of financial actors, markets, practices, measurements and narratives, resulting in a structural transformation of economies, firms, States and households" (Aalbers, 2019, p. 4). Over the past 20 years, social science research has shown the extension of the sphere of influence of private financial and banking actors, and their increasing ability to extract value from other businesses, the non-profit sector, governments and households alike. This comes with a general increase in debt for private households, governments and companies (Duménil and Lévy, 2001; Krippner, 2005; Mader, Mertens and van der Zwan, 2020).

The financialization of economies is a complex process that is inseparable from the policies pursued by governments (Baud and Chiapello, 2015; Krippner, 2011; van der Zwan, 2017). The situation in developing countries is no exception. Among the policies concerned, we focus specifically on development policies largely driven by organizations with headquarters in the Global North. The aim is to identify different avenues through which initiatives carried out in the name of development contribute to the financialization of Global South economies (*financialization by development policies*). This financialization can be described as a transformation of financial circuits both locally and globally. More and more populations are locally connected to private financial actors who offer them various financial products and these local circuits are also linked to global

DOI: 10.4324/9781003039679-1

finance. Our approach draws on the work of Mader (2015) on "the political economy of microfinance", which demonstrates how microfinance constitutes an extension of the financial system:

> Through such processes as the successive commercialization and deepening union with mainstream financial markets, and the expansion of microfinance into new fields such as credit for public goods, the system of microfinance has expanded the frontier of finance and opened up new terrains for capital in its restless and unrelenting search for opportunities to generate and extract surplus. Does this constitute development? Perhaps, but a thoroughly financialized capitalist variant of development.
>
> *(Mader, 2015, p. 6)*

The 15 case studies in this book extend the analysis to other practical types of development policies, beyond microfinance. Each chapter examines initiatives aimed at reducing poverty or increasing the access of populations in developing countries to essential goods such as health care, food or education. These actions involve both private and public aid and the engagement of development actors, such as public agencies, development banks, NGOs and foundations. We seek to understand how these types of initiatives contribute to financialization. Taken together, the cases show how actors around the globe shape new financialized solutions for development problems and help implement these solutions into local contexts in Africa, Latin America and Asia. The financialization by development policies is a decade-long, multifaceted process. It involves powerful global players, local governments and a myriad of actors and intermediate institutions to prepare the ground for financialization through the dissemination of narratives, resources and practices that make the world of development compatible with the world of finance. Given this multiplicity of intertwined financialization processes, we use the plural form "financializations" in the title of this book.

By development policies we mean policies propelled by Western countries, after the Second World War, directed at economic structures and state institutions in the countries of the Global South. Most of these countries were initially colonies or ex-colonies. After decolonization processes, loans provided by the World Bank (WB) were intended to develop the resources of the new developing countries, many of which were abundant in natural resources or had extensive agricultural potential. The original WB loans were complemented by various forms of aid (e.g. technical aid, concessional loans) distributed by national or multilateral public development institutions and banks, which had multiplied during that time. In order to ensure some degree of coordination and structuring of development policies around the globe, the WB set up the Development Assistance Committee (DAC) in 1960, as a further institution to be coordinated by the new Organisation for Economic Co-operation and Development (OECD). This committee brought together mostly public donors of the so-called "free world" when aid was increasingly used as a geopolitical tool in the context of the cold war. The collapse of the Soviet Union in the early 1990s marked the end of this formative period. In the aftermath of the cold war constellation, a considerable reduction in Official Development Assistance (ODA) occurred. The nature of aid gradually transformed, leading to a "triple revolution of goals, stakeholders and instruments" (Severino and Ray, 2009, p. 1). The goals shifted toward the fight against poverty. New actors emerged (e.g., NGOs and foundations) and played an increasing role in defining development policies and implementing programs (Davies, 2012). Philanthropy is one of the ways used by the private sector, namely large multinational firms, to become influential players in development policies (McGoey, 2015; Morvaridi, 2012). However, companies are also increasingly taking over development goals, at least discursively (Gresse and Preusser de Mattos, 2023, this volume). New types of financing instruments were tested and sometimes rolled out widely. The last 20 years have seen these trends continue and even become more pronounced after the 2007–2008 financial crisis. Mawdsley, Savage and Kim (2013) refer to a "paradigm shift in foreign aid and development cooperation" and the establishment of a "post-aid world" characterized by a decline in direct public aid from Global North countries. At the same time, new states such as China have entered the world of development as donor countries (Bergamaschi, Moore and Tickner, 2017), becoming very active while staying outside the DAC-OECD. The cases reviewed in this book take place in this broader landscape of transformations in development policies since the late 1990s.

What are the processes at play that cause certain initiatives in the field of development to support the increase in power and wealth of financial actors?

## Financialization processes

We have identified two main processes that affect both the content (formulation and objectives) of development policies and their implementation (type of actors involved and financing instruments chosen). These processes involve different actors and relate to different approaches to development. On the one hand, financialization is produced by the project to enroll private financial actors into the financing of development policies. On the other hand, financialization regards the wide development of financial activities considered as a development goal in the first place. Yet in both cases, the result is the same: a change of actor configurations and the arrival or growing importance of private finance actors that are enrolled in and associated with the conception and implementation of development policies. It also means that practices, theories and instruments stemming from the financial sector are nowadays used to frame the understanding of development, the design of the policies and their implementations.

These two forms of articulation between financialization and development policies organize the order of the cases and situations presented in this book (see below). Taken together, the 15 cases illustrate different financializations of development. We will see varying degrees of financialization, as well as different forms, leading to a huge spectrum of outcomes. Not all financialization processes actually penetrate and transform the intended sectors and spheres. Moreover, unintended consequences and side effects can be observed.

In order to refine this framework (see Figure 0.1), we have outlined a chronology of financializing processes and events, starting with the microfinance movement as it was reinvented in the 1980s, namely after the Grameen Bank foundation in Bangladesh (Mader, 2015, p. 53).

Microfinance is part of the older process of financialization according to which financial development *is* development (*finance as development*). This form encompasses policies that aim to develop financial activities in a given country. The establishment of a modern financial system and the financial inclusion of the population are seen as development objectives in their own right. They are considered as being able to promote both economic activities and access to other social services. This category includes microcredit, which in many ways was a precursor to what would happen more generally to development projects and policies in later stages (Doligez, 2017). Based on the promise that access to credit would enable micro-entrepreneurs to develop economic activity and escape poverty, microcredit was celebrated as a way to bring empowerment to the participants, especially to women. In the context of the Washington consensus (Gore, 2000) and the loans conditionalities of the Structural Adjustment Programs coordinated by the International Monetary Fund (IMF) and the WB, the microcredit movement was also highly compatible ideologically (Young, 2010, p. 614). In a neoliberal understanding of development processes, states should have only minimal social welfare institutions, therefore microcredit was used to alleviate the social problems generated by the liberalization of policies, while still celebrating people's ability to help themselves (Mader, 2015, p. 55).

Experimented with during the 1980s, microcredit became progressively one of the darling policies of development institutions. The WB founded the Consultative Group to Assist the Poor (CGAP) in 1995 to coordinate microfinance actors and to finance initiatives through its private sector arm, the International Finance Corporation (IFC). Consequently, CGAP contributed to "standardize and homogenize microfinance on a private sector template" (Mader, 2015, p. 59). In 1997, the first Microcredit Summit was held in Washington. In 2001, CGAP and private foundations launched the Mix Market, a website that provides financial data for investors about Microfinance Institutions (MFI). The first IPOs of MFIs took place in 2006–2007. The popularity of microfinance reached its peak in the mid-2000s. The UN declared 2005 as the International Year of Microcredit, and the founder of the Grameen Bank, Muhammad Yunus, was awarded the Nobel Peace Prize in 2006. Microcredit activities have been progressively complemented by banking, insurance, payment and savings services, an evolution that explains the wide use of the term microfinance rather than microcredit. The end of the 2000s was marked by a crisis of microcredit. Not only did over-indebted populations revolt in Morocco, Nicaragua and India (Guérin, Labie and Servet, 2015), but economic research also suggested that microcredit has no positive long-term effect on development (Bateman, 2010). However, despite these difficulties, the thesis that a priority of development should be to provide the populations of developing countries access to credit has not been challenged (Muhammad Yunus described it as a "human right" in a famous speech at UNESCO in 1997). In fact, only the narratives have changed. Nowadays, financial inclusion (i.e. the connection of a country's adults to the formal financial system) is considered an essential precondition of development, if not a development goal in itself. This can be achieved through standard banking networks, microfinance institutions or through the use of mobile money that can be handled by mobile phones. Kenya, known as the pioneer of mobile money since the launch of M-Pesa in 2007, serves in this plan as an advanced laboratory for all fintech inclusion initiatives (Natile, 2020; see also Al Dahdah, and Langevin, Brunet-Bélanger and Lefèvre, 2023, this volume).

As Mader (2015, p. 19) put it:

> the emergent doctrine of financial inclusion shifts the goalposts of microfinance, or almost removes them altogether, in that the process of expanding microfinance becomes the end in itself.

Financial inclusion is associated with a monetization of economic systems and an increase in market exchanges, both considered good for economic growth. Monetization and marketization of societies can also be accelerated by social policies that organize cash transfers to beneficiaries. Indeed, these schemes oblige beneficiaries to have a bank account and to make payments in money, and thus to become involved in money-based market exchanges. As Lavinas (2017) has shown, namely in the case of the Brazilian program Bolsa Familia, social cash transfer programs tend also to produce a rise of indebtedness in the formal banking system. People become indebted to bank intermediaries due to the regular payments organized by the social assistance system (see Gronbach, 2023, this volume, for the South African case). As in the case of microcredit, which promotes a representation of the poor as responsible and autonomous individuals, cash transfer policies are based on a liberal, non-paternalistic representation of the poor who, provided they have a minimum amount of money, can take charge of their own destiny and choose how to spend it. These policies of access to money and debt have been accused to be levers for over-indebtedness (see Kamath and Joseph, 2023, this volume). Therefore, they are now accompanied by financial literacy programs designed to explain the rules of the game to the target populations and to help them manage their budget (see Res, 2023, this volume). These various *microfinance, financial inclusion* and *financial education* programs make financialization a development objective. The more a population is bancarized (i.e., included in the financial system and educated to maneuver within it), the more positive the situation is considered to be in terms of development. This form of financialization leads to a financialization of everyday life (Langley, 2008; Martin, 2002), transforming the subjectivity of individuals (see Res, 2023, this volume). However, this active transformation of economic agents into responsible agents capable of taking on debt or being invested in by capital is itself seen as an integral part of the development work. This is why various development programs also aim to develop the *investment readiness* or the *capabilities* of actors, such as Small and Medium Enterprises managers or local authorities, so that they are better able to access finance to develop (see Grubbauer and Hilbrandt, and Bayliss and Van Waeyenberge, 2023, this volume).

A more recent form of financialization has arisen from the need to find new ways for financing development policies (*financing development*). This type of financialization concerns a reduction of the development objectives to problems of financing. To financialize a health policy is thus to consider that the main problem to be addressed is finding the money to carry it out (see Ehrenstein, or Al Dahdah, 2023, this volume). This kind of translation of development into a financial problem has developed hand in hand with an approach of development in terms of goals, such as the Millennium Development Goals established in 2000 or the Sustainable Development Goals adopted in 2015 (Bond, 2006; see Gresse and Preusser de Mattos, 2023, this volume). Once the goals are established, they are supposed to be taken on board by governments and development operators. Consequently, the main work of the international development community is to find the money for the realization of such development goals. International conferences for financing for development (the first took place in Monterrey in 2002, the third and latest in Addis Ababa in 2015) have then tackled the issue of finding ways to address the so-called financial gaps to achieve global development goals. Reports have been produced (e.g., the UN-Secretary General, 2019) to quantify those gaps (i.e., the sums required that the public aid system and the public development banks alone cannot mobilize; Mawdsley, 2018). Once financing development is constructed as the main development problem, the effort then consists of finding ways to mobilize private finance to supplement insufficient public finance (see Mah, and Ducastel, Bourblanc and Adelle, 2023, this volume). However, private finance actors (i.e., those who oversee the management of the world's savings and constantly look for new ways to valorize capital) are not going to be involved if there is no financial return. Therefore, various innovations had to be invented. They mainly consist of using money from the budgetary states' expenditures to leverage private finance. This means incentivizing private finance to invest in development. This may require tax waivers for philanthropists, the setting up of guarantee funds or various blended finance arrangements to de-risk private investments (see Bayliss and van Waeyenberge, 2023, this volume). The establishment of public-private partnerships (PPP; Bayliss and van Waeyenberge, 2018), development impact bonds (Alenda-Demoutiez, 2019; and Alenda-Demoutiez, 2023, this volume) or the issuance of bonds to prefinance investments (e.g., in vaccine research) that will be reimbursed by future public spending are also part of the so-called innovative methods that have been found to associate private finance with public funds (see Ehrenstein, 2023, this volume). The financialization of development that these different practices induce is a transformation of the policy's target beneficiaries. Indeed, the financial actors who need to be enrolled, seduced and convinced become the real targets of the development policy. It is their financial returns or risks that are taken care of and managed in the first place, since it is only on the condition that financial actors are willing to invest that development policies themselves can be conducted (Chiapello, 2017). Gabor (2021, p. 1) calls this "elaborate effort to reorganize development intervention around partnership with global finance" the "Wall Street Consensus". She describes the advent of a conception of development as de-risking the investments of private investors to help them making new investments. This second form of financialization consists of a transformation of the circuits and instruments for financing development policies. This process has accelerated particularly since the 2007 financial crisis (van Waeyenberge, 2016) and has transformed a wide range of development policies, including the financial inclusion projects discussed before. The willingness to enroll private finance means that development projects and initiatives need to be prepared in order to be invested in by for-profit investors or lenders. What has been described as a financialization of microcredit (Aitken, 2013; Mader, 2015; Young, 2010) is at the intersection of both processes of financialization. MFIs, which in the early decades were mainly NGOs or cooperatives, have themselves been invested in by investment funds, or have even been listed in stock markets (see Kamath and Joseph, 2023, this volume). The desire to generalize microfinance has led to regulatory changes allowing the development of for-profit microfinance organizations, whose arrival has not only led to an increase in interest rates but also to the over-indebtedness of populations (Guérin, Morvant-Roux and Villarreal, 2013).

Blended finance (first fund launched in 2007 by the EU) is part of the endeavor to enroll private finance in development projects (see Mah, 2023, this volume). It is now considered a good practice, standardized and rationalized by the OECD (OECD, 2021). Another example is the development of an impact investment market, where investors get a financial return while producing a social impact. This idea was pioneered by the Impact Investing Initiative launched in 2008 by the Rockefeller Foundation (Barman, 2015). Impact investing is now discussed all over the world, and many investment funds declare their commitment to these kinds of investment practices (Chiapello and Knoll, 2020; Ducastel and Anseew, 2020). The deployment of these multitudes of new financial arrangements to finance development has reached a sufficient degree of legitimacy today that the DAC-OECD has changed its statistical system to integrate all contributions, from philanthropic and private actors alike, into development finance statistics. This proposal was already made by Severino and Ray (2009). It became a reality in March 2021, with the publication of the first comprehensive set of Total Official Support for Sustainable Development (TOSSD) data for 2019 (see Mah, 2023, this volume).

The first type of financialization work (*finance as development*) aims to transform economic and social relations in the target countries, and involves *local actors* who must manufacture financial inclusion on the ground, even if they are financed by public or philanthropic programs formulated in the Global North. The second type of financialization work (*financing development*) essentially involves *actors from the Global North*. Development Finance Institutions (DFIs) and Development Banks are changing their policies and their ways of using the funds by creating, for example, guarantee funds or private equity funds designed to leverage and attract private investors who are also Global North actors (e.g., large foundations and institutional investors).

The two processes of financialization concern the global circuits for financing, as well as the local insertion of actors into the formal financing systems. They both produce an increase in the power and wealth of private financial actors and their ability to extract value from the economies, firms, states and households of developing countries. Private finance actors are more present both locally in the day-to-day activities of recipient countries, and they are more active in the spheres where global policies are formulated. Development policies have thus accentuated the general financialization of these economies. Some additional financialization has been produced by the development policies through the two processes we have identified: find money for development and create financial inclusion. At the local level, companies take charge of welfare distribution systems, are paid to operate payment systems or to distribute credit (see Villarreal or Gronbach, 2023, this volume). At the global level, largely tax-exempt multinational corporations and foundations obtain public guarantees or even subsidies for their investments in developing countries (see Langevin, Brunet-Bélanger and Lefèvre, 2023, this volume). Moreover, the involvement of large companies and big financial actors in international policy forums means that it is harder to implement any policies that would be contrary to their interests.

Figure 0.1 provides a synthesis of the two ways in which development policies, although formulated with the intention of serving development goals (e.g., poverty alleviation or access to health), contribute to the transformation of financial systems and to an increase in the power of private financial actors, as well as their capacity to extract money from developing countries' economies. They thus take

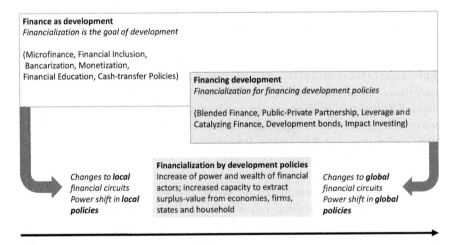

**FIGURE 0.1**  Two financialization processes by development policies (own aggregation).

their place in the concert of different monetary and financial transformations that together make up the Wall Street Consensus (Gabor, 2021).

## The content of the book

The contributions to this book present case studies at both global and local levels. They identify the actors, the narratives and the tools by which the two processes of financialization are brought forward, and they provide critical assessments of the effects and implications that the described changes bring with them.

The first part, entitled **Financing Development**, focuses on activities to enroll private finance to bridge the so-called "funding gap." Most cases are situated at the global level, involving mainly Global North actors who are trying to design new circuits for financing development. The second part, entitled **Finance as Development**, is dedicated to the older process of bringing more and more people into the monetary sphere and connecting them to the financial system. It gathers cases concerned with initiatives in Southern countries attempting to advance the insertion of people into formal financial circuits. We look at institutions and actors operating from sites in the Global North, and local case studies in Mexico, South Africa, Kenya, Cambodia and India.

### *Financing development*

Part I includes eight case studies. The first three chapters focus on the activities of Development Finance Institutions (DFIs) that are development banks dedicated to financing the private sector. As such, they play a key role in the efforts of large public development donors trying to attract private sector funds. In the case of microfinance, it is recalled that the WB used its DFI (IFC) to finance MFIs to steer them toward profit-making models that would make them attractive investment targets for international finance. The cases gathered here describe how, more recently, they seek to use their money to leverage private funds, in particular by using blended finance arrangements.

We start with a contribution by *Antoine Ducastel, Magalie Bourblanc* and *Camilla Adelle* who show how DFIs catalyze investments above and beyond public resources, and how this is promoted as a way to bridge the funding gap in agriculture. The chapter is based on a longitudinal analysis (from the year 2000 onward) of the agriculture portfolios of two DFIs. It clearly appears that the DFI contributions to close the funding gap is very limited. At the same time, the DFIs' governance and instruments are financialized as these institutions adopt financial practices and norms from private finance focused on risk management. While closing the funding gap would require more commitment to agriculture by DFIs, the adoption of standardized risk management procedures tends to annihilate such prospects. New blending finance initiatives come as an attempt to resolve this contradiction.

*Océane Ronal* looks at the complementary process of how DFIs have become involved in making development goals available to private investments since the early 2000s. This chapter analyses private equity funding as practiced by France's development aid policy operator, the French Development Agency Group (AFD Group–*Groupe Agence française de développement*) and its DFI Proparco. Private equity funding by public bodies is an attempt to solve the problem of a lack of development funding by turning the recipients into products for financial speculation. The chapter points to key consequences such as hybridizing the development interest logic with a purely financial investment logic and what it does to the concept of development that is performed by the institution.

*Luis Mah's* contribution looks at the EU as an important actor in the transformation of the development aid world. This chapter explores how the EU developed the first blended finance instruments and how this increasing financialization of development policy serves the EU's global strategic interests. As the world's leading donor, the EU plays an important role in the negotiation, design and implementation of the rules of the game underpinning the international architecture of the Official Development Assistance (ODA). Since 2007, the EU has been piloting blended finance initiatives to mobilize and de-risk private sector investments in developing countries. By combining public grants with private finance, blended finance represents the financialization trend of the EU's development policy.

The following two chapters focus on schemes promoted by major global donors to increase the "financial readiness" of cities and countries in the Global South so that they can more easily attract private investors, specifically by helping them to develop PPP projects.

*Monika Grubbauer* and *Hanna Hilbrandt* discuss the increasing entanglement of development finance and urban development agendas, particularly urban sustainability and green investment. The chapter focuses on activities of the World Bank's City Creditworthiness Initiative, which has been running (with interruptions) since 2014. The authors examine how the World Bank targets cities as partners and loan beneficiaries. This involves important institutional and programmatic shifts in development practices that serve to open new sites and economic sectors and moves development finance from the national to the local scale. This fragile process is fraught with hurdles and leads to potentially ambivalent outcomes for Southern municipalities. While the rescaling of power to the urban level may increase the room to maneuver for cities, they become exposed to new risks and sudden changes.

*Kate Bayliss* and *Elisa Van Waeyenberge* provide critical insights into the financialization of infrastructure in sub-Saharan Africa through PPPs that provide infrastructure. The chapter discusses the implications of interventions by donors and governments to construct infrastructure in a way that will attract private investors. Infrastructure as a physical spatial asset becomes condensed into financial metrics, seeking to offer secure revenue streams for investors. The role of the state is reconstructed as one of commissioner rather than the provider of services, effectively erasing the redistributive mandate with which infrastructure provisioning is associated. The specifics of the engagement with private finance vary substantially according to where an investment is located within the broader structure of global capitalism, with lower income countries relying heavily on external funding and foreign consultants.

The following case study by *Eduardo Gonçalves Gresse* and *Fernando Preusser de Mattos* allows us to understand how financial actors deal with the issue of sustainable development and the role played by the UN 2030 Agenda and its 17 Sustainable Development Goals (SDGs) in this process. In a case study of Brazil, Gresse and Preusser de Mattos demonstrate the financialization of sustainable development goals in practice. The chapter explores the narratives, resources and practices with which prominent financial actors in Brazil have engaged with the SDGs. This case allows us to understand how financial actors, whom policies aimed at maximizing finance for development seek to enlist, consider these issues, as well as the tools they equip themselves with.

The last two cases discussed in this section draw attention to innovative financial arrangements (procurement partnerships and impact bonds) invented and promoted mainly by large philanthropic foundations and private actors.

*Véra Ehrenstein* provides a case study on the procurement of vaccines involving a mega-foundation. She examines the ways in which the global health partnership Gavi transformed vaccine procurement for low-income countries. Set up by international organizations (WHO, UNICEF and the World Bank) and financed through philanthropic (Gates Foundation) and public donations, Gavi operates at the interface between the pharmaceutical industry and the resource-strained health administrations. This chapter explores one of Gavi's first market shaping initiatives for pneumococcal vaccines and shows how the initiative was designed to use aid funding to incentivize manufacturers to increase production capacity and sell new vaccines at a lower price. The effects are the redirection of local demands for vaccines and the channeling of funds to very few vaccine producers, mostly in the Global North.

With a case study on development impact bonds (DIBs), *Juliette Alenda-Demoutiez* critically analyses a new type of financial instruments. DIBs, and the actors supporting them, promise to solve so-called traditional issues in development projects by focusing on financial returns and a balance of power centered on the financial actors involved. The chapter shows that DIBs and the narratives behind them push a trajectory of governance that revolves more and more around financial motivations and an evolution in the way stakeholders involved in such programs interact. In the design of this governance, the idea of the DIB system is based on the enforcement of an investor's viewpoint, reformulating the notion of poverty as a problem to be invested in and bringing to the forefront the question of how to organize the repayment of funds, along with a return on investment for the investor.

## Finance as development

Part II includes seven chapters that address different initiatives to develop financial inclusion. The first two chapters continue the exploration of the role of private foundations as actors financializing development. We also discover the importance of private actors that are neither banks nor investors, but payment infrastructure providers (such as Mastercard or telecommunication companies).

The chapter by *Marie Langevin, Andréanne Brunet-Bélanger* and *Sylvain A. Lefèvre* provides the case study of the Mastercard Foundation advancing philanthrocapitalism by promoting an Africa-centered program that aims to maximize the economic participation of African youth through financialized solutions using digital payments. The foundation thus helps to build new platforms for the inclusion of the poor in financial circuits and the flow of resources from developing economies to the centers of accumulation. This type of strategic philanthropy is adopted by firms that conceive their philanthropic work as a commercial strategy in its own right. The chapter analyzes the foundation's practices and the links between its financial inclusion agenda and Mastercard's strategic interests of expanding the global digital payment system.

Providing a very concrete example, *Marine Al Dahdah* shows how the construction of new financial circuits can create specific risks for the poor. She analyses the case of a program in Kenya that involves private actors from the digital sector in the design of health policies. Such programs have particularly flourished in Africa in the past few years through mobile money services. Where banking enrolment is low, mobile banking services allow individuals to pay health expenses with mobile money. These services promise the first healthcare coverage to Africans, thus shedding light on the lack of a welfare state. Because mobile markets in Africa are dominated by prepaid users who repeatedly switch operators, mobile-based health insurance is strongly related to the construction of sustainable and profitable mobile markets in a competitive and unstable African context.

The next two chapters examine the role of social cash transfer programs, which have become a key instrument to tackle poverty and inequality, in the monetization and bancarization of vulnerable people and communities. They also highlight the contribution of these policies to the development of new forms of indebtedness and surplus extraction from the poor, as well as describe configurations that allow private financial actors to become operators of public policies.

*Lena Sophia Gronbach* shows how, as cash transfer programs are extended to additional beneficiaries, the manual disbursement of cash is increasingly replaced with digital, financially inclusive payments through formal financial channels. The business case for these financial service providers usually extends beyond the provision of payment services and includes the cross-selling of additional financial products to beneficiaries. In its most advanced form, it can lead to the collateralization of social cash transfers for the provision of credit, opening the door to rising household debt and financial exploitation. South Africa's experience with its former payment provider CPS/Net1 illustrates the manifestation of financialization in the sphere of social protection and highlights the adverse impact these processes can have on beneficiaries.

*Magdalena Villarreal* analyses a conditional cash transfer program in Mexico. She addresses the kinds of dilemmas that present themselves at the interface between different actors involved in the implementation of social policy, particularly regarding the participation of the private sector. Her analysis is based on the case of *PROIIF,* the integral program for financial inclusion in Mexico, which was part of the last conditional cash transfer program (*PROSPERA*) implemented in Mexico. She discusses the ways in which this social development policy facilitates a financialization processes related to the local circulation of money and resources.

The book concludes with three chapters that return to the case of microfinance, whose central importance in the history of financialization through development policies has been noted. These chapters explore how financialization processes have evolved from microcredit and its crises.

*Rajalaxmi Kamath* and *Nithya Joseph* provide a long-term case study on microfinance in a South Indian Town. This chapter describes how microfinance activities have been reconfigured over time. It analyses a group of field staff that moved together from an NGO that facilitated local self-help group activities, to a MFI and finally became a so-called "Small Finance Bank". As part of this process, the authors describe changes in their interactions with borrowers, community members, their employers, state officials and investors. Over time, the MFI staff turn into proxy-creditors, charged with drawing the poor into networks of global finance, producing debt and being responsible for its recovery without owning the capital. They thus switch from social workers helping groups to lend internally and apply for bank loans, to gatekeepers that attract credit.

*Phasy Res* examines financial literacy programs in Cambodia. These programs were set up in response to the microcredit crisis. The empirical analysis captures the process of forming subjectivities around risk and debt responsibility. It also reveals how the local community either accepts or contests these formations. MFIs attempt to construct a reality where risk and over-indebtedness are entirely the responsibility of the borrower. The MFIs further this narrative by portraying over-indebted households as "reckless" and "irresponsible." This chapter argues that by reorienting development as a lack of financial resources, the ability of citizens to imagine alternative possibilities for development can be impaired. In light of this, Res claims that alternatives need to be found for debt distressed households to allow debt forgiveness.

Finally, *Isabelle Guérin* shows that the logic of microcredit has spread widely to other activities, and that these new practices have the same flaws. She looks at the broad changes in pro-poor markets invented to both serve the poor and attract social investors. These markets are seemingly demand-driven, improve welfare and share value. The chapter links the shortcomings of these relatively new markets to the experiences with the older microcredit schemes. In both cases, the constraints of profitability and scaling up are incompatible with a quality offer adapted to local constraints, social norms and cultural practices. Many of these products do not bring the expected welfare. While social investment accounts form a growing share of the financing of anti-poverty policies, there is reason for concern regarding the excessive concentration of a few profitable markets and creditworthy customers to the detriment of the whole range of goods, services and infrastructures that are unprofitable, but desperately needed by the poor.

## References

Aalbers, M. (2019) 'Financialization,' in Richardson, D. (ed.), *The International Encyclopedia of Geography: People, the Earth, Environment, and Technology*. Oxford: Wiley, pp. 1–12.

Aitken, R. (2013) 'The Financialisation of Micro-credit,' *Development and Change*, 44(3), pp. 477–499. DOI:10.1111/dech.12027

Al Dahdah, M. (2023) '"Top up your healthcare access": mobile money to finance healthcare in sub-Saharan Africa,' in *Financializations of Development: Global Games and Local Experiments*, this volume.

Alenda-Demoutiez, J. (2019) 'A Fictitious Commodification of Local Development through Development Impact Bonds?,' *Journal of Urban Affairs*, 42(6), pp. 892–906. DOI: 10.1080/07352166.2019.1581029

Alenda-Demoutiez, J. (2023) 'Financialization in development projects and new modes of governance,' in *Financializations of Development: Global Games and Local Experiments*, this volume.

Barman, E. (2015) 'Of Principle and Principal: Value Plurality in the Market of Impact Investing,' *Valuation Studies*, 3(1), pp. 9–44. DOI: 10.3384/VS.2001-5592.15319

Bateman, M. (2010) *Why Doesn't Microfinance Work? The Destructive Rise of Local Neoliberalism*. London: Zed Books.

Baud, C. and Chiapello, È. (2015) 'How the Financialization of Firms Occurs: The Role of Regulation and Management Tools: The Case of Bank Credit,' *Revue française de sociologie*, 56, pp. 439–468. DOI: 10.3917/rfs.563.0439.

Bayliss, K., and van Waeyenberge, E. (2018) 'Unpacking the Public Private Partnership Revival,' *The Journal of Development Studies*, 54(4), pp. 577–593. DOI: 10.1080/00220388.2017.1303671

Bayliss, K., and van Waeyenberge, E. (2023) 'The financialization of infrastructure in sub-Saharan Africa,' in *Financializations of Development: Global Games and Local Experiments*, this volume.

Bergamaschi, I., Moore, P. and Tickner, A.B. (eds.) (2017) *South-South Cooperation Beyond the Myths. Rising Donors, New Aid Practices?* London: Palgrave Macmillan. DOI: 10.1057/978-1-137-53969-4.

Bond, P. (2006) 'Global Governance Campaigning and MDGs: From Top-Down to Bottom-Up Anti-Poverty Work,' *Third World Quarterly*, 27(2), pp. 339–354. DOI: 10.1080/01436590500432622.

Chiapello, E. (2017) 'La financiarisation des politiques publiques,' *Mondes en développement*, 45(178), pp. 23–40. DOI: 10.3917/med.178.0023.

Chiapello, E. and Knoll, L. (2020) 'Social Finance and Impact Investing. Governing Welfare in the Era of Financialization,' *Historical Social Research*, 45(3), pp. 7–30. DOI: 10.12759/hsr.45.2020.3.7-30.

Davies, T.R. (2012) 'The Transformation of International NGOs and Their Impact on Development Aid,' *International Development Policy|Revue internationale de politique de développement*, 3. DOI: 10.4000/poldev.994.

Doligez, F. (2017) 'La microfinance, précurseur de la financiarisation de l'aide au développement?,' *Mondes en développement*, 217/2(178), pp. 41–58. DOI: 10.3917/med.178.0041

Ducastel, A. and Anseew, W. (2020) 'Impact Investing in South Africa: Investing in Empowerment, Empowering Investors,' *Historical Social Research*, 45(3), pp. 53–73. DOI: 10.12759/hsr.45.2020.3.53-73

Ducastel, A., Bourblanc, M., and Adelle, C. (2023) 'Why development finance institutions are reluctant to invest in agriculture... And why they keep trying The financialization of development policies as an obstacle to invest in agriculture,' in *Financializations of Development: Global Games and Local Experiments*, this volume.

Duménil, G. and Lévy, D. (2001) 'Costs and Benefits of Neoliberalism. A Class Analysis,' *Review of International Political Economy*, 8(4), pp. 578–607. DOI: 10.1080/09692290110077593

Ehrenstein, V. (2023) 'Financial circuits of vaccine procurement in the era of global health,' in *Financializations of Development: Global Games and Local Experiments*, this volume.

Epstein, G.A. (2005) *Financialization and the World Economy*. Cheltenham: Edward Elgar Publishing.

Gabor, D. (2021) 'The Wall Street Consensus,' *Development and Change*, 52(3), pp. 429–459. DOI: 10.1111/dech.12645.

Gore, C. (2000) 'The Rise and Fall of the Washington Consensus as a Paradigm for Developing Countries,' *World Development*, 28(5), pp. 789–804. DOI: http://dx.doi.org/10.1016/S0305-750X(99)00160-6

Gresse, E.G., and Preusser de Mattos, F. (2023) 'The financialization of sustainable development goals,' in *Financializations of Development: Global Games and Local Experiments*, this volume.

Gronbach, L. (2023) 'Social cash transfers in sub-Saharan Africa: financialization, digitization and financial inclusion,' in *Financializations of Development: Global Games and Local Experiments*, this volume.

Grubbauer, M., and Hilbrandt, H. (2023) 'Shifts and hurdles in the urbanization of development finance: the case of the World Bank's city creditworthiness initiative,' in *Financializations of Development: Global Games and Local Experiments*, this volume.

Guérin, I., Labie, L. and Servet, J.M. (eds.) (2015) *The Crises of Microcredit*. London: Zed Book. DOI: 10.5040/9781350250932.0006.

Guérin, I., Morvant-Roux, S. and Villarreal, M. (eds.) (2013) *Microfinance, Debt and over-Indebtedness: Juggling with Money*. London and New-York: Routledge.

Kamath, R., and Joseph, N. (2023) 'From social workers to proxy-creditors to bank tellers: financialization in the work of microcredit field staff in a South Indian town,' in *Financializations of Development: Global Games and Local Experiments*, this volume.

Krippner, G. (2005) 'The Financialization of the American Economy,' *Socio-Economic Review*, 3, pp. 173–208. DOI: 10.1093/SER/mwi008

Krippner, G. (2011) *Capitalizing on Crisis: The Political Origins of the Rise of Finance*. Cambridge: Harvard University Press.

Langevin, M., Brunet-Bélanger, A., and Lefèvre, S. A. (2023) 'Financialization through payment infrastructure: the philanthrocapitalism of the Mastercard foundation,' in *Financializations of Development: Global Games and Local Experiments*, this volume.

Langley, P. (2008) 'Financialization and the Consumer Credit Boom,' *Competition & Change*, 12, pp. 133–147. DOI: 10.1179/102452908X289794

Lavinas, L. (2017) *The Takeover of Social Policy by Financialization: The Brazilian Paradox*. New York: Palgrave Macmillan.

Mader, P. (2015) *The Political Economy of Microfinance. Financialising Poverty*. London: Palgrave Macmillan.

Mader, P., Mertens, D. and van der Zwan, N. (2020) *The Routledge International Handbook of Financialization*. London: Routledge.

Mah, L. (2023) 'The financialization of EU development policy: blended finance and strategic interests (2007–2020),' in *Financializations of Development: Global Games and Local Experiments*, this volume.

Martin, R. (2002) *Financialization of Daily Life, Labor in Crisis*. Philadelphia, PA: Temple University Press.

Mawdsley, E. (2018) 'From Billions to Trillions': Financing the SDGs in a World "Beyond Aid,"' *Dialogues in Human Geography*, 8(2), pp. 191–195. DOI: 10.1177/2043820618780789

Mawdsley, E., Savage, L. and Kim, S.M. (2013) 'A "Post-Aid World"? Paradigm Shift in Foreign Aid and Development Cooperation at the 2011 Busan High Level Forum,' *Geographical Journal*, 180, pp. 27–38. DOI: 10.1111/j.1475-4959.2012.00490.x

McGoey, L. (2015). *No Such Thing as a Free Gift. The Gates Foundation and the Price of Philanthropy*. London and New York: Verso.

Morvaridi, B. (2012) 'Capitalist Philanthropy and Hegemonic Partnerships,' *Third World Quarterly*, 33(7), pp. 1191–1210. DOI: 10.1080/01436597.2012.691827.

Natile, S. (2020) 'Digital Finance Inclusion and the Mobile Money. "Social" Enterprise: A Socio-Legal Critique of M-Pesa in Kenya' *Historical Social Research*, 45(3), pp. 74–94. 10.12759/hsr.45.2020.3.74-94

OECD (2021) *The OECD DAC Blended Finance Guidance*. Paris: Éditions OCDE. DOI: 10.1787/ded656b4-en.

Res, P. (2023) 'Financial literacy training in Cambodia as a tool to form borrowers' subjectivities,' in *Financializations of Development: Global Games and Local Experiments*, this volume

Severino, J.-M. and Ray, O. (2009) 'The End of ODA: Death and Rebirth of a Global Public Policy,' *Center for Global Development*, Working Paper 167, [online]. Available at: https://www.cgdev.org/sites/default/files/1421419_file_End_of_ODA_FINAL.pdf. (Accessed: 20 June 2020).

UN Secretary-General (2019) *Roadmap for Financing the 2030 Agenda for Sustainable Development: 2019–2021* [online]. Available at: https://www.un.org/sustainabledevelopment/sg-finance-strategy/. (Accessed: 20 June 2020).

van der Zwan, N. (2014) 'Making Sense of Financialization,' *Socio-Economic Review*, 12(1), pp. 99–129. DOI: 10.1093/ser/mwt020.

van der Zwan, N. (2017) 'Financialisation and the Pension System: Lessons from the United States and the Netherlands,' *Journal of Modern European History*, 15(4), pp. 554–578. DOI: 10.17104/1611-8944-2017-4-554

van Waeyenberge, E. (2016) 'The Private Turn in Development Finance,' Working Papers wpaper140, Financialisation, Economy, Society & Sustainable Development (FES-SUD) Project [online]. Available at: https://ideas.repec.org/p/fes/wpaper/wpaper140.html. (Accessed: 20 June 2020).

Villarreal, M. (2023) 'Conditional cash transfer programs in Mexico,' in *Financializations of Development: Global Games and Local Experiments*, this volume.

Young, S. (2010) 'Gender, Mobility and the Financialisation of Development,' *Geopolitics*, 15, pp. 606–627. DOI: 10.1080/14650040903501104

# PART I
# Financing development

# 1

# WHY DEVELOPMENT FINANCE INSTITUTIONS ARE RELUCTANT TO INVEST IN AGRICULTURE... AND WHY THEY KEEP TRYING

## The financialization of development policies as an obstacle to invest in agriculture

*Antoine Ducastel, Magalie Bourblanc and Camilla Adelle*

## Introduction

Bilateral and multilateral Development Finance Institutions (DFIs), that is, government-backed institutions that invest in private-sector projects in low- and middle-income countries, take center stage in the development finance community. These institutions are not new, for instance, the British Commonwealth Development Corporation (CDC), the oldest European DFI, was established in 1948 (McWilliam, 2002). Historically, DFIs have to reconcile two objectives: ensure financial profitability, while fulfilling developmental goals and mandates. For a long time, DFIs remained largely at the periphery of development and cooperation policies. However, since the 2000s and particularly after the 2008s financial crisis they have attracted growing interest from decision-makers and have experienced a rapid increase in their activities (Institute of New Structural Economics, 2019; Overseas Development Institute, 2016).

In this chapter, we attempt to better understand what DFIs actually do in terms of development public policy. Rather than looking at DFIs' overall portfolio, we focus on financial flows targeting one specific asset class: agriculture. This is because the agricultural sector epitomizes the two contradictory logics in which DFIs seem to be caught. On the one hand, agriculture is recognized in development spheres as a very strategic sector to tackle food insecurity, climate change and/or (rural) poverty. As such, agricultural development is high on DFIs' political agenda. On the other hand, DFIs' investment officers have to deal with the specific characteristics of agriculture (weather variation, land and water management, etc.), which involve higher costs and uncertainties compared to DFIs' asset classes of choice: finance and infrastructure. Hence the question: how do DFIs deal with these contradictory logics? Looking at their agriculture

DOI: 10.4324/9781003039679-3

portfolios published over the last three decades, we show that DFIs tend to dis-invest from primary production agriculture companies in the Global South and to move to agriculture finance and agroindustry. While the existing literature on this topic has mostly engaged with particular risks associated with agriculture (Kenny et al., 2018), we move a step further by analyzing the financialization of development policies as the main obstacle to agricultural development.

In development studies, two different approaches examine the financializa-tion of public policies, that is, the idea that "new public policies are designed to capture the strengths of private finance, to engage its actors, and [also conform to] its techniques and forms of reasoning" (Chiapello, 2020, p. 22). First, ac-ademics analyze the increasing influence of financial actors over development institutions and ecosystems. In this emerging "beyond-aid world" (Mawdsley, 2018) or "Wall-Street consensus" (Gabor, 2019), decreasing traditional public resources for development, starting with ODA, have to be optimized in order to leverage private investors' capital flows. Second, scholars look at the spread of financial norms into development organizations and the specific (technical and relational) work that attempts to (re)frame development projects and programs as assets, that is, a thing with a specific risk and reward profile (Birch and Muniesa, 2020; Ducastel and Anseeuw, 2016). In this chapter, we build on our previous research (Ducastel, 2017, 2019) around the financialization of development pol-icies and turn to focus on the involvement of DFIs in the agricultural sector over the last four decades. After having paid specific attention to the narratives deployed and the preferred instruments used in development policies, we aim to direct our attention to DFIs financial flows in order to investigate how exactly the dissemination of financial norms within development institutions influences capital allocation.

Although DFIs have increasingly attracted the attention of policymakers, they have remained largely understudied by social scientists for a long time, even while reports by DFI managers and consultants have mushroomed (e.g. Institute of New Structural Economics, 2019; ODI and EDFI, 2019). This chapter seeks to fill this gap by focusing on major European bilateral DFIs (Proparco, DEG, FMO, CDC) and a few multilateral institutions (IFC, EIB and AfDB). While the analyzed DFIs differ widely in terms of shareholding structures, mandates, geographic areas and size, they currently face similar challenges and draw on a similar repertoire of instruments and expertise to address them. When it comes to their commitments to agricultural development, DFIs experience similar challenges and transformations. In the pages that follow, we focus the analysis on these common challenges and practices.

For this study, we collected a variety of data. We reviewed recent reports and grey literature dealing with agriculture development policies, in order to analyze mainstream institutional narrative and problematization. From 2017 to 2018, we conducted 18 interviews with representatives of DFI supervisory authorities, with DFI staff (executive managers, investment officers or social development specialists) and with DFI experts (e.g. staff of NGOs such as Oxfam and Counter

Balance), to better understand DFIs' internal organization and daily work. Finally, we analyzed DFI annual reports and other publications (internal reports, project factsheets, press releases, etc.) to identify and list DFIs' investments in agriculture from 2000 to 2020, with a particular focus on Proparco and the European Investment Bank (EIB).

In the first section, we briefly describe the recent evolution of agriculture development policies' narratives, which are increasingly focused on bridging the funding gap. We then present our findings from a longitudinal analysis from the year 2000 onward, of two DFIs' agriculture portfolios, to look at the underlying companies and activities encompassed under this "asset class". We conclude that DFIs' contribution to close the funding gap is very limited. In the last section, we seek to explain this shortfall by focusing on day-to-day agriculture investments.

## The new rhetoric of bridging the funding gap in agriculture for development

Historically, agriculture has been a priority sector for development agencies and banks. After the independence of former colonies, donor countries strongly supported the agricultural development banks in developing countries, and the share of the ODA going to the sector remained high until the end of the 1980s (FAO, 2018). Since then, however, there was a regular and inexorable decrease in development institutions' funding to agriculture. This represented a general trend for all development flows, including ODA (FAO, 2018), as agriculture was seen as a declining sector, and prices for agricultural products were on a long downward slope. Two decades later, the 2007/2008 world food crisis[1] pushed agriculture back onto the development agenda (McMichael, 2009). Not surprisingly, the World Bank dedicated its 2008 World Development Annual Report to agriculture, emphasizing that "in the 21st century, agriculture continues to be a fundamental instrument for sustainable development and poverty reduction" (World Bank, 2008, p. 1).

Recently, the 2030 Agenda for Sustainable Development launched an objective directly related to agriculture, namely the SDG 2: "end hunger, achieve food security and improved nutrition and promote sustainable agriculture".[2] Accordingly, the UN agenda reaffirmed how important the sector is for sustainable development. In the development sphere, agriculture is commonly recognized as a "unique instrument for development" for three main reasons: (1) as a major economic activity in countries of the global South, it is a source of growth, employment and income; (2) as a livelihood, it is a safety net for poor people in rural areas; and (3) "as a provider of environmental services" it is an important component of natural resources conservation (World Bank, 2008).

Despite this apparent consensus and long-term commitment in the development communities to the importance of targeting the agricultural sector, it seems that agriculture in developing countries has so far failed to meet development goals. Global food insecurity actually increased again in 2019 (FAO, 2020).

New narratives have emerged to explain existing obstacles in development policies' investments towards agriculture, and new solutions to bypass identified hurdles have recently been proposed. Such narratives mostly revolve around the issue of a large and persistent "funding gap", that is, a mismatch between the financial needs of agricultural actors and the allocation of financial resources to the agricultural sector by public or private financial institutions. Different cost assumptions estimated by international research centers circulate, such as "US$ 7.3 billion to improve both agriculture productivity and climate change adaptation" (SAFIN & Dalberg, 2020). Closing these gaps has become a top priority in global development communities, as illustrated by the proliferation of studies and reports, specifically on finance for agriculture in developing countries (e.g. FAO, 2018; World Bank, 2016).

We can list several explanations for such funding gaps: a significant decline in ODA for agriculture between 1973 and 2007/2008; a significant reduction in government spending on agriculture as part of structural adjustment programs; and the "inability of banks and other financial institutions to tailor products for the agricultural sector" (FAO, 2018). The funding gap's perimeter and borders are also open to debate. Some authors talk about a "missing middle", that is, the capital needs of farmers and agriculture players are too high for microfinance but too small for commercial banks (FAO, 2018, p. 59). Others argue that the gap is actually between public subsidies or concessional funding and commercial funding (Jenkins, 2019). Consequently, the solutions proposed differ, ranging from patient capital and private equity funds to "smart subsidies" (Dalberg, 2016). Yet, all solutions reveal that additional capital flows are urgently and massively required, particularly from institutional investors, such as pension funds or insurance companies, to fund 2030 SDGs as traditional public funding stagnates (United Nations, 2015).

Agriculture development policies thus tend to be financialized inasmuch as food insecurity or rural poverty are increasingly framed within national and global development spheres as essentially a financial issue. Consequently, policymakers are more concerned with how to leverage private investors' capital flows than with agriculture models, techniques and practices to support farmers (e.g. agroecology vs. agroindustry, corporate vs. family farming). Hence, the so-called right agriculture model is the one that is able to attract capital flows. In practice, this apparent politically agnostic approach actually works in favor of large-scale industrial and mechanized agriculture, meaning that existing mainstream agriculture players keep absorbing most of development finance's funding (Oxfam, 2020). Bilateral and multilateral development initiatives to promote agroecology exist. For instance, the French 2014 *Orientation and programming law on development policies and international solidarity* stipulates that "France promotes family farming, producing wealth and growth, supporting food-crop production, respecting biodiversity and ecosystems". However, these two debates – how to finance agriculture and which agriculture to finance – are completely separated. In sum, Development Banks and Development Finance Institutions are called upon to play a key role to help closing a funding gap, in line with their capacity to lever-age private finance. In the next section, we critically examine the outputs they can account for by taking stock of DFIs' concrete investments in sub-Saharan African agriculture.

## A historical overview of DFIs investments in agriculture

DFIs are development-oriented financial institutions, and as such they have a specific mandate dictated by their supervisory authorities to intervene in agriculture, particularly since the 2007/2008 food crisis. For instance, the FMO replaced "housing" with "agri-food" in its priority asset class in 2010, as its for-mer chief executive officer (CEO) reminded us:

> It was clear, however, that the Dutch government was also starting to focus more on this sector [agriculture] and that FMO had to contribute to a pressing worldwide problem. How else could we help to ensure that, with the same land area and less water use, there would be enough food for nine billion people in 2050?
>
> *(Kleiterp, 2017, p. 129)*

In this section, we look at DFIs' investments in agriculture from 1980 to 2020, and specifically those of two institutions[3]: the French bilateral DFI Proparco and the multilateral EIB's "African, Caribbean and Pacific Investment Facility",[4] and their investments from 2000 onwards in sub-Saharan African agriculture. In doing so, we go into details and describe DFIs' asset classes in order to shed light on which type of agriculture these DFIs actually support in terms of value chain, beneficiaries' profiles or localization. Over this period, we identified 47 new financial commitments to projects from Proparco, and 28 to projects labeled as "agriculture" from EIB. By looking at the evolution of their investment portfo-lio, we found two complementary trends: (1) a disinvestment from agriculture in general, and especially from agriculture primary production, partially offset by (2) increasing support to agriculture finance and entrepreneurs.

### *DFIs' disinvestment from agriculture primary production*

Agriculture and agribusiness are historically a strategic sector for DFIs. Until the 2000s, the Commonwealth Development Corporation, for instance, was a key financier of agribusiness in sub-Saharan Africa, where it pioneered several greenfield projects (Tyler and Dixie, 2013).

However, the share of overall agriculture projects in DFIs' portfolio decreased steeply from the 1980s onwards. Tyler and Dixie (2013) showed that the agri-cultural sector accounted for 48% of the CDC's global portfolio in 1951 and 53% in 1986, but only 20% in 2000. After a sharp decline in the late 1990s, when "finance" and "infrastructure" became DFIs' cherished asset classes, the share of agriculture in DFIs settled down at an almost insignificant level. Kenny et al. (2018) compared five bilateral DFIs' portfolios (CDC, DEG, FMO, OPIC, Proparco) plus IFC, looking at their commitments from 2012 to 2016. They noted that commitments in "agriculture, forestry, fishing, and hunting" accounted for only 1%–6% on average over this period (Kenny et al., 2018). Even after the 2007/2008 food crisis, while ODA flows to agriculture experienced a recovery, DFIs' involvement in the sector at large remained very scarce.

Our analysis of annual reports[5] shows a similar trend within Proparco's annual financial commitment to agriculture:

> 1986: 14 agriculture equity investments (38.7% of total commitments);
> 1995: six equity investments (38%) and 39 loans (44%);
> 2007: three loans (8%) and one equity investment (2.5%);
> 2019: three loans (5%).

Focusing on Proparco from 2000 onward, we note, on the one hand, a relative stability over the period in terms of the number of deals: each year (except for 2002), Proparco reported new commitments in sub-Saharan African agriculture with a peak at six new projects in 2013. Thus, we note a marginal but persistent exposure to agriculture. On the other hand, the average ticket size progressively increased: respectively from €2.5M in 2000 to €31.2M in 2018 for Proparco, and from €12.75 to €19.6M for the EIB. This significant trend is proportional to the sharp increase of DFIs' total commitments over the same period: from €201M in 2000, to €1.600M in 2018 for Proparco. In absolute value, DFIs injected more money into agriculture over the period, targeting larger deals, to keep pace with their total portfolio increase.

Historically, DFIs finance the capacities for the development and modernization of production in major and already well-developed enterprises requesting large amounts of patient capital,[6] typically for rent-seeking crop plantations with a manufacturing base producing sugar, palm oil, rubber tree or banana. By supporting cash crops, DFIs also actively promote a development model based on an export-oriented agriculture. It is interesting to highlight a continuous support for specific rent-seeking crop plantations from DFIs. Tyler and Dixie (2013) showed that one-third of CDC's investment from 1948 to 2000 targeted only three crops (tea, sugar, palm oil) and 80% were, at least partially, oriented toward exportation.

Over time, DFIs have also maintained a stable network of clients in sub-Saharan Africa, sometimes from colonial or early independence years. Therefore, beyond development policies and agendas (e.g. post-2008 food security crisis), it is noteworthy that they have their own inherited pipeline of companies. For instance, our analysis of Proparco and EIB commitments since 2000 shows the importance of large sugar companies in their investments in sub-Saharan Africa. From 2000 to 2013, these two DFIs undertook six new commitments (five loans and one equity operation) to restructure and modernize large agribusiness conglomerates, partly or exclusively producing and processing sugar, in Chad, Ivory Coast, Kenya, Mauritius, Malawi, Uganda and Swaziland. However, in recent years, less and less funding has gone to these large-scale agricultural companies. From 2013 onwards, we note only two loans to agribusiness conglomerates: large Ivorian and Ugandans sugar producers, in 2018. Thus, in the last decade DFIs progressively distanced themselves from agriculture primary production.

## DFIs' support to agriculture finance and entrepreneurs

While the share of primary production declines, DFIs turn to downstream or upstream agro-industries and agriculture finance intermediaries. Hence, DFIs support medium and large enterprises along the agricultural value chains, either in downstream activities (seeds and fertilizers) or upstream (processing and trading). From 2013 onwards, 13 out of 23 of Proparco's commitments in sub-Saharan Africa went to agroindustry companies with no or almost no primary production activities: a soft-drinks producer in West Africa (Gaselia), a manufacturer of fertilizer in Nigeria (Indorama), a wheat/maize miller in Mozambique, and a pan-African leading trader and exporter (ETG). Here, DFIs support entrepreneurs who are either African or in Africa, along agriculture value chains. Few projects in this category target African agri-food markets or support an endogenous development that would mean betting on an increasing local demand driven by a rising middle class. All the others are still in the very same rent-seeking crop value chains pursuing African agriculture extraversion (e.g. ETG and Indorama).

Moreover, in order to reach a larger scope of sub-Saharan African agribusinesses and to disburse larger tickets, DFIs increasingly support commercial financial institutions. Such indirect support to the sector is rapidly growing compared to DFIs' direct investments in agriculture. For instance, after 2013, 9 out of 11 of the EIB's commitments (i.e. €221M out of €252.2M) were with financial institutions, compared to only three from 2000 to 2013.

Among financial intermediaries, private equity funds, either specifically dedicated to agriculture or with a trans-sectorial approach, have attracted an increasing amount of DFI capital since the 2010s. This instrument is based on the principle of delegating management to a professional fund manager who invests the capital in a mutual fund on behalf of investor(s). In 2010, Proparco invested with a €10M equity investment in the African Agriculture Fund, alongside the French Development Agency and the African Development Bank, to support agricultural value chains in Africa (Ducastel, 2017). DFIs have played a decisive role in the structuring and organization of the African emerging private equity industry (Ronal, 2023, this volume). They are important capital providers in this financial industry, and in 2018 the EIB invested €88.5M in four different funds targeting sustainable forestry, sustainable fisheries and aquaculture projects, and sustainable land use projects in countries in the South. On the other hand, funds' managers and investment officers are often former DFI staff. For instance, the managing company of the African Agriculture Fund was created in South Africa in 2005 by two former employees of the Commonwealth Development Corporation Group (CDC), where they respectively held the positions of Director of the Africa division, and Private Equity Business Development Executive.

Alongside private equity funds, microfinance institutions and banks are other privileged intermediaries. DFIs grant credit lines to these institutions with specific aims and targets. Through microfinance institutions, DFIs attempt to reach (small-scale) farmers. The EIB granted €5M to Fefisol, targeting small biological and sustainable farmers in sub-Saharan Africa, while Proparco funded Advans, an Ivorian institution promoting innovative solutions for small-scale cacao producers. Development and commercial banks, such as the Agricultural Development Bank owned by the government and the central bank of Ghana, or the First Merchant Bank of Malawi, a subsidiary of a South African leading commercial bank, received large credit lines, respectively €15M and €17.5M to support agriculture export-oriented value chains (e.g. rubber, sugar). Contractual agreements frame the credit line allocation upstream, according to investee characteristics such as value chain, turnover, and so on. These intermediaries largely promote fintech and mobile banking to enhance farmers' financial inclusion and thus to strengthen agriculture value chains' efficiency. By outsourcing the work of identification, evaluation and supervision of investees in agriculture, DFIs tend to become a fund of funds, disbursing a large amount of capital to local financial intermediaries.

DFIs' commitments to agriculture evolved significantly in the last four decades: from the 1980s to 2000 their portfolio share dropped down to a marginal level, before leveling off in relative value although the profile of agriculture, that is, tangible underlying assets included in this category, evolved. DFIs agricultural portfolio currently reveals a singular picture: a narrow conception of agriculture populated by financial institutions and entrepreneurs, with very few growers and land; in other words, an offshore agriculture. In the next section, we explain these findings by analyzing the day-to-day making process of DFIs' agriculture investments, showing how the financialization of DFIs' investment practices might be at odds with the prospect of funding the agricultural (primary) sector.

## Opening DFIs agriculture investment black box: DFIs' financialized rules at odds with agriculture

In this section, we make the case that financialization, that is, the idea that "new public policies are designed to capture the strengths of private finance, to engage its actors, and [also conform to] its techniques and forms of reasoning" (Chiapello, 2020, p. 22), push DFIs far from agriculture as their staff face challenges of converting this sector into an asset class. However, DFIs cannot completely give up on agriculture as they still have to fulfill their supervisory authorities' requirements. They therefore implement circumvention schemes and promote innovative financial instruments such as blending facilities. We first briefly present recent DFIs' financialization process, then move to the making process of agriculture investments.

## DFIs financial rationalization and standardization

Two aspects illustrate the increasing influence of financial actors, norms and instruments over DFIs in the last two decades: the evolution of their governance structures and the professionalization of risk management.

In terms of governance, several DFIs have opened their supervisory boards – strategic spaces where DFIs' investment strategies and their budgets and monitoring are approved – to private shareholders and independent members from the financial industry. For instance, the FMO's board is made up of three representatives of Dutch banking and insurance companies, one representative of the private equity industry and two representatives of NGOs. In Proparco's board of directors, the French Agency for Development holds, on behalf of the State, a 57% share but only 7 out of the 16 board members, who are moreover minority shareholders (i.e. French commercial banks, foreign DFIs or development banks) reach a majority representation. Thus, DFIs' supervisory authorities (e.g. ministry of finance, agency/ministry of development, foreign office) have retreated from governing arenas. In addition, they tend to weaken their "political grip" over DFIs strategic plans, as described by a former Proparco CEO:

> When you have Caisses d'Epargne and Banques Populaires investing 30 million, the Caisse des Dépots et Consignations investing 20 million, etcetera, then it's difficult (for the supervisory authority) to say "shut up"! Compared to AFD board meetings, at Proparco, supervisory authorities have always been much more disciplined, because in front of them they have the private sector.
>
> *(Interview with former Proparco CEO, 18 January 2018)*

DFIs moreover adopted risk management procedures already in force in commercial banks and financial institutions. This meant that DFI managers engaged in portfolio diversification strategies (by asset-class, by financial product and by geography) and increasingly aligned their due-diligence – that is, ex ante investigation to assess investment proposal's risks and returns through audit, financial modeling and on-site visits, against standardized financial benchmarks. In parallel, new risk managers challenged investment officers deal by deal to assess their robustness. These professional norms have circulated and permeated DFIs with the evolution of banking regulations (Baud and Chiapello, 2017), the arrival of new profiles and positions from large banks, private equity firms or audit companies and the emergence of a DFI transnational community[7] (Ducastel, 2019).

These recent transformations have important material implications shifting and realigning DFIs' financial flows, as we see in the next section for the case of agriculture.

## *Making agriculture an asset class*

As Hoeser highlighted in his pioneering study on development banks in the 1990s, DFIs' investment or credit officers face one major issue: the lack of "good" projects to finance (Hoeser, 1998). DFI staff thus have to reconcile several, sometimes contradictory, objectives: to maintain, and often to increase, the volume of annual disbursement – for example Proparco had to double its commitments from 2017 to 2020 (Proparco, 2017); to ensure a financial return, for example FMO targets 6% (Kleiterp, 2017); to reach social and development impacts, that is a "social profitability" (Chiapello, 2014); and, last but not least, to identify and to mitigate risks.

The lack of appealing projects is even more critical in agriculture, which makes this sector unpopular and cumbersome for DFI staff. First, agriculture production, productivity and profitability depend on weather variations, specific technical and agronomic issues (e.g. land and water management), and the volatility of agricultural commodity prices. Second, agriculture in sub-Saharan Africa is characterized by a weaker standardization and normalization of practices, for instance regarding accounting or work issues. Consequently, from a DFI investment officer's perspective, agriculture has a very specific and high-risk profile compared to other asset classes, starting with finance and infrastructure, because of its unpredictability, the difficulties to assess the value of underlying assets, its lower profitability, the absence of liquid collateral, and so on. DFI staff therefore have to invest a lot of time in preparatory work to check and mitigate the economic and financial risks of agricultural projects. As a Proparco investment officer pointed out, agriculture financing requests "a specific technicity in terms of structuration, understanding of the sector. For instance, securitization of loans is sometimes complex" (Proparco, 2012).

In addition, DFIs' investment officers and managers consider agriculture to be a highly sensitive sector in terms of social and environmental risks. Recently, several cases have been raised by NGOs and/or local communities blaming DFIs, or companies supported by DFIs, for land grabbing, mismanagement or violation of labor laws, or the misuse of chemicals. Ferronia, a large palm oil producer in the Democratic Republic of Congo, is probably one of the most emblematic controversial cases. Through long-term loan facility or equity investment, five European DFIs (CDC, DEG, BIO, FMO and Proparco) financed this company in the 2010s. These DFIs were strongly criticized for the lack of transparency, the violation of national and international laws, and their misuse of public funding. To mitigate these risks, DFI officers have implemented several strategies. First, they prioritize capital-intensive activities (e.g. sugar or palm oil) in order to disburse larger tickets to formal and standardized companies. Second, DFIs externalize their activities in agriculture to financial intermediaries. This outsourcing strategy allows DFIs to disburse larger amounts of capital, as local and specialized intermediaries are believed to be in a better position to reduce transaction costs, that is, the time and resources needed to implement a financing project and to manage specific agricultural risks. This is also about blame avoidance, as it is hoped that financial intermediaries will, according to the vocabulary of the field, take the heat in case of social or environmental controversy – although recent experience, such as the Ferronia case mentioned earlier, has shown that this is wishful thinking: DFIs ultimately remain responsible. Third, DFIs favor existing partnerships and well-established companies rather than green field projects, and thus reduce the resources their teams would need to devote to asset evaluation. Fourth, they adopt environmental and social (E&S) guidelines to mitigate reputational risks. IFC Environmental & Social Performance Standards have become a standardized matrix shared by DFIs and DFIs' financial intermediaries. If this E&S rating is unsatisfactory, they set up a corrective action plan to mitigate negative impacts, for example a resettlement plan for displaced households. Fifth, DFIs adopted a proactive strategy on E&S issues, highlighting the impacts leveraged by DFIs' capital flow (Ducastel, 2019), through ex ante modeling and/ or case studies. In recent years, DFI teams have focused specifically on two indicators: "direct and indirect jobs created and/or support" and "tonnes of $CO_2$ equivalent avoided annually" (Kleiterp, 2017, p. 134).

Looking at DFIs' staff professional issues, we start to better understand the two trends highlighted in the previous section. Because risk management became the mainstream professional framework for capital allocation, agriculture started looking too risky. To conform to these professional norms, DFI teams drastically reduce their exposure to agriculture and favor an offshore agriculture. The evolution of DFIs' agriculture portfolios over the last three decades is therefore directly related to the financialization of these institutions.

## *A new era of farmer finance?*

Despite all these impediments deterring DFIs from investing in agriculture, they keep trying. Even if DFIs distance themselves from their supervisory government, their advantage compared to commercial banks or financial institutions relies on their access to cheap money, either through concessional loans or owing to their preferential access to financial markets. They benefit from an implicit guarantee from the state and, as such, their rating is the same as for sovereign debt, independently of their balance sheet. To maintain this advantage and the profitability of their business model, DFIs have to be in line with the 2030 Agenda for Sustainable Development without disrupting standardized capital allocation procedures. Therefore, DFIs cannot escape investing in agriculture, but according to their professional rules. They are therefore deeply engaged in a research and development process looking for "new business models" in agriculture. To this end, they enroll dedicated partners and financial intermediaries of global agricultural finance or the smallholder finance community (CSAF, 2018).

Over the last few years, a set of financial innovations has generated high expectations in the development community and particularly among European

DFIs, with the prospect of bridging SDGs' funding gaps. These innovations are known as blended finance (Mah, 2023, this volume), that is "the strategic use of development finance for the mobilization of additional finance towards sustainable development in developing countries" (OECD, 2016). ODA enables financial operators, starting with DFIs or investment fund managers, to take much higher risks without consequences on their organizations' balance sheet. After the first-generation blending facilities targeting infrastructure, agriculture now looks like a promised land for blended finance. Recently, European development institutions set up or supported several blended facilities targeting agriculture, such as AgriFI (https://www.agrifi.eu/). According to its promoters, blending finance would help to close the financial gap by de-risking agriculture investments that are departing from mainstream risk management norms. However, blended finance favors operators from DFIs or the investment industry. For instance, AgriFI's current manager and portfolio officer come from the Belgium and the French DFI, respectively. They will therefore most probably manage these facilities according to the very same financial norms and practices inherited from their professional and training background. As such, AgriFI's first investment was in the Fairtrade Access Fund, a fund offering lending products for agricultural exporters in Latin America, the Caribbean and Africa, alongside Fairtrade International, the Grameen foundation or the German development bank KfW. Looking at agriculture through the (narrow) lens of risk management inevitably leads to prioritizing financial intermediaries and lengthening the financial chain.

Through these blending finance arrangements, DFIs and their financial intermediaries increasingly tap into ODA flows at the expense of other historical ODA brokers such as development agencies. This illustrates their growing influence in development spheres, where their norms and devices, particularly in terms of risk management, overflow and tend to become predominant (Christiansen, 2021).

## Conclusion

Looking at DFIs' involvement in agriculture over the last three decades, we note a diminishing investment in primary production and an increasing focus on agriculture finance and agroindustry. This trend runs counter to contemporary agriculture development policies calling for more investment in the sector, particularly for small-scale farmers, in order to close the existing funding gap. We explain such an apparent paradox by looking at the making process of DFI investments. As minimizing risks is the first requirement of DFI investment officers, this work rationale tends to pull them away from agriculture. Recent transformations in DFIs' governance and internal organization further entrench this dynamic. By promoting innovative financing instruments, DFI staff try to counter-balance this tendency and to reconcile their supervisory authority's political demand with their capital allocation procedures.

In this chapter we presented and discussed two different, contradictory levels of financialization. First, global agriculture development policies are financialized insofar as policymakers increasingly focus on funding gaps. Closing these gaps through a combination of public and private resources, that is, capital market arrangements, becomes a top priority on the development agenda, at the expense of alternative public policy framing of what development is all about. Second, DFIs' governance and instruments are also financialized as these institutions adopt financial practices and norms from private finance, focused on risk management. It is striking that these different layers of financialization are pitted against one another: while closing the funding gap would require more commitment to agriculture by DFIs, the adoption of standardized risk management procedures tends to annihilate such prospects. Current blending finance initiatives therefore pose as an attempt to resolve this contradiction.

## Acknowledgment

This research is part of the AFGROLAND project funded jointly by the Agence Nationale de la Recherche, France; National Research Foundation, South Africa; and Swiss National Science Foundation, Switzerland, via the Belmont Forum and Joint Programming Initiative on Agriculture, Food Security and Climate Change (FACCE-JPI) (Grant Number: 40FA40_160405).

## Notes

1  In a few months the price of rice, wheat and many other agricultural commodities skyrocketed (e.g. +50% for rice) triggering food riots in several countries of the South (Clapp and Cohen, 2009).
2  Available online at: https://www.un.org/sustainabledevelopment/hunger/.
3  For each project we specify: (1) the identity and activity of the beneficiary; (2) the beneficiary's host country/region; (3) the amount granted – with potential co-investor; (4) the type of financial product; and (5) the purpose of the financing. The summary table is available online at: https://doi.org/10.18167/DVN1/EGZ5TL
4  To identify these projects we review DFIs' annual reports from 2000 to 2020, as well as internal databases (available online at: https://www.eib.org/en/projects/loans/index.htm) and interactive maps (available online at: https://www.proparco.fr/en/carte-des-projets). We have entered every project labelled as an agricultural, agri-food or agribusiness project by the DFIs themselves.
5  The summary table is available online at: https://agritrop.cirad.fr/603190/.
6  As DFIs can offer long-term financial products, up to 15 years for Proparco.
7  DFIs interact with each other, either through syndicated loans and cross-participations or through their own association such as the European Development Finance Institution (EDFI).

## References

Baud, C. and Chiapello, E. (2017) 'Understanding the disciplinary aspects of neoliberal regulations: The case of credit-risk regulation under the Basel Accords,' *Critical Perspectives on Accounting*, 46, pp. 3–23. DOI: 10.1016/j.cpa.2016.09.005.

Birch, K. and Muniesa, F. (2020) *Assetization. Turning things into assets in technoscientific capitalism.* Cambridge: MIT press.

Chiapello, E. (2014) 'Financialisation of valuation,' *Human Studies*, 38(1), pp. 13–35. DOI: 10.1007/s10746-014-9337-x.

Chiapello, E. (2020) 'Stalemate for the financialization of climate policy,' *Economic Sociology*, 22(1), pp. 20–30.

Christiansen, J. (2021) 'Fixing fictions through blended finance: The entrepreneurial ensemble and risk interpretation in the Blue Economy,' *Geoforum*, 120, pp. 93–102. DOI: 10.1016/j.geoforum.2021.01.013.

Clapp, J. and Cohen, M.J. (eds.) (2009) *The global food crisis: Governance, challenges and opportunities.* Waterloo: Wilfred Laurier University Press and Centre for International Governance.

Council on Smallholder Agricultural Finance (CSAF) (2018) *State of the Sector* [online]. Available at: https://www.csaf.org/wp-content/uploads/2018/08/CSAF_State_of_the_Sector_2018_FINAL.pdf. (Accessed: 30 June 2022).

Dalberg (2016) *Inflection Point: Unlocking Growth in the Era of Farmer Finance* [online]. Available at: https://mastercardfdn.org/research/inflection-point-unlocking-growth-in-the-era-of-farmer-finance/ (Accessed: 30 June 2022).

Ducastel, A. (2017) 'Le capital-investissement comme instrument de l'action publique ou la financiarisation du développement en Afrique subsaharienne,' *Politique Africaine*, 144, pp. 135–155. DOI: 10.3917/polaf.144.0135.

Ducastel, A. (2019) 'Une banque comme les autres? Les mutations de Proparco et de la finance administrée,' *Actes de la recherche en sciences sociales*, 229, pp. 34–45. DOI: 10.3917/arss.229.0034.

Ducastel, A. and Anseeuw, W. (2016) 'Agriculture as an asset class: Reshaping the South African farming sector,' *Agriculture and Human Values*, 33(1), pp. 1–11. DOI: 10.1007/s10460-016-9683-6.

FAO (2018) *Agricultural Investment Funds for Development* [online]. Available at: http://www.fao.org/policy-support/tools-and-publications/resources-details/en/c/1178689/. (Accessed: 30 June 2022).

FAO (2020) *The State of Food Security and Nutrition in the World* [online]. Available at: http://www.fao.org/publications/sofi/2020/en/. (Accessed: 30 June 2022).

Gabor, D. (2019) *Understanding the financialisation of international development through 11 FAQs.* Washington: Heinrich Boll Stiftung North America.

Hoeser, U. (1998) *À la recherche de projets. L'action aveugle des banques de développement.* PhD thesis. Paris: Science-Po.

Institute of New Structural Economics (2019) *Mapping Development Finance Institutions Worldwide: Definitions, Rationales and Varieties* [online]. Available at: https://www.nse.pku.edu.cn/docs/20190530090006692126.pdf. (Accessed: 30 June 2022).

Jenkins, R. (2019) *The Need for Private Equity, Patient and Donor Capital Coupled with Integrated Sector Strategies in Sub-Saharan Africa to Support the Development of Sustainable Businesses and Industry Sectors.* AFSIC Presentation [online]. Available at: https://www.afsic.net/wp-content/uploads/2019/05/Phatisa.pdf. (Accessed: 30 June 2022).

Kenny, C., Kalow, J., Leo, B. and Ramachandran, V. (2018) 'Comparing Five Bilateral DFIs and the IFC,' *CGD Policy Paper*, 116 [online]. Available at: https://www.cgdev.org/sites/default/files/comparing-five-bilateral-development-finance-institutions-and-ifc.pdf. (Accessed: 30 June 2022).

Kleiterp, N. (2017) *Banking for a better world.* Amsterdam: Amsterdam University Press.

Mah, L. (2023) 'The financialization of EU development policy: Blended finance and strategic interests (2007–2020),' in *Financializations of Development: Global Games and Local Experiments*, this volume.

Mawdsley, E. (2018) '"From billions to trillions": Financing the SDGs in a world "beyond aid,"' *Dialogues in Human Geography*, 8(2), pp. 191–195. DOI: 10.1177/2043820618780789.

McMichael, P. (2009) 'Banking on agriculture: A review of the world development report 2008,' *Journal of Agrarian Change*, 9(2), pp. 235–246. DOI: 10.1111/j.1471-0366.2009.00203.x.

McWilliam, M. (2002) *The development business: A history of the commonwealth development corporation.* New York: Palgrave.

ODI and EDFI (2019) *Impact of Development Finance Institutions on Sustainable Development* [online]. Available at: https://cdn.odi.org/media/documents/12892.pdf. (Accessed: 30 June 2022).

OECD (2016) *Development Co-operation Report 2016. The SDGs as Business Opportunities* [online]. Available at: https://www.oecd.org/dac/development-co-operation-report-2016.htm. (Accessed: 30 June 2022).

Overseas Development Institute (2016) *Development Finance Institutions Come of Age. Policy Engagement, Impact and New Directions* [online]. Available at: https://edfi-website-v1.s3.fr-par.scw.cloud/uploads/2017/10/Development-Finance-Institutions-Come-of-Age.pdf. (Accessed: 30 June 2022).

Oxfam (2020) *Une pincée d'agroécologie, pour une louche d'agro-industrie* [online]. Available at: https://www.oxfamfrance.org/wp-content/uploads/2020/11/mediabreief_nov2020_EXEOKBD.pdf. (Accessed: 30 June 2022).

Proparco (2012) 'Development Initiatives for Sub-Saharan Agriculture and Food Production Industries,' *Private Sector & Development*, 13 [online]. Available at: https://www.proparco.fr/en/ressources/development-initiatives-sub-saharan-agriculture-and-food-production-industries. (Accessed: 30 June 2022).

Proparco (2017) *Annual Report* [online]. Available at: https://www.proparco.fr/en/ressources/proparco-financial-report-2017. (Accessed: 30 June 2022).

Ronal, O. (2023) 'How private equity turns development finance into a market opportunity,' in *Financializations of Development: Global Games and Local Experiments*, this volume.

SAFIN & Dalberg (2020) *Blended Finance Tools to Catalyze Investment in Agricultural Value Chains. An Initial Toolbox* [online]. Available at: https://www.safinetwork.org/safinre-sources/Blended-finance-for-agriculture. (Accessed: 30 June 2022).

Tyler, G. and Dixie, G. (2013) *Investing in Agribusiness: A Retrospective View of a Development Bank's Investments in Agribusiness in Africa and Southeast Asia and the Pacific.* Washington: World Bank [online]. Available at: https://openknowledge.worldbank.org/handle/10986/16660. (Accessed: 30 June 2022).

United Nations (2015) *Addis Ababa Action Agenda of the Third International Conference on Financing for Development* [online]. Available at: https://sustainabledevelopment.un.org/index.php?page=view&type=400&nr=2051&menu=35. (Accessed: 30 June 2022).

World Bank (2008) *World Development Report 2008: Agriculture for Development* [online]. Available at: https://openknowledge.worldbank.org/handle/10986/5990. (Accessed: 30 June 2022).

World Bank (2016) *Financing Agribusiness in Sub-Saharan Africa: Opportunities, Challenges, and Investment Models* [online]. Available at: https://www.findevgateway.org/sites/default/files/publications/files/africa_agrifinance_2016.pdf. (Accessed: 30 June 2022).

# 2

# HOW PRIVATE EQUITY TURNS DEVELOPMENT FINANCE INTO A MARKET OPPORTUNITY

*Océane Ronal*

During the 2017 Spring Meeting of the World Bank Group and the International Monetary Fund, World Bank President Jim Yong Kim stated:

> We believe that everyone in the development community should be an honest broker who helps find win–win outcomes – where owners of capital get a reasonable return, and developing countries maximize sustainable investments.
>
> *(Jim Yong Kim, "Rethinking Development Finance"*
> *Speech, 11 April 2017, at the London School of Economics)*

The idea behind this support for funding development through investment, public and private, is that private equity funding (i.e. direct investment in private unlisted companies) can bring both a useful injection of financial capital to recipient countries of development aid and returns for public and private sector investors. In this discourse, development finance institutions themselves are encouraged, through the so-called honest broker image, to invest and thus leverage private investment. The objective is to use public investment as an incentive, to attract and guide private capital into companies in aid-recipient countries that are neglected by traditional financing markets. The words of the President of the world's leading public development bank, and the public brokerage practices he is advocating, are signs of the importance of the devices and actors associated with the rise of investment-based development finance. In view of this situation, this chapter examines private equity investment by public entities as a mode of development finance. Private equity was added to the aid toolbox via bi- and multilateral Development Finance Institutions (DFIs). DFIs are public or quasi-public organizations that manage the operational allocation of development aid on behalf of one or more states (e.g. the International Finance Corporation for

DOI: 10.4324/9781003039679-4

the World Bank Group), issued on market terms and intended to support the recipient countries' private sector. These private-oriented practices, especially private equity funding, became fashionable in the international development community in the early 2000s (United Nations, 2002, 2008, 2011). This chapter shows that they are part of a financialization process and transform conceptions of development.

Financialization must be understood here as defined by Eve Chiapello, "as a specific process of transforming the world, objects, organizations and the problems we encounter, by the introduction of 'financialized' practices, theories and instruments" (Chiapello, 2020, p. 81). Recent academic literature published in English (Brooks, 2016; Clapp, 2014; Mawdsley, 2018) and French (Ducastel, 2016; Gabas, Ribier and Vernières, 2017) has begun to examine the financialization of development aid policies as a political turn (see also Mah, 2023; Ducastel et al., 2023 and Alenda-Demoutiez, 2023, all in this volume). This chapter proposes to extend these reflections by studying private equity funding as practiced by France's development aid policy operator, the French Development Agency group (AFD group – *groupe Agence française de développement*) which consists of the eponymous French Development Agency (AFD – the French public development bank) and its subsidiary, a DFI named Proparco (*Société de Promotion et de Participation pour la Coopération économique* – society for the promotion and participation for economic cooperation). Based on this case study, I first aim to highlight the change in approach that led to private equity being promoted as a key channel of development finance in international aid policies – and to show how the French institution organized its distribution of aid accordingly. I then turn to the socio-technical devices and management tools (Chiapello and Gilbert, 2019) necessary for the practical implementation of private equity funding. These are examined by studying the financially-focused investment choice method, and Proparco's internal impact assessment tool. I shall underline how these devices produce a specific form of intervention that differs from more traditional lending and are redefining the form of aid that appears to be the furthest removed from the financial sector: grants. I argue that the financialization process, as reflected in the intensification of private equity funding, is contributing to a redefinition of development in commercial terms, as an object and as a public problem.

This chapter is based on semi-standardized in-depth oral interviews conducted with AFD group staff ($n = 38$); private equity actors, including asset managers, legal or strategic advisors and bankers ($n = 33$); and a few representatives of companies in which the institution has made equity investments ($n = 5$). It also draws on direct or semi-participant field observations at AFD and Proparco's respective headquarters, as well as 2 of its 85 offices abroad (one in East Africa and one in West Africa). Finally, written sources of information (international and national official papers and data banks) dealing with development aid and the specific issues of including public investment in this aid were also consulted.

## Public investment as a catalyst for private investment: the origins of a financialized policy and practical framework

This section describes the institutional forms of reasoning that promote and guide private equity funding by public entities at the international level. I then show how this global agenda-setting is embodied in the structure of Proparco's investment practices.

### *Establishing the private sector as a driver of development*

A strategy "to use public aid as a driver for private investment" (United Nations, 2013) has been in operation since the early 2000s, via the cycle of international conferences on financing for development (in Monterrey in 2002, Doha in 2008 and Addis-Ababa in 2015). Its advocates seek to demonstrate the profitability of public investment in aid-recipient countries, while at the same time trying to secure private investment and the associated returns. In theory, these ideas are part of a private sector development (PSD) strategy developed by the Inter-American Development Bank (2011). In practice, they lead to an increase in DFI activities, and the French DFI Proparco is no exception. This DFI is growing: it undertook three capital increases in the early 2000s (in 2001, 2003 and 2008), and its private equity operations have risen significantly (see Figure 2.1) both in absolute terms and relative to loans issued. In terms of cumulative balance sheet volume, from Proparco's public annual balance sheets (2001, 2003 and 2008), Proparco's equity investments represented about a quarter of loans (24%) in 2001, but almost half in 2008 (47%).

The rise of private equity investment by public institutions is one element of the "rise of mission-oriented state investment banks" described by Mazzucato and Penna (2015) in their work on public development banks in Germany (the KfW – *Kreditanstalt für Wiederaufbau*) and Brazil (the BNDES – *Banco Nacional de Desenvolvimento Econômico e Social*). It implies an acceptance that private interests, particularly financial interests, can legitimately play a role in the implementation of public action. To the traditional justifications for State intervention in the economy such as the public interest or correction of market failures, the PSD strategy adds the financialized and now legitimated argument of the profitability of public aid. The aim of achieving a return on public money, or a profit on aid operations, is justified on the grounds that this would reduce the development aid budget, and act as an incentive to attract private money (the leverage argument) while continuing to encourage development through public funding.

This focus on returns is not new in French development aid, as Gordon Cumming observed in a book published for the 75th anniversary of AFD. In fact, it is historically "deeply rooted in AFD's DNA" (Cumming, 2017, p. 49, author's translation) and structures relations between the supervisory ministries[1] (particularly the Ministry of Economy and Finance) and AFD as an income-generating operator for the state. The PSD strategy, one expression of which is the development of private equity funding, thus offers a fresh, although not new, policy framework for public-private hybridization. The following pages explore the implications of these financialized forms of reasoning for the case of French development aid policy, and their consequences.

### Putting private equity into development aid: the French case study

As long ago as the late 19th century, the need to support economic development in the colonies translated into support from the French empire for local private sectors, which at the time consisted of large colonial owners. In France, the primary channel for this support was constructing a local bank offering. French public investment initiatives in the colonies started in the 1920s with the so-called colony enhancement (*mise en valeur des colonies*) policy launched by the Sarraut plan of 1923. Sarraut proposed a major public investment plan for the productive sectors and infrastructures to increase colonial wealth while pursuing certain social objectives such as healthcare and education. This policy of public support through productive investment to bring about "creation and renewal of new wealth" (Sarraut, 1923, p. 85, author's translation) continued after the second world war through the formation of State-owned entities, and mixed-economy entities in which the state held most of the capital. After the colonies gained their independence, this policy changed. The French government, now dealing with separate sovereign states, sold its former colonial investments and a whole array of development aid was dedicated to specific support for commercial private sectors in these new countries. In France, the organization in charge of this was Proparco, a DFI set up in 1977 specifically to help the private sector grow, which was theoretically specialized in venture capital funding. Loans nonetheless remained the principal form of French aid during the 1980s and 1990s (concessionary loans made by the AFD to the public sector and non-profit private sector, or market-rate loans to the commercial private sector).

It was not until the start of the 21st century that private equity funding began to develop in DFIs. In France, the AFD group stepped up its equity investments in the private sector after the 14 February and 11 December 2002 meetings of the Interministerial Committee for International Cooperation and Development – *Comité Interministériel de la Coopération Internationale et du Développement*. In 2002, the question of development finance and the role of financial instruments able to leverage private investment was the central topic of the International Conference on Financing for Development at Monterrey (United Nations, 2002). In 2008, when the second international conference on financing for development was held in Doha, Proparco undertook a capital increase to support its growth. Its investment activities had risen by 264% between 2002 and 2008 (see Figure 2.1).

Also in 2008, the AFD group set up a new €250 million fund for support to Africa, the Investment and Support Fund for Businesses in Africa – *Fonds d'Investissement et de Soutien aux Entreprises en Afrique* (Fisea), France's first public investment fund. Its creation was announced by French President Nicolas Sarkozy in a speech to the South African parliament (Sarkozy, 2008), and materialized France's ambitions for promoting private equity funding. In April 2009,

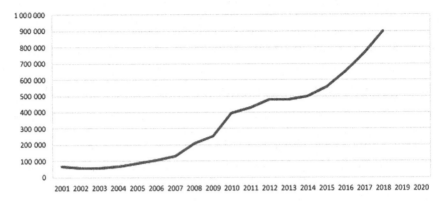

**FIGURE 2.1**   Equity and other investments by Proparco (in k€) from 2001 to 2018.
*Source:* Océane Ronal, 2021. The data presented here were collected from Proparco public annual balance sheets from 2001 to 2018.

in preparatory notes for the lunch of the fund, Fisea's board considered private equity funding as "a flagship, high-impact activity". Its operational importance was justified by the fact that African companies found it hard to increase their capital: "Equity is the most subsidiary mode of investment, and the scarcest re-source in most of our geographical zones of intervention" (ibid.). Fisea would thus add to the French public aid toolbox a new institutional instrument able to answer this unmet local demand for capital. More than ten years later, the men who were the CEOs of AFD (Jean-Michel Severino 2001–2010) and Proparco (Luc Rigouzzo 2006–2010) when Fisea was formed are still promoting the in-strumental relevance of this fund form, from their current positions at the head of two (private-sector) private equity firms that invest in Africa.

### Getting organized to invest

In the AFD group, Proparco is the only source of market-rate financial support to the private sector (as funding for the non-profit private sector – for example, NGOs, foundations – is issued by the AFD), and therefore the part of the group that handles private equity activities. However, the governance of these devices remains with AFD (as the legal parent company) and Proparco's two supervisory ministries (the Ministry of Economy and Finance and the Ministry of Europe and Foreign Affairs). In 2004, two years after the step-up in the AFD group's pri-vate equity investments, Proparco set up an *Equity and Sharing* team (now called *Equity Responsible Investments*), then, as the volumes of investment increased (see Figure 2.1), a so-called department was opened in 2018. This department, which included the initial team, institutionalized a more formal dedicated private eq-uity activity, with more human and financial resources. This change of scale normalized and organized the practice of private equity investment by public bodies, by bringing in outside skills (hiring staff from the private finance sector) and allocating financial resources (liquidities).

During the 2010s in particular, Proparco engaged finance professionals to re-inforce its teams. 150 new recruits joined Proparco in 2016 and it employs more than 300 people today, double the workforce of ten years ago. The larger teams working exclusively on private equity funding only account for a small part of this growth, but the institution has broadly renewed its socio-cultural base, with at least 50% of staff having previously worked in the private sector. One example is P.D.,[2] recruited in 2014 after working at a merchant bank, a private equity firm and an audit and consulting firm:

> I had met people from Proparco at the time, because I was already target-ing that kind of institution, not Proparco necessarily, but that finance and development ecosystem, and they had told me: "you have to learn the ropes in traditional finance."
>
> *(Interview with P.D., investment officer, Proparco, 12/04/2018)*

The idea was to hire new profiles from outside the AFD group in order to benefit from their experience in the private sector, particularly finance in the case of staff hired by the investment department. Among the group employees interviewed ($n =$ 38), 24 had joined Proparco from outside the public sector. Significantly, all of them had some previous experience in the commercial private sector. Only five of them had also worked in the public sector or non-profit private sector (see Table 2.1).

Private-sector banking is the most frequently-represented sector in the Proparco employees' backgrounds. The employees concerned mostly worked in the Corporate & Investment sections of banks and are specialists in corporate finance and financial markets. Financialization is thus reflected in a transfor-mation of the human resources mobilized for public action. Development aid is no longer simply implemented by the volunteers and engineers who were the traditional actors of the AFD group. Increasingly, it is also handled by finance professionals who previously worked in profit-seeking finance.

**TABLE 2.1** Proparco employees' background

| | *Proparco employees in the study with experience in[a]…* | | | | | |
|---|---|---|---|---|---|---|
| *Total Proparco employees in the study* | *The commercial private sector (n = 24)* | | | | *State-owned firms or administrations* | *NGOs* |
| | *Merchant banking* | *Private Equity firms* | *Audit and consulting firms* | *Commercial firms* | | |
| 24 | 16 | 10 | 7 | 13 | 2 | 3 |

*Source*: Océane Ronal, 2021. Based on an author's survey.
[a] One individual may have worked in more than one sector.

## Making development profitable

This section looks at the socio-technical devices that enable public action, and their consequences. Studying these devices provides a better understanding of the financialization induced by private equity funding (Baud and Chiapello, 2015; Chiapello, 2020) and the changes it generates in development-related practices and representations.

## Selecting bankable businesses, making profitable deals: the investment choice method

The rise in Proparco's private equity funding activities involves the use of financially-focused investment choice methods to select which projects will be financed.

Analysis of the practices by Proparco's investment officers at Project Committee meetings, and of internal files,[3] shows the role played in the investment decision by a series of financial indicators. These indicators describe the financial performance of a project (annual sales; gross margin; EBITDA[4]) and monitor progress on the execution of financial projects (generally over a seven-year period[5]). The investment files thus seek to quantify external growth (acquisitions) expected of the investment recipient companies, and also their organic growth (attrition rate, Opex[6] and Capex[7]). Forecast EBITDA and cash flow for the project are examined. Financial leverage and debt ratios are calculated. In the end, the value of the investment (i.e. the amount that would have to be paid to invest in the company under consideration) is determined by several standard financial approaches: comparisons with other files or calculations by the DCF – Discounted cash flow – method, which is a recognized sign of financialized reasoning (Chiapello, 2015, 2020; Doganova, 2015). The investment under consideration is summed up by its estimated profitability, expressed as the RoE – Return on Equity.

It is important to understand that this financial information differs from the information considered for a lending decision, which concentrates on estimating the borrower's capacity to repay and the appropriate interest rate. Private equity funding thus tends to transform the conventions of aid allocation, by financializing the way development projects are valued. To calculate an interest rate, the additional amount payable on a borrowed sum is calculated. Interest does not form part of the loan repayment as such; it is remuneration for the service rendered, the cost of the borrowing. But when RoE is calculated, reference is made to a positive or negative change over time in the capital invested. The return on the investment rewards (or sanctions) a speculative risk, the gamble taken on the change in value. The focus is less on managing a risk of default by the counterparty, and more on speculating on that risk in order to derive a financial return. For projects that might be granted finance, it is no longer enough to be bankable (i.e. demonstrate a future ability to repay their borrowing and its cost); they must also be able to provide financial returns (i.e. demonstrate a future ability to generate value through a positive change in the capital invested). Paradoxically, in favouring a selection process that chooses companies to finance based on their ability to provide returns, the practice of private equity funding by public bodies reinstates the obstacles it was originally designed to overcome.

### Assessing development impact: what Proparco's impact evaluation system tells us about development

The non-financial, more qualitative aspects of development projects tend to be invisibilized in the selection process explained above. Proparco's investment officers generally talk about those aspects in terms of the "impact" and "mandate" (see Panel 1). This section studies how they are taken into consideration.

---

### Panel 1. Proparco Project Committee meeting

A Project Committee meeting is a discussion on a specific investment opportunity for Proparco. On this occasion, different Proparco team members meet, usually sitting at tables arranged in a U shape. On one side sits the Project team (PT), consisting of two investment officers from the Investment department and one member each from the *Legal, Environmental, Social & Governance*, and *Impact measurement* departments. The PT is there to present the case for their investment projects. Facing them are two members from the *Risk and Second Opinion* (RSO) department and one member from the *Permanent Control and Compliance* (PCC) department. The role of the RSO members is to challenge the proposed investment project before issuing an "opinion". The role of the PCC members is to assess the project's level of risk through non-financial analysis (legal, country risk, etc.). In the middle sits the head of the Investment department, who chairs the meeting.

The PCC representative usually opens the meeting giving its analysis of the proposed investment's legal and technical structure, concluding in grading the project from "low" to "high" risk.

The chairman then may ask many questions about several specific points of the investment project. Each time the project managers reply, and a discussion starts: is there a market for this specific product or service? What are the characteristics of the consumer, and the required standards for putting the products on the market? What about growth prospects? Competition? Financial projections ("crash tests"), graphs of production and capacity for use of the products or services are commented on. The company's main shareholder and its funding options are also considered: is the company going to raise debt or not?

At the end, the RSO representative gives his conclusion. He gives his global assessment of the investment opportunity in terms of "risks" (especially financial or operational). It is usually at this point that it is said a little about how the project fits into Proparco's mandate and what the expected impacts are.

The chairman then closes the meeting with his proper conclusions and acknowledgments.

**Source:** *Océane Ronal, 2021. The data presented here were collected by the author through the observation of several Proparco Project Committee meetings, 2018, Proparco office in Paris.*

In the Proparco Project Committee meetings we observed, the non-financial results of the investment were usually not discussed. The terms "impact" and "mandate" were mentioned briefly at the end, but neither defined nor concretely described. However, Proparco has a standard system to evaluate the so-called impacts of its investment projects: the GPR – *Geschäftspolitisches Project Rating* or *Corporate Policy Project Rating* – system developed in 2002 by the German Investment Corporation DEG – *Deutsche Investitions- und Entwicklungsgesellschaft*. Proparco purchased this system, which was specifically designed for the evaluation of DFI investment portfolios, in 2008. It consists of a criterion-based scoring grid, leading to a final rating expressed out of 500 points. Nearly half of the total points (220) are awarded on financial criteria: the *level of investment risk* (rated out of 120) and the *investment profitability* (rated out of 100). *Impacts on development* (rated out of 165[8]) account for just over one-third of the final rating. The last rating category, *Investment fit with Proparco's Strategy* (rated out of 115) assesses the project's alignment with Proparco's strategic orientations (rated out of 46), the advisory role that the DFI can play in it (out of seven), its subsidiarity[9] (out of 29) and its ability to leverage other funds (out of 17 points).

Table 2.2 shows the rating for a specific project we call the Aurora project, which would involve a $10 million investment by Proparco to cofinance the creation of a private hospital. With a rating of 123 out of 165, this project is in the top category for impacts on development (DEV-1), corresponding to "significant" impacts according to Proparco's vocabulary. This is higher than most projects, which generally fall into category DEV-2, with a rating of around 100 out of 165. However, on financial criteria, the Aurora project is rated well below the average, with 40 out of 120 for the *level of investment risk* and 35 out of 100 for *investment profitability* (these ratings are generally both around 80).

By giving more weighting to financial criteria than to the impacts on development, the GPR system reinforces the financial nature of Proparco's investment project assessments. The Aurora project did not receive Proparco funding despite being classified DEV-1. The chosen impact measurement thus makes a further contribution to financializing the way a development project is evaluated. An impact measurement might be expected to complement the financial assessment by using different, non-financial points of evaluation; instead, the GPR system includes the financial assessment and increases its weighting, while marginalizing

**TABLE 2.2** Example of a GPR rating: the case of the Aurora project

| Criteria | Rating |
| --- | --- |
| 1. Level of investment risk (out of 120) | 40 |
| 2. Impacts on development (out of 165) | 123 (DEV-1) |
| 3. Investment fit with Proparco's Strategy (out of 115) | 52 |
| 4. Investment profitability (out of 100) | 35 |
| GPR Rating (out of 500) | 215 |

*Source:* Océane Ronal, 2021. Based on an author's survey.

the more qualitative dimensions of development. That marginalization is accentuated further by the latitude allowed by the *Investment fit with Proparco's strategy* criterion, and the lack of any detail about that strategy.

## What private equity does to grants: blended finance principle

Finally, it is important to examine the consequences of this financialization process on the mode of aid allocation that is generally considered the furthest removed from the financial sector: grants. Whether they are called "grants", "donations" or "facilities", the ways of using concessionary finance in development aid are changing as financialized solutions become more common. Such free funding, which in principle is only distributed by the AFD, is now being combined with financial instruments which, in contrast, aim to generate returns in the form of interest (on loans), fees (for services) or a return on investment (on private equity funding). By blending free funding with financing that comes at a cost, these combinations produce fungibility in funding modes, with the potential risk that the giving logic of donations and aid will be neutralized because it is subordinate to the goal of profitability. This phenomenon is particularly noticeable in so-called blended finance situations, in which a grant is used to support funding that seeks returns and this begins with the very first examination of the investment proposals.

Blended finance has attracted a lot of attention in development circles in recent years, due to the variety of financing arrangements involved, and their presumed benefits. In 2017 Development Assistance Committee (DAC) members of the Organization for Economic Co-operation and Development (OECD) adopted the *Blended Finance Principles for Unlocking Commercial Finance for SDGs (Sustainable Development Goals)* (2018). More recently, they actually set themselves up as a practice community, on a blended finance-themed platform consisting of the DAC members and representatives of the private sector, called the CoP-PFSD (the *DAC Community of Practice on Private Finance for Sustainable Development*). This new platform not only encourages contact between the public and private sectors, but it also aims to co-construct a new way of thinking about and issuing development aid that hybridizes sources of funding and "aligns" their underlying interests:

> The CoP-PFSD will focus on how to **optimise the use of ODA** [Official Development Assistance] and other sources of **development finance** in blended finance mechanisms to **mobilise private investments** that are aligned with the SDGs and achieve **real impact**. (OECD's brochure on blended finance)[10]

Blended finance consists of combining different types of financing (grants, loans, guarantees, private equity funding) and organizing it by tranches in order to improve an investment project's risk profile. Each tranche has its own guarantees (repayment guarantees or a loss limit, for example) and ranks payments by priority. Some elements of non-profit-seeking concessionary financing (which may be public, often via the state or the European Union, or private from a philanthropic source) mitigate the risk for the financial part of the operation (which is often privately-funded). By offering better-than-market investment conditions, this type of arrangement encourages private investment in businesses in development aid recipient countries. The favourable conditions are made possible by public funding that is prepared to bear more risk than private investors, greater losses/smaller gains, and/or to receive the benefits later, waiting more "patiently" for a return, to use the actor's vocabulary.

Public blended finance instruments bridge the gap between different modes of aid allocation and thus blur the lines between different aid policy regimes. They disrupt the way finance is provided, by making concessionary aid run the gauntlet of financially-focused project selection methods. In so doing, they divert concessionary aid away from its traditional and even "legally-defined"[11] beneficiaries – public or private non-profit organizations – and towards private for-profit organizations, which thus become legitimate beneficiaries of free public money.

Since the early 2000s, private equity funding by public bodies has established itself worldwide as one mode, if not *the* mode, of development finance. This reveals a change in the way the public authorities conceive and implement the aid they give. Public development aid for the private sector not only supports commercial markets (where goods and services are traded according to supply and demand), particularly banking markets; it also supports financial markets (where intangible assets are traded according to the actors' ability to make them profitable). The argument that there are not enough public resources to achieve common development objectives (currently the 2015–2030 SDGs) operates in favour of government-backed financial instruments that can lever support from private funds and generate a return on public money. Private equity funding by public bodies is thus an attempt to solve the problem of a lack of development funding resources by turning the recipient firms into products for financial speculation.

These changes have consequences. They bring new, financialized forms of reasoning (hybridizing the public intervention logic with the financial investment logic), resources (human and financial) and public action devices (founded on the calculation of financial value). These financialized practices go hand in hand with a different conception of development, sliding away from reasoning in terms of the public issue of improving quality of life and reducing poverty and inequality, towards a financialized approach to development understood as a financial market opportunity for profit accumulation. Financial profitability is taking precedence over the potential impacts of aid for enhancing local living conditions, as if financial markets had become prerequisites for development and public action (see also Guérin, 2023; Alenda-Demoutiez, 2023, both in this volume). Financial markets thus become modes of financing that emancipate private actors from mediation by the very public institutions whose role is to guarantee the collective dimension of development issues.

## Notes

1 The AFD Group has three French supervisory ministries: the Ministry of Economy and Finance, the Ministry of Europe and Foreign Affairs, and the Ministry of the Overseas (France) (their official names in 2019).
2 The names of people and firms quoted in the chapter have been modified to protect their anonymity.
3 Based on direct observation of 5 Project Committee meetings and documentary analysis of 3 preliminary investment files examined at those meetings, comprising 113, 87 and 92 pages respectively.
4 Earnings Before Interest, Taxes, Depreciation and Amortization.
5 This is a fairly standard timeframe for the private equity sector, in which most funds have an 8-year lifetime after which the invested funds are returned to investors.
6 Operational Expenditure.
7 Capital Expenditure.
8 The criteria considered are project effects on the market and production structures (35 points), public finances (28 points), employment (21 points), corporate performance and quality on environmental and social issues (18 points), technology and know-how transfer (17 points), training (15 points), governance (8 points), accessibility (8 points), company working conditions (6 points), environment (6 points), and on economic and social infrastructures (3 points).
9 The DFI's ability to support local private sector development if necessary, without replacing it.
10 Data available at: www.oecd.org/dac/financing-sustainable-development/development-finance-topics/Co-%20FSD-Brochure.pdf (Accessed: 1 December 2020).
11 Articles 107 and 108 of the Treaty on the Functioning of the European Union ban State aid as incompatible with the internal market. Development aid allocated outside the European Union is outside the scope of these articles. Nonetheless, the conception of public aid they carry raises questions about the idea of development aid, its conceptions and its consequences, particularly when it affects market conditions and reveals the existence of some form of remuneration.

## References

Alenda-Demoutiez, J. (2023). 'Financialization in development projects and new modes of governance,' in *Financializations of Development: Global Games and Local Experiments*, this volume.

Baud, C. and Chiapello, E. (2015) 'How the financialization of firms occurs: The role of regulation and management tools. The case of bank credit,' *Revue Française de Sociologie*, 56(3), pp. 439–468 [online]. Available at: http://www.cairn-int.info/article-E_RFS_563_0439--how-the-financialization-of-firms-occurs.htm. (Accessed: 20 May 2021).

Brooks, S.H. (2016) 'Private finance and the post-2015 development agenda,' *Development Finance Agenda*, 1(3), pp. 24–27 [online]. Available at: https://www.opendemocracy.net/en/openeconomy/private-finance-and-post2015-development-agenda/. (Accessed: 20 May 2021).

Chiapello, E. (2015) 'Financialization of valuation,' *Human Studies*, 1(38), pp. 13–35. DOI: 10.1007/s10746-014-9337-x.

Chiapello, E. (2020) 'Financialization as a socio-technical process,' in Mader, P., Mertens, D. and Van der Zwan, N. (eds.), *The Routledge international handbook of financialization*. London: Routledge, pp. 81–91. DOI: 10.4324/9781315142876.

Chiapello, E. and Gilbert, P. (2019) *Management tools: A social sciences perspective*. Cambridge: Cambridge University Press. DOI: 10.1017/9781108553858.

Clapp, J. (2014) 'Financialization, distance and global food politics,' *The Journal of Peasant Studies*, 41(5), pp. 797–814. DOI: 10.1080/03066150.2013.875536.

Cumming, G.D. (2017) 'La transformation de l'AFD et de l'aide française au cours des « années Severino » : vers une nouvelle compréhension des réformes de politiques publiques,' in Giraud, G. and Rioux, R. (eds.), *75 ans au service du développement - L'Agence Française de Développement des origines à nos jours*. Paris: Agence Française de Développement and Cliomédia, pp. 35–63 [online]. Available at: http://librairie.afd. fr/. (Accessed: 20 May 2021).

Doganova, L. (2015) 'Que vaut une molécule ? Formulation de la valeur dans les projets de développement de nouveaux médicaments,' *Revue d'Anthropologie des Connaissances*, 9(1), pp. 17–38. DOI: 10.3917/rac.026.0017.

Ducastel, A. (2016) 'Le capital-investissement comme instrument de l'action publique ou la financiarisation du développement en Afrique subsaharienne,' *Politique Africaine*, 144(4), pp. 135–155. DOI: 10.3917/polaf.144.0135.

Ducastel, A., Bourblanc, M. and Adelle, C. (2023). 'Why development finance institutions are reluctant to invest in agriculture… And why they keep trying The financialization of development policies as an obstacle to invest in agriculture,' in *Financializations of Development: Global Games and Local Experiments*, this volume.

Gabas, J.-J., Ribier, V. and Vernières, M. (2017) 'Présentation. Financement ou financiarisation du développement? Une question en débat,' *Mondes en Développement*, 178(2), pp. 7–22. DOI: 10.3917/med.178.0007.

Guérin, I. (2023). 'The financialization of the fight against poverty: from microcredit to social capitalism,' in *Financializations of Development: Global Games and Local Experiments*, this volume.

Inter-American Development Bank (2011) *Private sector development strategy: Fostering development through the private sector* [online]. Available at: https://www.cbd.int/financial/mainstream/idb-private.pdf. (Accessed: 20 May 2021).

Mah, L. (2023). 'The financialization of EU development policy: blended finance and strategic interests (2007–2020)' in *Financializations of Development: Global Games and Local Experiments*, this volume.

Mawdsley, E. (2018) '"From billions to trillions": Financing the SDGs in a world "beyond aid,"' *Dialogues in Human Geography*, 8(2), pp. 191–195. DOI: 10.1177/2043820618780789.

Mazzucato, M. and Penna, C.C.R. (2015) *The rise of mission-oriented state investment banks: The cases of Germany's KfW and Brazil's BNDES* [online]. Available at: http://www. isigrowth.eu/wp-content/uploads/2015/11/working_paper_2015_1.pdf. (Accessed: 20 May 2021).

Organization for Economic Co-operation and Development (2018) *OECD DAC blended finance principles for unlocking commercial finance for the sustainable development goals. Organisation for Economic Co-operation and Development* [online]. Available at: https://www. oecd.org/dac/financing-sustainable-development/development-finance-topics/ OECD-Blended-Finance-Principles.pdf. (Accessed: 20 May 2021).

Sarkozy, N. (2008) *Discours de M. le Président de la République française devant le Parlement Sud-Africain*, Cap Town (South Africa), 28 February [online]. Available at: https:// www.diplomatie.gouv.fr/IMG/pdf/PARLEMENT_AS.pdf. (Accessed: 20 May 2021).

Sarraut, A. (1923) *La mise en valeur des colonies françaises*. Paris: Payot.

United Nations (2002) *Monterrey consensus on financing for development* [online]. Available at: https://www.un.org/en/development/desa/population/migration/generalassembly/ docs/globalcompact/A_CONF.198_11.pdf. (Accessed: 20 May 2021).

United Nations (2008) *Doha declaration on financing for development: Outcome document of the follow-up international conference on financing for development to review the implementation of the Monterrey consensus* [online]. Available at: https://documents-dds-ny.un.org/doc/UNDOC/LTD/N08/630/55/PDF/N0863055.pdf?OpenElement. (Accessed: 20 May 2021).

United Nations (2011) *Busan partnership for effective development Co-operation* [online]. Available at: https://www.oecd-ilibrary.org/development/busan-partnership-for-effective-development-co-operation_54de7baa-en?_ga=2.136429872.1441606713.1621504111-886159194.1483457025. (Accessed: 20 May 2021).

United Nations (2013) *Public aid as a driver for private investment* [online]. Available at: https://www.un.org/en/ecosoc/newfunct/pdf13/dcf_switzerland_first_complete_draft_public_aid_as_a_driver_for_private_investment.pdf. (Accessed: 20 May 2021).

# 3

# THE FINANCIALIZATION OF EU DEVELOPMENT POLICY

## Blended finance and strategic interests (2007–2020)

*Luis Mah*

## Introduction

The European Union (EU) is the world's largest provider of Official Development Assistance (ODA) to developing countries, channeling more than half of the global ODA reported for 2019 by the Development Assistance Committee at the Organization for Economic Co-operation and Development (OECD-DAC) (EC, 2020a). In 2019, the total ODA provided by the EU reached €75.2 billion. The EU delegations across 141 countries offer not only direct support to partner countries, but also seek to help coordinate Member States' own development policy on a country level. The EU largesse affords it an important role in the negotiation, design and implementation of the rules of the game underpinning the international ODA architecture. Since the 1960s, this architecture has been led by richer nations grouped in the OECD-DAC, mostly from Europe and North America (Schmelzer, 2014). As the OECD-DAC states on its website: "We help set international principles and standards for development co-operation and monitor how donors deliver on their commitments" (OECD, 2022a).

In 2007, the EU launched the EU-Africa Infrastructure Trust Fund (AITF), an initiative blending grants from European donors and European Development Finance Institutions (DFIs) to support private investments in infrastructure in Africa. This blended finance initiative heralded a new direction in the international ODA architecture, with the most visible impact felt in 2020: from now on, ODA statistics measured by OECD-DAC will begin taking into account, for the first time, public grants supporting private sector investments. AITF was the first EU regional blended finance facility. For the EU, "blending is the strategic use of a limited amount of grants to mobilize financing from partner financial institutions and the private sector to enhance the development impact of investment projects" (EC, 2015). Between 2007 and 2012, the EU created seven other

DOI: 10.4324/9781003039679-5

regional facilities, each one for the strategic regions covered by EU development policy (Lundsgaarde, 2017).

In 2011, the EU officially adopted blended finance as part of its development policy tools (EC, 2011), turning the EU into the first leading donor to publicly embrace this approach, only a few years before it became part of the mainstream narrative within the development finance arena. Between 2007 and 2017, the eight EU regional blended finance facilities channeled an estimated €3.4 billion in grants. These grants leverage €26 billion in loans by European DFIs and regional multilateral banks to unlock investments in developing countries totaling around €57 billion (EC, 2017). The latest reforms in the EU development finance – a single finance mechanism for development policy or the Neighborhood, Development and International Cooperation Instrument (NDICI), the European Fund for Sustainable Development Plus (EFSD+) and the External Action Guarantee (EAG) (EP, 2018) – unveiled in the 2021–2027 budget signal the political will to continue the "blendification" trend and financialization of EU development policy (Bonizzi, Laskaridis and Toporowski, 2015; Van Waeyenberge, 2015). While the process of financialization of the EU development policy takes place, it has also begun to be used to service EU strategic interests. Following the 2007 Treaty of Lisbon (although it only became effective in 2009), EU development policy came under the control of EU foreign policy's vision, goals and operations (Mah, 2015). EU development policy would not only be about fighting poverty and tackling social injustices, but it would also follow the EU's strategic interests in a rapidly changing world order (Janus, Klingebiel and Paulo, 2015; Klingebiel, Mahn and Negre, 2016).

This chapter attempts firstly to explore how EU-blended finance has, since 2007, led to the financialization of EU development policy, and secondly how this "blendification" is now being used to address EU global strategic interests. The first section discusses the emergence of blended finance as the new development finance trend. The second section looks at the origins and evolution of EU blended finance since 2007. The third section discusses how the growingly financialized EU development policy is now being used to serve EU strategic interests in a changing world order. The conclusion discusses the main findings about the evolution of EU development policy and finance between 2007 and 2020. The research for this chapter begins by using discourse analysis to interpret relevant official statements, as well as documents related to a transforming EU development policy. Subsequently, the research attempts to trace the outcomes of such statements and documents by assessing the materialization of those changes. Secondary literature was used to cross-check information and to offer context and history to the research.

## Blended finance and the financialization of development policy

Blended finance has emerged as a key development finance policy in the past decade (UNCTAD, 2014). However, as pointed out by Attridge and Engen (2019,

p. 17), there are now a "myriad of definitions of blended finance". Common features of these definitions appear to be: (1) the use of concessional development finance (grants or loans with below-market rates); (2) the catalyzing effect aimed at attracting private commercial finance; and (3) the expected development impact of the investment (Attridge and Engen, 2019). Blended finance is "not an investment approach, instrument or end solution" (Convergence, 2020), but a structuring approach bringing together concessional public-oriented finance (mostly ODA but it can also come from philanthropic funders) and market-rate private capital. Multilateral and bilateral DFIs play an important role in this process as they are usually the ones managing such structures (Savoy, Carter and Lemma, 2016). It is this small share of concessional public-oriented finance, in particular ODA, that has attracted the attention and discussion of the international development community. ODA is expected to mobilize additional non-concessional finance, particularly private, and reduce risks in investments that address unmet needs in crucial sectors for economic growth, such as infrastructure, energy, water, industry or job-generating projects. In blended finance structures or mechanisms, ODA can take different formats. The most commonly practiced are investment grants and interest rate subsidies (to reduce the amount to be invested and the project costs), technical assistance (to support preparation and management of the investment project), risk capital contribution (equity or quasi-equity to attract private finance by co-investment) and structured finance-first loss piece or loans guarantees (to reduce the risk of other, mostly private, investors) (Pereira, 2017).

The growing embrace of blended finance is an answer to another trend led by multilateral organizations: the legitimation and validation of the private sector as a partner for development. While private sector development has been on the donor's agenda as a crucial step to help build markets to work for the "poor" since the 1990s (Langan, 2011; Schulpen and Gibbon, 2002), it is only during the 2011 Busan High Level Forum on Aid Effectiveness, organized by the OECD-DAC, that the private sector has acquired this central seat in the international development agenda (Mawdsley, 2015a; Mawdsley, Savage and Kim, 2014) – not only due to its financial capacity, but also because of its role in fostering economic growth, transforming economic structure and creating jobs. Blended finance emerges as the ideal development finance policy to attract investment and partnerships from the private sector.

Following the Busan Forum, several multilateral documents and international initiatives began to emerge, boosting the role of blended finance in the international development agenda: (1) the 2014 UN Report of the Intergovernmental Committee of Experts on Sustainable Development Financing (UN, 2014); (2) the 2015 Addis Ababa Action Agenda (UN, 2015); (3) the 2030 Agenda launched in 2015; (4) the 2015 OECD and World Economic Forum (WEF) Blended Finance Toolkit (WEF, 2015); and (5) the private sector-led blended finance platforms Sustainable Development Investment Partnership (SDIP, 2022) and Convergence (Convergence, 2022). Both platforms aimed at connecting public, private and philanthropic institutions to scale up private investment in developing countries to help achieve the Sustainable Development Goals (SDGs). Blended finance is now seen as a central mechanism to help the goal of turning "billions to trillions", as envisioned by the WB and IMF (2015), by using billions of public concessional development finance to catalyze trillions in commercial private finance. This push is being helped by estimates that developing countries alone (or even with the help of donors) will not be able to finance the achievement of key SDGs by 2030 (UNCTAD, 2014). The OECD-DAC has already launched the Blended Finance Principles Guidance in 2020 (OECD, 2020b), a policy tool proposing a common framework and guidance on the use of this financial mechanism.

However, this attempt to unlock commercial private finance remains elusive, according to available data. The OECD's latest 2019 Global Outlook on Financing for Sustainable Development shows how commercial private finance for development is failing to materialize three years after the launch of the SDGs: private investment decreased 30% in 2016–2017 and project finance the same percentage in the first semester of 2018 (OECD, 2018b). Additionally, the impact of the COVID-19 pandemic is expected to aggravate the situation. A recent note by the OECD (2020a) has estimated that external private finance flows to developing countries could drop by almost 700 billion USD in 2020 compared to the previous year.

Until recently, the international development debate was mostly focused on the quantity and quality of traditional development finance – ODA, remittances, Foreign Direct Investment (FDI) and debt. But the rising adoption of blended finance channeled through DFIs has had an important impact on the decades-old definition and measurement of ODA by the rich country-led OECD-DAC. DFI's financial support to private sector investments in developing countries has always been regarded as non-concessional and would not be considered as ODA by the OECD-DAC. But in 2016, after years of discussions, the OECD-DAC agreed that capital contributions provided by member states to private sector investments in recipient countries could count as ODA from 2018 onwards, under the label of Private Sector Instruments (PSIs).

The contributions to PSIs can take two formats: *institutional* and *instrumental*. In the *institutional* format, all capital contributions to DFIs by DAC member states are to be included in their ODA figures. In the *instrumental* format, loans and equity investments to private sector entities by DFIs can be reported as ODA (OECD, 2018a). In 2020, DAC released, for the first time, full data on ODA through PSIs by its members. The data (reported in 2018) shows that ODA through PSIs is still relatively small ($4.6 billion) compared with overall ODA figures reaching $147 billion for 2018 (Development Initiatives, 2020). Figures are expected to increase in the coming years with the mainstream continuation of blended finance by multilateral and bilateral DFIs (Caio and Craviotto, 2021; Development Initiatives, 2020). However, Attridge and Gouett (2021) show that multilateral and bilateral DFIs are falling short in mobilizing private investment as needed to achieve the SDGs.

The modernization of ODA measurement by OECD-DAC occurs as another discussion is taking place to forge a new international statistical standard: Total Official Support for Sustainable Development (TOSSD) (OECD, 2022b). The novelty of this new statistical standard, in comparison with the modernized ODA measurement, is that it includes all forms of development finance provided by not only OECD DAC members, but also by all non-OECD DAC bilateral and multilateral donors, including South-South Cooperation and Triangular Cooperation (OECD, 2022b). It aims to monitor cross-border public and private flows to promote sustainable development in developing countries as well as support global public goods and challenges. Since 2017, the discussion is led by an International TOSSD Task Force, an initiative that brings experts from donor countries, recipient countries and multilateral organizations together. The inclusive membership of this task force beyond OECD-DAC is potentially challenging the latter's decades-old leadership in the international ODA regime.

Since the 1960s, due to their global economic leadership, European and North American donors, grouped around the OECD-DAC, have led the narrative and practice of the ODA regime by setting specific normative goals and policy frameworks supported by spending targets (Führer, 1994; Hynes and Scott, 2013). As Schmelzer (2014) points out, the OECD-DAC has been important for (1) helping to build a community of rich donors who respect and share the principles and practices of an ODA regime (even if they lack the power to legally or economically sanction those who fail to abide by the rules of the system); (2) coordinating ODA flows (public and private) targeting developing countries; and (3) setting leading norms, standards and benchmarks on ODA provision and distribution. The OECD-DAC-led ODA regime has depended on voluntary but binding agreements made by consensus, rather than centralized enforcement (Wook and Rumsey, 2016). However, this regime is currently undergoing challenges as non-European and non-North American donors also began to play an important role in providing ODA. From the early 2000s, this has been usually called the *Rise of the South* built on a growing South-South Cooperation (SSC) (Benn and Luijkx, 2017; Gulrajani and Raphaëlle, 2019; Hackenesh and Janus, 2013; Mawdsley, 2015a; OECD, 2010; UNDP, 2013). The creation of TOSSD represents the acknowledgment of the growing importance of development finance provided by non-OECD-DAC members, particularly through SSC.

In sum, the emergence of blended finance in development policy has begun to disrupt and change a decades-old regime to open up the space for a new paradigm that Gabor (2021) calls "Development as De-Risking", according to which global private finance plays a critical role in the implementation of development policies. As a leading voice and practitioner in support of blended finance, for the past decade, the EU has played an important role in pushing for the financialization of the principles and practices of the ODA regime.

## The origins and evolution of EU blended finance (2007–2020)

Blended finance in EU development policy can be analyzed in three landmark periods: initiation (2007–2010), institutionalization (2011–2016) and consolidation (2017–2020). In 2007, the EU launched its first blended finance facility: the AITF. This facility was created in the aftermath of the 2007 EU-Africa Summit in Lisbon to support regional infrastructure projects in Africa. It was under the management of the European Investment Bank (EIB) and lasted until 2019. After the establishment of the AITF, the EU created four other similar facilities, each for a particular region covered by its development policy: the NIF or Neighborhood Investment Facility (2008), the WBIF or Western Balkans Investment Framework (2009), the LAIF or Latin American Investment Facility (2010) and the IFCA or Investment Facility for Central Asia (2010). Unlike the AITF, these four facilities came under the management of the EC.

But it was only with the 2011 *Agenda for Change* that the EU moved to institutionalize blended finance as part of its development policy:

> In selected sectors and countries, a higher percentage of EU development resources should be deployed through existing or new financial instruments, such as blending grants and loans and other risk-sharing mechanisms, in order to leverage further resources and thus increase impact.
>
> *(EC, 2011, p. 8)*

In the following year, the EC launched three other regional blended finance facilities: the CIF or Caribbean Investment Facility (2012), the AIF or Asian Investment Facility (2012) and the IFP or Investment Facility for the Pacific (2012). Within a five-year period, the EU had put in place eight blended finance facilities covering all partner regions benefitting from the EU development policy (see Table 3.1).

The eight blended finance facilities received their resources from the EU's two main ODA budget lines: the European Development Fund (EDF) (D'Alfonso, 2014) and the Development Cooperation Instrument (DCI) (EP, 2017). Together, they account for the biggest share of EU funding for international development (Gavas, 2012). With the institutionalization of blended finance in EU development policy in 2011, the EU continued to clarify and reinforce its intentions to engage the private sector in policymaking processes and with financial instruments to achieve its development policies. It did so by releasing the following strategies: *Improving EU Support to Developing Countries in Mobilizing Financing for Development* (EC, 2012) and *A Stronger Role of the Private Sector in Achieving Inclusive and Sustainable Growth in Developing Countries* (EC, 2014). The following year, the European Commission released the guidelines on EU blending operations, offering the following definition of blending: "Strategic use of a limited amount of grants to mobilize financing from partner financial institutions and the private sector to enhance the development impact of investment

**TABLE 3.1** Overview of EU regional blended finance facilities

| Facility | Established | Priority areas | EU funding to date (EUR) |
|---|---|---|---|
| EU-Africa Infrastructure Trust Fund | 2007 | Regional infrastructure, sustainable energy | 815 million |
| Neighbourhood Investment Facility | 2008 | Energy, private-sector financing | 1,678 million |
| Western Balkans Investment Framework | 2009 | Transport, energy, social sectors, environment | 480 million |
| Latin America Investment Facility | 2010 | Water and sanitation, energy | 305 million |
| Investment Facility for Central Asia | 2010 | Environment, water, energy | 143 million |
| Caribbean Investment Facility | 2012 | Energy, water and sanitation | 83.6 million |
| Asian Investment Facility | 2012 | Energy, environment | 147 million |
| Investment Facility for the Pacific | 2012 | Timor-Leste, Fiji | 10 million |

*Source*: Lundsgaarde (2017).

*Note*: The figure for the EU-Africa Infrastructure Trust Fund represents grant pledges from the European Commission and 13 member states contributing to the trust fund. The NIF funding figure reflects contributions from the EU budget. The WBIF figure reflects funding commitments from the European Commission to date. In the remaining facilities, the figures refer to funding for approved projects. These figures do not include estimates of funding leveraged from DFIs and private investors in addition to EU contributions.

projects" (EC, 2015, p. 3). Between 2007 and 2018, the EU granted almost €6.63 billion in ODA to these blended facilities, though it represented a relatively small share of the total EU ODA for this period (Bayliss et al., 2020).

2017 marks the consolidation period of blended finance as a central approach in EU development policy with the launch of the EU External Investment Plan (EIP), a new blended finance initiative aimed at encouraging private sector investments in Africa and the EU Neighborhood (EP, 2019; Gavas and Timmis, 2019). The EIP introduces two novelties in the European development finance architecture. First, the €4.1 billion European Fund for Sustainable Development (EFSD) that includes a financial guarantee offered to a diversity of actors (EIB, European DFIs, private investors from EU Member States and partner countries). Second, technical assistance to help investors design bankable projects and partner countries improve their regulatory environments to become more supportive of business and investment (EC, 2018; Gavas and Timmis, 2019).

In June 2018, the EC proposed a new framework for EU development finance to be included in the 2021–2027 EU budget. It was justified as a need to simplify the ongoing architecture and to scale up the impact of EIP (Gavas and Timmis, 2019). This new framework included, firstly, the merger of all ODA instruments into a single one, the NDICI; and, secondly, the launch of an

EFSD+ (an expanded version of the previous EFSD) and the EAG with a ceiling of €60 billion. The EFSD+ and the EAG were to be supported financially by the NDICI, and this clearly shows an EU willingness to further "blendify" its development policy.

In October 2019, a High-Level Group set up by the Council of the European Union released its report on the future of the European financial architecture for development (Council of the EU, 2019b). The High-Level group not only saw the creation of NDICI as a potential "catalyst for improvement" of EU development finance, but also proposed the establishment of a single entity to "strengthen the EU's presence, role and long-term capacity to deliver EU development priorities": the European Climate and Sustainable Development Bank (Council of the EU, 2019b, pp. 3–4). In late December 2020, the European Parliament and the EU member states in the Council agreed to set up the €79.5 billion NDICI (EC, 2020b). The evolution of events in the past decade reveals that the EU has embraced blended finance as a core approach to its development policy. By de-risking private sector investments in partner countries through EFSD+ and the EAG, it has contributed to increasingly financialize its development policy. While the EU consolidated blended finance as a development finance mechanism, it also launched the 2016 EU Global Strategy (EGS) in which development policy is seen as playing an important role in promoting EU strategic interests. This move would then have relevant implications for the functioning of EU-blended finance.

## Blended finance and EU strategic interests

In 2016, Federica Mogherini, then EU High Representative for Foreign Affairs and Security Policy, launched the EU Global Strategy (EGS). The EGS set five main external priorities: (1) the security of the Union; (2) state and societal resilience in the EU Neighborhood and Africa; (3) an integrated approach to conflicts; (4) cooperative regional orders; and (5) global governance for the 21st century (EEAS, 2016). But more interestingly, Mogherini stated unequivocally that "development policy will become more flexible and aligned with our strategic priorities" (EEAS, 2016). This was a very clear public statement on the future of EU development policy: less about global solidarity to fight poverty and tackle social injustices and more about EU strategic interests. This vision has been supported by institutional reforms in the EU following the 2007 Lisbon Treaty, namely the creation of the High Representative for Foreign Affairs and Security Policy (HRFASP) and the European External Action Service (EEAS) or the EU diplomatic corps. With the Treaty, the EU development policy was placed under the guidance of the HRFASP (Mah, 2015). The creation of the new post of HRFASP (who is also vice-president of the European Commission) and the EEAS opened up the opportunity for the EU to provide its foreign policy with more strength, coherence and consistency (Vanhoonacker and Pomorska, 2013).

Right after the presentation of the EGS, the EU launched the EIP, the new blended finance initiative to support private investments in Africa and Neighborhood countries. In the 2016 State of the Union, Mogherini could not have been more explicit about the role of the EIP in supporting EU strategic interests:

> While creating the conditions for Europeans to expand their business and move into new countries, the new External Investment Plan (EIP) will support our partners' economies and societies, as well as our strategic foreign policy goals, from security to global development.
>
> *(EC, 2016)*

The EIP not only consolidates blended finance as a core feature of a financialized EU development policy, but also as a financial mechanism to support EU strategic interests. The EIP is expected to help EU private sector investments in partner countries revealing not only "high up-front investments, high risk exposure" but also often "unfair international competition that require action to ensure a level playing field" (EC, 2014, p. 10). SSC is a particularly competitive challenge. It is based on an alternative ideological framework supported by usually plentiful material resources (Mawdsley, 2015b). Unlike the EU development policy aimed at developing countries, SSC has favored: (1) loans over aid; (2) public-private partnerships in infrastructure and production development aimed at economic growth over social investments to fight poverty; and (3) national interests over global agenda goals. SSC has also helped South-South trade relations (UNCTAD, 2015), with China playing a leading role. Beijing has recently launched two new multilateral DFIs showing the country's willingness to increase development finance to developing countries: the Asian Infrastructure Investment Bank (AIIB) and the New Development Bank (NDB) or BRICS development bank (Jiang, 2016). For the past two decades, China has strongly benefited from SSC, allowing it to become the top trading partner for many African and Latin American countries. The 2016 EU Global Strategy, the EIP and, more recently, the proposal of the MFF 2021–2027 are signs that the European bloc is responding to global challenges as development policy becomes increasingly enmeshed with strategic national political and economic interests. For example, in its strategic outlook for EU-China relations released in March 2019, the EC noted:

> China is, simultaneously, [...] an economic competitor in the pursuit of technological leadership, and a systemic rival promoting alternative models of governance. This requires a [...] pragmatic whole-of-EU approach enabling a principled defence of interests and values.
>
> *(EC, 2019a, p. 1)*

In September 2019, Ursula von der Leyen presented her new European Commission (EC) team. This commission has already self-identified as geopolitical. During his hearing at the European Parliament in October 2019, Josep Borrell, the current HRFASP, stated that "Europe needs to learn the language of power" and, more recently, he reinforced this vision with an essay at Project Syndicate entitled *Embracing Europe's Power* (Borrell, 2020). One of the noticeable changes related to this self-identification was the re-labelling of the former Commissioner for International Development and Cooperation as a Commissioner for International Partnerships. In the mission letter to the new Commissioner, President-elect Jutta Urpilainen emphasized the need to guarantee a strategic and effective "European model of development that creates value for money and contributes to our wider political priorities" (EC, 2019b, p. 4). Absent from the letter was poverty reduction, and eventually its extinction, enshrined in the 2009 Treaty of Lisbon as the main goal of the EU's development policy and humanitarian aid (EU, 2007). This re-labeling, together with the mission letter, shows the continuation and strengthening of a process initiated in the former Commission to place EU development policy at the service of EU strategic interests (Teevan and Sherriff, 2019, p. 4).

## Conclusion

This chapter explored how EU blended finance has, since 2007, led to the financialization of EU development policy, and how this "blendification" is now being used to serve the EU global strategic interests. From a decades-old focus on providing mostly ODA, over the last decade the EU development policy has moved rapidly towards embracing the blended finance structure, bundling together ODA and commercial private finance. From eight regional blended finance facilities between 2007 and 2012, and then the NDICI, EFSD+ and EAG between 2017 and 2020, the EU development policy has become increasingly financialized as it began to offer more ODA to help de-risk private sector investments in developing countries. With the "blendification" in progress and growing strongly, the EU development policy apparatus came slowly under the control of EU foreign policy following the 2007 Lisbon Treaty. With the launch of the 2016 EGS, the EU development policy was publicly turned into a tool at the service of EU strategic interests. In other words, the EU-blended finance has turned into a geopolitical instrument.

## References

Attridge, S. and Engen, L. (2019) 'Blended finance in the poorest countries: The need for a better approach,' *ODI Report* [online]. Available at: https://www.odi.org/publications/11303-blended-finance-poorest-countries-need-better-approach. (Accessed: 4 February 2021).

Attridge, S. and Gouett, M. (2021) 'Development finance institutions: The need for bold action to invest better,' *ODI Report* [online] Available at: https://odi.org/en/publications/development-finance-institutions-the-need-for-bold-action-to-invest-better/. (Accessed: 10 April 2021).

Bayliss, K., et al. (2020) 'The use of development funds to de-risk private investment: How effective is it in delivering development results,' *A paper requested by the European Parliament's Committee on Development* [online]. Available at: https://www.europarl.

europa.eu/RegData/etudes/STUD/2020/603486/EXPO_STU(2020)603486_EN.pdf. (Accessed: 5 February 2021).

Benn, J. and Luijkx, W. (2017) 'Emerging providers' international co-operation for development,' *OECD Development Co-operation Working Papers*, 33. Paris: OECD Publishing. DOI: 10.1787/15d6a3c7-en.

Bonizzi, B., Laskaridis, C. and Toporowski, J. (2015) 'EU development policy and the promotion of the financial sector,' *FESSUD: Working Paper Series 120* [online]. Available at: http://fessud.eu/wp-content/uploads/2015/03/EU-Development-Policy-And-The-Promotion-Of-The-Financial-Sector-FESSUD-working-paper-120.pdf. (Accessed: 17 August 2020).

Borrell, J. (2020) 'Embracing Europe's power,' *Project Syndicate* [online]. Available at: https://www.project-syndicate.org/commentary/embracing-europe-s-power-by-josep-borrell-2020-02?barrier=accesspaylog. (Accessed: 21 March 2021).

Caio, C. and Craviotto, N. (2021) 'Time for action: How private sector instruments are undermining aid budgets' [online]. Available at: https://www.eurodad.org/time_for_action. (Accessed: 4 February 2021).

Convergence (2020) 'The state of blended finance,' *Convergence* [online]. Available at: https://www.convergence.finance/resource/1qEM02yBQxLftPVs4bWmMX/view. (Accessed: 13 April 2021).

Convergence' (2022) 'Convergence blending global finance' [online]. Available at: https://www.convergence.finance/about. (Accessed: 15 June 2022).

Council of the European Union (2019b) 'Europe in the world: The future of the European financial architecture for development,' *An independent report by the High-Level Group of Wise Persons on the European financial architecture for development* [online]. Available at: https://www.consilium.europa.eu/media/40967/efad-report_final.pdf. (Accessed: 5 August 2020).

D'Alfonso, A. (2014) 'European development fund: Joint development cooperation and the EU budget: Out or in?' [online]. Available at: https://www.europarl.europa.eu/EPRS/EPRS-IDA-542140-European-Development-Fund-FINAL.pdf. (Accessed: 14 April 2021).

Development Initiatives (2020) 'Final ODA data for 2018: what does the data tell us?'. Factsheet [online]. Available at: https://devinit.org/resources/final-oda-data-2018/#note-B97iwgg4a. (Accessed: 4 February 2021).

EC (2011) 'Increasing the impact of EU development policy: An agenda for change,' *COM (2011) 637 final* [online]. Available at: http://eur-lex.europa.eu/LexUriServ/LexUriServ.do?uri=COM:2011:0637:FIN:EN:PDF. (Accessed: 5 August 2020).

EC (2012) 'Improving EU support to developing countries in mobilizing Financing for Development' [online]. Available at: http://eur-lex.europa.eu/legal-content/EN/TXT/PDF/?uri=CELEX:52012DC0366&from=EN. (Accessed: 20 August 2020).

EC (2014) 'A stronger role of the private sector in achieving inclusive and sustainable growth in developing countries' [online]. Available at: http://eur-lex.europa.eu/legal-content/EN/TXT/PDF/?uri=CELEX%3A52014DC0263&qid=1400681732387&-from=EN. (Accessed: 20 August 2020).

EC (2015) 'Guidelines on EU blending operations' [online]. Available at: https://op.europa.eu/en/publication-detail/-/publication/4a5eaccd-10f1-11e6-ba9a-01aa75ed71a1/language-en. (Accessed: 15 April 2021).

EC (2016) 'State of the union: Strengthening European investments for jobs and growth' [online] Available at: https://ec.europa.eu/commission/presscorner/detail/en/IP_16_3002. (Accessed: 4 September 2020).

EC (2017) 'EU external investment plan factsheet' [online]. Available at: https://ec. europa.eu/info/sites/info/files/external-investment-plan-factsheet_en.pdf. (Accessed: 12 April 2021).

EC (2018) 'Towards a more efficient financial architecture for investment outside the European Union,' *Communication from the Commission to the European Parliament, the European Council, the Council and the European Investment Bank, COM (2018) 644 Final* [online]. Available at: https://eur-lex.europa.eu/legal-content/EN/TXT/HTML/ ?uri=CELEX:52018DC0644&from=EN. (Accessed: 12 April 2021).

EC (2019a) 'EU-China – A strategic outlook' [online]. Available at: https://ec.europa.eu/ info/sites/default/files/communication-eu-china-a-strategic-outlook.pdf. (Accessed: 12 July 2021).

EC (2019b) 'Mission letter to Jutta Urpilainen, Commissioner-designate for International Partnerships, from Ursula von der Leyen, President-elect of the European Commission' [online]. Available at: https://ec.europa.eu/info/sites/info/files/mission-letter-jutta-urpilainen_en.pdf. (Accessed: 28 September 2020).

EC (2020a) 'The European Union remains world's leading donor of Official Development Assistance with €75.2 billion in 2019' [online]. Available at: https://ec.europa. eu/commission/presscorner/detail/en/IP_20_674. (Accessed: 20 June 2020).

EC (2020b) 'European Commission welcomes political agreement on future €79.5 billion for a new instrument to finance the EU external action and lead the global recovery through international partnerships' [online]. Available at: https://ec.europa.eu/com-mission/presscorner/detail/en/IP_20_2453. (Accessed: 14 April 2021).

EEAS (2016) 'Shared vision, common action: A stronger Europe, A global strategy for European union's foreign and security policy' [online]. Available at: https://eeas.europa. eu/archives/docs/top_stories/pdf/eugs_review_web.pdf. (Accessed: 12 March 2021).

EP (2017) 'Development cooperation instrument' [online]. Available at: https:// www.europarl.europa.eu/RegData/etudes/BRIE/2017/608764/EPRS_ BRI(2017)608764_EN.pdf. (Accessed: 20 July 2020).

EP (2018) 'Guarantee fund for external actions' [online]. Available at: https:// www.europarl.europa.eu/RegData/etudes/BRIE/2018/630338/EPRS_ BRI(2018)630338_EN.pdf. (Accessed: 20 July 2020).

EP (2019) 'European fund for sustainable development' [online]. Available at: https://www.europarl.europa.eu/RegData/etudes/BRIE/2019/637893/EPRS_ BRI(2019)637893_EN.pdf. (Accessed: 20 July 2020).

EU (2007) 'Treaty of Lisbon,' *Official Journal of the European Union*, vol. 50 (17 December 2007) [online]. Available at: https://eur-lex.europa.eu/legal-content/EN/TXT/PDF /?uri=OJ:C:2007:306:FULL&from=EN. (Accessed: 14 April 2021).

Führer, H. (1994) 'The story of official development assistance – A history of the development assistance committee and the development co-operation directorate in dates, names and figures,' *OCDE/GD* (94)67 [online]. Available at: https://www.oecd.org/ dac/1896816.pdf. (Accessed: 10 April 2021).

Gabor, D. (2021) 'The wall street consensus,' *Development and Change* [online]. Available at: https://onlinelibrary.wiley.com/doi/10.1111/dech.12645. (Accessed: 12 April 2021).

Gavas, M. (2012) 'The European Commission's legislative proposals for financing EU Development Cooperation,' *ODI Background Note* [online]. Available at: https://odi. org/en/publications/the-european-commissions-legislative-proposals-for-financing-eu-development-cooperation/. (Accessed: 14 August 2020).

Gavas, M. and Timmis, H. (2019) 'The EU's financial architecture for external investment: Progress, challenges, and options' [online]. Available at: https://www.

cgdev.org/publication/eus-financial-architecture-external-investment-progress-challenges-and-options. (Accessed: 18 September 2020).

Gulrajani, N. and Raphaëlle, F. (2019) 'Donors in transition and the future of development cooperation: What do the data from Brazil, India, China and South Africa reveal?,' *Public Administration and Development*, 39(4–5), pp. 231–244.

Hackenesh, C. and Janus, H. (2013) 'Post 2015: How emerging economies shape the relevance of a new agenda,' *German Development Institute GDI Briefing Paper* 14/2013 [online]. Available at: https://www.econstor.eu/bitstream/10419/199714/1/die-bp-2013-14.pdf. (Accessed: 15 July 2020).

Hynes, W. and Scott, S. (2013) 'The evolution of official development assistance: Achievements, criticisms and a way forward,' *OECD Development Co-operation Working Papers*, no. 12 [online]. Available at: https://www.oecd.org/dac/financing-sustainable-development/development-finance-standards/Evolution%20of%20ODA.pdf. (Accessed: 13 April 2021).

Janus, H., Klingebiel, S. and Paulo, S. (2015) 'Beyond aid: A conceptual perspective on the transformation of development cooperation,' *Journal of International Development*, 27, pp. 155–169.

Jiang, Y. (2016) 'China's new development banks and infrastructure-led growth,' NUPI Policy Brief No. 18, Oslo: NUPI [online]. Available at: https://www.nupi.no/en/Publications/CRIStin-Pub/China-s-New-Development-Bank-and-Infrastructure-led-Growth. (Accessed: 1 July 2021).

Klingebiel, S., Mahn, T. and Negre, M. (2016) 'Fragmentation: A key concept for development cooperation,' in Klingebiel, S., Mahn, T. and Negre, M. (eds.), *The fragmentation of aid: Concepts, measurements and implications for development cooperation*, 1st ed. London: Palgrave Macmillan, pp. 1–18.

Langan, M. (2011) 'Private sector development as poverty and strategic discourse: PSD in political economy of EU-Africa trade relations,' *The Journal of Modern African Studies*, 49, pp. 83–113.

Lundsgaarde, E. (2017) 'The European fund for sustainable finance: Changing the game?', *Discussion Paper 29/2017* [online]. Available at: https://www.die-gdi.de/uploads/media/DP_29.2017.pdf. (Accessed: 20 August 2020).

Mah, L. (2015) 'Reshaping European Union's development policy: Collective choices and the new global order,' *Revista Brasileira de Política Internacional*, 58(2), pp. 44–64.

Mawdsley, E. (2015a) 'DFID, the private sector and the re-centring of an economic growth agenda in international development,' *The Geographic Journal*, 180, pp. 27–38.

Mawdsley, E. (2015b) "Development geography I: Cooperation, competition and convergence between 'North' and 'South,'" *Progress in Human Geography*, 41(1), pp. 108–117.

Mawdsley, E., Savage, L. and Kim, S.M. (2014) "A 'post-aid world'? Paradigm shift in foreign aid and development cooperation at the 2011 Busan High Level Forum," *Geographical Journal*, 180, pp. 27–38.

OECD (2010) *Perspectives on global development: Shifting wealth*. Paris: OECD Publishing.

OECD (2018a) 'Reporting methods for private sector instruments,' *DCD/DAC (2018)47/ Final* [online]. Available at: https://www.oecd.org/officialdocuments/publicdisplay-documentpdf/?cote=DCD/DAC(2018)47/FINAL&docLanguage=En. (Accessed: 4 February 2021).

OECD (2018b) 'Global outlook on financing for sustainable development 2019: Time to face the challenge' [online]. Available at: https://www.oecd-ilibrary.org/sites/9789264307995-en/1/1/5/index.html?itemId=/content/publication/978926 4307995-en&_csp_=725b6399c64abff9e585c75195c4e8ea&itemIGO=oecd&item ContentType=book. (Accessed: 20 July 2020).

OECD (2020a) 'The impact of coronavirus (COVID-19) crisis on development finance' [online]. Available at: https://read.oecd-ilibrary.org/view/?ref=134_134569-xn1go1i113&title=The-impact-of-the-coronavirus-(COVID-19)-crisis-on-development-finance. (Accessed: 3 September 2020).

OECD (2020b) 'Blended finance principles guidance' [online]. Available at: http://www.oecd.org/officialdocuments/publicdisplaydocumentpdf/?cote=DCD/DAC(2020)42/FINAL&docLanguage=En. (Accessed: 4 February 2021).

OECD (2022a) 'Development co-operation directorate' [online]. Available at: https://www.oecd.org/dac/. (Accessed: 16 June 2022).

OECD (2022b) 'TOSSD: Total official support for sustainable development' [online]. Available at: https://www.tossd.org/. (Accessed: 15 June 2022).

Pereira, J. (2017) 'Blended finance for development – Background Paper. Intergovernmental Group of Experts on Finance for Development 1st Session' [online]. Available at: https://unctad.org/system/files/official-document/tdb_efd1_bp_JP_en.pdf. (Accessed: 4 February 2021).

Savoy, C., Carter, P. and Lemma, A. (2016) 'Development finance institutions come of age: Policy engagement, impact and new directions,' *A Report of the CSIS Project on Prosperity and Development and Overseas Development Institute (ODI)* [online]. Available at: https://csis-website-prod.s3.amazonaws.com/s3fs-public/publication/161021_Savoy_DFI_Web_Rev.pdf. (Accessed: 4 February 2021).

Schmelzer, M. (2014) 'A club of the rich to help the poor? The OECD, "Development", and the hegemony of donor countries,' in Frey, M., Kunker, S. and Unger, C. (eds.), *International organizations and development 1945–1990*, 1st ed. Basingstoke: Palgrave Macmillan, pp. 171–195.

Schulpen, L. and Gibbon, P. (2002) 'Private sector development: Policies, practices and problems,' *World Development*, 30(1), pp. 1–15.

SDIP (2022). 'Sustainable development investment partnership' [online]. Available at: http://sdiponline.org/. (Accessed: 15 June 2022).

Teevan, C. and Sherriff, A. (2019) 'Mission impossible? The geopolitical commission and the partnership with Africa,' *Briefing No.113* [online]. Available at: https://ecdpm.org/work/mission-possible-the-geopolitical-commission-and-the-partnership-with-africa. (Accessed: 27 September 2020).

UN (2014) *UN report of the intergovernmental committee of experts on sustainable development financing*. New York: UN [online]. Available at: https://www.un.org/esa/ffd/wp-content/uploads/2014/12/ICESDF.pdf. (Accessed: 15 June 2022).

UN (2015) *Addis Ababa Action Agenda*. New York: UN [online]. Available at: https://www.un.org/esa/ffd/wp-content/uploads/2015/08/AAAA_Outcome.pdf. (Accessed: 15 June 2022).

UNCTAD (2014) 'World investment report: Investing in the SDGs: An action plan' [online]. Available at: https://unctad.org/en/PublicationsLibrary/wir2014_en.pdf. (Accessed: 16 May 2020).

UNCTAD (2015) 'Global value chains and south-south trade, economic cooperation and integration among developing countries' [online]. Available at: https://unctad.org/system/files/official-document/gdsecidc2015d1_en.pdf. (Accessed: 1 July 2021).

UNDP (2013) *Human development report 2013, the rise of the South: Human progress in a diverse world*. New York: UNDP Publishing.

Vanhoonacker, S. and Pomorska, K. (2013) 'The European External Action Service and agenda-setting in European foreign policy,' *Journal of European Public Policy*, 20(9), pp. 1316–1331.

Van Waeyenberge, E. (2015) 'The private turn in development finance,' *FESSUD: Working Paper Series 140* [online]. Available at: https://eprints.soas.ac.uk/22273/. (Accessed: 17 August 2020).Wook, S.W. and Rumsey, J.G. (2016) 'The development aid regime at fifty: Policy challenges inside and out,' *International Studies Perspectives*, 17, pp. 55–74.

World Bank and IMF (2015) 'From billions to trillions: Transforming development finance post-2015 financing for development: Multilateral development finance' [online]. Available at: https://pubdocs.worldbank.org/en/622841485963735448/DC2015-0002-E-FinancingforDevelopment.pdf. (Accessed: 14 April 2021).

World Economic Forum (2015) *Blended finance Vol. 1: A Primer for Development Finance and Philanthropic Funders* [online]. Available at: https://www3.weforum.org/docs/WEF_Blended_Finance_A_Primer_Development_Finance_Philanthropic_Funders.pdf. (Accessed: 15 June 2022).

# 4

# SHIFTS AND HURDLES IN THE URBANIZATION OF DEVELOPMENT FINANCE

## The case of the World Bank's city creditworthiness initiative

*Monika Grubbauer and Hanna Hilbrandt*

## Introduction

With the World Bank and other development institutions increasingly pushing for capital market involvement in municipal finance,[1] we are currently witnessing what we term the urbanization of development finance. This urban turn in the financialization of development has become evident in key global policy programs including the United Nations' Financing for Development and Habitat III processes. While the first of these processes sets the terms of financial cooperation to implement the Sustainable Development Goals (SDGs) of the Addis Ababa Action Agenda (United Nations, 2015), Habitat III, the most recent iteration of the UN-Habitat program, works to localize SDGs at the urban scale, with the New Urban Agenda as its central policy framework (United Nations, 2017). Together, these processes that have come to be known as the post-2015 urban agenda (Barnett and Parnell, 2016) have highlighted and reinforced the increasing relevance of cities as actors and sites of global climate and development policy. To operationalize this agenda in policy and financial practice, development institutions have worked to change the interactions between finance and urban management through a range of policy programs that promote municipal reform and financing through improving the access of municipalities to capital borrowing for investment in purportedly sustainable growth. This chapter discusses the City Creditworthiness Initiative (CCI), a World Bank initiative aimed at facilitating private investment at the municipal level, in order to examine the increasing entanglement of development finance in the post-2015 urban agenda.

Whereas the formation of the post-2015 urban agenda has attracted much attention in recent years, its entanglement with the "acceleration and deepening of [the] financialization-development nexus" (Mawdsley, 2018, p. 265; see also Mader, 2014) has gone largely unnoticed. Yet, crucially, this process has been

DOI: 10.4324/9781003039679-6

accompanied by efforts to open up new sites and economic sectors in so-called emerging-market cities to the conversion of their assets into products of financial value. Political economists and critical development scholars have long analyzed capitalism's continuous need for market expansion to offset crises of overaccumulation. In this view, the post-2015 urban agenda's focus on the sustainable development of cities and local authorities in what are termed emerging markets can be read as the opening of a new frontier of capital accumulation (Hilbrandt and Grubbauer, 2020). But, to create pathways for extracting profit from this realm requires a reform of urban and fiscal policy as well as an organizational transformation of municipal institutions. In examining the rollout of the CCI as well as its implementation, this chapter contributes to understanding how this program has attempted to create pathways for capital flows to the urban level.

Implemented by the World Bank and its private-sector arm, the International Finance Corporation (IFC), the CCI has been operating, with interruptions, since 2014. In order to secure private investment in the urban infrastructure of so-called emerging-market cities, this initiative encompasses three elements that aim at improving municipal creditworthiness: training academies, an online assessment tool and technical assistance. In examining the rationalities behind the rollout of the CCI as well as its development, implementation and key features, our analysis pinpoints institutional and programmatic shifts implied by the World Bank's increasing engagement at the level of municipal policy. Institutional shifts involve the inclusion of new actors in the World Bank's development activities and new means of intervention. Programmatic shifts concern the development of novel policy targets regarding municipal financialization. In analyzing these shifts and the potential conflicts involved, we argue that the rollout of the CCI is not only fraught with hurdles in implementing these shifts in the World Bank itself, but that it can also lead to ambivalent outcomes for Southern municipalities. Although this program is rescaling power to the urban level and may increase the room for maneuver available to some cities, possible power gains remain fragile and highly unclear, whereas adoption of the program is potentially risky for the participating cities and subject to drastic and sudden change. In teasing out these ambivalences, our discussion is limited to the institutional and programmatic shifts in which the CCI is entangled. Due to the lack of empirical data and limited length of this chapter, we omit a discussion of the CCI's wider effects on citizens as well as on the urban development and ecological sustainability of targeted cities. As these aspects are critical for a holistic discussion of the urbanization of climate and development finance, further empirical research is needed to understand the potentially detrimental effects of this process.[2]

This chapter is based on the analysis of strategic documents and six interviews, conducted between July 2019 and March 2020, with key actors involved in the CCI rollout. Interviewees included: the program's former director; a key advisor and contributor to the program; two officials in partner organizations [the C40 Finance Facility and the German Development Corporation (GIZ)] partially in charge of implementing CCI-affiliated workshops; a staff member in the World Bank; and an expert on municipal rating. Data from these interviews are complemented with insights from two research projects, both addressing the expansion of financial markets into Southern cities (Grubbauer, 2020; Hilbrandt and Grubbauer, 2020). The CCI is then framed within the context of debates on development finance, linking this literature to accounts of the financialization of municipal budgets. We trace the background, objectives and development of the CCI in a second section and advance a discussion of the challenges that become evident in the program's implementation in a third. We conclude by outlining a research agenda that focuses on the urban effects of initiatives such as the CCI.

## Literature review: conceptualizing the CCI in the context of development and municipal finance

The CCI and other attempts by development institutions to improve municipal creditworthiness are usefully contextualized by two strands of literature in development studies and financial geography. Against the background of theoretical approaches that capture the "financialization-development nexus" (Mawdsley, 2018, p. 265) and the financialization of municipal policy (Hilbrandt and Grubbauer, 2020), these literatures focus more narrowly on the global institutional changes and municipal restructurings that accompany and reinforce capitalist market expansion.

The first body of work addresses the crucial and changing role of the World Bank and other global players in advancing structural reforms on national and municipal levels (Clegg, 2017; Goldman, 2005; Grubbauer and Escobar, 2021; van Waeyenberge, 2018) and contextualizes the CCI in a history of development policy. Seen in this context, the new generation of World Bank initiatives that target cities as partners and sites of investment builds on a longstanding agenda of urban structural adjustment (Fabricius and Harris, 1996), decentralization (Fox and Goodfellow, 2016) and efforts to promote sustainable urbanism (Seto, Solecki and Griffith, 2016). Moreover, literatures that discuss the recent programmatic shifts of World Bank policies and their institutional underpinnings vis-à-vis earlier development approaches are central for understanding what we refer to as the urbanization of climate and development finance. In the structural adjustment programs of the 1980s and 1990s, loans and debt restructuring were conditioned upon deep policy reforms that aimed at opening up the markets of debtor countries but frequently led to a debt crisis in the receiving states. With the end of those programs and the emergence of the Post-Washington Consensus in the early 2000s, Bigger and Webber (2020, p. 1) posit that "the Bank [transitioned] to a more explicit focus on poverty alleviation and state capacity building." Put differently, recent shifts in World Bank policy are marked by a strategic reorientation toward a pro-poor rhetoric, as well as a stronger focus on institution-building and organizational reforms inside the World Bank itself (Clegg, 2017). However, this more inclusive and cooperative approach of the past two decades has been characterized by an increasingly important role of financial instruments and financial markets (Carroll and Jarvis, 2015; Soederberg, 2013). Mader (2017, p. 462) concludes that "the emergent development orthodoxy of financial inclusion [has served] as a core pro-poor private-sector led development intervention."

Research finds the current financialization agenda of development policy to be reviving key policy tropes of the 1980s while using them to different ends: on the one hand, the World Bank's green finance agenda has brought a return to former structural adjustment policies. As Bigger and Webber (2020, pp. 1–2) note, this new era of what they term "Green Structural Adjustment" couples ecological and financial measures to produce "new geographies of rent extraction." In distinction to earlier structural adjustment programs, contemporary policies are now explicitly labeled as green and are targeting cities through new financial instruments that aim at spatially fixing Northern capital in the global South (Bigger and Webber, 2020). Yet, similarly to the conditionalities of earlier structural adjustment policies, these programs push for investor-friendly reform (although this time addressing munici-pal governments) to create "enabling conditions" (Bigger and Webber, 2020, p. 12) that allow the World Bank to catalyze global private finance into urban develop-ment. On the other hand, the literature finds that recent interest in private-sector investment in infrastructure provision in Southern cities revives the privatization agenda of the 1980s (Bayliss and van Waeyenberge, 2018). Although these efforts are justified by demands to improve public-service provision in low-income coun-tries, as Bayliss and van Waeyenberge (2018) argue, the motives behind efforts to involve the private sector have changed. As a burgeoning literature has pointed out, this financialized approach to infrastructure (Bayliss, 2014; Silver, 2017) seeks to enable private-sector investment in infrastructure projects (Pieterse, Parnell and Haysom, 2018). Bayliss and van Waeyenberge (2018, p. 577; see also 2023, their contribution to this volume) highlight the problems of this approach, including "high costs, the long-term and rigid nature of contracts, the difficulty in finding sufficient appetite on behalf of private investors, and varying assessments of their performance in terms of efficiency, risk transfer and social impact."

The second body of work that explores the entanglement of local government in global financial markets shines a light on the expected effects of the CCI at the urban scale (Hendrikse and Lagna, 2017; Pike et al., 2019). In particular, studies in urban and economic geography analyzing the financialization of urban policy have offered crucial insights into the consequences of local governments' increasing ac-cess to capital markets, as well as into the role of sub-sovereign rating and municipal debt (Kirkpatrick, 2016; Lake, 2015; O'Brien and Pike, 2019). Accordingly, mu-nicipal budget cuts and resultant urban fiscal crises have moved financial reasoning and calculating into the sphere of urban public policy. This research documents how municipalities' experiments with (global) finance have transformed core state functions in unprecedented ways and with far-reaching effects (Hendrikse and Lagna, 2017). It has evidenced how state institutions have adopted financial log-ics, thereby shifting the culture of the bureaucracy so that "traditional cultures of risk aversion in city hall are gradually infused by novel practices of active risk management" (Deruytter and Möller, 2019, p. 411). Municipalities have advanced financial innovation through newly invented financial instruments, such as social impact bonds or interest rate swaps; they have embraced financial accumulation by building state incomes on financial assets; and they have directly financialized citizens' lives, for instance through the financialization of pensions and social infrastructures (Karwowski, 2019, p. 1002). Pike et al. (2019, pp. 24–25; emphasis by the authors) conclude that "rather than passive and inactive, […] national *and* local states have been subject to *as well as* led the financialising process."

Literatures that examine the financialization of municipalities also document the scalar and horizontal power shifts that the discussed processes of municipal restructuring entail (Hendrikse and Lagna, 2017, p. 11). First, the financialization of municipal government is inscribed into a process of *vertically* rescaling state functions to both sub- and supranational levels. The devolution of state functions to the metropolitan scale has also downscaled operational and financial risks to the local level (Silver, 2017, p. 1486) – although, as Sbragia (1996, p. 85) points out, strictly controlled judicial limits on local borrowing restrict local governments' fiscal autonomy. At the same time, municipal governance is inscribed into the upscaling of state functions. Driven by global market organizations (e.g. the World Bank) and transnational financial associations (e.g. the International Capital Market Association, ICMA), the widespread creation of regulatory agencies at the global scale has entwined urban policies into supranational governance regimes over the past 15 years (Silva and Trono, 2020). Second, these developments are entangled in *horizontal* power shifts, characterized most prominently by the increasing leverage of financial elites over public policy and regulation (Tsingou, 2015). Whereas urban entrepreneurialism has long fostered speculative development and involved cities in public-private partnerships, the literature describing the financialization of municipalities notes an increased shareholder interest in urban governance or the provision of municipal services (Pryke and Allen, 2013). Moreover, municipalities' speculation with financial instruments has made them subject to the influence of rating agencies, which are increasingly gaining power over urban policy (Interview, 24 July 2019).

The two strands of literature this section has discussed illustrate the deepening involvement of financial markets in global development policy as well as processes of municipal fiscal restructuring in the wider context of financialization. Yet while the literature on development finance fails to address how the described shifts in the work of development institutions are actually implemented, research examining the financialization of municipalities remains largely focused on cities in consolidated financial markets (for exceptions, see Datz, 2004). Moreover, there is little research exploring the intersection of these two lines of debate: the involvement of global development institutions in the urban realm and the intended institutional transformations of Southern cities. As a result, the mechanisms through which global development finance is linked to and rolled out at the urban scale remain largely unknown. In demonstrating how global policy programs target cities, our analysis of the CCI offers insights into the institutional and programmatic shifts underlying the operationalization of relevant initiatives.

## Case Study: CCI-related institutional and programmatic shifts

The CCI emerged from an umbrella program called Public-Private Infrastructure Advisory Facility (PPIAF), a multi-donor technical assistance facility integrated into the World Bank (World Bank, 2020). Since 1999, PPIAF has served to conduct technical assistance in so-called developing countries, with a particular focus on realizing infrastructure projects with private-sector participation (PPIAF, 2021).[3] Under this umbrella, the World Bank created an additional subprogram termed Subnational Technical Assistance (SNTA) in 2007.[4] This subprogram provides financial support for technical assistance to subnational entities such as municipalities and state-owned utilities in order to "attract finance for sustainable infrastructure solutions by developing bankable projects, strengthening financial systems, and building creditworthiness" (PPIAF, 2021, p. 5). As the former director of the CCI explains, the CCI was established as one program line within the broader SNTA program in 2014,[5] with the specific objective "to strengthen their [the municipalities'] creditworthiness and ideally to tap capital markets as a result" (Interview, 14 January 2020). The CCI ran from 2014 to 2017, paused and was resumed for another three-year term in 2019; however, the second term was under new leadership and without some of the initial elements of the program (Interview, 25 February 2020). Our analysis in this paper refers to the first cycle of the CCI.

A key motivation for the establishment of the SNTA program, and later the CCI, was to circumvent the articles of agreement of the World Bank (Interview, 17 January 2020). These articles prohibit the World Bank from providing financial services to sub-sovereign entities without the approval of national governments and without a sovereign guarantee by them. Around the mid-2000s, two concerns led the World Bank to identify this prohibition of lending directly to sub-sovereign entities as a constraint: first, the World Bank became increasingly aware that cities were becoming crucial for development in the face of climate change, global urbanization and migration dynamics and were, at the same time, increasingly in need of improved infrastructure provisioning. Second, the World Bank posited bringing cities to creditworthiness more explicitly as part of its own development agenda. We identify this as a programmatic shift. As constitutional change in its restrictive articles of agreement proved unrealistic, the World Bank identified the IFC as a vehicle for its aims. To qualify for the services of the IFC and other private providers, the World Bank was "to lead the technical assistance efforts in order to prepare cities and sub-nationals to become creditworthy" (Interview, 14 January 2020). This constitutes an institutional shift vis-à-vis the ways in which earlier programs were structured. When the World Bank instituted the SNTA program in 2007, the

PPIAF budget totaled around $15 million annually, with the SNTA making up roughly one-third of that total. Over the past 13 years, a total of $43 million have been invested through the SNTA program (PPIAF, 2021).

Apart from the strategic aim of putting the creditworthiness of cities on the agenda of the World Bank, the initiation of the CCI in 2014 also had another more practical reason: the CCI was to overcome what were perceived as difficulties the World Bank faced in identifying opportunities for providing technical assistance within the SNTA program and in justifying (to donors) the selection of cities receiving resources and assistance. The former program director, responsible for the implementation of this program at the time, illustrates this point:

> So why would you put the money in [City X] instead of Istanbul? Why not cities in Turkey as opposed to the capital or the economic powerhouses? What about the low-income countries? It's easy to talk about subnational sovereign financing in the upper- or upper-middle-income countries. But what about sub-Saharan Africa and so on?
>
> *(Interview, 14 January 2020)*

The CCI responded to these questions through a more effective methodology that helped reach out to the municipalities and gather information that could serve as a basis for the selection of cities that the World Bank considered suitable for further funding and the consequential exclusion of other cities not considered worthy of support.

The initiative consisted of two elements: training academies and an online assessment tool. City Creditworthiness Academies were set up to reach out to municipal practitioners from finance, infrastructure and planning departments and national government officials to unite and improve the collaboration of practitioners in central positions. The first academy event took place in Nairobi (Kenya) in October 2013, before the official launch of the CCI in 2014. Other academies, in Seoul (South Korea), Arusha (Tanzania), Kampala (Uganda) and Addis Ababa (Ethiopia), amongst others, followed between 2014 and 2017. The academies brought together officials from multiple cities from a single country or from multiple countries for several days, offering lectures and workshops held by academics and World Bank advisors; however, participants had to pay for their travel costs themselves. The program covered different aspects of municipal finance, with a focus on capital investment plans, debt management and best practices for generating own-source revenue. The centerpiece of the academies was an online tool for self-assessment and project planning.[6] Based on the analytics used by this tool, participants were asked to fill out a questionnaire at the end of each day, sharing information on their cities related to the topics covered (Interview, 17 January 2020). At the end of the academy, practitioners used the information to develop action plans that could justify the World Bank's engagement and convince donors, that is national governments and international development institutions, to fund their proposals:

> That's when we would use the information gathered in these self-assessments, that's how we call them, in order to prioritize interventions. And again, it would help the participants prioritize interventions, identify specific actions. We would bring all of this information home and it would allow us to work with our donors and other donors and other partners.
>
> *(Interview, 14 January 2020)*

Based on the collected data, the World Bank sought to implement technical assistance activities. The precise type of activities depended on the preferences of the World Bank and its donors, including regional preferences, specifically targeted sectors and industries and existing projects that could complement or be integrated into planned interventions. Moreover, the likelihood of delivering successful effective results was to be critically assessed and failures to be avoided, as the director of the C40 Finance Facility explained (Interview, 17 January 2020).[7] Typically, the World Bank's technical assistance aimed, first, at identifying and enhancing revenue sources through enhancement plans that considered the whole process of billing, collecting and managing revenues, an aim which could be described as urban structural adjustment. In the second step, the program sought to target projects that were already in the pipeline and to offer support in terms of project selection, design and financing. The third step focused on the assessment of overall debt management policy and included the preparation of a shadow or public rating of the city or selected utilities and support of the World Bank's local partners in procuring the services of rating agencies.

In the years between 2013 and 2017, the CCI trained around 700 participants from around 300 cities in 40 countries (Interview, 14 January 2020). Only roughly one-tenth of the cities that attended the academies further engaged in SNTA-funded technical assistance programs. So far, according to the same interviewee, merely a small number are reported to have closed a PPP deal and to have established projects by tapping into capital markets, receiving sub-sovereign loans, or using other financial instruments, such as municipal bonds (Interview, 14 January 2020). However, detailed results on the long-term impact of the CCI and the geographical distribution of the SNTA-funded technical assistance activities that resulted from the CCI are not publicly available.

## Discussion of empirical findings: hurdles in the implementation of the CCI

Despite its limited success in delivering effective closings of financial transactions, the CCI has contributed to the described institutional and programmatic shifts in development finance. Visible in the governance constellations and mechanisms through which the CCI is organized and delivered, these shifts mirror and promote the scalar and horizontal transformation of power described in the literature review (Hendrikse and Lagna, 2017). Yet, our findings provide nuance to an understanding of the ways in which the redistribution of influence, risks and responsibilities between international financial institutions, national governments and local states are put into practice. Looking closer at the described stages of implementation, we argue that rather than a smooth rollout, the introduction of the CCI must be understood as a bumpy road with potentially ambivalent outcomes for local institutions. In particular, we discuss three challenges on different institutional levels that complicate the CCI's implementation, namely the hurdles (1) in the course of the reorganization of the World Bank itself, (2) between the municipal and national levels of government and (3) within the local bureaucracy of the targeted cities.

The first challenge results from contradicting goals of the different actors involved in the promotion of the CCI within and on behalf of the World Bank. As evident in PPIAF's SNTA program, the CCI's aim of enhancing municipal creditworthiness is implemented by channeling international donor resources into training academies, an online assessment tool and local technical assistance. The objective of these measures has been to enable sub-sovereign entities to tap into and take out credit from national (and to a lesser degree international) capital markets, thus creating new direct links between municipalities and local capital markets. Yet these shifts are contested within the World Bank and the financial development community. World Bank loans have long served to generate revenues for donors while, at the same time, their attendant policy prescriptions have provided the means to push for structural adjustment and implementation of market-driven agendas (Grubbauer and Escobar, 2021; van Waeyenberge, 2018). Clearly, opening up and diversifying other options of financing decreases this kind of policy influence. Moreover, by assisting cities in lending from capital markets, the CCI provides competition with their very own business model of providing loans.

Consequently, a World Bank advisor involved in the design of the CCI and its implementation reported that the initiative experienced resistance from parts of the Washington-based World Bank teams:

> Now the World Bank … its fundamental *raison d'*être is to be a financial institution. It needs to demonstrate that it's making loans; that it's getting those loans repaid; and that it's making money through this process. So, what we were talking about is putting cities on a path that would open up […] direct competition to the fundamental function of the World Bank.
>
> *(Interview, 17 January 2020)*

While the CCI was designed to circumvent the restrictions of lending to sub-sovereign entities, it also worked to overcome established World Bank policies "to crowd out the private sector" (Interview, 14 January 2020) and cause capital flight by undercutting the prices of private-sector loans. In contrast, fostering municipal lending from national capital markets would make cities less dependent upon World Bank financing, particularly if cities turn to local capital markets for borrowing in the local currency. As we were told, conflicts within the World Bank around these strategic questions led to the CCI being temporarily paused then continued only in a limited manner (Interview, 25 February 2020). Yet, the global picture looks different: one interviewee involved in strategizing at the C40 Finance Facility reports that several global actors are considering the establishment of a new development bank, tailor-made to meet the financial needs of cities (Interview, 12 February 2020). Moreover, other UN institutions are mainstreaming the municipal finance agenda across UN programs in ways that mirror and build on the experiences of the CCI (Interview, 14 January 2020, see also UNIDO, 2017; UN-Habitat, 2018, 2021).

The second hurdle in implementing the CCI and its wider agenda arises from differences in the interests and the political and regulatory competences of municipal and national institutions. For cities, becoming creditworthy often involves the federal state guaranteeing sub-sovereign lending, thus hindering municipal bankruptcy. In providing additional advantages for cities, these guarantees potentially improve the conditions for the uptake of capital market loans. However, municipal fiscal autonomy is not always in the national interest. That the CCI has pushed cities to assume new roles as potentially creditworthy financial actors and has promoted the devolution of fiscal autonomy to the local level has opened up new lines of conflict with federal state institutions. Anecdotal evidence suggests that national-scale institutions have even undermined cities' attempts to raise money through capital markets (Gorelick, 2018a). For instance, Gorelick, key advisor to the CCI, reports of the CCI's failures in Dakar (Senegal) and Kampala (Uganda), stating that

> political conflicts between the local and national levels led to Dakar's bond issuance being cancelled at the last minute [...] in the case of Kampala, national regulation has capped the city's borrowing at a prohibitively low amount. This limit means that the city cannot borrow enough money to make bond issuance worthwhile.
>
> *(Gorelick, 2018b)*

In line with this statement, our interviewees stressed that the dependency of cities on the central government potentially undermines the attempts of initiatives such as the CCI to empower cities and expand their room for maneuver. Hence, strategically, the CCI Academies made sure to jointly invite national and local officials. Yet, negotiations with the central governments about follow-up projects were complicated in multiple dimensions, including unclear institutional competencies and jurisdictions, election cycles, shifting political priorities in terms of targeted sectors and regions and varying attitudes toward decentralization and sub-sovereign financing.

The third challenge in the rescaling of risks and responsibilities concerns the administrative capacities for implementing change at the municipal level. As cities are institutionalized as supposed partners in direct technical assistance, capacity-building activities of municipal officials have gained in relevance. Officials who have participated in the CCI are key personnel, subordinate to the political level of mayors and the executive branch of government. The World Bank and other organizations have been actively trying to involve these individuals through formats such as the City Creditworthiness Academies, as well as communication platforms and the support of horizontal networking and sharing of learning resources between practitioners based on online tools (see Clegg, 2017). However, involving operative personnel is challenged by the fact that knowledge, if not institutionalized, is fleeting. The director of the C40 Finance Facility at the GIZ emphasizes:

> What doesn't work is when capacity development is focused solely on training and education of individuals. The fluctuation in the municipal bureaucracy is too high for this to work. […] This is a bottomless pit. This might even become the problem. The more skills they [municipal officials] have the more attractive they are for the private sector. […] Capacity development needs to be institutionalized, has to be thought of in much broader terms.
>
> *(Interview, 17 January 2020)*

It follows that attempts to effectively train municipal officials are frequently short-dated. This is aggravated by the fact that the public sector in low-income countries is notoriously understaffed, which makes the effective and long-term involvement of individuals from the bureaucracy difficult. Moreover, attempts at capacity-building run the risk of thwarting their intended effect. As interviewees in development finance and cooperation reported, local bureaucracies frequently undermine the capacity-building strategies of development organizations and actually expect foreign experts to relieve the local staff from additional workloads and deliver ready-made solutions and projects (Interviews, 17 January 2020; 25 July 2019).

## Conclusion

This empirical account of the rollout of the CCI sharpens our understanding of the institutional and programmatic shifts that the initiative promotes and of the hurdles and challenges that attended its implementation: diverging objectives within the World Bank; conflicts arising between national and municipal levels; and limited resources and capacities within municipal bureaucracies complicate the financialization of development in the urban context. We have argued that the CCI's implementation holds ambivalent outcomes for the targeted municipalities. Municipalities may gain in agency by expanding their fiscal autonomy; yet this opens up new external lines of conflict vis-à-vis federal states. In sum, the effective room for cities to maneuver is highly unclear and subject to unpredictable and major change (e.g. Gorelick, 2018b). The long-term 'on the ground' effects of this program lie beyond the scope of this paper, which has focused on the CCI rollout and its attendant challenges. Yet, the ambiguities that the introduction of this program has entailed raise key questions regarding the wider consequences of the CCI, including through its geographically uneven engagement, the foreseen structural adjustments and policy changes in urban institutions and, most crucially, its effects on urban populations. These questions call for a threefold research agenda.

First, the urbanization of development finance raises critical questions regarding the ways in which international development finance (i.e. multilateral development banks and their development institutions) reshape global urban geographies. There is an urgent need to understand the selected inclusion of cities in global development strategies, the uneven transnational reach of development finance institutions into local space, and the regional and urban imbalances between and within cities. Second, it is necessary to account for the legal, regulatory and financial processes of municipal restructuring these programs promote. In-depth empirical research on how these programs have landed and are shaped, as well as contested, in particular geographical contexts could show the varieties of these changes on the urban scale. Third and most crucially, how the institutional and programmatic shifts we discussed shape the city as a living space largely fails to be understood. As holding the private sector accountable for urban development increases private corporate influence over what gets built where and by whom, it is crucial to examine who profits and who gets excluded at the local scale. Clearly, urban residents bear the risks of creditworthiness, including the consequences of risky urban policy and potential municipal indebtedness.

## Notes

1 These programs targeting Southern cities and their urban and fiscal policy include, for example, the GIZ's FELICITY project, the World Bank's City Creditworthiness and Low-Carbon Livable Cities Initiatives, and the International Finance Corporation's Breathe Better Bond program.

2 Our ongoing research project *The Urbanization of Global Climate Finance*, funded by the Swiss National Science Foundation and conducted at the University of Zurich, addresses this gap through a case-study analysis of processes of municipal restructuring in Mexican and Indian cities.

3 PPIAF has been in existence since 1999. Donors include numerous national governments and national development agencies, the European Commission and international development organizations such as the IFC and the Asian Development Bank. In 2020, it operated with a total budget of $46.96 million and provided a total of $8.80 million for technical assistance activities.

4  Around $1.25 million were dedicated in total to the SNTA program in 2020 (PPIAF, 2021). Donors specifically listed for the SNTA trust fund include Australia, France, Italy, Switzerland, the United Kingdom and the IFC (PPIAF, 2021).
5  Funding specifically dedicated to the City Creditworthiness Initiative in 2020 was $270,000, or 2% of the overall budget of PPIAFF (PPIAF, 2021). Active partners for the program in 2020 included the World Bank's Urban Global Practice, the Rocke-feller Foundation, the Korea Green Growth Trust Fund, and the C40 Network.
6  The tool was accessible online at www.citycred.org. By the time of writing it was still accessible but no longer active (last accessed April 22, 2021).
7  The C40 Cities Finance Facility is a partnership between C40 and the GIZ, amongst other development cooperations, that focuses on three goals: the preparation of in-vestment projects, the building of capacities at the municipal level, and the promotion of knowledge and learning (Interview, 12 February 12, 2020).

## References

Barnett, C. and Parnell, S. (2016) Ideas, implementation and indicators: Epistemologies of the post-2015 urban agenda, *Environment and Urbanization*, 28(1), pp. 87–98. DOI: 0956247815621473.

Bayliss, K. (2014) The financialization of water, *Review of Radical Political Economics*, 46(3), pp. 292–307. DOI: 0486613413506076.

Bayliss, K. and van Waeyenberge, E. (2018) Unpacking the public private partnership re-vival, *The Journal of Development Studies*, 54(4), pp. 577–593. DOI: 10.1080/00220388.2017.1303671.

Bayliss, K. and van Waeyenberge, E. (2023). 'The financialization of infrastructure in sub-Saharan Africa,' in *Financializations of Development: Global Games and Local Exper-iments*, this volume.

Bigger, P. and Webber, S. (2020) Green structural adjustment in the World Bank's re-silient city, *Annals of the American Association of Geographers*, 111(1), pp. 1–16. DOI: 24694452.2020.1749023.

Carroll, T. and Jarvis, D.S.L. (2015) The new politics of development: Citizens, civil society, and the evolution of neoliberal development policy, *Globalizations*, 12(3), pp. 281–304. DOI: 14747731.2015.1016301.

Clegg, L. (2017) Constrained experimentalism and the World Bank, in Clegg, L. (ed.), *The World Bank and the Globalisation of Housing Finance: Mortgaging Development*. Cheltenham, UK: Edward Elgar Publishing, pp. 13–41.

Datz, G. (2004) Reframing development and accountability: The influence of sovereign credit ratings on policy making in developing countries, *Third World Quarterly*, 25(2), pp. 303–318. DOI: 0143659042000174824.

Deruytter, L. and Möller, S. (2019) Cultures of debt management enter City Hall, in Mader, P., Mertens, D. and van der Zwan, N. (eds.), *Routledge International Handbook of Financialization*. London: Routledge, pp. 400–410.

Fabricius, I. and Harris, N. (1996) *Cities and Structural Adjustment*. London: UCL Press.

Fox, S. and Goodfellow, T. (2016) *Cities and Development*. London: Routledge.

Goldman, M. (2005) *Imperial Nature: The World Bank and Struggles for Social Justice in the Age of Globalization*. New Haven, CT: Yale University Press. DOI: 978-0-300-13209-0.

Gorelick, J. (2018a) Supporting the future of municipal bonds in sub-Saharan Africa: The centrality of enabling environments and regulatory frameworks, *Environment and Urbanization*, 30(1), pp. 103–122. DOI: 0956247817741853.

Gorelick, J. (2018b) The Real Reason Why Cities in Sub-Saharan Africa Aren't Issu-ing Municipal Bonds, *The Conversation*, February 14 [online]. Available at: https://

theconversation.com/the-real-reason-why-cities-in-sub-saharan-africa-arent-issuing-municipal-bonds-91688. (Accessed: April 22, 2021).

Grubbauer, M. (2020) Assisted self-help housing in Mexico: Advocacy, (micro)finance and the making of markets, *International Journal for Urban and Regional Research*, 44(6), pp. 947–966. DOI: 1468-2427.12916.

Grubbauer, M. and Escobar, L. (2021) World Bank experiments in housing: Microfinance for self-organized housing in Mexico in the era of financial inclusion, *International Journal of Housing Policy*, 21(4), pp. 534–558. DOI: 10.1080/19491247.2021.1898897.

Hendrikse, R. and Lagna, A. (2017) State financialization: A multi-scalar perspective, *SSRN Electronic Journal*, n. p. DOI: ssrn.3170943.

Hilbrandt, H. and Grubbauer, M. (2020) Standards and SSOs in the contested widening and deepening of financial markets: The arrival of Green Municipal Bonds in Mexico City, *Environment and Planning A: Economy and Space*, 52(7), pp. 1415–1433. DOI: 0308518X20909391.

Karwowski, E. (2019) Towards (de-)financialisation: The role of the state, *Cambridge Journal of Economics*, 43(4), pp. 1001–1027. DOI: cje/bez023.

Kirkpatrick, L.O. (2016) The new urban fiscal crisis, *Politics & Society*, 44(1), pp. 45–80. DOI: 0032329215617464.

Lake, R.W. (2015) The financialization of urban policy in the age of Obama, *Journal of Urban Affairs*, 37(1), pp. 75–78. DOI: 10.1111/juaf.12167.

Mader, P. (2014) Financialisation through microfinance: Civil society and market-building in India, *Asian Studies Review*, 38(4), pp. 601–619. DOI: 10357823.2014.963507.

Mader, P. (2017) Contesting financial inclusion, *Development and Change*, 49(2), pp. 461–483. DOI: dech.12368.

Mawdsley, E. (2018) Development geography II: Financialization, *Progress in Human Geography*, 42(2), pp. 264–274. DOI: 0309132516678747.

O'Brien, P. and Pike, A. (2019) "Deal or no deal?" Governing urban infrastructure funding and financing in the UK City Deals, *Urban Studies*, 56(7), pp. 1448–1476. DOI: 0042098018757394.

Pieterse, E., Parnell, S. and Haysom, G. (2018) African dreams: Locating urban infrastructure in the 2030 sustainable developmental agenda, *Area Development and Policy*, 3(2), pp. 149–169. DOI: 23792949.2018.1428111.

Pike, A., O'Brien, P., Strickland, T., Thrower, G. and Tomaney, J. (2019) *Financialising city statecraft and infrastructure*. Cheltenham, UK: Edward Elgar Publishing.

PPIAF (Public Private Infrastructure Advisory Facility) (2021). Annual Report 2020.

Pryke, M. and Allen, J. (2013) Financialising household water: Thames Water, MEIF, and "ring-fenced" politics, *Cambridge Journal of Regions Economy and Society*, 6(3), pp. 419–439. DOI: cjres/rst010.

Sbragia, A.M. (1996) *Debt Wish: Entrepreneurial Cities, U.S. Federalism, and Economic Development*. Pittsburgh, PA: University of Pittsburgh Press.

Seto, K.C., Solecki, W.D. and Griffith, C.A. (eds.) (2016) *The Routledge Handbook of Urbanization and Global Environmental Change*. London: Routledge.

Silva, C.N. and Trono, A. (eds.) (2020) *Local Governance in the New Urban Agenda*. Cham: Springer.

Silver, J. (2017) The climate crisis, carbon capital and urbanisation: An urban political ecology of low-carbon restructuring in Mbale, *Environment and Planning A: Economy and Space*, 49(7), pp. 1477–1499. DOI: 0308518X17700393.

Soederberg, S. (2013). Universalising financial inclusion and the securitisation of development, *Third World Quarterly*, 34(4), pp. 593–612. DOI: 01436597.2013.786285.

Tsingou, E. (2015) Club governance and the making of global financial rules, *Review of International Political Economy*, 22(2), pp. 225–256. DOI: 09692290.2014.890952.

UN-Habitat (2018) *Finance for City Leaders Handbook*. Nairobi: UN-Habitat.

UN-Habitat (2021) Marco Kamiya, UN-Habitat's Integrated Municipal Finance Programme – Part 2, Urbanet, August 22 [online]. Available at: https://www.urbanet. info/un-habitats-integrated-municipal-finance-programme-partii/. (Accessed: May 5, 2021).

UNIDO (2017) Sustainable Cities and Investments: Addressing the Bottlenecks to Urban Infrastructure Development. Issue Paper No. 3. Vienna: UNIDO.

United Nations (2015) Addis Ababa Action Agenda of the Third International Conference on Financing for Development [online]. Available at: https://sustainabledevelopment.un.org/content/documents/2051AAAA_Outcome.pdf. (Accessed: April 22, 2021).

United Nations (2017) New Urban Agenda [online]. Available at: https://habitat3.org/ wp-content/uploads/NUA-English.pdf. (Accessed: April 22, 2021).

Van Waeyenberge, E. (2018) Crisis? What crisis? A critical appraisal of World Bank housing policy in the wake of the global financial crisis, *Environment and Planning A: Economy and Space*, 50(2), pp. 288–309. DOI: 0308518X17745873.

World Bank (2020) City Creditworthiness Initiative: A Partnership to Deliver Municipal Finance [online]. Available at: https://www.worldbank.org/en/topic/urbandevelopment/brief/city-creditworthiness-initiative. (Accessed: April 22, 2021).

# 5

# THE FINANCIALIZATION OF INFRASTRUCTURE IN SUB-SAHARAN AFRICA

*Kate Bayliss and Elisa Van Waeyenberge*

## Introduction

Over the last decade, development discourse and practices have witnessed a dramatic ramping up of advocacy of public-private partnerships (PPPs) in infrastructure provision (see Bayliss and Van Waeyenberge, 2018).[1] While building on the pro-privatization rhetoric of the past three decades, the current PPP revival represents a departure from previous privatization policy due to the central role played by global finance. This has led to a growing financialization of infrastructure. Diverse physical investments across an extensive range of spatial environments have become condensed into financial metrics seeking to offer secure revenue streams for investors. Infrastructure policy has become increasingly focused on reconstructing sector investment requirements around the interests of potential investors.

Financialization gained momentum with the UN Sustainable Development Goals (SDGs) in 2015 which called for global private resources to fill the "financing gap", in particular through the deployment of PPPs. As part of this private turn in development finance (see Van Waeyenberge, 2015), donor efforts have become (increasingly) oriented around mobilizing funds from institutional investors, with the explicit promotion of developing country infrastructure as private (and financial) assets (see Bayliss and Van Waeyenberge, 2018). In a further elevation of private finance, the Billions to Trillions report (World Bank and IMF, 2015) and the follow-up Maximizing Finance for Development (MFD) strategy (World Bank and IMF, 2017a) called for public funds to be used to "leverage" private finance, such as by "de-risking" potential PPP projects (Jomo and Chowdhury, 2019). The logic of this approach is that public funds are in short supply and so bringing in private finance is essential both to finance infrastructure and to increase fiscal space (World Bank and IMF, 2017a, p. 5). Private finance is now

DOI: 10.4324/9781003039679-7

deemed essential and "barriers" to private investment are presented as a reason for infrastructure failings. These narratives have been influential in shaping a policy agenda centered around the needs of private finance.

This chapter sheds light on the actors and processes involved in the attempts to increase the role of private finance in infrastructure across sub-Saharan Africa (SSA) and to assess the implications of PPP-promoting measures for development policies and practices in the context of shifting structures of global capitalism. We see PPPs as a wedge in reconceptualizing the meaning of infrastructure as well as redefining the policy space around infrastructure provision, with important repercussions over and above their (relatively small) immediate financial significance. The particular way in which PPPs are promoted across developing countries highlights the consolidation of a development policy regime that relies on ostensibly neutral sets of benchmarks, standards and various other instruments. The modalities of this policy regime have been in the making since development agencies sought to redefine their role in the wake of the private turn in development finance and have been further strengthened with the advent of the global financial crisis and an emerging glut of global finance (see Bayliss and Van Waeyenberge, 2018).

This chapter draws on an extensive review of academic and grey literature and datasets. The following section focuses on the interventions by international agencies to support developing country governments in attracting private finance to infrastructure investment. Section 3 then considers the implications of this, in light of a wide body of literature showing weak evidence of benefits from private finance. We show that this policy framing is associated with a shift in understandings of infrastructure and a refocusing of the role of the state. Moreover, these developments are consistent with broader transitions in the structures of global capitalism. The chapter shows that the construction of infrastructure policy in terms of creating attractive commercial investments may result in a reorientation of development policy to meet the needs of global finance rather than improving conditions for the world's poorest.

## Boosting private infrastructure investment

New narratives with regard to infrastructure and development have emerged over the last decade (see Bayliss and Van Waeyenberge, 2018; Romero and Van Waeyenberge, 2020). These put the private sector and PPPs at the center of infrastructure finance. PPPs take different forms and are often represented on a spectrum from traditional public procurement to outright privatization or divestiture, capturing differences in the nature and extent of the involvement and relations between private and public agents. However, the various forms of PPPs can be grouped together as manifestations of a push for the increased involvement of the private sector (and finance) in public service provision (see Romero and Van Waeyenberge, 2020). Using private finance for infrastructure investment has become the default option while the use of allegedly scarce public finance is seen as a last resort.

PPPs are supposedly associated with far-reaching benefits. The African Development Bank (AfDB) highlights how PPPs

> can offer a solution to increase investments and efficiencies in public infrastructure. PPPs leverage private sources of finance, optimize the quality and the value for money by leveraging private innovation and capital to provide public services more efficiently.
>
> *(AfDB, 2021, p. 1)*

An additional benefit is that PPPs provide off-budget finance. According to the G20 Compact with Africa (CwA) initiative, launched in 2017 to promote private investment in Africa,

> Reforming public utilities and commercializing them will shift their borrowing and performance risks off the public balance sheet, thereby creating fiscal space for non-commercial public infrastructure.
>
> *(G20, 2017a, p. 16)*

Given the desirability of private finance, the stumbling block to development becomes the capacity of governments to attract such funds. For example, the founding document of the G20s CwA declares that:

> Meeting Africa's infrastructure financing needs crucially depends on countries' ability to prepare, execute and monitor project contracts, including through public-private partnerships.
>
> *(G20, 2017a, p. 25)*

A major challenge to the rollout of this financing mechanism has been attracting interest from the private sector, particularly in poorer countries. Figure 5.1 shows that private participation in infrastructure has declined from a peak in 2012.

Private investment accounted for less than 0.4% of GDP in emerging market and developing economies in 2017 (down from just over 0.5% between 2008 and 2012) (World Bank, 2018a). It remains stubbornly skewed toward middle-income countries (MICs), with China, Indonesia, Mexico, Brazil and Pakistan accounting for nearly 60% of all private infrastructure investment (World Bank, 2019). It is predominantly allocated toward the energy and transport sectors which together accounted for 95% of all Private Participation in Infrastructure (PPI) in 2017 (World Bank, 2018a). PPI in low-income countries (LICs) saw a steep drop in 2018 falling to its lowest level in the past ten years (World Bank, 2019, p. 14). In SSA, private infrastructure investment has been volatile. It declined steeply from 2013 and it was barely significant in 2016, accounting for only a small fraction of infrastructure investment (just over 4% in 2016), the bulk of which is allocated to energy and transport (ICA, 2017). Private investment recovered in 2018, but this was driven mainly by a surge in renewable energy projects in South Africa (World Bank, 2019, p. 11).

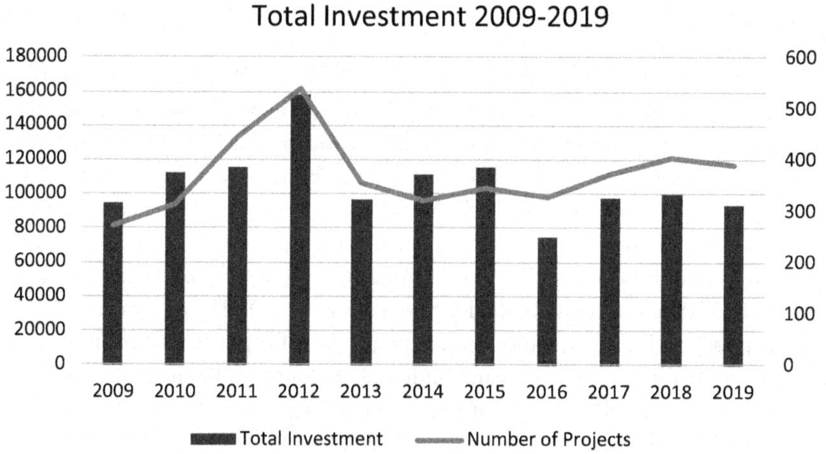

## Total Investment 2009-2019

**FIGURE 5.1** Investment commitments in infrastructure projects with private sector participation in emerging market and developing economies (EMDEs), 2009–2018.

*Source*: World Bank (2019).

The relatively low level of interest from private finance in LIC infrastructure has led to renewed donor efforts to make such investments more attractive. With PPPs promoted as the solution to infrastructure finance, the problem becomes one of a lack of "bankable" projects, for which read profitable (AfDB, 2018, p. 100).[2] Donor responses have been oriented around enhancing the role of private sector (see Bhattacharya et al., 2018, p. 10; G20, 2017b; World Bank and IMF, 2017b). A plethora of initiatives and mechanisms have emerged. The rest of this section discusses the different measures that the donor community deploys to promote private financial involvement in infrastructure. These include upstream measures that assist in transforming policy landscapes to ready them for PPPs, and downstream measures that mobilize development finance in support of specific PPP investments.

### Upstream measures: project pipelines, standardization and creating markets

Upstream policies are oriented around project preparation, an area where state capacity limitations are deemed most prevalent (World Bank, 2014). Governments are required to implement reforms to create a so-called enabling environment for private infrastructure investment. Attention is needed to the institutional, legal, political, financial, regulatory and engineering contexts and specific analyses that translate an infrastructure concept into a "well-defined and properly structured project, with clear identification and allocation of risk" (G20, 2107a). The cost of project preparation can be high – estimated to be in the range of 5%–16% of total cost – and is often overlooked in the budgets of both investors and governments (G20, 2017a).

Countries are urged to design pipelines of projects in which investors can participate. A number of donor initiatives have emerged to help developing country governments with upstream measures (see the World Bank's PPP Knowledge Lab, and their PPP Reference Guide (World Bank, 2017b) for an extensive range of resources[3]). Specific initiatives include the World Bank's Global Infrastructure Facility (GIF)[4] which offers support for governments to develop a project pipeline with its Upstream Project Preparation Window. Similarly, a group of multilateral development banks (MDBs) have established a platform called SOURCE, which provides online support with infrastructure project preparation for governments. The facility offers standardized project preparation templates for 40 different infrastructures, from irrigation to hospitals. The platform is offered for free to developing country government agencies and, while primarily funded by MDBs and donors, it has benefited from increasing financial contributions from private sector infrastructure players. SOURCE is managed by the Swiss-based Sustainable Infrastructure Foundation (SIF). While intended to bring "transparency and consistency to the project development cycle" (SIF, 2018, p. 1), the SIF Strategic Committee includes private sector investors such as Microsoft, Bouygues, Autodesk and KPMG (SOURCE, n.d).

Standardization of the provisions in concession agreements or other PPP contracts is intended to reduce transactions costs and overcome capacity constraints (G20, 2017a; Schmidt-Traub and Sachs, 2015, p. 14). The Compact with Africa for example suggests that standardization is a way to overcome governmental institutional constraints such as a lack of legal and commercial skills to negotiate with the private sector (G20, 2017a). Adopting standard contractual documentation is intended to increase investor interest. However, such measures are typically oriented around the needs of investors, for example, by offering regulatory certainty (AfDB, 2018, p. 99).

### Downstream measures: support for specific projects

Donor efforts in downstream support for PPPs are focused around improving the conditions for investors with regard to specific projects. Key in this area is the notion of de-risking, where donor interventions aim to reduce specific project risks that might deter investors. This is also known as blending, where donors contribute directly to project finances, and leveraging, which includes mechanisms like guarantees which insulate investors from certain project risks. Development finance institutions such as the World Bank's International Finance Corporation (IFC) might take an equity stake in projects or provide concessional loan finance to "crowd in" private financing sources to projects and locations where private financiers may not be comfortable with the perceived level of risk (Chao and Saha, 2015). These measures have been gaining support in recent years among donors and governments, as for example in the G20s Compact with Africa (Bayliss et al., 2020; G20, 2017a).

A specific incarnation of de-risking takes the form of donor or public grant funding, known as viability gap funding to make projects commercially viable. For example, in Ghana, a Viability Gap Scheme fills capital investment funding gaps required to make infrastructure PPP projects profitable for investors (World Bank, 2012). In this vein, the World Bank's Private Sector Window was established in 2017 to catalyze private sector investment in low-income countries with a focus on fragile and conflict-affected states. The program provides World Bank support to ramp up de-risking measures to attract private investment to these locations. The EU's External Investment Plan, launched in 2016 is another example of downstream donor activity. This combines a guarantee scheme with other "blending" activities to unblock bottlenecks to private investment in Africa and other target countries (Bayliss et al., 2020).

While PPPs are presented as a source of infrastructure finance, they can place considerable demands on the public sector and rely on public resources. For example, the much-celebrated PPP toll road between Dakar and Diamniadio in Senegal heavily depended on various sources of official support (including via public sector loans, MDB concessional loans and non-concessional loans) for ultimately a private sector participation stake of less than 20% (Bayliss, Romero and Van Waeyenberge, 2021). Similarly with donor efforts to promote private investment in solar energy in Zambia, over 70% of project finance in the two solar PPPs was from development institutions to attract a minority equity stake from European investors for two solar power generation plants. These projects were furthermore underpinned by commitments by the state for a fixed payment to investors for 25 years (Bayliss and Pollen, 2021).

## PPPs as a wedge: the capture of infrastructure policy by finance

The PPP agenda has led to major reconfigurations of developing country infrastructure policy landscapes toward creating conditions that are acceptable to global finance. Indeed, the drive for PPPs and private finance in infrastructure has translated into a series of legislative and regulatory reforms. In its review of the National Development Plans (NDPs) of 35 African countries, UNCTAD (2016) finds that 29 of these national plans link PPPs to national development goals. And the World Bank (2018b, p. 27) reveals that stand-alone PPP laws have been enacted in a large number of SSAn countries (see also Ambani et al., 2018).[5] Across various SSAn countries, the interest in PPPs has also manifested itself in the institution of PPP units. This reflects a common trend across the developing world, as it is perceived that these units can "facilitate the development of PPPs by centralizing PPP expertise in a single government agency" (World Bank, 2018b, p. 30). The specific form these units take as well as their formal place within the policy-making landscape, varies across countries, but, as local transmitters of a broader agenda, PPP units tend to share a set of characteristics. These include the following: responsibility for PPP regulation policy and guidance, capacity building for other government entities, promotion of PPP programs, technical support in implementing PPP projects and oversight in PPP implementation. The PPP unit hence performs an advisory (and promotion) role in support of specific procurement decisions located within relevant line ministries (World Bank, 2018b, p. 30).[6] PPP units emerge both with and without direct support from external agencies, although the fast-growing web of facilitation platforms and benchmarking exercises discussed above has increased the likelihood of their being established across countries [see the Annex of the G20s CWA for examples of the range of specific donor-funded initiatives in support of PPPs (G20, 2017a)].

Institutional and regulatory changes in support of PPPs have given rise to a proliferation of lists of "bankable" projects across SSAn countries which seek to advertise to (foreign) investors how different infrastructure projects provide attractive investment opportunities. These lists include a host of projects across sectors (e.g., from transport, hospitals, prisons, power to schools, universities) that have been prepared so that private investors can express interest. Kenya's pipeline, for instance, includes 64 projects (in June 2022; Government of Kenya, 2022).

Despite such enthusiasm in local development policies for PPPs, the outcomes of PPPs in practice have been problematic. The issues are well documented and widely known. They include high costs, limited efficiency gains, failure to address poverty, and cherry-picking from the private sector leading to fragmentation. Furthermore, measures to reduce private sector risk simply transfer this to the public sector (see Bayliss and Van Waeyenberge, 2018; Jomo et al., 2016; Romero, 2015 and references therein). Moreover, PPPs and private finance are not substitutes for public funds. PPPs bring investment that is repaid with a profit. They may bring advantages over public finance in terms of the speed of allocation, or predictability of financial flows but they are not a source of funding. Countries with weak fiscal positions, such as highly indebted poor countries, may be likely to seek private infrastructure finance for large projects due to their constraints (Arezki et al., 2018) but these then can lead to even greater fiscal liabilities in the long term. Policy advocacy is noticeably vague when it comes to the wider benefits of PPPs. For UNCTAD (2016, p. 111) many of the formulations in support of PPPs across NDPs lack specificity, and, although PPPs are promoted as conduits of development across these NDPs, it remains unclear how PPPs are likely to fulfill this function. Yet, despite well-documented limitations, infrastructure policy continues to be oriented around the creation of bankable opportunities.

However, the continued promotion of PPPs in the absence of substantive evidence of their benefits is associated with some more fundamental transitions in global capitalism. In the pages that follow, we focus on how infrastructure has been reframed, whose interests it comes to represent, and how a bias in favor of private investors is furthered.

### Reframing infrastructure

First, the framing of infrastructure needs in terms of lack of finance has led to a fundamental shift in understandings of infrastructure, from a physical construction of pipes and bricks to a financial revenue stream. This process has necessitated the "erasure" of a history of infrastructure as public works so that different sectors, locations and timings can all be converted into single, ahistorical asset class, or a "universal global thing called 'infrastructure'", regardless of history, context or material form (Bear, 2020, p. 46).

As PPP advocacy has gathered momentum, the underlying nature of public infrastructure is obscured. Rather than reflecting a standard product, infrastructure by its nature is intended to induce change so, for example, a road is expected to have social and economic benefits and lead to changes in transportation that will have an impact on spatial developments. Hence, infrastructure needs to be understood in terms of a fluid integrated system rather than discrete segments (see Helm, 2013). As Appel, Anand and Gupta (2018, p. 12) point out,

> Rather than being a singular thing, infrastructure is instead an articulation of materialities with institutional actors, legal regimes, policies and knowledge practices that is constantly in formation across space and time.

A system of infrastructure itself is located in a social dimension assuring the conditions of social reproduction of households across sectors. Indeed, households do not face water and energy and housing bills in isolation. Justifying an increase in tariffs (as an infrastructure project is made bankable) on the basis of alleged willingness to pay fails to take into consideration the implications for other dimensions of social reproduction and deprivation. Yet, once infrastructure needs are framed (almost exclusively) in terms of a lack of funds, private finance is easily promoted as the solution, and policy becomes focused on attracting the private sector.

## Rethinking the role of the state in infrastructure

This leads to a second point. The shift in infrastructure policy cultures is associated with a transformation in understanding the role of the state and the public good. The expansion of PPP policies has consolidated a view of the state as commissioner of services rather than provider, as the notion of infrastructure-as-asset displaces previous notions of infrastructure as the "structural underpinning of the public realm" (Hildyard, 2016, p. 22), framed by overall imperatives of accessibility and quality for all (see Romero and Van Waeyenberge, 2020). The state is increasingly seen as fulfilling a residual role, providing for those most difficult to serve, rather than infrastructure policy being situated as part and parcel of the broader redistributive mandate of the state in which infrastructure is governed by "collective and universal principles and practices of delivery" (Bayliss and Fine, 2016, p. 6). Furthermore, with a focus on PPP pipelines, the ambition is no longer to design comprehensive infrastructure plans but to prepare lists of separate projects, each of which offers profitable opportunities to (typically foreign) investors.

The promotion of PPPs prejudices alternatives and risks compromising the wider public good. For example, Aizawa (2018) carried out a review of 12 PPP guidelines published by major regional or international organizations.[7] She highlights the significant gaps across PPP guidelines, including how these "leave out the viewpoint of the public or non-commercial stakeholders" and have little interest in issues of public benefit or public good (Aizawa, 2018, p. 4). Interestingly, Aizawa (2018, p. 4) finds that "most [guidelines] lack helpful guidance on the circumstances under which PPPs should be used or avoided". The author adds that, in the persistent absence of evidence that PPPs have a strong positive impact on public service delivery, including in terms of improving access, the issue arises as to whether the panoply of resources in support of PPPs could not have been better directed in support of the public financing and provision of infrastructure.

### Persistent bias

Finally, the policy turn to PPPs is part of a wider structural shift that promotes the interests of global capital in development. The prioritization of PPPs has led to a reconfiguration of the policy realm in support of purportedly technocratic measures such as bankability, yet these incorporate an inherent bias. Proposals to standardize contracts provide a good example. The World Bank's Guidance on Contractual Provisions (World Bank, 2017a) has attracted negative criticism from the advocacy community for favoring investors over citizens and the environment, and offering investor protection that exceeds provisions under much-contested investment treaties. For the Heinrich Boll Foundation the guidelines contradict Principle 8 of the UN Guiding Principles on Business and Human Rights following which governments should maintain sufficient policy space to meet their human rights obligations (Alexander, 2017 and see also Shrybman and Sinclair, 2015) Bayliss and Van Waeyenberge (2018) also note that the proposals for standards tend to be devoid of sector-specific features, with sectoral specificities subordinate or incidental to the broader purpose of generating revenue streams for financial investors.

Indeed, PPP advocacy entrenches an approach to development policy that has been promoted since the Washington Consensus (WC), characterized by capital account openness, low levels of taxation, encouraging foreign investment, discouraging State Owned Enterprises, etc. But, while during the original era of the WC in the 1980s, reforms were imposed through conditionalities regulating access to much-needed (official) development finance, a different regime of policy adoption has come to prevail governed by standards, benchmarks, etc. Policy reforms are no longer necessarily integrated into conditionalities but promulgated via an insidious web of policy governance as development finance shifts to emphasize the role of the private sector. This regime of policy influence has been in the making since the turn to private finance in the mid-1990s, as traditional donors increasingly project roles for themselves as "brokers between the global market system and the interests of emerging countries and poor people" (Kim, 2017) rather than providing funding to governments for the direct financing and provision of infrastructure (see Van Waeyenberge and Fine, 2011). This switch in policy emphasis has been strengthened, since the Global Financial Crisis, as direct and indirect official (public) support for private participation in infrastructure has massively increased (see Romero and Van Waeyenberge, 2020).

The progression of the private finance agenda has cast infrastructure in a generic form not just across sectors, but also across locations. Yet, the ways in which private finance is engaged in infrastructure vary substantially according to where an investment is located within broader structures of global capitalism. Low-income countries tend to fare worst in terms of attracting investment and capacity to ensure beneficial outcomes (World Bank, 2018b). Indeed, lack of capacity is widely cited as a constraint to the effective implementation of PPPs and numerous donor programs have been launched to address such limiting factors. Clearly many countries lack the expertise to negotiate and monitor contracts on a scale to match that of international capital. Smaller economies such as Rwanda, Uganda, Zambia and Ghana face a broader shortage of staff with expertise in areas such as risk evaluation, contract design, project preparation and financing, and economic analysis of PPP benefits compared with alternatives (EIU, 2015). Low-income countries are often reliant on external funding and foreign consultants which means that interventions take a standard form rather than being rooted in the development constraints that are faced locally. However, blaming capacity for weak implementation has echoes of wider narratives related to so-called good governance. For Best (2014, p. 122),

> the good governance agenda … allowed the IFIs to shift significant responsibility for those failures [of development finance] onto low-income governments while at the same time developing new forms of expertise to respond to the "problem" of governance.

With PPPs, a focus on capacity constraints appears to be neutral and suggests that these can be overcome by training, technical expertise and standardization. Such a focus can negate more problematic questioning of whether the original policy is appropriate.

## Conclusion

So far, PPPs play a relatively small role in infrastructure investment in developing countries. But over the last decade, the development finance community has increased its efforts, both financial and non-financial, to further the private sector's role in infrastructure. This has been emblematic of the promotion of PPPs as a way to finance large infrastructure needs in developing countries. These needs are understood in terms of a financial gap and, combined with arguments regarding fiscal constraints, the private sector emerges as the way forward. Establishing a PPP Unit is seen as a sensible part of infrastructure policy. Yet PPPs create fiscal risks for governments. While the impact so far is marginal in low-income countries, efforts to de-risk PPPs such as with guarantees, create contingent liabilities, usually in foreign currency that are akin to debt. In the long-term PPPs often lead to financial outflows as debt repayments or shareholder profits. This has significant overarching distributional implications, with essential infrastructures in developing countries possibly offering a basis for revenue extraction in the service of private (and often foreign) finance (see Bayliss and Van Waeyenberge, 2018).

Furthermore, in low-income countries, including in SSA, private finance for infrastructure has not responded as intended by the development finance community, with very low shares of infrastructure privately financed in practice. Nevertheless, the implications of the international policy direction have been pervasive. These relate to the way in which infrastructure policy has become conceptualized, with previous notions of infrastructure as "structural underpinning of the public realm", or as serving the public good, rapidly evaporating in favor of "profitable business opportunity" or "financial asset". Such displacement strongly bears on the way in which infrastructure projects are designed, on the criteria that govern the particular shape of an infrastructure plan (e.g., access versus profitability), on the perceived and actual role of the state, the scope for accountability, and so on. As such, while PPP policies are yet to bear financial fruits, they operate as a powerful wedge in the financialization of public policy.

The benefits of PPPs then are far from obvious, yet policy remains framed in terms of how to overcome implementation constraints. PPPs are not the only solution proposed to address the financing gap. Other avenues for raising development finance include curbing tax evasion and limiting capital flight. But international institutional innovation around these solutions has been minimal, in contrast with efforts to boost private sector finance which is "where the energy lies" in development finance debates and reforms (Mawdsley, 2018, p. 192). These initiatives elevate the roles played by international finance, as development institutions partner with venture capital, hedge funds, investment banks and sovereign wealth funds (Mawdsley, 2018). Moreover, the emphasis on raising private finance distracts from other aspects of development finance such as raising aid flows (Jomo and Chowdhury, 2019).

Best (2014, p. 4) describes how development institutions approach their ultimate objective of improving policies and outcomes in developing countries "far less directly than in the past". This is clearly demonstrated in the case of PPPs. The pathways by which these might lead to equitable sustainable development are not charted. Best (2014) notes that, in the face of persistent failures of development policies, international agencies shift the terms of the debate. The financialization of infrastructure finance in SSA is a prime example of this. Social outcomes can be set aside when the goal has become simply one of raising finance.

# Notes

[1] There are multiple definitions of infrastructure and these have themselves been subject to change. We adopt a broad definition to include both what is, on the one hand, sometimes referred to as economic (or "hard"), such as roads, ports, airports, and so forth, and, on the other, social (or "soft") infrastructure such as education and health provision. PPPs tend to take the form of long-term contractual arrangements for the private sector to provide infrastructure assets and services that traditionally would have been provided by governments.

[2] For the AfDB (2018, p. 100) a project is "bankable" when "it provides clear incentives for lenders to consider financing it".

[3] See https://pppknowledgelab.org/tools/tools-assess-whether-implement-project-ppp?ref_site=kl#source.

[4] The Global Infrastructure Facility (GIF) was set up by the World Bank as a PPP "facilitation platform" that seeks to connect global financial flows with infrastructure needs in developing countries (see https://www.globalinfrafacility.org/). Other such platforms include the Global Infrastructure Hub set up by the G20 (see https://www.gihub.org/), see Bayliss and Van Waeyenberge (2018) for a discussion.

[5] This compares to 41% for OECD HICs.

[6] Aizawa (2018, p. 22) notes that most discussions of PPP units do not acknowledge the way in which these units perpetuate a policy bias in favor of PPPs.

[7] In Annex 1, Aizawa (2018) provides a list of PPP documents from which she selected 12 specific guidelines for her review.

# References

AfDB (2018) 'Financing Africa's Infrastructure: New Strategies, Mechanisms and Instruments' in *African Economic Outlook*. Report by African Development Bank, pp. 95–124 [online]. Available at: https://www.afdb.org/fileadmin/uploads/afdb/Documents/Publications/2018AEO/African_Economic_Outlook_2018_-_EN_Chapter4.pdf. (Accessed 9 September 2020).

AfDB (2021) 'African Development Bank Group PPP Strategic Framework 2021–2031,' African Development Bank [online]. Available at: https://www.afdb.org/en/documents/african-development-bank-group-ppp-strategic-framework-2021-2031. (Accessed 9 September 2020).

Aizawa, M. (2018) 'A Scoping Study of PPP Guidelines,' UN DESA Working Paper No. 154 [online]. Available at: http://www.un.org/esa/desa/papers/2018/wp154_2018.pdf. (Accessed 9 September 2020).

Alexander, N. (2017) 'Globalization and the State's Sovereign Right to Regulate in the Public Interest: The Case of Public-Private Partnerships (PPPs) in Infrastructure' [online]. Available at: https://us.boell.org/2017/05/15/globalization-and-states-sovereign-right-regulate-public-interest-case-public-private. (Accessed 15 June 2022).

Ambani, P., et al. (2018) 'Sustainable Development and Public-Private Legislation. A Technical Review of Domestic Legislation in 18 Countries in SSA.' International Economic Law Clinic. Monash University.

Appel, H., Anand, N. and Gupta, A. (2018) 'Introduction: Temporality, Politics and the Promise of Infrastructure,' in N. Anand, A. Gupta and H. Appel (eds.). *The Promise of Infrastructure*. Durham, NC: Duke University Press, pp. 1–38.

Arezki, R., Bolton, P., Peters, S., Samama, F. and Stiglitz, J. (2018) 'From Global Savings Glut to Financing Infrastructure: The Advent of Investment Platforms,' IMF Working Paper WP/16/18.

Bayliss, K., Bonizzi, B., Dimakou, O., Laskaridis, C., Sial, F. and Van Waeyenberge, E. (2020) The Use of Development Funds for De-risking Private Investment: How Effective Is It in Delivering Development?, Report for The European Parliament [online]. Available at: https://www.europarl.europa.eu/thinktank/en/document. html?reference=EXPO_STU(2020)603486. (Accessed 10 September 2020).

Bayliss, K. and Fine, B. (2016) 'Theoretical Framework for Assessing the Impact of Finance on Public Provision,' *FESSUD Working Paper Series*, 192. [online] Available at: https:// eprints.soas.ac.uk/23418/1/FESSUD_WP192_Theoretical-Framework-for-Assessing-the-Impact-of-Finance-on-Public-Provision.pdf. (Accessed 4 February 2021).

Bayliss, K. and Pollen, G. (2021) 'The power paradigm in practice: A critical review of developments in the Zambian electricity sector,' *World Development*, 140. DOI: 10.1016/j.worlddev.2020.105358.

Bayliss, K., Romero, M.-J. and Van Waeyenberge, E. (2021) 'The private sector and development finance: Equity and sustainability,' *Development in Practice*, 31(7), pp. 934–945.

Bayliss, K. and Van Waeyenberge, E. (2018) 'Unpacking the public private partnership revival,' *The Journal of Development Studies*, 54(4), pp. 577–559. DOI: 10.1080/00220388. 2017.1303671.

Bear, L. (2020) 'Speculations on infrastructure: From colonial public works to a post-colonial global asset class on the Indian railways 1840–2017,' *Economy and Society*, 49(1), pp. 45–70. DOI: 10.1080/03085147.2020.1702416.

Best, J. (2014) *Governing Failure: Provisional Expertise and the Transformation of Global Development Finance*. Cambridge: Cambridge University Press.

Bhattacharya, A., et al. (2018) 'The New Global Agenda and the Future of the Multilateral Development Bank System,' Report for Brookings/Center for Global Development/Centre for Global Development and ODI [online]. Available at: https:// www.brookings.edu/wp-content/uploads/2018/02/epg_paper_on_future_of_mdb_ system_jan301.pdf. (Accessed 3 February 2021).

Chao, J. and Saha, D. (2015) 'Sources of Financing for Public-Private Partnership Investments in 2015,' PPP Database, World Bank [online]. Available at: https:// ppi.worldbank.org/content/dam/PPI/resources/ppi_resources/topic/2015-PPP-Investments-Sources.pdf. (Accessed 21 December 2022).

EIU (2015) 'Evaluating the Environment for Public Private Partnerships in Africa,' The 2015 Infrascope. An Index and Study by The Economics Intelligence Unit.

G20 (2017a) 'The G20 Compact with Africa,' A Joint AfDB, IMF and WBG Report. G-20 Finance Ministers and Central Bank Governors Meeting, March 17–18, 2017 [online]. Available at: https://www.compactwithafrica.org/content/dam/ Compact%20with%20Africa/2017-03-30-g20-compact-with-africa-report.pdf. (Accessed 6 October 2020).

G20 (2017b) 'Principles of MDBs' Strategy for Crowding-in Private Sector Finance for Growth and Sustainable Development,' IFA WG, April 2017 [online]. Available at: https://www.bundesfinanzministerium.de/Content/EN/Standardartikel/Topics/ world/G7-G20/G20-Documents/Hamburg_reports-mentioned/Principles-of-MDBs-strategy.pdf?__blob=publicationFile&v=3 (Accessed 21 December 2022).

Government of Kenya (2022) 'PPP Project List,' Public Private Partnerships Unit, Kenya National Treasury, Nairobi [online]. Available at http://portal.pppunit.go.ke. (Accessed 15 June 2022).

Helm, D. (2013) 'British infrastructure policy and the gradual return of the state,' *Oxford Review of Economic Policy*, 29(2), pp. 287–306. DOI:10.1093/oxrep/grt018.

Hildyard, N. (2016) *Licensed Larceny. Infrastructure, Financial Extraction and the Global South*. Manchester University Press. DOI: 10.7228/manchester/9781784994266.001.0001.

ICA (2017) 'Infrastructure Financing Trends in Africa – 2016,' Report by Infrastructure Consortium for Africa [online]. Available at: https://www.icafrica.org/fileadmin/documents/IFT_2016/Infrastructure_Financing_Trends_2016.pdf. (Accessed 10 February 2021).

Jomo, K., Chowdhury, A., Sharma, K. and Platz, D. (2016) 'Public Private Partnerships and the 2030 Agenda for Sustainable Development: Fit for Purpose?,' *UN Department of Economic and Social Affairs DESA Working Paper*,148, ST/ESA/2016/DWP/148.

Jomo, K.S. and Chowdhury, A. (2019) 'World Bank financializing development,' *Development*, 62, pp. 147–153. DOI: 10.1057/s41301-019-00206-3.

Kim, J.Y. (2017) 'Rethinking Development Finance,' Speech by World Bank Group President Jim Yong Kim [online]. Available at: http://www.worldbank.org/en/news/speech/2017/04/11/speech-by-world-bank-group-president-jim-yong-kim-rethinking-development-finance. (Accessed 15 June 2022)

Mawdsley, E. (2018) '"From billions to trillions": Financing the SDGs in a world "beyond aid,"' *Dialogues in Human Geography*, 8(2), pp. 191–195. DOI: 10.1177/2043820618780789.

Romero, M.J. (2015) 'What Lies Beneath? A Critical Assessment of PPPs and their Impact on Sustainable Development,' Report for European Network on Debt and Development, Brussels [online]. Available at: https://www.eurodad.org/what_lies_beneath. (Accessed 21 December 2022).

Romero, M.J. and Van Waeyenberge, E. (2020) 'Beyond Typologies. What Is a Public Private Partnership?' in J. Gideon and E. Unterhalter (eds.). *Critical Reflections on Public Private Partnerships*. London: Routledge, pp. 39–63.

Schmidt-Traub, G. and Sachs, J. (2015) 'Financing Sustainable Development: Implementing the SDGs through Effective Investment Strategies and Partnerships,' Working Paper, *Sustainable Development Solutions Network*, Paper prepared for Third Conference on Financing for Development, Addis Ababa, July 2015.

Shrybman, S. and Sinclair, S. (2015) 'A Standard Contract for PPPs the World Over: Recommended PPP Contractual Provisions Submitted to the G20,' Report for Heinrich-Böll-Stiftung [online]. Available at: https://us.boell.org/sites/default/files/ppp-web_1.pdf. (Accessed 10 February 2021).

SIF (2018) 'SIF and Leading Canadian and G7 Investors to Collaborate on the G7 Infrastructure Fellowship Program,' Press Release, Sustainable Infrastructure Foundation, Switzerland [online]. Available at: https://public.sif-source.org/wp-content/uploads/2018/06/Press-Release_SIF.pdf. (Accessed 10 February 2021).

SOURCE (n.d.) SOURCE Brochure [online]. Available at: https://public.sif-source.org/wp-content/uploads/2020/03/SOURCE-Brochure.pdf. (Accessed 16 February 2021).

UNCTAD (2016) 'Economic development in Africa Report,' United Nations Conference on Trade and Development, Geneva.

Van Waeyenberge, E. (2015) 'The Private Turn in Development Finance,' FESSUD Working Paper Series 140 [online]. Available at: https://eprints.soas.ac.uk/22273/. (Accessed 21 December 2022).

Van Waeyenberge, E. and Fine, B. (2011) 'A Knowledge Bank?' in B. Fine, et al. (eds.). *The Political Economy of Development: The World Bank, Neoliberalism and Development Research*. London: Pluto, pp. 26–46.

World Bank (2012) 'Project Appraisal Document on Proposed Credit to the Republic of Ghana for the PPP Project,' Report No.: 66198-GH, Washington, DC: World Bank.

World Bank (2014) 'World Bank Group Support to Public-Private Partnerships: Lessons from Experience in Client Countries,' Report by Independent Evaluation Group of the World Bank Group. Washington, DC: World Bank.

World Bank (2017a) 'World Bank Guidance on Contractual Provisions, 2017 Edition' [online]. Available at: https://ppp.worldbank.org/public-private-partnership/library/guidance-on-ppp-contractual-provisions-2017-edition. (Accessed 3 February 2021).

World Bank (2017b) PPP Reference Guide World Bank, Washington DC [online]. Available at: https://library.pppknowledgelab.org/documents/4699/download. (Accessed 18 June 2022).

World Bank (2018a) '2017 Private Participation in Infrastructure Annual Report.' Washington, DC: World Bank.

World Bank (2018b) 'Procuring Infrastructure Public Private Partnerships Report 2018: Assessing Government Capability to Prepare, Procure, and Manage PPPs,' World Bank Report [online]. Available at: https://openknowledge.worldbank.org/handle/10986/29605. (Accessed 5 February 2021).

World Bank (2019) '2018 Private Participation in Infrastructure Annual Report.' Washington, DC: World Bank.

World Bank and IMF (2015) 'From Billions to Trillions: Transforming Development Finance. Post-2015,' DC2015-0002 [online]. Available at: https://olc.worldbank.org/system/files/From_Billions_to_Trillions-Transforming_Development_Finance_Pg_1_to_5.pdf. (Accessed 4 March 2021).

World Bank and IMF (2017a) 'Maximizing Finance for Development: Leveraging the Private Sector for Growth and Sustainable Development,' DC-2017–0009 [online]. Available at: https://www.devcommittee.org/sites/dc/files/download/Documentation/DC2017-0009_Maximizing_8-19.pdf. (Accessed 4 March 2021).

World Bank and IMF (2017b) 'Forward Look. A Vision for the World Bank Group in 2030 – Progress and Challenges,' DC2017-0002 [online]. Available at: http://www.devcommittee.org/sites/dc/files/download/Documentation/DC2017-0002.pdf. (Accessed 4 March 2021).

# 6

# THE FINANCIALIZATION OF SUSTAINABLE DEVELOPMENT GOALS

*Eduardo Gonçalves Gresse and Fernando Preusser de Mattos*

Sustainable development goals have existed since the concept was coined by the Brundtland Report in the late 1980s (WCED, 1987). However, the first concrete global framework consisting of goals, targets and indicators for sustainable development was only established in 2015, when UN Member States ratified the 2030 Agenda for Sustainable Development. The global agenda originates from the 2012 UN Conference on Sustainable Development, also known as Rio+20, when world leaders agreed on an intergovernmental process toward global and time-bound goals for sustainable development (UNGA, 2012, §§ 245–251). Building on the Millennium Development Goals (MDGs), the 2030 Agenda consists of 17 Sustainable Development Goals (SDGs), 169 targets and over 200 indicators developed during a wide negotiation process (Kanie and Biermann, 2017; UNGA, 2015b).

The establishment of the 2030 Agenda marks the creation of a global framework for sustainable development governance, hereby understood as "the coordination of policies and programs for sustainable development by multiple social actors through a system of rules and cooperation" (Gresse, 2022, p. 2). This process has also resulted in the emergence of financialized goals for sustainable development. We regard *financialized goals* as any goals established in a way that fits specific aims, norms and practices with the narratives and techniques of finance. While financial actors have played important roles as the entrepreneurs of financial norms and the catalysts of private investments since the transition from the MDGs to the SDGs (Mendez and Houghton, 2020), the advent of the SDGs culminates in a systematic attempt by the UN to engage financial actors and private funding in worldwide initiatives for sustainable development.

Before the ratification of the 2030 Agenda, world leaders had already agreed upon a global framework for financing sustainable development – the Addis Ababa Action Agenda (AAAA) – which seeks to support the implementation of

DOI: 10.4324/9781003039679-8

the SDGs (UNGA, 2015a). Since then, UN institutions have launched numerous initiatives to attract private investments for sustainable development programs (e.g. SDG Philanthropy Platform, SDG Bonds, Sustainable Stock Exchanges initiative), highlighting in particular the systemic importance of banks and other financial institutions on the path toward the realization of the SDGs (Cosma et al., 2020). Financial actors have responded supportively to the incentives to engage with the 2030 Agenda and embed the SDGs in their strategies, narratives and disclosure practices, driven in no small part by an estimated $12 trillion per year in business opportunities associated with the global goals (Business and Sustainable Development Commission, 2017; van Zanten & van Tulder, 2018). In this sense, the 2030 Agenda plays a dual role as both a product of the financialization of sustainable development goals and a catalyst for that process.

In Brazil, leading financial actors have adopted the 2030 Agenda as a strategic instrument to guide their investments, report their alleged contributions to the realization of the SDGs and structure financial circuits based on sustainability norms. In doing so, they have actively promoted a range of financialized solutions for sustainable development. Exploring how this phenomenon has unfolded in Brazil is therefore particularly interesting for the purposes of unveiling and critically discussing the financialization of sustainable development goals. Two main questions arise: first, how does the financialization of sustainable development goals work in practice? Second, what are the implications of this process for sustainable development governance?

To address these questions, this chapter builds on the empirical findings of a qualitative research on the diffusion of the 2030 Agenda in Brazil (Gresse, 2022). In particular, the chapter draws on insights from participant observations at dozens of sustainability-related events in Brazil and from semi-structured interviews conducted with representatives from UN institutions, academia and private organizations in numerous sectors (finance, consulting, energy, philanthropy), between September 2017 and February 2018 (Gresse, 2022). In addition, the argument relies on a systematic document analysis (Bowen, 2009) and interpretation of a wide range of investor relations material collected from online databases of two major Brazilian financial actors: the Brazilian stock exchange B3 S.A. – Brasil, Bolsa, Balcão (hereinafter B3) and Latin America's largest financial services conglomerate, Itaú Unibanco Holding S.A. (hereinafter Itaú).

To examine the financialization of sustainable development goals and discuss its main implications for sustainable development governance, special attention is given to the ways in which influential financial actors in Brazil engage with the SDGs. In doing so, we draw on Chiapello's approach to study the "work of financialization" (Chiapello, 2020). We regard the *financialization of sustainable development goals* as a socio-technical process that involves the increasing role of the financial sector in promoting solutions for sustainable development through its narratives, resources and practices. In this sense, financializing requires not only discursive and ideological work, that is importing new thought frameworks and relabeling sustainable development issues, activities, or public policies by using the language of investment. It also involves deliberate efforts by financial actors to capture resources and re-organize financial circuits in such a way that financialized rules can be applied.

As such, the financialization process works through three interconnected operations, namely *problematization, tangibilization,* and *financial structuring.* The three categories of operation involve logically ordered stages: categorizing and interpreting the world using the words and perspectives of an investor; giving embodiment to these visions by identifying what is worth investment, assigning values and incorporating them into calculations; and, finally, organizing monetary flows by building new financial circuits (Chiapello, 2020). According to Chiapello, the process of financialization is "weak" when it involves superficial transformations and the decoupling between narratives and practices; "strong" financialization, in turn, encompasses the creation of new financial circuits that are connected to private investors or financial markets and operated under financialized rules (Chiapello, 2020, p. 83).

This chapter presents striking examples of how the financialization of sustainable development goals works in practice. We focus on leading operators of Brazil's capital markets, exploring how the financialization of sustainable development goals involves the interpretation of problems and solutions for sustainable development through the lenses of finance (*problematization*) as well as the adoption of time-bound, investable goals (*tangibilization*) and the creation of financial circuits to attract private investments aligned with sustainability norms (*financial structuring*). Finally, we discuss the main implications of this financialization process for sustainable development governance.

## The financialization of sustainable development goals in Brazil

Financial actors have promoted a wide array of financialized solutions for sustainable development inspired by the SDGs in Brazil. Leading banking institutions and investment management companies, not to mention the Brazilian stock exchange, have not only incorporated the 2030 Agenda and the SDGs into their strategies and operations, but also developed technicalities and devices to transform the language and instruments of sustainable development, thus reinforcing the power of the financial sphere. As explored below, analyzing the narratives, resources and practices of some of the key "workers" of the financialization of sustainable development goals in the country helps us understand how this process works in practice. Moreover, it illustrates how the engagement of leading financial actors with the UN Agenda involves all three stages making up the work of financialization according to Chiapello (2020; i.e. *problematization, tangibilization* and *financial structuring*), in one of the world's largest economies and a key player in global sustainability governance.

To gauge empirical evidence on that matter, the present section concentrates on two leading actors operating within Brazil's financial system: the Brazilian stock exchange, B3, and Latin America's largest financial services conglomerate, Itaú. This section draws on the analysis of numerous investor relation resources, available through the online databases of both organizations. Primary textual sources include, for example, annual, sustainability and bond issuance reports; corporate sustainability policies and Environmental, Social and Corporate Governance (ESG) guidelines; infographics, white papers and conference presentations, among other publicly available financial and non-financial information disclosed by the two financial institutions. Adding to the body of evidence are transcripts from semi-structured interviews and field notes taken during participant observations at dozens of sustainability-related events.

Based on the analysis of the extensive primary source material, we argue that both B3 and Itaú go beyond the initial stage of the work of financialization (i.e. re-framing problems and solutions for sustainable development from the investors' viewpoint, thereby imprinting on the topic new thought frameworks backed up with financialized devices; *problematization*). In fact, B3 and Itaú have engaged in explicitation and quantification work when dealing with the SDGs, by identifying assets and liabilities, assigning monetary value to SDGs and their respective targets, and incorporating them into reports and calculations (*tangibilization*). In addition, both financial organizations have promoted investment vehicles that are able to attract investors to new financial circuits of so-called sustainable financial products by trading various types of "environmental intangibles", such as carbon or decarbonization credits (Chiapello and Engels, 2021), issuing ESG-related bonds (e.g. green, social, sustainable and sustainability-linked bonds) or creating topic-specific funds, such as water or clean energy funds in order to promote the associated SDGs (*financial structuring*; see Table 6.1).

Yet there are important differences between B3 and Itaú concerning their respective roles in the financialization of sustainable development goals in Brazil. As a marketplace organizer (or financial market infrastructure), B3 is primarily involved in coordinating efforts to settle non-binding and agenda-setting measures or collective rules, and disseminating financialized narratives and practices among investors, companies and other stakeholders. Hence the reason why it primarily operates at the first stage of the financialization process, namely problematization. Leading banking institutions such as Itaú are better positioned to create new ways to encourage investors to incorporate the SDGs into their portfolios, thereby structuring what has become an ever-increasing Brazilian SDG financing circuit. The ways in which these operations unfold in practice are addressed in the ensuing sections.

### SDGs on the capital markets: evidence from the Brazilian stock exchange

One of the key workers of the financialization of sustainable development goals in Brazil is the Brazilian stock exchange, B3. As a financial market infrastructure, B3 plays a pivotal role in all three operations, positioning itself at the forefront of the debate on sustainable finance in the country and coordinating efforts with different actors to disseminate a financialized narrative on the 2030 Agenda. B3's involvement in the successive stages of the financialization of sustainable development goals in Brazil manifests itself in essentially two ways: first, as a catalyst for the incorporation of the SDGs into listed companies' material information[1] and disclosure methodologies, thus playing a key role in the *problematization* stage (BM&FBOVESPA, 2016). Second, as an architect and a steward of new financial circuits in which financialized rules and practices can also be applied to matters of sustainability. For example, by providing the registration environment for carbon credit issuances in the country or trading different investment vehicles such as green, social and sustainability bonds (i.e. *financial structuring*; B3 S.A., 2021d).

B3's prominent role in the field of responsible investment and sustainable finance in the country is reflected in the series of initiatives to which it subscribes both in Brazil and abroad. B3 was the world's first stock exchange to adhere to the UN Global Compact in 2004 and the first emerging-market exchange to be a signatory to the Principles of Responsible Investment (PRI) in 2010. B3 is also one of the founding signatories to the Sustainable Stock Exchanges (SSE) initiative, established in 2012, and since 2014 has been a member of the World Federation of Exchanges' Sustainability Working Group (WFE) (BM&FBOVESPA, 2016). The Brazilian stock exchange was also a pioneer in the sector when it launched the Corporate Sustainability Index (*Índice de Sustentabilidade Empresarial, ISE B3*) in 2005, the fourth stock index of its kind in the world.

ISE B3 is one of the leading performance indicators of the stocks traded on B3 (B3 S.A., 2022a). It is designed to track changes in the stock prices of companies recognized for their commitment to corporate sustainability. Such companies are integrated into the ISE portfolio after successfully completing a three-step voluntary selection process in which their commitments, performance and reporting standards on seven sustainability-related dimensions are thoroughly assessed. With its sustainability index, B3 also intends to encourage listed companies to adopt best ESG practices, support both individual and institutional investors in their decision-making process and thus attract those in line with responsible investment principles to the shares selected in the ISE portfolio. The 2022 portfolio for ISE B3 includes 46 companies from 27 different sectors (B3 S.A., 2022b, 2022c).

Over the last decade, B3 has stepped up its engagement with transnational networks and global corporate sustainability initiatives, as well as with domestic stakeholders, in order to establish itself as an obligatory passage point in the process of translating the 2030 Agenda to Brazil's capital markets. In doing so, it has pushed forward its *problematization* work by incorporating the SDGs into ISE B3's methodology to assess business sustainability performance and select which B3-listed issuers will join the index's portfolio. This is an ongoing process with which

> ISE B3 expects to increasingly broaden its direct conversations with organizations, investors and other stakeholders … to enhance business sustainability practices in light of the 2030 Agenda.
>
> *(B3 S.A, 2019, p. 27)*

Every year, ISE B3 methodology takes additional steps toward a new conceptualization of corporate sustainability, based on the 2030 Agenda. Figure 6.1 shows a timeline of ISE B3's incorporation of the 2030 Agenda and the SDGs into its questionnaire. The timeline is illustrative of B3's *problematization* work insofar as it shows how the stock index situates the SDGs as a problem to be dealt with from an investor's perspective, not only at the level of a company's strategic planning, but also in their public communication to stakeholders. With such a narrative, B3 seeks to translate the essence of the 2030 Agenda to a company's scale and leverage ISE B3's role as an "articulator and trend indicator in the business sustainability area" (B3 S.A., 2019, p. 3). Also, it seeks to induce financialized practices by respondent companies which will purportedly consolidate the SDGs as a "guidance and common language for actors in all industries, all over the world" (B3 S.A., 2019, p. 3).

Results from the 63 companies who filled out the 2019 ISE B3 questionnaire bring some evidence on how B3's *problematization* work resonates among respondent companies. Among the multiple dimensions of the assessment report, two issues in particular stand out. First, the question as to whether companies use the 2030 Agenda and the SDGs as a reference to identify and incorporate relevant aspects of sustainability into their business practices – which 94% of respondents claim to do. The second crucial dimension refers to whether the SDGs are deemed a priority by the company for their "*direct and relevant relationship* between the impacts of their activities and that topic" (B3 S.A., 2019, p. 20, emphasis in original). Here, the least prioritized goals are a telling indicator of how companies perceive their role in supporting the realization of sustainable development goals: 71% of respondent companies saw no impact of their activity on SDG 10 (reduced inequalities); 69% left SDG 2 (zero hunger) out of their priority list, as did 61% of respondents with SDG 1 (no poverty). On the other hand, SDGs 9 (industry, innovation, and infrastructure) and 8 (decent work and economic growth) stand out as top priorities for 96% and 83% of the companies, respectively. The concluding section further elaborates on this point.

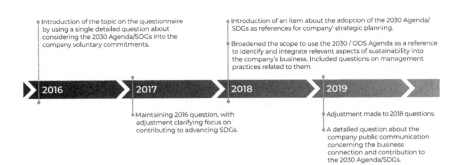

**FIGURE 6.1** *Problematization*: ISE B3 and the 2030 Agenda.
*Source*: B3 S.A. (2019, p. 14).

A leading sustainability scholar, who assisted B3's sustainability team in designing ISE B3 and updating its portfolio selection process, explained how the performance of participating companies is evaluated in terms of their contributions to the 2030 Agenda. In his words, a major concern when conducting this process was to infuse into ISE B3's questionnaire and methodology a different rationale other than the "sticker-album" logic dictating companies' usual misperception toward the 2030 Agenda and the SDGs:

> Companies' most immediate logic is that of the sticker album ...They want to be able to put the seal of each SDG in their sustainability report and then claim, "I have at least one action that contributes to at least one of the SDGs, so I am committed to the SDGs, look how cool I am" ... I must confess, companies don't really understand what I am talking about. They read the [ISE] questions, they tick the boxes, but they don't actually think about what that implies ... I think very few people understand this.
>
> *(Interview sustainability scholar, January 2018)*

Another example of B3's prominent role in disseminating the 2030 Agenda among Brazilian financial actors, and advancing such a narrative shift in corporate sustainability, is the *Report or Explain for the Sustainable Development Goals (SDGs)* initiative. Launched by B3 in 2012 at Rio+20, in partnership with the Global Reporting Initiative (GRI), the project was originally titled *Report or Explain for Sustainability or Integrated Reporting* and consisted of a series of efforts made by B3 to encourage listed companies to report their alleged contributions toward sustainability, while disclosing financial information (BM&FBOVESPA, 2016; B3 S.A., 2017; B3 S.A., 2018). The Report or Explain project therefore came into being with essentially two objectives: first, to urge listed companies to either voluntarily disclose ESG information or, if they opted not to do so, to explain the reasons why sustainability issues were not included in their annual reports at that point. Second, to compile a dedicated database with the main findings of the survey to "facilitat[e] rapid access to this information by the investors" (B3 S.A., 2021a).

Four years later, in 2016, the Report or Explain project left its mark on Brazil's Securities and Exchange Commission (*Comissão de Valores Mobiliários*, CVM). The institution in charge of ensuring the regular and efficient operation of Brazil's stock market, as well as monitoring the disclosure of information on securities traded and the companies that issued them, has refined its own supervisory practices inspired by this initiative. It did so by adding a specific item for companies to state whether they disclose social and environmental data in the so-called Reference Form, a mandatory assessment tool that publicly held companies must submit to CVM periodically. In the following year, the Report or Explain initiative was then calibrated to assess whether companies were disclosing their reports considering the SDGs. As part of the transition, B3 launched – together with CVM, GRI and the UN Global Compact – specific guidelines on how to align the reporting standards required by domestic supervisory frameworks, such as CVM's Reference

Form, with both GRI norms and the SDGs (B3 S.A., 2018). In the words of B3, the fact that national supervisory entities such as CVM began directly requesting companies to state their SDG-related practices not only "proves that measures to encourage the voluntary adoption of an ESG agenda are highly effective in the Brazilian market", but also represents a "victorious conclusion" of the Report or Explain project, which ended in 2020 (BM&FBOVESPA, 2016, p. 14).

Non-binding, agenda-setting measures like the ones adopted by the B3 relate directly to the initial stages of the work of financialization of the SDGs in Brazil. Its efforts to push forward the theme of sustainable finance and the 2030 Agenda among supervisory entities and leading operators of Brazil's capital markets are clothed with narratives and ways of thinking that appeal to investors' concerns for return, risk and liquidity. As Chiapello (2020, p. 86) notes,

> [t]hanks to problematization, special narratives using the language of investment and its returns, of capital and its risks, make thinkable the possibility of attracting financial actors and persuading them to finance what is under-invested.

B3 itself acknowledges that discursive practices are key to effectively mobilizing stakeholders around business sustainability practices aligned with the SDGs:

> Although SDGs are positioned and recognized as the main global reference in the sustainable development agenda … using proper language is a critical aspect to disseminate that agenda, as well as building narratives and perspectives that are understood, relevant and able to mobilize different audiences.
>
> *(B3 S.A., 2019, p. 27)*

And yet *problematization* is but one of the stages at which B3 operates in the process of financializing the SDGs in Brazil. In fact, the Brazilian stock exchange has played a key role in the two other types of activities involved in the work of financialization aside from discursively constructing sustainable development as a problem to be addressed by investors and framing the incorporation of the 2030 Agenda and the SDGs into companies' strategies, operations and disclosure practices as a possible solution. Performing both *tangibilization* and *financial structuring* work, B3 also opens its over-the-counter (OTC) platform to so-called ESG Thematic Bonds, as well as registering and trading carbon credits. In so doing, it has identified and promoted what is worth investing, describing the qualities, risks and returns of different types of social or environmental assets and impact commodities, among other types of investment vehicles.

ESG Thematic Bonds are debt instruments created to enable "the channeling of capital to finance sustainable economic activities", and include various types of sustainability-related bonds (B3 S.A., 2021d). In 2020, a total of 20 such instruments were available from B3's OTC market; 14 debentures and 6 so-called agribusiness receivable certificates (CRAs), totaling an issue value of R$6 billion (B3 S.A., 2021d). In addition, B3 provides the emissions trading and registration platform for Decarbonization Credits (CBIOs) issued by biofuel producers and importers. This is one of the instruments implemented by the 2017 National Bi-ofuels Policy (RenovaBio, Law No. 13,576/2017) to increase the bioenergy share in Brazil's energy mix to approximately 18% by 2030 (B3 S.A., 2021b, 2021c).

## SDGs as an "asset allocation guide": evidence from Itaú Unibanco

Brazil's leading banking institution and largest financial services conglomerate, Itaú Unibanco, provides us with another notable example of how the financial-ization of sustainable development goals operates. Not unlike B3, the company has a long track record of corporate sustainability practices. Itaú has been part of ISE B3's portfolio since 2005 and is the only banking institution in Latin America to ever be included in the Dow Jones Sustainability Index since it was launched in 1999 (Itaú Unibanco Holding S.A., 2021a). In addition, it is a signatory to benchmark sustainable finance and reporting frameworks, such as the Equator Principles, the PRI, the GRI and the CDP (Itaú Unibanco Holding S.A., 2020c).

With the adoption of the SDGs in 2015, the financial conglomerate started a three-year internal review process aimed at redefining its material topics and setting goals that would guide its strategies and operations from that point on-ward toward ESG issues. This review process culminated in the elaboration of a so-called strategic sustainability vision, launched in 2019 as Itaú's *Positive Impact Commitments*. The same year, Itaú became a signatory to the Principles for Responsible Banking (PRB) at the UN Headquarters in New York, thus "align-ing our business with the Sustainable Development Goals (SDGs)", as stated in different investor relations resources (Itaú Unibanco Holding S.A., 2019, p. 10, 2020a, 2021a). The relevance of the SDGs in the financial sector was stressed by a representative of Itaú's sustainability department:

> There is a lot of pressure on the financial sector for … the impact it gener-ates depending on the amount of credit it provides or not. This also entails a very powerful role to the financial sector … I can claim "if you are in doubt whether you should adopt [the SDGs] or not, as a company or as a client, be aware that this affects your credit score" … When you do that, you generate a lot of influence on the market.
>
> *(Interview Itaú Unibanco representative, January 2018)*

The three-year internal review process also paved the way for the financializa-tion of sustainable development goals by Itaú. This is evident, for instance, in a 2018 report titled *Responsible Investment through the SDG Lens: The Itaú Asset Management Approach* (Itaú Asset Management, 2018). The unit responsible for managing conglomerate funds at Itaú outlines in the paper the

> investors' perspective on how the SDGs can produce better returns, align-ing risks with the positive impact on society, and bring[ing] benefits to the environment and the business, based on the balance between investment initiatives to reach goals and targets.
>
> *(Itaú Asset Management, 2018, p. 10)*

Although asset management is but one of the activities performed by the Brazilian banking conglomerate, and ESG-related funds are only a fraction of the unit's overall investment strategy, the report provides a telling illustration of both *problematization* and *tangibilization* work.

The SDGs are referred to throughout the entire publication as a "framework for investment analysis, impact assessment or an asset allocation guide", a "new approach for investors to improve their investment decisions" and a "common language to shape and articulate responsible investment strategies" (Itaú Asset Management, 2018, pp. 5, 12–13). In addition, the paper explores the synergies and trade-offs between 15 "investable sustainable development goals" and their 57 "investable sub-goals" (i.e. SDG targets) (Itaú Asset Management, 2018, p. 11). Interestingly, SDGs 16 (peace, justice and strong institutions) and 17 (partnerships for the goals), as well as 112 out of 169 targets are not deemed "investable" (i.e. "subject to incorporation into investment decisions"), with a footnote informing, as the only justification for the exclusion, that this is what "leading institutional investors" claim (Itaú Asset Management, 2018, p. 11).

A valuation method to assess how investable targets correlate with so-called ESG drivers (i.e. the impacts related to different ESG issues affecting companies' future market value) is then laid out in the final part of the paper. In a clear move to quantification, the valuation method put forward by Itaú is designed as a tool to assign values and to incorporate the SDGs and their targets into companies' present and future financial performance (Itaú Asset Management, 2018, pp. 11–12). As such, it is both a core component of Itaú Asset Management's own investment strategy and a purported standard-setting valuation practice, yet the valuation method is described in the report as a general method to be used by any so-called sustainable investor. The report illustrates such a financialized practice applied to SDG 7 (affordable and clean energy) by relying on a hypothetical case of a pulp and paper company willing to improve energy efficiency in its production process in the following years (for more details, see Itaú Asset Management, 2018, p. 13).

The adoption of the Paris Agreement and the SDGs sparked an internal review process at Itaú, which culminated in the elaboration of a systematic effort to incorporate global norms for sustainable development within the organization, the so-called Positive Impact Commitments. With the launch of the Positive Impact Commitments and its strategic sustainability approach in 2019, the SDGs have become an integral part of the communications from the holding company and its affiliates (e.g. annual and ESG reports, guidelines, white papers), serving as a key component of their corporate narratives and disclosure practices. In fact, referring to each one of the goals considered as priorities to the banking sector has helped Itaú embark on a labeling operation, thereby financializing social and environmental issues deemed worthwhile of investment and offering products and services specifically designed to increase financing for so-called positive impact (i.e. sustainability-related) sectors.

As laid out in Itaú's 2021 *Sustainability Finance Framework*, such investment opportunities include green, social and sustainability bonds or loans, with which the company expects to contribute to

> the development of sustainable financing solutions, with the objective of raising funds for new and existing projects with environmental or social benefits.
> *(Itaú Unibanco Holding S.A., 2021b, p. 5)*

For renewable energy generation and services alone, the conglomerate intends to allocate R\$15 billion by 2025. Overall, Itaú has committed to raise R\$100 billion via bond issuances and/or loan disbursements to positive impact sectors by 2025 (Itaú Unibanco Holding S.A., 2021b). As of December 2020, these targets were met by 84% and 48%, respectively (Itaú Unibanco Holding S.A., 2020d, p. 89).

Yet these are not the only services offered or products traded by Itaú within the ever-increasing Brazilian SDG financing circuit. In 2020, Itaú launched a new set of ESG and Sustainable Investment Funds, creating new ways to encourage investors to incorporate the SDGs into their portfolios (Itaú Asset Management, 2021). Two investment opportunities stand out in this regard: the Itaú ESG Water Index Fund and the Itaú ESG Clean Energy Index Fund. While the former aims at "fostering positive externalities to society and the environment" by investing in 50 companies operating worldwide in the water segment, the latter targets 30 companies in the biofuels, solar and wind energy segments (Itaú Asset Management, 2021, p. 9). Most importantly, both share the explicit association with the relevant SDGs (SDGs 6 and 7, respectively) and attest to how Itaú has been one of the key workers of the financialization of sustainable development goals in Brazil.

Nevertheless, the share of ESG transactions is still relatively small considering the overall volume of operations structured in the local and foreign capital markets by Itaú BBA, the unit responsible for business with large companies and investment banking operations. In 2020, only 18.9% of the total amount of R\$62 billion in structured operations corresponded to the issuing of green, social and sustainable bonds, climate transition and sustainability-linked transactions (Itaú Unibanco Holding S.A., 2020b). This implies that the incorporation of the SDGs in financial narratives and practices does not necessarily lead to fundamental changes in the financial sector. Quite the contrary, engaging with the SDGs not rarely represents a market opportunity to communicate half-baked sustainability-related initiatives to shareholders eager for any statement on the matter, given investor, consumer and/or regulatory pressures.

The two cases discussed above indicate a strong degree of financialization, inasmuch as leading financial actors such as B3 and Itaú do not merely interpret problems and solutions for sustainable development through the lenses of finance (*problematization*), but also adopt time-bound, investable goals (*tangibilization*) and structure financial circuits imbued with their reasoning methods, valuation techniques and financialized rules to attract investments aligned with sustainability

**TABLE 6.1** The financialization of sustainable development goals in Brazil

| Operations | B3 | Itaú |
|---|---|---|
| **Problematization** Re-framing of problems and solutions for sustainable development from the investor's viewpoint | • Incorporation of SDGs into business sustainability performance assessment <br> • New conceptualizations of corporate sustainability <br> • SDGs as a problem to be dealt with in strategic planning and communication <br> • "Report or Explain" initiative | • Internal review process, aligning own business with SDGs <br> • Framing responsible investments through the SDG lens <br> • SDGs regarded as an investment analysis framework <br> • SDGs as part of communication strategies |
| **Tangibilization** Explicitation and quantification work when dealing with the SDGs as "investable" goals | • Identification and promotion of attractive SDG-linked investments | • Valuation method to assess investable SDG targets and to incorporate SDGs into calculations of financial performance for companies |
| **Financial structuring** Promotion of investment opportunities able to attract investors to new financial circuits of "sustainable financial products" | • Provision of registration environment for carbon credit issuances <br> • Trading platform for sustainability-related investment vehicles | • Offering products and services to leverage sustainability-related investments <br> • Trading sustainability-related investment vehicles <br> • Launching of ESG and Sustainable Investment Funds |

norms (*financial structuring*). Indeed, the financialization of sustainable development goals in Brazil reveals that the 2030 Agenda, and particularly the SDGs, have become a key component of the narratives, disclosure methodologies and investment decisions of investors (cf. Table 6.1). The main implications of such a financialization process for sustainable development governance are discussed below.

## Implications for sustainable development governance

The financialization of sustainable development goals has taken place in parallel to decades-long transformations in the capitalist economic system. Since the Brundtland Report coined the notion of sustainable development in the late 1980s (WCED, 1987), the world has witnessed a continuous and unprecedented growth in the influence of financial actors on world politics due to state deregulation and the rise of global financial markets underpinned by new, financialized types of regulations (Chiapello, 2015; Deutschmann, 2020). The launch of the 2030 Agenda and the SDGs, in turn, marks the establishment of a global framework that plays a dual role as both a product of the financialization of sustainable development goals and a catalyst for that process.

In Brazil, financial actors have promoted various financialized solutions for sustainable development inspired by the SDGs. As the examples presented above reveal, leading financial actors have widely incorporated the 2030 Agenda and the SDGs into their strategies and operations. Most importantly, they have relied on financialized narratives and practices which, combined with the resources they mobilize, transform the language and instruments of sustainability and reinforce the power of the financial sphere in sustainable development governance, denoting a strong financialization process. The ways in which this occurs in practice allow us to reflect on three implications of this process for sustainable development governance.

First, the SDGs are financialized goals that provide stakeholders with a concrete framework to guide their investments and to report their practices as so-called sustainable ones. As the Brazilian case shows, the adoption of the SDGs by powerful financial actors involves deliberate efforts to promote sustainability solutions that are conditioned to the logic and rules of financial markets. Such an approach has important implications for sustainable development governance since it privileges the diffusion of voluntary initiatives focused on short-term gains at the expense of structural transformations for sustainable development, such as tackling social inequalities and implementing climate-friendly regulations and infrastructures (Hickel, 2019; Gresse, 2022; Stammer et al., 2021).

Second, whereas financial actors explicitly prioritize specific goals and targets they deem investable, the interconnections among sustainable development goals – and above all the necessary transformations for the realization of those goals (Sachs et al., 2019) – are largely overlooked. Indeed, the incorporation of sustainable development goals in financial narratives and practices does not necessarily lead to structural changes within financial flows or in the financial sector as a whole. The adoption of the SDGs by financial actors involves a number of strategic efforts and voluntary add-on initiatives focused on sustainability finance and not on pursuing sustainable development in the first place. Hence, the prioritization of investable goals and targets established by the 2030 Agenda shows how engaging with sustainable development goals represents marketing opportunities and a way to promote financial businesses without changing them or other finance activities.

Finally, the empirical evidence indicates that financialized solutions for sustainable development seek to couple sustainability (as a norm, a goal and a value) with the way investors live and perceive the world. Those financialized solutions, along with the narratives and practices behind them, shift the meaning of sustainable development as a development process that couples human well-being with environmental protection toward an understanding of sustainability in the context of private businesses. By focusing on profit-making, they also represent the colonization of human lives and ecosystems (Krenak, 2020) through the deliberate attempts to create convenient, profitable solutions that dovetail sustainability aims, norms and practices with the narratives and techniques of finance.

The arguments and conclusions laid out above are limited in terms of scope and geographical coverage and derive mostly from the interpretation of publicly available sources obtained from a small sample size. Nevertheless, the cases of B3 and Itaú indicate how the SDGs can be conveniently incorporated by financial actors to support their own businesses and promote solutions for sustainable development that do not challenge the unsustainable pathways that brought us into the Anthropocene.

## Note

1 The accounting concept "material" is defined as follows by the International Accounting Standards Board:

> Information is material if omitting, misstating or obscuring it could reasonably be expected to influence the decisions that the primary users of general purpose financial statements make on the basis of those financial statements, which provide financial information about a specific reporting entity.
>
> (IFRS Foundation, 2018)

## References

B3 S.A. – Brasil, Bolsa, Balcão (2017) *B3 Discloses Results of the 'Report or Explain for the Sustainable Development Goals (SDGs)*, São Paulo, September 22, 2017 [online]. Available at: http://www.b3.com.br/data/files/D8/90/A4/93/73E7061099BE5706790D8AA8/B3%20discloses%20results%20of%20the%20Report%20or%20Explain%20for%20Sustainable%20Development%20Goals%20_SDGs_.pdf. (Accessed: 28 August 2021).

B3 S.A. – Brasil, Bolsa, Balcão (2019) *ISE B3 Experience with the 2030 Agenda and Its SDGs*, São Paulo, December 2019 [online]. Available at: https://iseb3-site.s3.amazonaws.com/eng-ISEB3_e_Agenda2030-pdf.pdf. (Accessed: 28 August 2021).

B3 S.A. – Brasil, Bolsa, Balcão (2021a) *Transparency* [online]. Available at: http://www.b3.com.br/en_us/b3/sustainability/at-b3/transparency/. (Accessed: 28 August 2021).

B3 S.A. – Brasil, Bolsa, Balcão (2021b) *Annual Report 2020*, São Paulo, 2021 [online]. Available at: https://ri.b3.com.br/en/financial-information/annual-report/. (Accessed: 28 August 2021).

B3 S.A. – Brasil, Bolsa, Balcão (2021c) *ESG Products and Services: Decarbonization Credit (CBIO)*. [online]. Available at: http://www.b3.com.br/en_us/b3/sustainability/esg-products-and-services/decarbonization-credit-cbio/. (Accessed: 28 August 2021).

B3 S.A. – Brasil, Bolsa, Balcão (2021d) *ESG Products and Services: ESG Thematic Bonds* [online]. Available at: http://www.b3.com.br/en_us/b3/sustainability/esg-products-and-services/green-bonds/. (Accessed: 28 August 2021).

B3 S.A. – Brasil, Bolsa, Balcão (2022a) *Bovespa Index (Ibovespa)* [online]. Available at: https://www.b3.com.br/en_us/market-data-and-indices/indices/broad-indices/ibovespa.htm. (Accessed: 21 January 2022).

B3 S.A. – Brasil, Bolsa, Balcão (2022b) *Corporate Sustainability Index (ISE B3)* [online]. Available at: https://www.b3.com.br/en_us/market-data-and-indices/indices/sustainability-indices/corporate-sustainability-index-ise-b3.htm. (Accessed: 21 January 2022).

B3 S.A. – Brasil, Bolsa, Balcão (2022c) *Raio-x das 46 empresas que compõem a carteira ISE B3 2022*, 4 January [online]. Available at: https://www.b3.com.br/pt_br/noticias/ise-b3-2022.htm. (Accessed: 21 January 2022).

B3 S.A. – Brasil, Bolsa, Balcão, Comissão de Valores Mobiliários, Global Reporting Initiative, and Rede Brasil do Pacto Global (2018) *Mercado de Capitais e ODS – Objetivos de Desenvolvimento Sustentável*, São Paulo, 2018 [online]. Available at: http://www.b3.com.br/data/files/51/94/4D/DC/A4887610F157B776AC094EA8/Mercado_de_Capitais_e_ODS.pdf. (Accessed: 28 August 2021).

BM&FBOVESPA (2016) *New Value – Corporate Sustainability: How to Begin, Who to Involve, and What to Prioritize*, 2nd edition, revised and updated. São Paulo: BM&FBOVESPA [online]. Available at: http://www.b3.com.br/data/files/96/D0/37/3C/0F07751035EA4575790D8AA8/GuiaNovoValor_SustentabilidadeNasEmpresas_EN.PDF. (Accessed: 28 August 2021).

Bowen, G.A. (2009) 'Document Analysis as a Qualitative Research Method,' *Qualitative Research Journal*, 9(2), pp. 27–40. DOI: 10.3316/QRJ0902027.

Business and Sustainable Development Commission (2017) *Valuing the SDG Prize: Unlocking Business Opportunities to Accelerate Sustainable and Inclusive Growth.* London: Business and Sustainable Development Commission [online]. Available at: http://s3.amazonaws.com/aws-bsdc/Valuing-the-SDG-Prize.pdf. (Accessed: 28 August 2021).

Chiapello, E. (2015) 'Financialisation of Valuation,' *Human Studies*, 38(1), pp. 13–35. DOI: 10.1007/s10746-014-9337-x.

Chiapello, E. (2020) 'Financialization as a Socio-Technical Process,' in Mader, P., Mertens, D. and van der Zwan, N. (eds.), *The Routledge International Handbook of Financialization.* London: Routledge Taylor & Francis Group, pp. 81–91.

Chiapello, E. and Engels, A. (2021) 'The Fabrication of Environmental Intangibles as a Questionable Response to Environmental Problems,' *Journal of Cultural Economy*, 14(5), pp. 517–532. DOI: 10.1080/17530350.2021.1927149.

Cosma, S., Venturelli, A., Schwizer, P. and Boscia, V. (2020) 'Sustainable Development and European Banks: A Non-financial Disclosure Analysis,' *Sustainability*, 12(15), p. 6146. DOI: 10.3390/su12156146.

Deutschmann, C. (2020) 'Entrepreneurship, Finance and Social Stratification,' in Mader, P., Mertens, D. and van der Zwan, N. (eds.), *The Routledge International Handbook of Financialization* (Routledge international handbooks series). London: Routledge Taylor & Francis Group, pp. 31–42.

Gresse, E. G. (2022). *Non-State Actors and Sustainable Development in Brazil: The Diffusion of the 2030 Agenda* (1st ed.). Abingdon and New York: Routledge. https://doi.org/10.4324/9781003128816

Hickel, J. (2019) 'The Contradiction of the Sustainable Development Goals: Growth versus Ecology on a Finite Planet,' *Sustainable Development*, 27(5), pp. 873–884. DOI: 10.1002/sd.1947.

International Financial Reporting Standards Foundation – IFRS Foundation (2018) *Amendment Issued: IASB Clarifies Its Definition of 'Material'* [online]. Available at: https://www.ifrs.org/news-and-events/news/2018/10/iasb-clarifies-its-definition-of-material/. (Accessed: 20 January 2022).

Itaú Asset Management (2018) *Responsible Investment through the SDGs Lens: The Itaú Asset Management Approach*, São Paulo, 2018 [online]. Available at: https://www.itau.com.br/download-file/v2/d/42787847-4cf6-4461-94a5-40ed237dca33/19d26550-6790-0820-0e83-a7978e83926b?origin=2. (Accessed: 20 December 2022).

Itaú Asset Management (2021) *Sustainable Investment: Itaú Asset Management*, March 2021 [online]. Available at: https://www.itau.com.br/download-file/v2/d/42787847-4cf6-4461-94a5-40ed237dca33/f730ccc7-82aa-e6ef-947b-c6957542947d?origin=2. (Accessed: 20 December 2022).

Itaú Unibanco Holding S.A. (2019) *2018 Sustainability Report*, São Paulo [online]. Available at: https://www.itau.com.br/download-file/v2/d/7e52c211-7192-4231-abba-b349721b6a07/63ad46ee-94b5-4e31-b47f-e0e42e9d7a58?origin=2. (Accessed: 20 December 2021).

Itaú Unibanco Holding S.A. (2020a) *Positive Impact Commitments: Itaú Positive Impact* [online]. Available at: https://www.itau.com.br/download-file/v2/d/42787847-4cf6-4461-94a5-40ed237dca33/26112dbc-e266-262b-c51d-0de27a599b2b?origin=2. (Accessed: 28 August 2021).

Itaú Unibanco Holding S.A. (2020b) *2020 ESG Products and Services Results* [online]. Available at: https://api.mziq.com/mzfilemanager/v2/d/42787847-4cf6-4461-94a5-40ed237dca33/e5b33d2e-7a62-f40b-066a-ed1eb45fae53?origin=2. (Accessed: 20 December 2022).

Itaú Unibanco Holding S.A. (2020c) *2020 ESG Report* [online]. Available at: https://www.banktrack.org/download/esg_report_2020/itauunibancoesgreport2020.pdf. (Accessed: 20 December 2022).

Itaú Unibanco Holding S.A. (2020d) *2020 Integrated Annual Report* [online]. Available at: https://www.itau.com.br/download-file/v2/d/7e52c211-7192-4231-abba-b3497 21b6a07/3f5a2a56-c428-42a9-b58c-bef3a8571018?origin=2. (Accessed: 20 December 2022).

Itaú Unibanco Holding S.A. (2021a) *Amazon Region* [online]. Available at: https://www.itau.com.br/sustentabilidade/show.aspx?idCanal=lnVF1ApDIrEh13B5pE9jdA==&linguagem=en. (Accessed: 28 August 2021).

Itaú Unibanco Holding S.A. (2021b) *Sustainability Finance Framework* [online]. Available at: https://www.itau.com.br/download-file/v2/d/42787847-4cf6-4461-94a5-40ed237dca33/eeed2822-9900-4f42-a7be-0f9d4714f404?o. (Accessed: 21 January 2022).

Kanie, N. and Biermann, F. (eds.) (2017) *Earth System Governance. Governing through Goals: Sustainable Development Goals as Governance Innovation.* Cambridge, MA: MIT Press.

Krenak, A. (2020) *A vida não é útil*, 1ª ed. São Paulo: Companhia das Letras.

Mendez, A. and Houghton, D.P. (2020) 'Sustainable Banking: The Role of Multilateral Development Banks as Norm Entrepreneurs,' *Sustainability*, 12(3), p. 972. DOI: 10.3390/su12030972.

Sachs, J.D., Schmidt-Traub, G., Mazzucato, M., Messner, D., Nakicenovic, N. and Rockström, J. (2019) 'Six Transformations to Achieve the Sustainable Development Goals,' *Nature Sustainability*, 2(9), pp. 805–814.

Stammer, D., Engels, A., Marotzke, J., Gresse, E., Hedemann, C. and Petzold, J. (eds.) (2021) *Hamburg Climate Futures Outlook 2021. Assessing the Plausibility of Deep Decarbonization by 2050.* Hamburg: Cluster of Excellence Climate, Climatic Change, and Society (CLICCS).

UN (2015) *Addis Ababa Action Agenda of the Third International Conference on Financing for Development*[online]. Available at: https://www.un.org/en/development/desa/population/migration/generalassembly/docs/globalcompact/A_RES_69_313.pdf. (Accessed: 21 January 2022).

UNGA (2012). *Report of the United Nations Conference on Sustainable Development.* Rio de Janeiro, Brazil. 20–22 June 2012. A/CONF.216/16.

UNGA (2015a) *Addis Ababa Action Agenda of the Third International Conference on Financing for Development (Addis Ababa Action Agenda).* United Nations General Assembly (A/RES/69/313).

UNGA (2015b) *Transforming Our World: The 2030 Agenda for Sustainable Development.* United Nations General Assembly (A/RES/70/1).

van Zanten, J.A. and van Tulder, R. (2018) 'Multinational Enterprises and the Sustainable Development Goals: An Institutional Approach to Corporate Engagement,' *Journal of International Business Policy*, 1(3), pp. 208–233. DOI: 10.1057/s42214-018-0008-x.

WCED (1987) *Our Common Future.* World Commission on Environment and Development, United Nations (WCED). Oxford: Oxford University Press [online]. Available at: https://sustainabledevelopment.un.org/content/documents/5987our-common-future.pdf. (Accessed: 21 January 2022).

# 7

# FINANCIAL CIRCUITS OF VACCINE PROCUREMENT IN THE ERA OF GLOBAL HEALTH

*Véra Ehrenstein*

In 2020, during the COVID-19 pandemic, vaccines dominated the news cycle. Pharmaceutical firms raced to license vaccines against the novel coronavirus, as governments tried to secure enough doses with the hope of a quick return to normalcy. To prevent resource-strained nations from being left behind, an organization known as Gavi stepped into the scramble for vaccines. At a virtual pledging event hosted by the United Kingdom (UK), it announced the "Gavi Covax AMC":

> a $2bn procurement fund aimed at ensuring that poorer countries can access doses of a potential coronavirus vaccine.
>
> *(Wintour, 2020)*

This Advance Market Commitment (AMC) is inspired by the pilot AMC for pneumococcal vaccines (Gavi, 2020, p. 5). Launched in 2007, the latter aimed to ensure that new vaccines against pneumococcus, a bacterium responsible for respiratory diseases, were made available concurrently in both poor and wealthy countries. The AMC for pneumococcal vaccines sought to pioneer a finance model that is described in this chapter. Aid was channeled toward vaccine procurement to obtain low prices and long-term supply from the pharmaceutical industry. As I will suggest, this example of soft financialization highlights the interplay between multilateral aid funding and market thinking in the field of global health.

The chapter will first indicate how the idea of an AMC for vaccines was brought about. It will then examine the decision to target pneumococcal vaccines, the pricing and legal structure and some of the challenges that arose during its implementation. A critical discussion of the pilot AMC's wider implications will precede the conclusion. The case study is based on research conducted from 2014 to 2016.[1] Interviews (31) were done in person in Geneva and London, and

DOI: 10.4324/9781003039679-9

remotely in the US, with current and former staff members of the Gavi secretariat, current and former staff members of the UK Department for International Development (DFID) and the British Treasury, legal experts, economists and epidemiologists. Observations were also carried out in an African biomedical institution based in Burkina Faso.

Gavi's stated objective is to support child immunization by improving access to new vaccines in countries with low GDP per capita. The organization was established in 2000 at the initiative of experts from the World Health Organization (WHO), the United Nations Children's Fund (UNICEF) and the World Bank. The Bill and Melinda Gates Foundation provided seed money, a five-year $750 million grant, which was quickly supplemented by governmental donations from the UK, Norway and the United States. Twenty years after its creation, Gavi is thriving. From 2016 to 2020, funding pledges reached $8 billion, with the UK alone committing $2 billion and the Gates Foundation $1.5 billion. Strategic decisions are made by the Board, where the founding partners (WHO, UNICEF, the World Bank and the Gates Foundation) are represented alongside other partners (donor and recipient governments, the pharmaceutical industry, civil society organizations and research institutions) and independent professionals (Gavi, 2022a). The Gavi secretariat in Geneva and Washington, DC oversees day-to-day operations. Unlike UNICEF, there are no Gavi country offices. The organization functions as a global coordinator. It "aggregates demand from the world's poorest countries" and secures funding, which "[sends] a clear signal to manufacturers of a large and viable market for vaccines" (Gavi, 2022b). Gavi is at the interface between supply and demand. On the one hand, it pools grants from donors and collects requests for vaccines from health administrations eligible for financial support. On the other hand, it develops procurement strategies to engage the pharmaceutical industry and obtain affordable prices and long-term supply.

An example of philanthrocapitalism (Langevin et al., 2023, this volume), Gavi is one of those "global health partnerships" where governmental donors, international organizations, philanthropists and companies come together around a health problem (Buse and Harmer, 2007). The motivations behind such partnerships vary; it may support existing treatments (e.g. the Global Fund to fight AIDS, tuberculosis and malaria) or finance biomedical innovation (e.g. the Dengue Vaccine Initiative). Social scientists have demonstrated that the emergence of these new actors in the field of public health accompanied an ever more protective intellectual propriety regime, the decline of the WHO and a focus on technological fixes, performance metrics and economics (Adams, 2016; Birn, 2009; Reubi, 2018; Storeng, 2014). As a contribution to this literature, this chapter examines the financial circuits underpinning a collaboration between public donors and the private sector. The language used at Gavi to talk about immunization – "public-private business model", "market shaping", "demand forecast", "investment", "portfolio" – denotes a soft version of financialization (Chiapello, 2015). The pilot AMC was one of Gavi's first so-called market-shaping efforts. Public resources were to support for-profit activities through market transactions while trying not to "overpay" private companies with tax-payers' money (McGoey, 2014, p. 120).

In the pilot AMC, a group of donors (the UK, Italy, Norway, Canada, Russia and the Gates Foundation) committed to procure new pneumococcal conjugate vaccines according to a specific pricing structure: a fixed number of doses were purchased at a subsidized price, after which manufacturers supplied their vaccine for the long term at a lower price. The offer, made by wealthy sponsors on behalf of strained health administrations, came with the promise of saving many children's lives. The fact that making vaccines widely available was reduced to a simple market exchange warrants further attention. A look at the history of immunization policy and development economics will help understand how the stage was set for an AMC.

## Immunization policy and economics setting the stage for an AMC

Since the second half of the 20th century, vaccines and immunization have achieved great success through cooperation. The eradication of smallpox in 1980 is still heralded as a major achievement in the improvement of people's health across the world (Packard, 2016). In the 1970s, under the leadership of the WHO and UNICEF, routine immunization had received strong international support. As production was increasingly privatized, manufacturers sold vaccines at a few cents per dose to use excess capacity and short-term supply contracts were awarded to the lowest bidders (Robbins and Freeman, 1988). Vaccines procured through that system had been available for a long time (e.g., DTaP, measles). Yet, when novel, more expensive products (e.g. vaccines against hepatitis b and Haemophilus influenzae type b) came to market in the 1980s in the United States and Europe, these were not added to the immunization programs in poorer nations (Greenwood, 2014). This unequal access to the vaccines gradually started to raise concerns within the public health community, where humanitarian ethics had fused with business ethos. Every child ought to be granted the same access to vaccination, and innovative ways to involve the private sector were required to buy recently patented products (Hardon and Blume, 2005; Muraskin, 1996; Roalkvam, McNeill and Blume, 2013). The Global Alliance for Vaccines and Immunization (later renamed Gavi) was created in 2000 to address such concerns.

In the early years at Gavi, the assumption was that pooling funds would "pull demand, then [the] price [of vaccines] would drop" (interview, former Gavi staff member 1). This action model proved too simplistic. Gavi managed to raise aid funding to expand the use of hepatitis b and Haemophilus influenzae type b vaccines; however, an evaluation of the partnership's first five years concluded that its influence on reducing prices was limited (Chee et al., 2008). Additional manufacturers had entered the market, making the vaccines cheaper. Gavi would need to do more to influence vaccine prices and supplies, and this is how the pilot AMC for pneumococcal vaccines was developed.

The concept underpinning the AMC stems from the early work of Michael Kremer, one of the 2019 Nobel laureate development economists (along with Esther Duflo and Abhijit Banerjee). Kremer was concerned with public funding and vaccine innovation in the field of neglected diseases. His argument assumed that public authorities could not be trusted. Commitments might be made to support the creation of a vaccine at any cost, but "once firms have sunk their research investments and developed a vaccine", the latter might not be purchased or only at low prices (Kremer, 2000, p. 16). Anticipating this, pharmaceutical firms "invest less in research than they otherwise would" (Kremer, 2000, p. 17). Their distrust may, however, be mitigated through so-called pull mechanisms. A purchase commitment could legally bind donors to live up to their promises. From academia the concept transformed into aid policy (for an example of performativity, see MacKenzie, Muniesa and Siu, 2007). A Washington, DC think tank decided to explore the idea and set up a working group with economists (including Kremer), health experts, biotech executives, World Bank officials, British government officials and the finance director of Gavi. The term "Advance Market Commitment" was coined in a report that detailed a

> commitment to buy vaccines if and when they are developed [that] would create incentives for industry to increase investment in research and development.
>
> *(Levine, Kremer and Albright, 2005, p. x)*

The term *market* replaced *purchase* as the commitment was to be conditional on market demand (i.e. donors would pay for the vaccines if aid recipients requested them).

In the world of aid policy, political momentum gathered for piloting an AMC. From 2005 to 2007, it was a topic of high-level discussion at G7/G8 summits in London, Saint Petersburg and Rome (Interview 1, former staff member of the British Treasury). Gordon Brown, then Chancellor of the Exchequer, was a strong advocate of an AMC for vaccines. Innovative financing fit well with the pre-austerity of the new Labour government. Treasury's support to the AMC (and Gavi) was further motivated by taking UK's aid spending up to 0.7% of its GNP (Interview 2, former staff member of the British Treasury). The minister's cabinet worked hard to secure the buy-in of other governments, leading to the launch of an AMC for pneumococcal vaccines in February 2007 (Gavi, 2007). The UK, Italy, Norway, Canada, Russia and the Gates Foundation pledged a total of $1.5 billion to be disbursed over the lifetime of the program (up to two decades). Enforcing it would require coordination between the WHO, the World Bank and UNICEF. Gavi occupied a pivotal position in this process as it would forecast demand, gather requests for the vaccine and agree upon supply offers. The AMC provided the partnership with an opportunity to finally intervene in the vaccine markets.

## Investing aid to shape vaccine markets

To understand how shaping vaccine markets was to be achieved, three aspects of the pilot AMC for pneumococcal vaccines will be examined: (1) the selection of the target disease; (2) the design of the pricing system and the associated legal terms and conditions; and (3) the implementation of vaccine procurement.

### Selecting the target disease and raising demand

Epidemiological considerations were instrumental in selecting pneumococcal vaccines to develop a pilot AMC. The donors to the initiative established an expert committee responsible for reviewing six potential diseases: malaria, human immunodeficiency virus, human papillomavirus, tuberculosis, pneumococcus and rotavirus. It concluded that pneumococcal vaccines were "the most suitable candidate" due to

> their ability to demonstrate quickly that the AMC concept works and their potential impact on the health of the target populations.
> *(Independent Expert Committee Recommendation for AMC Pilot, no date, p. 2)*

The committee did include a few representatives from low- and middle-income countries (e.g. a public health official from Malawi's Ministry of Health and the President of the Medical Research Council of South Africa). Overall, however, potential beneficiaries of the program had limited input into the decisions related to the AMC. These decisions were made based on global epidemiology statistics (disease and mortality rates) and donor economics (cost-benefit calculations). The AMC's donors defended the "one-sided dialogue" by emphasizing that it was primarily a matter of financing, as the funds would not be handed over to health administrators (interview, former staff member of the British Treasury 2). What counted was an anticipated health impact that could justify channeling aid into transactions with private manufacturers.

When the AMC was launched in 2007, the pneumococcal conjugate vaccines were not, strictly speaking, new. In wealthy countries, children were already immunized against the bacterium as the American company Wyeth had been selling a first-generation vaccine licensed in 2000. Wyeth's product was molecularly designed to cover pneumococcal strains prevalent in the United States. Although the vaccine fit disease profiles in Europe, epidemiological studies indicated that it did not cover the strains responsible for the high disease and mortality rates in sub-Saharan Africa (Ehrenstein and Neyland, 2018). While other firms were trying to develop their own pneumococcal vaccines, Wyeth enjoyed a production monopoly for approximately ten years. In the mid-2000s, a couple of new vaccines suitable for a wider range of epidemiological characteristics was on its way to commercialization. Since these vaccines would be better suited to the countries eligible for its support, Gavi launched an initiative called

PneumoADIP to prepare for their roll out (Levine et al., 2004). Epidemiologists at Johns Hopkins University in the United States led this evidence-gathering work, which aimed to accelerate access to the second-generation vaccines. The decision to focus the AMC on pneumococcus was, eventually, based on the evidence provided by PneumoADIP.

The PneumoADIP Initiative produced, along with the WHO, an assessment of the global burden of disease attributed to pneumococcus and inquired into the industry's vaccine pipeline. It also disseminated information about the vaccine to health experts and policymakers at regional meetings. This awareness-raising activity stemmed from a market-focused perspective. The PneumoADIP team considered that, if it were able to "create predictable demand", manufacturers "could scale up [their] capacity" and this would "bring down the prices" (interview, former head of PneumoADIP team). Market thinking was also oriented toward donors. The latter needed to be mobilized early on given that they held the resources for the demand to be solvent. Cost-effectiveness analyses were carried out, whereby different prices were tested against projected health outcomes. These sought to capture what would happen if new vaccines were used that targeted "the top 3 ranked serotypes [strains] occurring in the GAVI-eligible countries" (O'Brien, 2008, p. 5). The obtained estimates justified the purchase of pneumococcal vaccines up to 5$ a dose (Sinha et al., 2007). This price was higher than the few cents at which Gavi was buying existing vaccines, but significantly lower than the price of the first-generation pneumococcal vaccine in the United States (around $50 a dose at the time).

The evidence laid out what the PneumoADIP team called "the investment case" for pneumococcal vaccines (interview, former head of PneumoADIP team). *Investment* was defined as the use of public money in an intervention yielding returns in the form of health impacts. Pneumococcal vaccines appeared to be a low-risk, high-gain investment. This was instrumental in shifting the focus of the AMC away from its initial purpose of incentivizing research on novel vaccines for neglected diseases, to incentivizing the production of second-generation vaccines to ensure wider use. In the British administration, the belief was that the "pilot [AMC] need[ed] to work because there [were] some political reputations at stake"; trying to tackle a disease like malaria was deemed too "risky" (interview, former DFID staff member 1). There was a preference for rapid success easy to demonstrate. Once the AMC pricing structure was agreed upon (see below), DFID assessed the "value for money" of the UK contribution to the pilot; it came out as "good enough", further supporting the government in its decision to commit public money to the initiative (interview, former DFID staff member 2).

The announcement of the pilot AMC in 2007 was an example of "evidence-based advocacy" (Storeng and Béhague, 2014). It came with a series of statistics: the severity of pneumococcal diseases was put forward (killing 1.6 million people globally every year), together with an estimate of the number of children whose lives could be saved (5.4 million by 2030). The new market demand was represented by epidemiological evidence that could be used in cost-benefit analyses. These numbers signaled the distribution and scale of suffering caused by pneumococcus (Gaudillière and Gasnier, 2020), while giving donors sufficient guarantees of success.

### Designing a pricing system and the contractual terms to incentivize suppliers

Diplomacy and evidence gathering were followed by discussions on how to structure the commitment. The process of operationalizing Gavi's first major market-shaping effort took two years, from 2007 to 2009. The AMC was eventually comprised of a pricing mechanism embedded in a set of legal terms and conditions. Ad hoc financial circuits were created to incentivize manufacturers to produce more vaccines and sell them at an affordable price.

The core idea of the commitment was that vaccine producers initially received a subsidized price for a fixed number of doses. In exchange, they supplied their products at a lower price over the long term. The subsidy was expected to help manufacturers quickly recover the cost of investing in additional capacity to satisfy the new demand. Economic experts were engaged to develop economic models and to consult with vaccine manufacturers to develop the mechanism. Their aim was to predict the industry's potential response to the AMC, to make assumptions about costs, to calculate discounted cash flows and to test prices. Given the secretive nature of pharmaceutical companies (McGoey, 2014), the experts designing the pricing structure had limited data to inform their modeling. Some useful information came from a consultancy conducted for the PneumoADIP initiative. Interviews with scientists and patent holders indicated that the average cost of producing one vaccine dose revolved around $2. This high production cost was due to the technical challenges associated with manufacturing a molecule capable of targeting several strains at once. Drawing on economics and anecdotal evidence, the AMC would ultimately make "an offer to the world" (i.e. the pricing and its legal conditions) to which companies might or might not respond positively (interview, legal expert for DFID).

In addition to pricing incentives, the donors' pledges needed to be credible. Legally binding commitments are unusual for aid grants, especially at DFID. The latter's financial donations would always acknowledge the existence of "a political environment" allowing "ministers [to] change their mind anytime about anything" (interview, former staff member of British Treasury 1). Economists define this as "time inconsistency" and the AMC sought to prevent it (Kremer, 2000). In this case, the commitment needed to be bankable, allowing companies to sue donors if they did not live up to their promises. UK commercial law was chosen due to its frequent use in business transactions. The aim was to give manufacturers enough certainty that they could enforce the AMC if necessary. Another condition designed to reassure them concerned the currency. Contributions were made in US dollars and donors bore the risk of currency fluctuation. To make the AMC even more predictable, the World Bank managed the $1.5

billion fund, instead of Gavi. The latter was deemed too young as an organiza-tion, whereas the triple A financial institution provided solid guarantees. The World Bank agreed to place the commitment on its balance sheet. Even if gov-ernments defaulted, the money would be made available to companies according to the AMC's terms and conditions. The World Bank entered into an agreement with each donor, attuning to its budgeting practices. For example, DFID had "a principle of not paying in advance of needs" (interview, DFID staff member 1). Therefore, a protocol using demand projections for pneumococcal vaccines two years into the future would trigger the UK's payments. This ensured that the flexibility the donor requested did not impede the credibility of the AMC.

The pilot AMC eventually worked as follows (Cernuschi et al., 2011). The Gavi secretariat was responsible for publishing regular demand forecasts for pneumococcal vaccines at least 15 years into the future. On this basis, UNICEF's supply division issued calls for supply offers (UNICEF remained the procure-ment agency for immunization programs, managing the logistics of vaccine pur-chases and deliveries). Companies with vaccines effective against the pertinent pneumococcal strains were invited to register and agreed to the terms and con-ditions of the AMC. They could then commit to a ten-year supply offer with a minimum of 10 million doses per year, starting not later than five years after the issuance of the call. The price was capped at $3.5 a dose and topped up by a subsidy of an additional $3.5 per dose. The total amount of subsidy received by a manufacturer depended on its supply offer. The volume of supplied doses was compared to an indicative target of 200 million doses (Gavi and UNICEF estimated this to be a good indicator of the total annual volume needed). The proportion of the target demand covered by the offer equaled the percentage of the $1.5 billion subsidy the manufacturer would receive. As an example, if a manufacturer made a supply offer of 10 million doses per year, this accounted for 5% of the indicative target (i.e. 200 million doses). Therefore, the company re-ceived 5% of the $1.5 million subsidy or $75 million. The subsidy was disbursed during the first years of supply as a $3.5 top-up per dose (for the first 21 million doses procured in the first two years).

The mechanism was expected to have an incentivizing effect on vaccine production. Companies should be willing to supply large volumes and invest in extra capacity to produce them, as they had guarantees their investments would be paid off. The terms and conditions of the AMC specified that the donors, Gavi and UNICEF were bound to honor the ten-year supply offer and pay for the subsidy with one specific condition: health administrations must request the vaccines. As manufacturers could then end up with oversized capac-ity, further assurance was provided. Each supply agreement contained a small purchase guarantee and the Gavi secretariat was expected to refine the demand forecasts, based on which calls for offers were released. Lastly, it was said that PneumoADIP had convinced health officials in eligible countries of the vac-cine's importance.

## Implementing the AMC by balancing supply and demand

The AMC became operational in 2009 when UNICEF's supply division released the first call for offers. Two companies had suitable vaccines about to be licensed. Pfizer, having bought Wyeth in part to acquire its lucrative pneumococcal business (interview, head of an immunology lab), and GlaxoSmithKline (GSK), each agreed to supply 30 million doses annually from 2012, in return for 15% of the subsidy. As new calls were issued to meet a growing demand, additional supply offers were signed in 2012, 2013 and 2018, with the same two companies (Gavi, 2022c). The pneumococcal vaccine is said to have been the quickest rollout of a new vaccine in Gavi's history. However, balancing supply and demand to implement the AMC proved challenging.

A first problem emerged in relation to the solvency of the demand. The $1.5 billion commitment was meant to pay for the subsidy, while Gavi would bear the rest of the cost (capped at $3.5 a dose). The consequences of the partnership had not been fully anticipated. In the early discussions, donors assumed that the beneficiary governments might use their own budgets to finance the long-term price, which was expected to be lower (around $1 a dose). As the AMC took shape, it became clear that Gavi's support would be essential.[2] In times of global financial and debt crises, its budget seemed fragile as it depended on non-binding grants (interview, former Gavi staff member 2). Large and reliable funding was needed to pay for a product that was 10 to 20 times more expensive than other vaccines. In 2011, DFID hosted a pledging conference in London, where Prime Minister David Cameron praised Gavi, a "top-perform[ing] agency for the delivery of aid that demonstrates tangible results", and Bill Gates urged participants "to ensure that all children – no matter where they live – have equal access to life-saving vaccines" (Gavi, 2011). The event raised $4 billion, allowing Gavi to carry on.

Another issue concerned the supply side. In the first years, GSK and Pfizer shipped fewer doses than agreed upon in the supply contracts. Both companies reported technical failures. Given the complexity of the manufacturing process, the claims could be true (Boston Consulting Group, 2015). However, shortages might also indicate that the AMC had not convinced company executives to sufficiently invest in extra capacity. Whether or not the pricing mechanism has had the intended incentive seemed unclear. The fact that only two companies provided the vaccine was a further disappointment. The AMC was supposed to create a market with several suppliers. In 2010, it was believed that the Serum Institute of India would commercialize a pneumococcal vaccine by 2016. In 2018, as the fourth procurement took place, its product was still not licensed.

The market logic underpinning the AMC assumed that competition would decrease prices. The long-term $3.5 a dose was only a cap. Companies could offer lower prices to obtain larger shares of the forecasted demand and the subsidy. In 2012 (third tender), GlaxoSmithKline agreed to supply its vaccine at $3.40 a dose from 2013, and $3.05 after 2017. Pfizer offered $2.95 a dose after 2018 and committed to retroactively apply the new price to pending doses. The deal with Pfizer, which was contracted for more doses than its competitor, involved concessions from Gavi. The latter agreed to further front load the subsidy and guarantee the purchase of a larger volume than set in the AMC. Gavi had consolidated itself financially and could take on more risks, thereby replacing the competitive dynamic that had not materialized.

## Ethical calculations

The AMC opened a new market for pneumococcal vaccines, in which Gavi established its necessity. The organization Médecins Sans Frontières (MSF) repeatedly criticized the pilot initiative for that. The subsidy system was considered a waste of money and a useless strategy to tackle high vaccine prices (MSF, 2011). In many middle-income countries, and in humanitarian emergencies, pneumococcal vaccines continued to be unaffordable. In 2019, MSF urged Gavi not to offer any remaining subsidy to the "duopoly" that had already made substantial profits by selling vaccines in wealthier markets (MSF, 2019). They asked Gavi to wait for the imminent commercialization of a $2 per dose product by the Serum Institute of India (with funding from the Gates Foundation) (Serum Institute of India, 2019). This would cost the partnership less, while helping progress toward broader global access to the vaccines and self-financing for low-income countries (i.e. they would not need to rely so much on Gavi). In June 2020, Gavi signed a contract with the Serum Institute of India for 5% of the AMC subsidy, a small amount compared to the 82.5% that has been transferred to Pfizer and GSK (Gavi, 2022c).

When the AMC pricing structure was discussed executives from emerging companies argued to keep some of the subsidies aside, so that more manufacturers could participate once their vaccines were approved. The donors refused. They considered the request not "ethically viable", as it would imply that "vaccines [are] available that we know are cost-effective, but we are not going to vaccinate children" (interview, former DFID staff member 1). As the AMC aimed to speed up access to pneumococcal vaccines, a sense of urgency offset the argument about market competition. Quickly rolling out the new vaccine was central to Gavi's ethical calculations. The partnership had not been created to transform the landscape of vaccine production, only to act at arm's length by shaping the market (Neyland, Ehrenstein and Milyaeva, 2019).

Gavi ought to make new vaccines available in the poorest regions of the world; this is the objective against which interventions like the pilot AMC are to be assessed. Vaccine procurement lends itself well to metrics, and Gavi's website is full of numbers accompanied by images of so-called beneficiaries. For public health experts working "on the ground", these numbers amounted to "donor phraseology"; a language donors like to use and hear, even though it is detached from the realities of healthcare (interview, immunization expert): where children are vaccinated against pneumococcus, hospitals might lack basic equipment and

medicine to diagnose and treat curable diseases like pneumonia (fieldwork observation in Burkina Faso). Gavi does provide grants to "strengthen health systems"
(Storeng, 2014), but these are limited to the logistics of vaccination. The partnership and its donors work within a narrow mandate, which is to secure vaccine
supply and increase immunization rates.

## Conclusion

As ever-increasing amounts of funds are spent on global health (Dieleman
et al., 2016), donors have been engaging the pharmaceutical industry through
sophisticated financial circuits. This chapter examined the Gavi partnership that
sought to support immunizations by shaping vaccine markets. Specifically, Gavi
attempted to lower the price of new vaccines while securing long-term supplies.
The chapter traced the development of one of such effort: the pilot Advance
Market Commitment for pneumococcal vaccines. In the AMC, aid financing
was structured as an incentive expected to encourage manufacturers to increase
production *and* an investment expected to yield returns in the form of health
impacts.

The sum of money at stake is substantial. Of the $1.5 billion of AMC funds,
87.5% has been spent as of December 2020 to subsidize the purchase of pneumococcal vaccines. From 2010 to 2019, 1 billion vaccine doses were procured. In
2019, the cost of buying 161 million doses of pneumococcal vaccines represented
40% of Gavi's annual disbursements for new and underused vaccines. The total
budget ($1.3 billion) was assigned to also cover ten other products, including
the widely requested pentavalent, rotavirus and polio vaccines. Despite reaching
a unitary price below $3, which in 2020 was 50 times less than in the United
States, pneumococcal vaccines are still a liability for the partnership.

This chapter on Gavi illustrated a soft form of financialization that centers on
the negotiation and implementation of financial transfers, whereby public money
subsidizes private activities to address a market failure. The AMC for pneumococcal vaccines, now a model for the Covax AMC, added a new vaccine to the
immunization programs of more than 60 countries, thereby purportedly fixing
this failure. In his Nobel Lecture, Kremer (2020, p. 1975) cites it as a successful
example of "meta-innovation": new institutions harnessing science and technology to meet human needs. But what about the specifics? The subsidy was considered too generous by many; the initiative's impact on scaling up manufacturing
capacity remained unclear; resource-strained health administrations could not
afford the vaccines; competition between suppliers was limited; and the push for
pneumococcal immunization based on global epidemiology may have sidelined
discussions about other national health priorities. In addition, the term *partnership*
promised a dialogue among equals. This may capture the relationship between
Gavi, its donors and the vaccine companies, wherein guarantees were provided
and conditions imposed in return. However, those for whom these transactions
took place remained at the margins. Social scientists have noted that "donor

countries are prominent policy-makers in the global domain on immunization issues, while recipients of assistance feature largely as policy-takers" (Roalkvam, McNeill and Blume, 2013, p. 96). This chapter on vaccine procurement further highlighted the market thinking that now pervades immunization issues: the needs of Gavi-eligible countries were reduced to a 'demand' depicted by statistics and fed into donors' economics. It also showed that large sums were transferred to two companies in the hope of influencing their investment and market decisions. While donors make immunization policy, the oligopolistic vaccine industry can decide whether or not to implement it. Tracing the financial circuits of overseas aid in public-private partnerships can thus instruct us on the way in which global corporate actors shapes people's health.

## Notes

1 This research was supported by the European Research Council (grant 313173) and I would like to thank Daniel Neyland, who was the Principal Investigator of the research project "Market-based Initiatives as Solutions to Techno-Scientific problems". I would also like to thank Noémi Tousignant for the useful references she suggested when reading an early version of this text. Finally, I am very grateful to Ève Chiapello, Anita Engels and Eduardo Gresse for putting together this volume and for their thorough comments throughout the entire editing process.
2 According to Gavi's co-financing policy, health administrations were expected to contribute to the transaction, but the amount is small – 20 cents a dose.

## References

Adams, V. (ed.) (2016) *Metrics: What counts in global health.* Durham, NC: Duke University Press.

Birn, A.E. (2009) 'The stages of international (global) health: Histories of success or successes of history?,' *Global Public Health*, 4(1), pp. 50–68. DOI: 10.1080/17441690802017797.

Boston Consulting Group (2015) The Advance Market Commitment Pilot for Pneumococcal Vaccines: Outcomes and Impact Evaluation [online]. Available at: http://www.gavi.org/results/evaluations/pneumococcal-amc- outcomes-and-impact-evaluation/. (Accessed: 28 June 2021).

Buse, K. and Harmer, A.M. (2007) 'Seven habits of highly effective global public–private health partnerships: Practice and potential,' *Social Science & Medicine*, 64(2), pp. 259–271. DOI: 10.1016/j.socscimed.2006.09.001.

Cernuschi, T., Furrer, E., Schwalbe, N., Jones, A., Berndt, E.R. and McAdams, S. (2011) 'Advance market commitment for pneumococcal vaccines: Putting theory into practice,' *Bulletin of the World Health Organization*, 89(12), pp. 913–918. DOI: 10.2471/BLT.11.087700.

Chee, G., Molldren, V., His, N. and Chankova, S. (2008) Evaluation of the GAVI Phase 1 Performance (2000–2005). Bethesda, MD: Abt Associates Inc. [online]. Available at: https://www.gavi.org/our-impact/evaluation-studies/gavi-first-evaluation-report. (Accessed: 28 June 2021).

Chiapello, E. (2015) 'Financialisation of valuation,' *Human Studies*, 38(1), pp. 13–35. DOI: 10.1007/s10746-014-9337-x.

Dieleman, J.L., Schneider, M.T., Haakenstad, A., Singh, L., Sadat, N., Birger, M. and Murray, C.J. (2016) 'Development assistance for health: Past trends, associations, and the future of international financial flows for health,' *The Lancet*, 387(10037), pp. 2536–2544. DOI: 10.1016/S0140–6736(16)30168-4.

Ehrenstein, V. and Neyland, D. (2018) 'On scale work: Evidential practices and global health interventions,' *Economy and Society*, 47(1), pp. 59–82. DOI: 10.1080/03085147.2018.1432154.

Gaudillière, J.-P. and Gasnier, C. (2020) 'From Washington DC to Washington State: The Global Burden of Diseases Data Basis and the Political Economy of Global Health,' in Leonelli, S. and Tempini, N. (eds.), *Data Journeys in the Sciences*, Springer Open, pp. 351–369 [online]. Available at: https://doi.org/10.1007/978-3-030-37177-7_1. (Accessed: 28 June 2021).

Gavi, the Vaccine Alliance (Gavi) (2007) *Five Nations and the Bill and Melinda Gates Foundation Launch Advance Market Commitment for Vaccines* [online]. Available at: https://www.gavi.org/five-nations-and-the-bill-and-melinda-gates-foundation-launch-advance-market-commitment-for-vaccines. (Accessed: 17 June 2022).

Gavi, the Vaccine Alliance (Gavi) (2011) *Donors Commit Vaccine Funding to Achieve Historic Milestone* [online]. Available at: https://www.gavi.org/donors-commit-vaccine-funding-to-achieve-historic-milestone-in-global-health. (Accessed: 17 June 2022).

Gavi, the Vaccine Alliance (Gavi) (2018) *Advance Market Commitment for Pneumococcal Vaccines: Annual Report, 1 January 2018 – 31 December 2018* [online]. Available at: http://www.gavi.org/library/gavi-documents/amc/. (Accessed: 28 June 2021).

Gavi, the Vaccine Alliance (Gavi) (2020) *The Gavi Covax AMC: An Investment Opportunity* [online]. Available at: https://www.gavi.org/sites/default/files/2020-06/Gavi-COVAX-AMC-IO.pdf. (Accessed: 28 June 2021).

Gavi, the Vaccine Alliance (Gavi) (2022a) *Gavi, the Vaccine Alliance Board* [online]. Available at: https://www.gavi.org/our-alliance/governance/gavi-board. (Accessed: 17 June 2022).

Gavi, the Vaccine Alliance (Gavi) (2022b) *Gavi's Business Model* [online]. Available at: https://www.gavi.org/our-alliance/operating-model/gavis-business-model. (Accessed: 17 June 2022).

Gavi, the Vaccine Alliance (Gavi) (2022c) *Supply Agreements* [online]. Available at: https://www.gavi.org/investing-gavi/innovative-financing/pneumococcal-amc/manufacturers/supply-agreements. (Accessed: 17 June 2022).

Greenwood, B. (2014) 'The contribution of vaccination to global health: Past, present and future,' *Philosophical Transactions of the Royal Society of London B: Biological Sciences*, 369(1645). DOI: 10.1098/rstb.2013.0433.

Hardon, A. and Blume, S. (2005) 'Shifts in global immunisation goals (1984–2004): Unfinished agendas and mixed results,' *Social Science & Medicine*, 60(2), pp. 345–356. DOI: 10.1016/j.socscimed.2004.05.008.

Independent Expert Committee Recommendation for AMC Pilot (no date) [online]. Available at: https://www.gavi.org/sites/default/files/document/independent-expert-committee-recommendation-for-amc-pilotpdf.pdf. (Accessed: 17 June 2022).

Kremer, M. (2000) Creating Markets for New Vaccine, Part 1: Rationale, *NBER Working Paper Series*, Working Paper 7716, Cambridge, MA: National Bureau of Economic Research [online]. Available at: https://www.nber.org/papers/w7716. (Accessed: 28 June 2021).

Kremer, M. (2020) 'Experimentation, innovation, and economics,' *American Economic Review*, 110(7), pp. 1974–1994. DOI: 10.1257/aer.110.7.1974.

Langevin, M., Brunet-Bélanger, A. and Lefèvre, S. A. (2023) 'Financialization through payment infrastructure,' in *Financializations of Development: Global Games and Local Experiments*, this volume.

Levine, O.S., Cherian, T., Shah, R. and Batson, A. (2004) 'PneumoADIP: An example of translational research to accelerate pneumococcal vaccination in developing countries,' *Journal of Health, Population and Nutrition*, 22(3), pp. 268–274.

Levine, R., Kremer, M. and Albright, A. (2005) *Making Markets for Vaccines: Ideas to Action. The Report of the Center for Global Development Advance Market Commitment Working Group.* Washington, DC: Communications Development Incorporated [online]. Available at: https://www.cgdev.org/sites/default/files/archive/doc/books/vaccine/MakingMarkets-complete.pdf. (Accessed 28 June 2021).

MacKenzie, D.A., Muniesa, F. and Siu, L. (eds.) (2007) *Do economists make markets? On the performativity of economics.* Princeton, NJ: Princeton University Press.

McGoey, L. (2014) 'The philanthropic state: Market–state hybrids in the philanthrocapitalist turn,' *Third World Quarterly*, 35(1), pp. 109–125. DOI: 10.1080/01436597.2014.868989.

Médecins Sans Frontières (MSF) (2011) *GAVI Money Welcome but Could It Be More Wisely Spent?* [online]. Available at: https://www.msf.org/gavi-money-welcome-could-it-be-more-wisely-spent. (Accessed: 28 June 2021).

Médecins Sans Frontières (MSF) (2019) *Pharma Giants Shouldn't Receive Multi-million Dollar Pneumonia Vaccine Subsidy* [online]. Available at: https://www.msf.org/pfizer-and-gsk-should-not-get-huge-subsidy-pneumonia-vaccine. (Accessed: 17 June 2022).

Muraskin, W. (1996) 'Origins of the children's vaccine initiative: The intellectual foundations,' *Social Science & Medicine*, 42(12), pp. 1703–1719. DOI: 10.1016/0277–9536(95)00328-2.

Neyland, D., Ehrenstein, V. and Milyaeva, S. (2019) *Can markets solve problems? An empirical inquiry into neoliberalism in action.* London: Goldsmiths Press.

O'Brien, K. (2008) *Pneumococcal Regional Serotype Distribution for Pneumococcal AMC TPP.* Washington, DC: Johns Hopkins Bloomberg School of Public Health [online]. Available at: https://www.gavi.org/sites/default/files/document/tpp-codebookpdf.pdf. (Accessed: 28 June 2021).

Packard, R.M. (2016) *A history of global health: Interventions into the lives of other peoples.* Baltimore, MD: Johns Hopkins University Press.

Reubi, D. (2018) 'Epidemiological accountability: Philanthropists, global health and the audit of saving lives,' *Economy and Society*, 47(1), pp. 83–110. DOI: 10.1080/03085147.2018.1433359.

Roalkvam, S., McNeill, D. and Blume, S. (eds.) (2013) *Protecting the world's children: Immunisation policies and practices.* Oxford: Oxford University Press.

Robbins, A. and Freeman, P. (1988) 'Obstacles to developing vaccines for the Third World,' *Scientific American*, 259(5), pp. 126–133.

Serum Institute of India (2019) *A New Pneumococcal Vaccine Is Here! Why This Matters* [online]. Available at: https://www.seruminstitute.com/news_pneumococcal_vaccine.php. (Accessed 17 June 2022).

Sinha, A., Levine, O.S., Knoll, M.D., Muhib, F. and Lieu, T.A. (2007) 'Cost-effectiveness of pneumococcal conjugate vaccination in the prevention of child mortality: An international economic analysis,' *The Lancet*, 369(9559), pp. 389–396. DOI: 10.1016/S0140–6736(07)60195-0.

Storeng, K.T. (2014) "The GAVI Alliance and the 'Gates approach' to health system strengthening," *Global Public Health*, 9(8), pp. 865–879. DOI: 10.1080/17441692.2014.940362.

Storeng, K.T. and Béhague, D.P. (2014) "'Playing the numbers game": Evidence-based advocacy and the technocratic narrowing of the safe motherhood initiative,' *Medical Anthropology Quarterly*, 28(2), pp. 260–279. DOI: 10.1111/maq.12072.

Wintour, P. (2020) $2bn Global Coronavirus Vaccine Fund Announced at Gavi Summit, *The Guardian*, 4 June. Available at: https://www.theguardian.com/world/2020/jun/04/2bn-global-coronavirus-vaccine-fund-announced-at-gavi-summit. (Accessed: 28 June 2021).

# 8

# FINANCIALIZATION IN DEVELOPMENT PROJECTS AND NEW MODES OF GOVERNANCE

## The case of development impact bonds

*Juliette Alenda-Demoutiez*

## Introduction

In the process of achieving the United Nations Sustainable Development Goals (SDGs), many mechanisms have been created to secure the increased involvement of international private funds. Financial arrangements have become increasingly sophisticated, drawing on multiple sources of public and private funding and bringing together a wide range of actors and instruments. This multiplication of actors has led to innovative financial engineering. There is a growing systematic use of decision criteria based on financial profitability and financial needs logic that now involves sectors such as agriculture, education and health (Gabas, Ribier and Vernières, 2017). In line with this, various systems that pay for successful results or performance in development contexts have grown in popularity and are increasingly backed by international development donors. A variety of Payment by Results programs have been developed, including so-called impact bonds.

Impact bonds have grown to represent a significant market across the world. According to the Brookings Global Impact Bonds Database, 194 impact bonds have been contracted in 33 countries across six sectors, representing over $421 million in upfront investment in social services and $460 million in total outcome funding committed (Gustafsson-Wright, 2020). The present chapter is focused on one specific type of impact bond, namely Development Impact Bonds (DIBs), which effectively illustrate the financialization tendency in development governance. Through this mechanism, financial investors fund development programs upfront, expecting a return on their investments, a return that depends on the achievements of service providers in the field and is generally paid by international aid donors, as discussed below. The goal is thus to generate profit for private financial investors willing to take the risk to support development projects. The first DIB, the Educate Girls DIB, was launched in 2014 and

DOI: 10.4324/9781003039679-10

became effective in 2015. The number of actors interested in the developing world is growing; it now includes the World Bank, the United States Agency for International Development (USAID), the UK Department for International Development (DFID, now part of the Foreign, Commonwealth and Development Office) and the Global Fund. In 2021, there were 13 DIBs in developing countries. Table 8.1 provides a list of currently existing programs.

The growing financialization of development requires one to understand the impact of power relationships between international, national and local stakeholders, illustrated in this chapter by the example of DIBs. In light of the emergence of DIBs as financialized solutions for development, what does the governance of such mechanisms look like? And what are the implications of DIBs for the design and implementation of development programs? DIBs and the actors supporting them promise to solve traditional issues in development projects, such as clientelism, corruption and the lack of accountability when managing flows of aid (DIB-WG, 2013), with a focus on the financial return and a balance of power centered on the financial actors. To understand this evolution, the focal point of this chapter is on the governance of DIBs.

There is a general shift in development programs (as elsewhere) from a hierarchical vision, where the state imposes almost immutable rules, toward a hybrid vision of different power structures, specifically regarding governance. This concept is based on the intervention of institutions and actors outside the

**TABLE 8.1** Current DIBs as of April 2021. Based on investigations by the author and Brookings Global Impact Bonds Database

| DIB | Stage of development | Countries | Sector |
| --- | --- | --- | --- |
| Educate Girls DIB | Complete | India | Education |
| Sustainable Cocoa and Coffee Production DIB | Complete | Peru | Agriculture |
| Village Enterprise/Graduation Model DIB | Complete | Kenya and Uganda | Poverty Reduction |
| Cameroon Cataract DIB | Implementation | Cameroon | Health |
| Utkrisht DIB for Maternal and Newborn Health | Implementation | India | Health |
| ICRC Program for Humanitarian Impact Investment (PHII) | Implementation | Mali, Nigeria, DRC | Health |
| Palestine (West Bank and Gaza) Employment DIB-F4J | Implementation | Palestine | Employment |
| Cambodia Sanitation DIB | Implementation | Cambodia | Environment |
| Palestine Type II Diabetes Mellitus (T2DM) DIB | Implementation | Palestine | Health |
| Chile Reading Comprehension DIB | Implementation | Chile | Education |
| Cameroon Kangaroo Mother Care DIB | Implementation | Cameroon | Health |
| Quality Education India DIB | Implementation | India | Education |
| Kenya SRH DIB (In Their Hands) | Implementation | Kenya | Health |

governmental sphere and the interdependence between these actors, leading to different institutional arrangements and thus different standards and policies (Abbott and Snidal, 2009; Stoker, 1998). Governance takes into account changes in the constellation of actors (during both the formulation and the implementation of policies) and in the method of political steering (Treib, Bähr and Falkner, 2007). Consequently, power relations are at the center of governance processes. As stated by Ducastel and Anseeuw (2020), impact investing studies in general tend to decontextualize these mechanisms; in reality, however, both promoters and practitioners are part of particular social, economic and political structures.

DIBs and the narratives behind them seem to be pushing a view of governance increasingly related to financial motivations, supporting the dominant role of financial investors and the logics of the market in development governance. DIBs are promoted as solutions to the problems of governments with regard to closing such as funding gaps and overcoming the lack of funder trust in recipient states. This promotion is accomplished by proposing a model that prioritizes private actors and bypasses governments. The model also insists on payment for results, with the expectation that this will lead to better monitoring and accountability. DIBs are thus a financialized model designed to respond to these problems by providing a form of discipline imposed by investors that are interested in their investment. In this chapter, I discuss the implications of DIBs for development governance, with particular attention to the fact that they were designed in Western countries and intended to be used in developing ones.

This chapter is divided into two sections. In the first section, I focus on the actors involved in DIB governance, including both promoters and participants. In the second, I address the impacts of the governance that is put in place, through the analysis of a discourse that promotes them and with a specific and concrete example, the Educate Girls DIB, which has been chosen because it was the first DIB to be established. In addition to there being more information about it than other DIBs, it is also considered a successful example that initiatives in other contexts can emulate. Methodologically, I rely on an analysis of the grey literature published by the actors involved in the development of DIBs. The research draws on reports from institutions and experts promoting DIBs,[1] actors involved in their application (see Table 8.1) and complementary sources such as blog posts, articles and debriefings of major events where DIBs are presented. This chapter aims at investigating the justifications given by the actors involved in DIBs for their involvement and the types of development programs that are drawn to DIBs.

## The takeover of development programs by financial investors

### Who is promoting DIBs?

The origin of DIBs can be found in a 2013 report entitled *Investing in Social Outcomes: Development Impact Bonds* (hereafter referred to as the 2013 Report or DIB-WG, 2013). DIBs are a subset of Social Impact Bonds (SIBs), originating mostly in developed countries since 2010 for use in developing countries (Maier and Meyer, 2017). A working group (hereafter DIB-WG) was created in 2012 to adapt SIBs for development programs. This DIB-WG was initiated by two organizations in particular, the Center for Global Development (CGD) and Social Finance UK. The CGD is a US think tank based in Washington, founded in 2001 by Nancy Birdsall, former executive vice-president of the Inter-American Development Bank, Edward Scott, an American philanthropist and former senior US government official, and Fred Bergsten, an American economist and political advisor. Social Finance UK, a not-for-profit consultancy, started up in 2007 and was involved in crafting the first SIB in 2010, a reoffending prevention program at the Peterborough Prison in the UK. Social Finance UK is mainly supported by philanthropists and foundations, such as the Rockefeller Foundation, a pioneer in impact investing, and the Esmée Fairbairn Foundation. The DIB-WG was designed to involve multiple actors (see Table 8.2).

As Table 8.2 clearly shows, international investment companies, such as the Overseas Private Investment Corporation (co-directing the DIG-WG) and Lion's Head Global Partners (participating member), have been involved in the working group from the outset, along with institutions such as the World Bank and certain foundations (e.g. Rockefeller) that have gained expertise in development over a long period of time. Note that actors from developing countries, the typical target of development programs, are conspicuously absent. Many of these DIB-WG participants are also considered to be part of the so-called venture philanthropy, driven by an entrepreneurial spirit that focuses on achieving social impacts while borrowing their practices and vocabulary from the world of finance and venture capital (Grenier, 2006; Pepin, 2005). In addition to the original promoters, other institutions have taken a more recent interest in DIBs, including the Brookings Institute, an influential Washington-based think tank that plays an important role in policymaking in the US and internationally.

This increasing interest led to the formation of another more formal working group in January 2018: the Impact Bonds Working Group (IBWG), which was initiated by the UBS Optimus Foundation and hosted by the World Bank. The UBS Optimus Foundation has become a leading actor in the evolution of DIBs since its important involvement in the first program of this kind, the Educate Girls DIB. The IBWG is also supported by the Swiss Agency of Development and Cooperation, the Swiss State Secretariat for Economic Affairs and the Inter-American Development Bank. The IBWG's objectives are to design a strategy for the establishment of DIBs, to assemble good practices related to DIBs and to help launch new IDB projects. In the space of two years, the IBWG saw its members increase from 23 to 70, including bilateral and UN agencies (e.g. DFID, USAID and UNICEF), financial institutions and investors (including banks, e.g. BNP Paribas, and fund managers, e.g. Bridges Fund Management), foundations (e.g. Shell and UBS Optimus), companies (e.g. Unilever and Ikea), evaluation firms (e.g. Philanthropy Advisors), impact intermediaries (e.g. Total Impact Capital) and others (IBWG, 2020).

**TABLE 8.2** Actors in the DIB-WG that produced the 2013 Report on DIBs

| DIB-WG participants | CGD | Social Finance UK | Overseas Private Investment Corporation | DFID, Swedish Ministry of Foreign Affairs, USAID | World Bank | Omidyar Network, Rockefeller Foundation, Bill and Melinda Gates Foundation, Kepler | Citigroup, Lion's Head Global Partners |
|---|---|---|---|---|---|---|---|
| Role in the DIB-WG | Instigator | Instigator | Co-chair, 2013 Report | Discussion participant | Discussion participant | Discussion participant | Discussion participant |
| Type of organization | US think Tank, focused on aid effectiveness | UK Inventors of SIBs | Self-sustaining US governmental agency, focused on investments in emerging markets | Governmental agencies | Donors | US philanthropic organizations | Private companies |

DIBs are therefore attracting more and more attention. The market for DIBs is supported by both old and new actors in the development sector (e.g. Social Finance UK), impact investing experts (e.g. Instiglio and Total Impact Capital), and investment bank and financial services corporations (e.g. UBS Optimus and Citigroup), with the private financial sector playing an increasing role in designing and funding DIBs, as well as in general decision-making.

### Governance oriented toward private investors

Investors occupy a central position among all DIB stakeholders. According to the guidelines established in the 2013 Report, the intended structure of a DIB can be schematized as in Figure 8.1.[2]

The governance of a DIB occurs within the context of a development impact partnership. Investors provide upfront funding to service providers and outcome funders are responsible for reimbursing investors if the objectives are achieved. To secure their rate of return and the reliability of personnel and management, investors are encouraged to be vigilant regarding the progress of the DIB, which they can do either themselves or through an intermediary. Governance is therefore oriented around the investors, who are thus in a position to control the service provider. Table 8.3 presents the main actors involved in the design of DIBs.

Outcome payers are mainly international organizations already familiar with outcome-based contracts in developing countries (or on a more global scale, with the development sector), such as USAID, the United Nations and various philanthropic organizations. The presence of the Global Financing Facility, an initiative created in 2015 by the United Nations and the World Bank as part of an effort to transform how governments in developing countries finance health and nutrition, is particularly noteworthy.

The majority of the investors are private foundations, especially from the banking sector (e.g. the UBS Optimus Foundation). Foundations traditionally place their capital in a financial market and use the returns to finance grants and programs; however, today they increasingly develop so-called mission-related

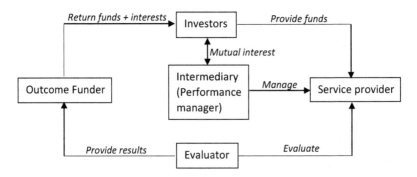

**FIGURE 8.1** Structure of a development impact partnership (illustration by the author).

**TABLE 8.3** List of actors involved in existing DIBs (location, type)

| Investors | Outcome payers | Intermediaries | Service providers (NGOs) |
|---|---|---|---|
| **Private foundations** | **Governmental agencies** | **Consultancies** | Rainforest UK |
| Schmidt Family Foundation (US) | The Common Fund for Commodities (United Nations) | Instiglio (Colombia) | Foundation (International) |
| Delta Fund (US) | | Social Finance (UK) | Educate Girls (India) |
| Bridges Impact Foundation (UK) | United States Agency for International Development | Kois Invest (Belgium) | International Committee of the Red Cross |
| Silicon Valley Social Venture Fund (US) | UK Department for International Development | MaRS Centre for Impact Investing (Canada) | (International) |
| Netri Foundation (Spain) | Government of Cameroon | | Village Enterprise (International) |
| Palestine Investment Fund | Global Financing Facility (United Nations) | Dalberg (Switzerland and International) | Kangaroo Foundation (Cameroon) |
| Stone Family Foundation (UK) | Swiss Agency for Development and Cooperation | | Population Services International |
| Children's Investment Fund Foundation (UK) | Belgian Development Agency | **Companies and venture capital firms** | (International) and Hindustan Latex Family Planning |
| **Banks/foundations affiliated to banks** | Italian Agency for Development Cooperation | Palladium Foundation | Promotion Trust (India) |
| UBS Optimus Foundation (Switzerland) | World Bank | Let's Make It Possible (US) | Magrabi ICO Cameroon |
| New Reinsurance Company Ltd (Switzerland) | Palestinian Ministry of Finance and Planning | Volta Capital (UK) | Eye Institute (Cameroon) |
| Lombard Odier (Switzerland) | **Foundations** | | DAI (International) |
| European Bank for Reconstruction and Development | Children's Investment Fund Foundation (UK) | | iDE (International) |
| | La Caixa Foundation (Spain, banking foundation) | | Juzoor for Health and Social Development (Palestine) |
| Dutch Entrepreneurial Development Bank | The Fred Hollows Foundation (Australia) | | |
| Bank of Palestine | Conrad N. Hilton Foundation (US) | | Gyan Shala (India) |
| **NGOs/governmental agencies** | British Asian Trust (UK) | | Kaivalya Education Foundation (India) |
| Grand Challenges Canada | Michael and Susan Dell Foundation (US) | | Society for All Round Development (India) |
| Overseas Private Investment Corporation (US) | Ellison Medical Foundation (US) | | Triggerise (US) |
| iDE (International) | Mittal Foundation (India) | | Marie Stopes Kenya |
| The Common Fund for Commodities (United Nations) | Comic Relief (UK) | | |
| | **NGOs** | | |
| | Nutrition International (Canada) | | |
| | MSD for Mothers (US) | | |
| | Sightsavers (UK) | | |

*Sources:* Based on Belt (2015), Instiglio (2015), Gustafsson-Wright, Gardiner and Putcha (2015), Cox et al. (2019), websites of Village Enterprise, International Committee of the Red Cross, USAID, the Palladium group, Brookings, F4J, ideglobal, Children's Investment Fund Foundation and the World Bank.

investments (MRIs) and program-related investments (PRIs) (Salamon, 2014). In such investments, capital is used directly to support a charity project through impact investment.

Service providers are NGOs. They may operate at an international level, such as Rainforest UK or Village Enterprise, or at the national level, such as Educate Girls in India. Finally, the presence of local or national governments is typically limited to supporting the projects; there is usually little if any active government participation and therefore little capacity to intervene. The governments of developing countries occupy a peculiar place in this scheme, as explained in the 2013 Report:

> As with any development program, wherever possible, Development Impact Bonds should be structured to avoid setting up systems that are parallel to a government's own systems.
>
> *(DIB-WG, 2013, p. 87)*

National and local governments can intervene to support DIBs, but they are not usually parties to the contract. The target populations are the beneficiaries, but they are not themselves partners. It is not unusual to find that the voices of the beneficiaries, often vulnerable low-income people, are often completely missing in programs conducted by social entrepreneurs or venture philanthropists, "where things seem to be done to, for, or around, but never with or by them" (Edwards, 2010, p. 72).

### Attracting impact investors and the central position of foundations

Attracting investors to this kind of emerging market is not an easy task. The problem is twofold. Projects must be able to yield sufficient incentives for investment and be relatively predictable, so as to reduce risk (Drew and Clist, 2015).

> Although this is slowly beginning to change, social services – particularly those aimed at the world's poorest, most vulnerable people – do not yield sufficiently high financial returns to attract private investment, despite their obvious benefits to society.
>
> *(DIB-WG, 2013, p. 22)*

DIBs are a kind of impact investment, designed to attract impact investors, who expect lower financial returns than traditional financial investors (Maier and Meyer, 2017). Nevertheless, to compensate for the risks taken by impact investors, impact bonds in general present a higher rate of return than traditional public debt (Tortorice et al., 2020).

To give some examples, the Educate Girls DIB was designed with a 10% return rate, 15% if the project goals were exceeded (Instiglio, 2015), which has been the case. Another DIB, the Village Enterprise DIB, was designed with a return rate of 16%, 18% if objectives were exceeded (Cox et al., 2019). The first

DIBs were small in scale – $110,000 upfront investment for the Rainforest UK DIB, aimed at supporting local farmers in Peru, and $267,000 for the Educate Girls DIB; but following these first successful experiences, some DIBs have been developed on a much larger scale. For example, $5.26 million for the Village Enterprise DIB, $4.8 million for the Utkrisht Impact Bond and $10 million for the Cambodia Rural Sanitation DIB (Belt, 2015; Cox et al., 2019).

Overall, this market situation can explain the strong presence of private foundations as investors in DIBs, as well as the evolution from financing through grants to financing through impact investment. In 2018, pfc Social Impact Advisors gave their report on the matter a revealing title: *UBS Optimus Foundation: From Giving to Investing*. Along with their philanthropic activities, foundations have a critical role in developing impact investing (Koh, Karamchandani and Katz, 2012), echoing the concept of philanthrocapitalism developed in the next chapter of the present book (Langevin, Brunet-Bélanger and Lefèvre, 2023, this volume). DIBs provide the opportunity to invest capital in projects that generate both a social and a financial return (Bolton and Saville, 2010; Carè, Rania and De Lisa, 2020). The funds advanced are ultimately reimbursed, along with a return generated mainly by international aid donors (i.e. from taxes raised in developed countries). Since most of the upfront financiers are foundations from Western countries, the financial cycle set in motion results in international aid donors being reimbursed, along with a return, by institutions in Western countries. DIBs are thus fueled by not only the financialization of philanthropy (the development of MRIs and PRIs), but also the financialization of aid, with aid money being used to provide a return to philanthropic foundations in Western countries (Hughes and Scherer, 2014).

## The impacts of finance-centered governance

As demonstrated above, DIBs provide the private financial sector, especially private foundations, with a central governance position. Having analyzed the promoters and actors involved in the governance of DIBs, let us move on to consider the impact of this approach to governance on development outcomes. The first sub-section focuses on the potential impacts as conceived and presented by actors who promote DIBs, and the second on the actual impacts of such programs.

### *The promotion of impact investing as a means to improve development programs*

DIBs are envisioned as a way of addressing the chronic lack of sufficient funds for development projects and the consequent allocation issues arising from this lack. Two trends have become evident: greater transparency and accountability through stronger monitoring and outcome evaluation controls along with the growing involvement of the private sector. According to this narrative, DIBs are presented as "innovative", a "revolution" and "a paradigm shift in how we fund social programmes" (DIB-WG, 2013, p. 21). The mechanism is thus presented as an opportunity to attract investors who will fund projects with social and environmental benefits, to better adapt to the local context and avoid mechanisms that are too standardized.

According to the 2013 Report, DIBs are considered to be solutions to the following problems of bad governance in development financing: poor targeting of beneficiaries, lack of prevention policies, outcomes that are not controlled for, poor tracking of funds, inadequate adaptation to multiple contexts and lack of opportunities for innovation (DIB-WG, 2013). This narrative is in line with the rhetoric of good governance in development programs, which insists on the idea that poverty reduction requires a reallocation of aid, based not only on poverty levels in specific countries but also on the quality of institutions and policies in those countries. DIBs were rapidly seen as an effective new mechanism for these purposes, fitting well into the search for financial innovation in development, as demonstrated by the World Bank's *Maximising Finance for Development Program* (World Bank, no date).[3] In 2015, the international financial institution wrote on its website that DIBs and SIBs were "among the more exciting and potentially promising instruments to recently enter the innovative financing market" (World Bank, 2015, para. 4).

To solve what are considered to be traditional issues of development programs, DIBs promote private investors as a solution, "in a clear management and governance structure", a value-added approach, contrasting with traditional aid (DIB-WG, 2013, p. 40). As stated in a 2015 UNDP report which focused more generally on impact investing in Africa, the continent is "poised to realize the benefits of Impact investment" (UNDP, 2015, p. 9). Again, we see an optimistic narrative and an emphasis on the necessity of accepting this approach to development work. The narrative continues, affirming that, in order to see this revolution take place and to improve the allocation of funds, "DIBs transform social problems into investible opportunities by monetizing the benefits of tackling social problems" (DIB-WG, 2013, p. 7). In fact, the goal is to attract investors to a new market by monetizing social and environmental impacts on development. The idea is that, in the process, private (and international) investors would disseminate best practices (DIB-WG, 2013). In the OECD's report entitled *The Social Development Goals as Business Opportunities*, Julie Sunderland, director of Program-Related Investments at the Bill and Melinda Gates Foundation, explained the importance of "align[ing] incentives for social and financial goals" (OECD, 2016, p. 116). Impact bonds, including DIBs, enable this sort of achievement. This idea of aligning different interests, as well as reconciling financial and social outcomes, is present in not only the working groups but also in the actors involved. According to the IBWG, impact bonds offer "a powerful tool for mobilizing some of the world's most creative capital and know-how to make optimal use of scarce public resources and official development assistance" (IBWG, no date, para. 1). Impact bonds, and impact investing more generally, are thus seen as a way of reshaping capitalism for a better world.

## What are the development implications of DIBs?

In essence, what happens with DIBs is that power changes hands. In traditional development programs, it is public donors who define the way forward, but in the case of DIBs, it is private investors (specifically, private foundations utilizing PRIs or MRIs). Let us take the example of the Educate Girls DIB, the first of its kind, to understand how this governance works and what the potential implications for the actors participating in DIBs are. The idea behind the project arose in 2012. Safeena Husain, Executive Director of the Indian NGO Educate Girls, founded the organization in 2007 and aimed at improving the educational enrollment of girls in Rajasthan. She contacted Avnish Gundadurdoss, co-founder and managing director at Instiglio, in order to apply for a DFID Payment by Results initiative. This initiative did not succeed. Faced with the need to acquire financing, Husain investigated other options. Interested in the possibilities offered by DIBs, she met with the CEO of the UBS Optimus Foundation (pfc Social Impact Advisors, 2018). From this point on, UBS took the lead as a potential investor. Its CEO asked the Children's Investment Fund Foundation, a partner on past venture philanthropic projects, to assume the role of outcome payer. Government agreement was necessary, since the DIB was being implemented in public schools. Other than that, there was no government involvement. Instiglio became not only the intermediary but also a central actor, alongside UBS Optimus, in the scheme. The organization helped to design the bond, determining which outcomes to measure, how to monetize it and how to structure the needs of each partner in order for them to agree on the terms of contract (Saldinger, 2016). The idea of performance management attached to these initiatives played an important role, ensuring that the interests of the investors were well understood. As is common in DIB reports, the intermediary (Instiglio in this case) was described as the "manager" (Instiglio, 2015).

The achievement of both social and financial objectives is central to the idea of DIBs. Accordingly, the investment of $267,000 in Educate Girls was made in two separate payments. The first took place in June 2015, with the final signing of the contract, while the second took place in June 2016, based on the performances of Educate Girls. For the evaluation, a price was associated with a learning payment metric, which was measured based on the student performance on the ASER test and the number of girls enrolled in school overall.[4] In the end, the program surpassed both target outcomes that were measured, reaching 160% of its learning target and 116% of its final enrollment target. To encourage Educate Girls to reach these goals, thus ensuring the desired social and financial outcomes, an incentive payment from UBS Optimus was designed in the event of success. As this example illustrates, the voice and role of private investors are indeed central to the governance of DIBs. As stated on the CGD website:

> DIBs are not meant to be only a financing instrument for social programmes, but rather a new model for how services are delivered. DIBs

create partnerships that give private sector actors incentives to improve the efficiency and effectiveness of service delivery, and the financing mechanism allows this to happen.

*(CGD, no date, para. 32)*

In order to better allocate aid, governments in developing countries are expected to support DIBs. This has certainly been the case with the Educate Girls DIB. There is thus a tendency to avoid political aspects when DIBs are involved. Moreover, the role and voice of NGOs as service providers are also limited. According to an evaluation report for DFID from Ecorys (Cox et al., 2019), the likelihood that a DIB will be launched at all is increased by having a sector with strong service providers. Furthermore, to attract investors, reliance on service providers with the capacity to achieve expected results is necessary (Goodall, 2014). This understandably leads to tensions in the role of NGOs as service providers in DIBs. These tensions are illustrated by the following remarks about one of the program managers of Educate Girls:

[He] manages the extraordinary pressure of delivering on the DIB's ambitious targets while not losing sight of Educate Girls' core mission. In one of our hallway conversations, he shared his fear that the DIB could reduce the NGO's work to a simple exercise of accounting for results.

*(Gungadurdoss, 2016)*

Rather than different stakeholders involved in the governance of DIBs having complementary roles, there is a clear hierarchy in these relationships.

The governance of DIBs in the field reveals the dominance of private financiers in the overall design of such schemes, a dominance that continues to affect the selection of service providers and supported institutions. Even if the funds returned to investors are reinvested in other philanthropic projects, the use of DIBs nonetheless impacts how the different actors in development work interact with each other.

## Conclusion and perspectives

Chiapello and Knoll (2020, p. 8) have recently stated that "in times of financialized capitalism, rent-seeking capital is turned into a solution to social problems, instead of being identified as their source". Replacing the words "capitalism" and "social" with the word "development" in this quote, we can say that DIBs are strongly related to this developing global narrative. Generally speaking, a DIB is a mechanism contributing to the financialization of development programs, through an approach to governance that is centered on private investors, mainly private and banking foundations. This process is reflected in the narratives behind those mechanisms, in the actors promoting them and in the way that governance works out in practice. By trying to align social impact with return on investment,

DIBs link ethical concerns to finance and globalization, thus contributing to legitimizing the place of financial actors at the center of development work.

The DIB system is based on the enforcement of an investor's viewpoint that reformulates questions of poverty as problems to be invested in, thus bringing to the forefront the question of how to organize the repayment of funds that have been advanced, along with a return on investment. This is in fact the main point of DIBs. They originate in a vision of the financial world, thus making the question of return on investment central. Although conceived as a solution for traditional problems in development programs, DIBs do not allow local governments, the workers who run the services delivered or the beneficiaries to actively participate in the design of such programs. The view of development work in DIBs is one that is envisioned and conceived in Western countries, not developing ones. Simply put, foundations invest their capital in developing countries and are reimbursed by public development aid. Moreover, DIBs have been developed in the context of major change in the approaches of large foundations, from the traditional grants to more MRIs and PRIs now; in short, they are the result of the financialization of philanthropy itself. DIBs are also supported by banking foundations that seem to be recycling their financial perspectives into philanthropic activities.

This development raises many questions. The strong focus on contractualization and partnerships in DIBs tends to erase conflicts between actors in development projects. However, DIBs cannot be implemented without considering the power relations and political contexts involved. Although potential relationship conflicts are addressed in DIBs by the use of contracts, the imbalanced power relations that DIBs encourage are generally not acknowledged. DIBs function with a strong hierarchy that separates the actors at the level of decision-making from those working in the field. With an increased influence from investors that want to make sure their money is being used according to the contract, a desire for more involvement in the delivery of social services arises, with some investors even wanting to see NGOs adopt a style of delivery more typical of businesses. The decreased role of governments in DIBs also raises questions, as international donors and investors intervene with their own strategies, objectives, philosophy and vision. The resultant fragmentation of actions, actors and institutions hinders the goal of coordinated development over a longer period of time.

## Notes

1 Center for Global Development and Social Finance UK, UK Department for International Development, Brooking Institute, KIT Royal Tropical Institute, Impact Bonds Working group, United Nations Development Programme (UNDP).
2 Interestingly, in every figure made by different institutes and websites on DIBs, the investors are always placed at the top.
3 Maximizing Finance for Development is aimed at leveraging sources of finance, expertise and solutions to support the sustainable development goals.
4 The Annual Status of Education Report is an Indian rapid assessment of children's ability to read simple text and do basic arithmetic.

# References

Abbott, K. and Snidal, D. (2009) 'The Governance Triangle: Regulatory Standards Institutions and the Shadow of the State,' in Mattli, W. and Woods, N. (eds.), *The Politics of Global Regulation*. Princeton, NJ: Princeton University Press, pp. 44–88.

Belt, J. (2015) *Autonomous and Sustainable Cocoa and Coffee Production by Indigenous Asháninka People of Peru*. Amsterdam: KIT [online]. Available at: http://www.commonfund.org/wpcontent/uploads/2017/05/Verification_Report.pdf. (Accessed: 11 April 2021).

Bolton, E. and Saville, L. (2010) *Towards a New Social Economy: Blended Value Creation through Social Impact Bonds*. London: Social Finance [online]. Available at: https://www.socialfinance.org.uk/sites/default/files/publications/towards-a-new-social-economy-web.pdf. (Accessed: 11 April 2021).

Carè, R., Rania, F. and De Lisa, R. (2020) 'Critical Success Factors, Motivations, and Risks in Social Impact Bonds,' *Sustainability*, 12(18), pp. 72–91. DOI: 10.3390/su12187291.

CGD (no date) *Investing in Social Outcomes: Development Impact Bonds. FAQs* [online]. Available at: https://www.cgdev.org/page/investing-social-outcomes-development-impact-bonds-0. (Accessed: 13 June 2022).

Chiapello, E. and Knoll, L. (2020) 'Social Finance and Impact Investing. Governing Welfare in the Era of Financialization,' *Historical Social Research*, 45(173), pp. 7–30. DOI: 10.12759/hsr.45.2020.3.7–30.

Cox, K., Ronicle, J., Lau, K. and Rizzo, S. (2019) *Independent Evaluation of the UK Department for International Development's Development Impact Bonds (DIBs) Pilot Programme*. London: Ecorys [online]. Available at: https://golab.bsg.ox.ac.uk/knowledge-bank/resources/ecorys-evaluation-dfid-dibs/. (Accessed: 11 April 2021).

DIB-WG (2013) *Investing in Social Outcomes: Development Impact Bonds. A Report of Development Impact Bond Working Group*. Washington, DC: Center for Global Development and London: Social Finance [online]. Available at: https://www.socialfinance.org.uk/sites/default/files/publications/cgd-sf-dibreport_online.pdf. (Accessed: 11 April 2021).

Drew, R. and Clist, P. (2015) *Evaluating Development Impact Bonds*. London: DFID [online]. Available at: https://assets.publishing.service.gov.uk/media/57a0896b40f0b64974000092/DIB_Study_Final_Report.pdf. (Accessed: 11 April 2021).

Ducastel, A. and Anseeuw, W. (2020) 'Impact Investing in South Africa: Investing in Empowerment, Empowering Investors,' *Historical Social Research*, 45(173), pp. 53–73. DOI: 10.12759/hsr.45.2020.3.53–73.

Edwards, M. (2010) *Small Change: Why Business Won't Save the World*. San Francisco, CA: Berrett-Koehler Publishers Inc.

Gabas, J.-J., Ribier, V. and Vernières, M. (2017) 'Financement ou financiarisation du développement? Une question en débat,' *Mondes en développement*, 178, pp. 7–22. DOI: 10.3917/med.178.0007.

Goodall, E. (2014) *Choosing Social Impact Bonds. A Practitioner's Guide*. Washington, DC: Bridges Impact [online]. Available at: http://socialinnovation.se/wpcontent/uploads/2015/02/ChoosingSocialImpactBonds_APractitionersGuide.pdf. (Accessed: 11 April 2021).

Grenier, P. (2006) *Venture Philanthropy in Europe: Obstacles and Opportunities*. Weybridge, UK [online]. Available at: https://www.oecd.org/dev/Venture%20Philanthropy%20in%-20Development-BAT-24022014-indd5%2011%20mars.pdf. (Accessed: 11 April 2021).

Gungadurdoss, A. (2016) 'Lessons from a Development Impact Bond,' *Stanford Social Innovation Review*, August [online]. Available at: https://ssir.org/articles/entry/lessons_from_a_development_impact_bond. (Accessed: 11 April 2021).

Gustafsson-Wright, E. (2020) *What Is the Size and Scope of the Impact Bonds Market?* Washington, DC: Brookings. [online]. Available at: https://www.brookings.edu/multi-chapter-report/measuring-the-success-of-impact-bonds/. (Accessed: 11 April 2021).

Gustafsson-Wright, E., Gardiner, S. and Putcha, V. (2015) *The Potential and Limitations of Impact Bonds.* Washington, DC: Brookings [online]. Available at: https://www.brookings.edu/wp-content/uploads/2015/07/impact-bondsweb.pdf. (Accessed: 13 June 2022).

Hughes, J. and Scherer, J. (2014) *Foundations for Social Impact Bonds: How and Why Philanthropy Is Catalyzing the Development of a New Market.* Boston, MA: Social Finance US [online]. Available at: https://thegiin.org/research/publication/foundations-for-social-impact-bonds-how-and-why-philanthropy-is-catalyzing-the. (Accessed: 11 April 2021).

IBWG (no date) *Impact Bonds Working Group* [online]. Available at: http://www.ib-wg.com/. (Accessed: 13 June 2022).

IBWG (2020) *3rd Annual Conference.* Online Report [online]. Available at: http://www.ib-wg.com/. (Accessed: 11 April 2021).

Instiglio (2015) *Educate Girls Development Impact Bond.* Bogotá: Instiglio [online]. Available at: https://www.instiglio.org/impact/educate-girls-development-impact-bond/. (Accessed: 11 April 2021).

Koh, H., Karamchandani, A. and Katz, R. (2012) *From Blueprint to Scale: The Case for Philanthropy in Impact Investing.* Monitor Group and Acumen Fund [online]. Available at: https://acumen.org/wp-content/uploads/2017/09/From-Blueprint-to-Scale-Case-for-Philanthropy-in-Impact-Investing_Full-report.pdf. (Accessed: 11 April 2021).

Langevin, M., Brunet-Bélanger, A. and Lefèvre, S. A. (2023) 'Financialization through payment infrastructure,' in *Financializations of Development: Global Games and Local Experiments*, this volume.

Maier, F. and Meyer, M. (2017) 'Social Impact Bonds and the Perils of Aligned Interests,' *Administrative Sciences*, 7(3), pp. 1–10. DOI: 10.3390/admsci7030024.

OECD (2016) *Development Co-operation Report 2016. The Sustainable Development Goals as Business Opportunities.* Paris: OECD Publishing [online]. Available at: https://www.oecd.org/dac/development-co-operation-report-2016.htm. (Accessed: 11 April 2021).

Pepin, J. (2005) 'Venture Capitalists and Entrepreneurs Become Venture Philanthropists,' *The International Journal of Nonprofit & Voluntary Sector Marketing*, 10, pp. 165–173. DOI: 10.1002/nvsm.10.

Pfc Social Impact Advisors (2018) *UBS Optimus Foundation: From Giving to Investing.* Oxford, UK: Pfc [online]. Available at: https://www.sbs.ox.ac.uk/sites/default/files/2020-03/2018-11-12%20UBSOF%20case%20study%20FINAL.pdf. (Accessed: 11 April 2021).

Salamon, L. (2014) *New Frontiers of Philanthropy: A Guide to the New Tools and New Actors that Are Reshaping Global Philanthropy and Social Investing.* Oxford, UK: Oxford University Press. DOI: 10.1093/acprof:oso/9780199357543.001.0001.

Saldinger, A. (2016) 'Have Development Impact Bonds Moved beyond the Hype?', *Devex*, 8 July [online]. Available at: https://www.devex.com/news/have-development-impact-bonds-moved-beyond-the-hype-88372. (Accessed: 11 April 2021).

Stoker, G. (1998) 'Governance as Theory: Five Propositions,' *International Social Science Journal*, 50, pp. 17–28. DOI: 10.1111/issj.12189.

Tortorice, D., Bloom, D., Kirby, P. and Regan, J. (2020) *A Theory of Social Impact Bonds.* Working Paper, Cambridge, MA: National Bureau of Economic Research [online]. Available at: http://www.nber.org/papers/w27527. (Accessed: 11 April 2021).

Treib, O., Bähr, H. and Falkner, G. (2007) 'Modes of Governance: Towards a Conceptual Clarification,' *Journal of European Public Policy*, 14(1), pp. 1–20. DOI: 10.1080/135017606061071406.

UNDP (2015) *Impact Investment in Africa: Trends, Constraints and Opportunities*. Addis Ababa: UNDP [online]. Available at: https://www.africa.undp.org/content/rba/en/home/about-us/AFIM/impact-investment-in-africa--trends--constraints-and-opportuniti.html. (Accessed: 11 April 2021).

World Bank (no date) *Maximizing Finance for Development* [online]. Available at: https://www.worldbank.org/en/region/eca/brief/programs#1. (Accessed: 13 June 2022).

World Bank (2015) 'Results-focused Impact Bonds Can Improve Development Outcomes by Involving the Private Sector,' *World Bank*, 21 December [online]. Available at: http://www.worldbank.org/en/news/feature/2015/12/21/results-focused-impact-bonds-can-improve-development-outcomes-by-involving-the-private-sector. (Accessed: 11 April 2021).

# PART II
# Finance as development

# 9

# FINANCIALIZATION THROUGH PAYMENT INFRASTRUCTURE

## The philanthrocapitalism of the Mastercard foundation

*Marie Langevin, Andréanne Brunet-Bélanger and Sylvain A. Lefèvre*

## Introduction

The work of mega-foundations is a phenomenon that marks the evolution of capitalism and the neoliberal development model by helping to reinforce and deepen its financialization process. Associated with the practices of venture philanthropy, these charitable institutions are increasingly the focus of attention by critical development scholars (Al Dahdah, 2019; Burns, 2019; McGoey, 2015; Mediavilla and Garcia-Arias, 2019; Mitchell and Sparke, 2016; Morvaridi, 2012; Poruthiyil, 2019; Thompson, 2014, 2018; Wilson, 2014). Along with other mega-foundations, the Mastercard Foundation (MF)[1] first appeared on the global political economy landscape in 2006 when Mastercard International, one of the largest payment technology firms, went public. MF's mission is "to advance education and financial inclusion to catalyze prosperity in developing countries" (Mastercard Foundation, 2019). When the foundation was created, Mastercard donated Class A shares representing 10% of the firm's equity (and voting equivalent) with an initial value of approximately $500 million, in addition to $20 million to cover its operating expenses (SEC, 2007). Since then, following Mastercard's financial growth, MF's capitalization has also grown, with its assets reaching CAN$35.8 billion in 2019 (CRA, 2021).

The MF deserves attention. On the one hand, despite its substantial economic power – it is the largest philanthropic organization in Canada and one of the largest foundations in the world[2] – it has been the subject of almost no research. On the other hand, the MF displays the distinctive features of an emerging phenomenon in the contemporary political economy: philanthrocapitalism, which is shaking up practices in several domains, particularly in international development. Concretely, philanthrocapitalism refers to the creation of foundations that use the vocabulary, vision and market tools (specifically those of finance)

DOI: 10.4324/9781003039679-12

to solve societal or environmental problems (Bishop and Green, 2008; McGoey, Thiel and West, 2018; Rogers, 2011). We have studied the practices and discourse of the MF to analyze its action program and understand its goals. The notion of goals is not incidental here, as philanthrocapitalism aligns with the paradigm of strategic philanthropy, rooted in the dominant managerial discourse of shared value (Porter and Kramer, 2011), where philanthropic work is no longer conceived alongside a firm's productive operations, but becomes a commercial strategy in its own right. Mastercard explicitly fits into this paradigm and in fact received the *Shared Value Award* in 2017, given out by the Global Action Platform and KPMG.

In this chapter, we seek to understand how the foundation's actions and programs serve Mastercard's interests. We show that the MF has chosen to focus its efforts on the inclusion of poor African populations in the formal and digitalized financial circuits and we explain that this sector is a core component of the firm's business model from which it reaps its profits. While this integration into formal finance is not necessarily a guarantee of an increase in the well-being of the beneficiary populations, the MF's practices contribute to global financialization. They facilitate the extraction of value from the populations at the bottom of the pyramid for the benefit of financial powers at the center of the capitalist system. We demonstrate that the manner in which the MF designs its action in the service of the development of African countries in fact serves to enhance the power and profits of the Mastercard firm, and that most of the charitable financial transfers have been received by North American organizations since its inception. Through the little-studied case of the MF, this chapter documents the action of new development actors, namely the large foundations claiming to be philanthrocapitalists and their role in the financialization of marginalized African populations.

In the next section, we present our philanthrocapitalism analytical framework, which contextualizes this phenomenon within the critical political economy of financialization and was used in our case study to understand the relationship between the MF's mission and the strategic interest of the firm Mastercard by looking at its business model. The second section focuses on the foundation's activities to explain how its financial inclusion practices in sub-Saharan Africa stem from strategic philanthropy. The third section discusses one of the foundation's programs – *Fund for Rural Prosperity* – in detail, to illustrate the configuration of financial actors, institutions and technologies that contribute to broadening the financialization process by forming new platform economies on the African continent.

### Philanthrocapitalism, financialization of development and Mastercard's strategic interests

Philanthrocapitalism has developed since the early 2000s with the arrival into the philanthropic field of actors who had made their fortunes in information technology and finance (Abelès, 2002), such as the foundations created by the new millionaires and billionaires from Silicon Valley's venture capitalism (Chan Zuckerberg Initiative, Bezos Family Foundation, etc.). As a body of practice and as a cultural and ideological framework associated with neoliberal development, philanthrocapitalism involves

> a transmutation of terms – from philanthropy to investment – and a new cultural model of investment in social problems – commodification, deep marketization.
>
> *(Mediavilla and Garcia-Arias, 2019, pp. 870–871)*

Philanthrocapitalism participates in financialization by giving a special place to actors who relay financial expertise, implement market tools and frame a whole range of issues under the prism of return on investment; the donation must generate benefits, which in addition must be measurable and made visible by means of indicators.

These emerging practices are further distinguished by a very clear emphasis

> on the provision of opportunities for people to "lift themselves" out of their own social and economic difficulties so that they can be better integrated into all facets of global capitalist life.
>
> *(Mitchell and Sparke, 2016, p. 733)*

Firms such as Mastercard and its foundation seek to reconcile capitalism with a moral vision of the economy by creating products and services intended for "bottom of the pyramid" markets (Prahalad, 2004). This type of approach frames the problem of development not in political terms of inequality and power issues, but as a matter of market opportunity, engaging poor people not as citizens, but rather as consumers and entrepreneurs. These practices bring together organizations and technologies that forge infrastructures that can capture the resource flows generated by the economic activities of the poor (the micro circuits of value circulation) to move them up to the center of the system (the macro circuits of financialized capitalism) (Al Dahdah, 2019, Mawdsley, 2018). Philanthrocapitalism thus contributes to the financialization of the margins (Aitken, 2015), a dynamic that is specific to financialized capitalism that tends to incorporate into its system new sources of accumulation located in the periphery of that system (Harvey, 1982; Leyshon and Thrift, 2007). This expansion of financial capitalism proceeds by means of, among other things, tools designed to insert marginalized people and communities into the market processes of accumulation.

Mastercard, through its foundation, specifically encourages the development of one of these types of tools: microfinance. Microfinance refers to financial services (credit, savings and insurance) intended for people who do not have access to formal finance. This device is a core component of the financial inclusion program, a flagship project of the neoliberal development agenda that aims to bring the 1.7 billion still unbanked people into the formal channels (Asli et al., 2018).

The evolution of microfinance in recent decades has been marked by the commercialization of practices and the integration of tens of millions of households in poor countries into the formal financial system. This pathway of inclusion has in turn made possible forms of profit extraction from these populations by collecting fees or interest (Hudson, 2008; Langevin, 2017). The current focus is on electronic money, digitized financial services and other fintechs to massify inclusion. This technological solutionism (Morozov, 2013), in which Mastercard and its foundation are involved, as we will see in the following sections, is developing while microfinance has proven to be a profitable investment niche,[3] even though it is not always conclusive in terms of social benefits (Duvendack and Mader, 2020). Other opportunities for profit are then added to microfinance-related services, such as banking and mobile technologies, credit risk assessment and electronic money (Langevin, 2019).

Mainstream finance players, including Mastercard, are now active in these markets, signaling a strategic interest in the financialization of margins. To understand more specifically how the MF's mission to advance financial inclusion in developing countries is strategically linked to Mastercard, we need to look at its business model, which is based on the expansion of the global digital payment system. As a basis for our analysis of Mastercard's commercial strategy, we relied on documents produced by the company and available on its website as well as the website of the US Securities and Exchange Commission (SEC).

Mastercard was founded back in 1966 with the creation of a service association in the US that consisted of the dominant banks of the day that came together to develop a shared technology infrastructure that would facilitate the flow of payments in the US banking system. The organization went global a few years later when it merged with the Europay payment platform. In 2002, it dropped its legal status as an interbank services cooperative to become a privately owned company and a few years later, in May 2006, the company went public. This change provided the company with an additional public capitalization of nearly $2.4 billion. Since the initial public offering (IPO), the company's market value has seen an explosive growth, reaching $296.8 billion in 2020 (SEC, 2020a).

Mastercard is not a financial institution, it does not extend credit, nor does it collect interest fees. It is a payment technology company that builds, owns and manages one of the largest financial communications networks that enable payments to flow within the economy. Mastercard's business model is based on the notion of a world beyond cash (meaning coins and banknotes) according to the firm's vocabulary. Its business strategy is supported by a series of technological innovations as evidenced by the number of patents it has filed for instant electronic payment and mobile money methods and devices. Between 1983 and 2019, the company has issued over 100 patents primarily geared toward cashless technologies (Justia Patents, 2020; LexInnova Technologies, 2015). The second largest player in the global payments industry after Visa, Mastercard processed $4.8 trillion in transactions in 2019, putting 1.2 billion debit cards and 882 million credit cards into circulation in 200 countries (SEC, 2020b).

With each transaction using Mastercard technology, whether through the medium of a card bearing the brand's logo or a dematerialized circulation of money and information, the company collects a usage fee, usually as a percentage of the monetary value of the transaction. Its revenues ($16.9 billion in 2019) and profits ($8.1 billion in 2019) are mainly generated by the volume of transactions carried out in the payment system it controls (SEC, 2020b). This means that it has a vested interest in seeing more transactions and users of its payment system on a global scale, and therefore in seeing poor individuals, households, and countries brought into the formal dematerialized payment channel. Another major component of the company's business model is based on the data that circulates through its network. As this Mastercard-orchestrated network expands and its volume of digitized transactions grows, the company collects massive data from a myriad of markets and develops new products that exploit the market value of these transactional data.

The MF's charitable goal of fostering the economic participation of poor people serves Mastercard's interests in the global development of financial inclusion, both in terms of the increased volume of financial transactions and the quantity of transactional data that is generated.[4] This company is at the core of the global payments system infrastructure on which critical development studies need to focus more thoroughly than it has to date (Maurer, 2015, p. 139). This infrastructure forms a part of the backstage for the extractive, agricultural, financial and other sectors to tap into the flows of resources that circulate within the global economy. Whereas the payments infrastructure dovetails with the flagship financial inclusion program through the Mastercard Foundation, it is important to grasp what is being organized in order to understand how these transformations participate in the financialization process and shape a singular vision of development.

## Development according to Mastercard foundation

In this section, we focus on the foundation's activities from the standpoint of their consistency with the firm's interests and business strategy. Our analysis is based on an exhaustive collection of documents posted on its website from its launch in 2008 until January 2020. This database consists of 431 documents (approximately 570 pages) produced by the MF: blog articles, press releases, interviews with partners, program descriptions, etc. From an initial content analysis, we were able to identify the types of programs, the domains (agriculture, finance, education, etc.), the instruments (platform economy, big data, etc.), the amounts invested, and the geographical areas favored by the MF. We also collected and analyzed financial reports, the foundation's legal registration documents and the data submitted annually to the Canada Revenue Agency. In a second phase, we conducted a systematic coding with NVivo software, with a focus on its vision of development, financial inclusion, poverty and entrepreneurship.

Generally speaking, our analysis of MF's programs reveals that the foundation operates on African soil through multiple partnerships in the education, finance, agriculture, energy and tourism sectors. These partnerships link the foundation to private companies, including many fintech startups, local and international financial institutions, other foundations, NGOs and some UN agencies. These types of hybrid trade and development strategies reflect an emerging trend in the neoliberal development field where technology platforms are being used to connect, for example, farmers to seed, energy, finance, education or health markets (Al Dahdah, 2023, this volume; Shrader, Morawczynski and Karlyn, 2018).

An analysis of the breakdown of donations made by the MF in 2018 illustrates this unique partnership dynamic guided by a top-down vision of development. For an international development foundation, NGOs[5] logically appear first among its beneficiaries, capturing 37% of the amounts distributed. However, more than 80% of this category of donations in 2018 were made to NGOs whose head offices are in the Global North.[6] An examination of all the funding distributed since its inception (CAN\$2.256 billion) underscores the paradoxical situation of a mission turned toward Africa, with keywords such as empowerment and entrepreneurship, but which granted less than 20% (CAN\$418 million) of its donations to beneficiary organizations (of all types) whose head offices are located in the continent.[7] Moreover, of all the types of African organizations (NGOs as well as private companies) supported by the MF, KPMG East Africa received the most funding in 2018 (a total of eight donations totaling CAN\$25,950,671). Charitable practices that prioritize support for private companies such as KPMG or M-KOPA (see the following section for detailed information) are rooted in an exogenous and financialized vision of development that does not contribute to supporting local infrastructure for socioeconomic development, nor does it help create local technological expertise (Al Dahdah, 2019; 2023, this volume; Natile, 2020). Mastercard's development vision is rather to build consumer platforms for various products and services that are connected to the digital payment infrastructure of global finance.

## Financial inclusion and inclusive growth as a course of action

One of the two areas of focus prioritized by the MF, in addition to education, is financial inclusion. After supporting partnerships with Kiva (a major international microfinance player) for several years and providing significant financial support to leading organizations in the field such as ACCION and MixMarket, the foundation is currently pursuing its investment in financial inclusion with a program aimed at "helping microfinance institutions increase access by exploring alternative channels to deliver services" (Mastercard Foundation, 2020) such as digital financial services and mobile banking. The MF sees in these types of technologies the ability to generate alternative data that could advance access to financial services through transaction tracking and understanding customer behavior, data that are used by startups to produce alternative credit scores, for example.

The MF programs the enrolment of poor people in the formal economy by encouraging the creation of multiple devices, which often take the form of digital platforms that connect consumers not only to financial services, but also to energy, health, education or agriculture markets. Building these digital ecosystems in Africa is closely aligned with Mastercard's business plan, as it states in its most recent financial report:

> We [Mastercard] diversify our business by: working with new customers …; scaling our capabilities and business into new geographies …; broadening financial inclusion for the unbanked and underbanked.
>
> *(SEC, 2020b, p. 7)*

To achieve this, the firm is developing strategic partnerships to "help national and local governments drive increased financial inclusion" (SEC, 2020b, p. 7). Financial inclusion is therefore embedded in the firm's business plan and is not simply an action for social responsibility. As this business strategy is simultaneously a core component of its foundation's mission, Mastercard appears to be an exemplary case of the shared value paradigm, where the creation of social value and profit are inseparable.

Another overlapping element between the firm and the foundation that helps strengthen the financialization of developmental and economic practices in general concerns transactional data. Mastercard leverages complementary Data Analytics and Consulting services and collaborates with financial institutions, corporations and governments to incorporate Mastercard's solutions and know-how into platforms. The firm's consulting services help to exploit the value of transactional data:

> By observing patterns of payments behavior based on billions of transactions switched globally, [Mastercard] leverage anonymized and aggregated information and a consultative approach to help our customers.
>
> *(SEC, 2020b, p.12)*

At the same time, the MF is involved in the creation of these same markets by supporting practices that generate transactional data in the African countries where it operates.

A cross-analysis of the discourse and practices of the two organizations shows that Mastercard pursues a commercial goal of integrating new income geographies, in particular poor populations, into the circuits of global finance. The foundation is a standard-bearer for financial inclusion, which specifically aims to massively increase the participation of these populations in formal finance. It emphasizes the participation of youth in the formal economy by focusing on technological solutions and financial services. These two organizations are therefore helping to transform the channels through which resource flows circulate and direct them toward the infrastructures that are at the center of the global digitized payments system.

## *The African terrain and the information and communications technology revolution*

The MF clearly favors a geopolitical zone of action, sub-Saharan Africa, where it is present in 28 countries. Africa is a geopolitical zone at the heart of the inclusive growth strategies promoted by the Organisation for Economic Co-operation and Development (OECD), the World Bank and the International Monetary Fund (IMF) (Better than Cash Alliance, 2014; UNCDF, 2018; World Bank, 2014). The continent is simultaneously attracting private investors with its abundant reservoir of raw resources and its new consumer markets supported by the emergence of a middle class and a young population (Mann, 2018; Melber, 2017). New combinations of actors are organizing there to implement strategies to create inclusive markets by leveraging technological solutions to increase production capacity and create new job opportunities for poor populations (Andoh-Baidoo, Osatuyi and Kunene, 2014; Polikanov and Abramova, 2003).

The MF justifies targeting sub-Saharan Africa by pointing to the fact that it has the youngest population in the world and that in some regions, more than 60% of its youth live below the poverty line. The foundation emphasizes that by 2023, these young people will become the largest workforce in the world and that they can lift themselves, their families and their communities out of poverty through access to financial services and quality education. The MF views technological innovations as means by which these young people can be brought into the formal economy: digitized financial inclusion would foster employability (primarily self-employment) and entrepreneurship (mostly small-scale) in in-demand sectors, such as farming or construction.

Ghana, followed by Uganda, Tanzania, Rwanda, Kenya and Malawi are the countries in which the MF is mainly present in Africa. The foundation's real work consists mostly of helping young entrepreneurs in the information and communications technology (ICT) sectors, by selecting promising initiatives via competitions or calls for projects. Following the selection process, the MF offers financial support, and sometimes technical expertise, to these innovative companies so they can develop products and services that promote various aspects of the economic integration of young Africans, and microentrepreneurs in particular.

The MF's positioning in the African continent is consistent with Mastercard's business interests. This becomes particularly evident when one considers the case of Kenya, the main hub from which fintechs and mobile telephony companies are developing digital finance services (Asli et al., 2018; Buku and Meredith, 2013; Costa and Tilman, 2015; Graham and Mann, 2013; Kendall et al., 2012). Mastercard has in fact established one of its business innovation hubs in Nairobi, the *Mastercard Lab for Financial Inclusion*, which collaborates closely with governments, NGOs and the academic community to test new financial inclusion intervention tools. In Mastercard's vision, the shared value created through its initiatives benefits African individuals and communities, as they are provided with greater opportunities to participate in the economy, but also the company's stakeholders who benefit from the increased stock market value and enhanced symbolic capital created by its actions in favor of social good.

## The *Fund for Rural Prosperity* program and the construction of financialized digital ecosystems in Africa

In this section, we analyze a specific program led by the MF, the *Fund for Rural Prosperity* (FRP). It is the foundation's financial inclusion program for which we have access to the most relatively detailed information over an extended period. This program is especially strongly promoted by the MF: of the 241 documents published on the website between the program's inception in 2016 and 2019, 93 (39%) are related to this program.

The foundation launched the FRP program in 2015 to encourage the ingenuity of African businesses in the agricultural sector. The program is based on a contest titled the *Scaling Competition,* which has driven the MF to invest (as of 2019) more than $26 million in 21 businesses from eight countries. The general objective of the FRP is to facilitate access to financial services for smallholder farmers in order to alleviate poverty in rural communities. Winning businesses receive financial support from the MF and benefit from a mentoring program to assist them in implementing or scaling up their project. Since its creation, all winning businesses have been from the financial products and services sector, with 78% operating in credit services.

Many direct relationships are established between the businesses that are supported by this competition and Mastercard for what is qualified as their innovative ideas. An analysis of the results shows that the winners often become Mastercard partners. All of the winning businesses work in the field of financial inclusion, whether through lending, credit or digital payments platforms. The majority now do as much business with the firm as they do with the MF. Many of them are focused on interests that align with those of the firm and all are based on mobile technologies or payments. The cases where the business relationships between the winners and Mastercard are most evident are Kifiya, M-KOPA, Copia Kenya, Juhudi Kilimo, Inuka, Letshego Holdings Limited, Musoni Kenya, ECA and CRDB Bank.

From these cases, we selected the company M-KOPA to illustrate this positioning of the foundation as this is a case that clearly illustrates how the MF and Mastercard intertwine their actions. M-KOPA targets populations at the bottom of the pyramid to roll out an offering of pay-as-you-go grid energy solutions. Founded in 2011 by former M-PESA executives (the global mobile payments platform launched by the mobile telephony network Safaricom, a subsidiary of Britain's Vodafone), M-KOPA sells solar energy collectors on credit, the costs of which are reimbursed on a daily or weekly basis via an app installed on a cell phone. The product is designed to provide consumers with access to what is qualified as affordable energy and an opportunity to build a credit history. Reimbursement of the solar collector's loan fee is contingent on its operation. By making payments on a regular basis, consumers generate transactional data that a credit bureau, fintech or bank can then use to estimate the risk of extending them another form of credit. *Kopa,* in fact, means "borrow" in Swahili. M-KOPA also offers other products on credit, including phones, household equipment and consumer loans.

The startup won the *Scaling Competition* in 2015, thereby benefiting from the support of the MF. In 2018, it managed to launch a technology platform to expand access to its products by partnering with Mastercard. M-KOPA then aligned itself with Mastercard's technology, *Quick Response Masterpass*, dedicated to payments by mobile telephony. This partnership affords a commercial advantage to M-KOPA by facilitating its integration into the multiple payment infrastructures of various African countries where *Quick Response Masterpass* technology has been implemented. For its part, Mastercard has partnered with M-KOPA in a network linking banks and mobile telephony operators. The Mastercard firm's interest here is to be able to replicate this model with other service providers (Takahashi, 2018). It explains this as follows in a press release touting this achievement:

> Following a successful pilot, Mastercard and M-KOPA plan to extend the program across East Africa. Mastercard will also work with mobile network operators to extend this model to other utilities like water and gas in developing markets across the world. This digital service innovation will open up new business opportunities for telecommunication companies and mobile network operators and evolve their business model beyond providing airtime and data services.
>
> *(Mastercard, 2018)*

This case illustrates how the MF supports companies in the creation of innovative services that are subsequently recovered by Mastercard. Consistent with the shared value model, as revealed in other assemblages in the South in which financial technology and mobile telephony firms are involved (Al Dahdah, 2019; 2023, this volume; Natile, 2020), these platforms structure resource flows in a manner that serves the interests of powerful firms in a way that contributes to the financialization of development practices and the lives of poor individuals and households.

## Conclusion

Mastercard is a financial technology firm that serves as an electronic bridge between consumers, banks, businesses, financial institutions and states by using technology and data to make electronic payments more practical, secure and efficient. The firm's business model is based on the flow of digital data associated with financial transactions. The firm created a foundation as it launched its IPO in 2006 with the mission of working toward the inclusion of poor people into the formal economy through education, technology and financial services. The symbol could hardly be better chosen to illustrate the fusion between charitable intentions and the commercial business end purpose. In its discourse, Mastercard positions itself as an agent of inclusive growth: the firm aims to "do well by doing good" and vice versa. It capitalizes on new customer segments in order to insert them into its payment systems and on a myriad of data produced when these customers use these systems, as it presents this business model as achieving social good through the economic and digital integration of disadvantaged populations. The design of the MF's development is focused on technological and commercial solutionism conceived in partnership with actors at the center of the system so as to reinforce financialization in a way that benefits the dominant interests.

## Notes

1 To avoid confusion, we use Mastercard in reference to the firm and MF for the Foundation.
2 To situate it among the most well-known foundations in the world, in 2019, the Bill & Melinda Gates Foundation had $46.8 billion in assets, the Ford Foundation $13.7 billion, and the Rockefeller Foundation $4.2 billion. In Canada, the second richest foundation, the Lucie and André Chagnon Foundation, has 15 times less capital, with CAN$2 billion in assets. In comparison to the CAN$35.8 billion of the MF, Canada's 10,000 foundations total $60 billion in assets.
3 The average return on equity (ROE) for MFIs was 11.9% in 2017. Over ten years (2009–2018), MFIs have posted an average increase in ROE of 2.9 percentage points (Microfinance Barometer, 2019).
4 The framework of this chapter does not allow for a detailed discussion of the political economy of transactional data in the digitized payment industry. See Maurer (2015) and Westermeier (2020) on this topic.
5 We have placed under this category a set of non-profit organizations that use various terms to refer to themselves (nonprofit, charity, NGO, social enterprise, etc.).
6 The variable used here is the location of the subsidized organization's head office. This does not, of course, indicate where the NGO conducts its operations.
7 Since its inception, through 2018, the MF allocated the vast majority of its donations to organizations of the Global North. However, this trend was reversed in 2019 when it distributed 53% of its funds to Global South organizations. It is too early to tell whether this trend will continue. Moreover, 2019 did not reverse the uneven distribution of donations specifically intended for NGOs: only 26% of the funds distributed to NGOs in this last year for which data are available were allocated to African organizations.

**Funding:** This work was supported by the Social Sciences and Humanities Research Council of Canada, Insight Development Grants.

## References

Al Dahdah, M. (2019) 'Between Philanthropy and Big Business: The Rise of Health in the Global Health Market,' *Development and Change*, 0(0), pp. 1–20. DOI: 10.1111/dech.12497.

Al Dahdah, M. (2023) '"Top up your healthcare access": mobile money to finance health-care in sub-Saharan Africa' in *Financializations of Development: Global Games and Local Experiments*, this volume.

Abelès, M. (2002) *Les nouveaux riches, un ethnologue dans la Silicon Valley*. Paris: Odile Jacob.

Aitken, R. (2015) *Fringe Finance: Crossing and Contesting the Borders of Global Capital*. London: Routledge/Ripe Series in Global Political Economy.

Andoh-Baidoo, F.K., Osatuyi, B., and Kunene, K. (2014) 'ICT Capacity as the Invest-ment and Use of ICT: Exploring Its Antecedents in Africa Information,' *Technology for Development*, 20(1), pp. 44–59. DOI: 10.1080/02681102.2013.804399.

Asli, D.-K., Klapper, L., Singer, D., Ansar, S., and Hess, J. (2018) *The Global Findex Database 2017: Measuring Financial Inclusion and the Fintech Revolution*. Washington, DC: World Bank.

Better than Cash Alliance (2014) *The Journey toward Cash Lite. Addressing Poverty, Saving Money and Increasing Transparency by Accelerating the Shift to Electronic Payments*. Somer-ville, MA: Better Than Cash Alliance.

Bishop, M., and Green, M. (2008) *Philanthrocapitalism. How the Rich Can Save the World*. New York: Bloomsbury Press.

Buku, M.W., and Meredith, M.W. (2013) 'Safaricom and M-Pesa in Kenya: Financial Inclusion and Financial Integrity,' *Washington Journal of Law, Technology and Arts*, 8(3), pp. 375–400.

Burns, R. (2019) 'New Frontiers of Philanthro-capitalism: Digital Technologies and Humanitarianism,' *Antipode*, 15(4), pp. 1101–1122. DOI: 10.1111/anti.12534.

Canada Revenue Agency (CRA) (2021) *Mastercard Foundation T3010 Registered Charity Information Return* [online]. Available at: https://apps.cra-arc.gc.ca/ebci/hacc/srch/pub/dsplyBscSrch?. (Accessed: 1 May 2021).

Costa, A., and Tilman, E. (2015). 'A Market-Building Approach to Financial Inclusion,' *Innovations*, 10(1–2), pp. 53–59. DOI: 10.1162/inov_a_00229.

Duvendack, M., and Mader, P. (2020) 'Impact of Financial Inclusion in Low- and Middle-Income Countries: A Systematic Review of Reviews,' *Journal of Economic Sur-veys*, 34(3), pp. 594–629. DOI: 10.1111/joes.12367.

Graham, M., and Mann, L. (2013) 'Imagining a Silicon Savannah? Technological and Conceptual Connectivity in Kenya's BOP and Software Development Sectors,' *The Electronic Journal of Information Systems in Developing Countries*, 56(2), pp. 1–19. DOI: 10.1002/j.1681-4835.2013.tb00396.x.

Harvey, D. (1982) *The Limits to Capital*. Oxford: Blackwell.

Hudson, J. (2008) 'Developing Geographies of Financialisation: Banking the Poor and Remittance Securitisation,' *Contemporary Politics*, 14(3), pp. 315–333. DOI: 10.1080/13569770802396360.

Justia Patents (2020) *Patents Assigned to MasterCard International, Inc.* [online]. Available at: https://patents.justia.com/assignee/mastercard-international-inc. (Accessed: 20 July 2020).

Kendall, J., Maurer, B., Machoka, P., and Veniard, C. (2012) 'An Emerging Platform: From Money Transfer System to Mobile Money Ecosystem,' *Innovations*, 6(4), pp. 49–64.

Langevin, M. (2017) 'L'agencement entre la haute finance et l'univers du développe-ment : Des donséquences multiples pour la formation des marchés (micro)financi-ers,' *Canadian Journal of Development Studies/Revue canadienne d'études du développement*, 38(4), pp. 487–506. DOI: 10.1080/02255189.2017.1294529.

Langevin, M. (2019) 'Big Data for (Not So) Small Loans: Technological Infrastructures and the Massification of Fringe Finance,' *Review of International Political Economy*, 26(5), pp. 790–814. DOI: 10.1080/09692290.2019.1616597.

LexInnova Technologies (2015) *War of the Wallets: Patent Landscape Analysis. San Francisco* [online]. Available at: https://www.wipo.int/edocs/plrdocs/en/war_of_wallets.pdf. (Accessed: 1 June 2020).

Leyshon, A., and Thrift, N. (2007) 'The Capitalization of Almost Everything,' *Theory, Culture & Society*, 24(7–8), pp. 97–115. DOI: 10.1177%2F0263276407084699.

Mann, L. (2018) 'Left to Other Peoples' Devices? A Political Economy Perspective on the Big Data Revolution in Development,' *Development and Change*, 49(1), pp. 3–36. DOI: 10.1111/dech.12347.

Mastercard (2018) *Mastercard and M-KOPA Solar Partner to Light Up Homes and Businesses. Press Release, Barcelona, Spain, February 26* [online]. Available at: https://newsroom. mastercard.com/press-releases/mastercard-m-kopa-solar-partner-light-homes-businesses-africa/. (Accessed: 1 June 2020).

Mastercard Foundation (2019) *Our Mission* [online]. Available at: https://mastercardfdn. org/foundation/mission-vision/. (Accessed: 1 June 2019).

Mastercard Foundation (2020) *Expanding Access to Financial Services in Africa* [online]. Available at: https://mastercardfdn.org/work/expanding-access-to-financial-services/. (Accessed: 29 April 2020).

Maurer, B. (2015) 'Data-Mining for Development? Poverty, Payment, and Platform,' in Roy, A., and Crane, E.S. (eds.), *Territories of Poverty: Rethinking North and South*. Athens, Georgia: University of Georgia Press, pp. 126–143.

Mawdsley, E. (2018) 'Development Geography II: Financialization,' *Progress in Human Geography*, 42(2), pp. 264–274. DOI: 10.1177/0309132516678747.

McGoey, L. (2015) *No Such Thing as a Free Gift. The Gates Foundation and the Price of Philanthropy*. London and New York: Verso.

McGoey, L., Thiel, D., and West, R. (2018) 'Le philanthrocapitalisme et les «crimes dominants»,' *Politix*, 121(29), pp. 29–54. DOI: 10.3917/pox.121.0029.

Mediavilla, T., and Garcia-Arias, J. (2019) 'Philanthrocapitalism as a Neoliberal (Development Agenda) Artefact: Philanthropic Discourse and Hegemony in (Financing for) International Development,' *Globalizations*, 16(6), pp. 857–875. DOI: 10.1080/14747731.2018.1560187.

Melber, H. (2017) 'The African Middle Class(es) – In the Middle of What,' *Review of African Political Economy*, 44(151), pp. 142–154. DOI: 10.1080/03056244.2016.1245183.

Microfinance Barometer (2019) *10th Edition* [online]. Available at: https://www.convergences.org/wp-content/uploads/2019/09/Microfinance-Barometer-2019_web-1. pdf. (Accessed: 1 September 2020).

Mitchell, K., and Sparke, M. (2016) 'The New Washington Consensus: Millennial Philanthropy and the Making of Global Market Subjects,' *Antipode*, 48, pp. 724–749. DOI: 10.1111/anti.12203.

Morozov, E. (2013) *To Save Everything, Click Here: The Folly of Technological Solutionism*. New York: Public Affairs.

Morvaridi, B. (2012) 'Capitalist Philanthropy and Hegemonic Partnerships,' *Third World Quarterly*, 33(7), pp. 1191–210. DOI: 10.1080/01436597.2012.691827.

Natile, S. (2020) 'Digital Finance Inclusion and the Mobile Money "Social" Enterprise,' *Historical Social Research/Historische Sozialforschung*, 45(3), pp. 74–94. DOI: 10.12759/ hsr.45.2020.3.74–94.

Polikanov, D., and Abramova, I. (2003) 'Africa and ICT: A Chance for Breakthrough,' *Information, Communication & Society*, 6(1), pp. 42–56. DOI: 10.1080/1369118032000068778.

Porter, M., and Kramer, M. (2011) 'Creating Shared Value,' *Harvard Business Review*, 89(1/2), pp. 62–77.

Poruthiyil, P.V. (2019) 'Semantic Dilution of Inequality: A Smoke-Screen for Philanthrocapitalism,' *Critical Discourse Studies*, 17(3), pp. 308–326. DOI: 10.1080/17405904.2019.1567365.

Prahalad, K. (2004) *The Fortune at the Bottom of the Pyramid: Eradicating Poverty through Profits*. State College, PA: Wharton School Publishing.

Rogers, R. (2011) 'Why Philanthro-Policymaking Matters,' *Society*, 48(5), pp. 376–381. DOI: 10.1007/s12115-011-9456-1.

SEC (2007) *Mastercard Incorporated Fiscal Year 2006 Form 10-k Annual Report* [online]. Available at: https://www.sec.gov/Archives/edgar/data/1141391/000119312507042384/d10k.htm. (Accessed: 1 June 2020).

SEC (2020a) *Mastercard Inc SEC CIK #000114139. Securities and Exchange Commission* [online]. Available at: https://sec.report/CIK/0001141391. (Accessed: 1 November 2020).

SEC (2020b) *10K Form. Annual Report for the Fiscal Year 2019 Mastercard International*. U.S. Securities and Exchange Commission (the "SEC") [online]. Available at: https://www.sec.gov/Archives/edgar/data/1141391/000114139119000013/ma12312018-10xk.htm. (Accessed: 1 November 2020).

Shrader, L., Morawczynski, O., and Karlyn, A. (2018) *Super Platforms: Connecting Farmers to Markets in Africa*, CGAP Blog [online]. Available at: http://www.cgap.org/blog/super-platforms-connecting-farmers-markets-africa. (Accessed: 1 June 2020).

Takahashi, D. (2018) Mastercard Tests Pay as You Go for Solar Energy in Africa. *Venture Beat Blog* [online]. Available at: https://venturebeat.com/2018/02/26/mastercard-tests-pay-as-you-go-for-solar-energy-in-africa/. (Accessed: 1 June 2020).

Thompson, C.B. (2014) 'Philanthrocapitalism: Appropriation of Africa's Genetic Wealth,' *Review of African Political Economy*, 41(141), pp. 389–405. DOI: 10.1080/03056244.2014.901946.

Thompson, C.B. (2018) 'Philanthrocapitalism: Rendering the Public Domain Obsolete?' *Third World Quarterly*, 39(1), pp. 51–67. DOI: 10.1080/01436597.2017.1357112.

UNCDF (2018) *Building Inclusive Digital Economies* [online]. Available at: http://www.uncdf.org/fr/mm4p/dfs4what/home. (Accessed: 30 June 2020).

Westermeier, C. (2020) 'Money Is Data – The Platformization of Financial Transactions,' *Information, Communication & Society*, 23(14), pp. 2047–2063. DOI: 10.1080/1369118X.2020.1770833.

Wilson, J. (2014) 'Fantasy Machine: Philanthrocapitalism as an Ideological Formation,' *Third World Quarterly*, 35(7), pp. 1144–1161. DOI: 10.1080/01436597.2014.926102.

World Bank (2014). *Global Financial Development Report: Financial Inclusion*. Washington, DC: World Bank Group.

# 10

# "TOP UP YOUR HEALTHCARE ACCESS"

## Mobile money to finance healthcare in sub-Saharan Africa

*Marine Al Dahdah*

## Introduction

This chapter analyzes the adoption of mobile payment devices to ensure health-care accessibility, and the increased role of private actors from the digital sector in the design of health policies. In developing countries, where banking enrolment is low, several healthcare programs use mobile banking services (called mMoney or mBanking) to allow individuals to pay or cover their health expenses via mobile money. The GSMA that represents the telecommunication sector broadly defines mobile money as "a service in which the mobile phone is used to access financial services" (GSMA, 2010, p. 3). In 2017, it identified over 690 million mobile money accounts, half of them in sub-Saharan Africa, where one in three mobile connections were linked to a mobile money account (GSMA, 2017). East Africa recorded the highest level of mobile money penetration (55%), with Kenya showing the highest level of adults using mMoney worldwide (75%). The vast majority were Safaricom M-PESA wallet users. Thus, sub-Saharan Africa, and Kenya in particular, has been the world epicenter of mMoney (Jung and Feferman, 2014). Presented as a cost-effective technology by its promoters, mMoney could rationalize and even reduce healthcare expenditures, simplify payments and avoid unpaid bills for healthcare institutions (PwC and GSMA, 2013). For healthcare advocates, mobile money offers improved access to healthcare through creating public-private partnerships (PPP) and interoperability across systems. For example, businesses offering micro-insurance products partner with public institutions like the Kenyan National Hospital Insurance Fund (NHIF; Business Call to Action, 2016). Thus, the conjunction of health and mMoney has given birth to a new form of health coverage presently flourishing in sub-Saharan Africa.

This chapter analyzes the M-TIBA program initiated in Kenya, the mMoney champion of Africa. M-TIBA is a mobile wallet dedicated to healthcare expenses,

DOI: 10.4324/9781003039679-13

backed by the world's most famous mobile money platform M-PESA (Natile, 2020). Launched nationally in 2016 by the main mobile network operator, Safaricom, M-TIBA brought together more than 2.3 million subscribers in 2020, and aims to facilitate financial accessibility to healthcare in Kenya. Working on health issues in Kenya since 2011, I was able to observe the arrival and evolution of this project during two fieldwork sessions in Nairobi, carried out six months apart in 2018. I conducted interviews with approximately 30 stakeholders in charge of implementing the program, a dozen health professionals affiliated with the system and 15 M-TIBA users.[1] Far from being a marginal model, M-TIBA was invited in 2017 to the Forum on Universal Health Coverage (UHC) in Tokyo. It was presented there as "a solution to set up UHC in Africa and has attracted the attention of world leaders" (PharmAccess Foundation, 2017). Since 2018, M-TIBA has been placed at the center of the UHC implementation in Kenya. Recent research has confirmed the findings of this chapter and has demonstrated that using such digital platforms is the new model of choice in East Africa (Prince, 2020).

In this chapter, I will explore the following questions: How does this mobile-money-based health coverage system operate? How can this for-profit, digital platform that relies heavily on philanthropic and donor money be considered a development program? And finally, how are digital actors constructing new markets and new ways of accessing healthcare through mobile money? Structured in four parts, this chapter describes (1) the M-TIBA service, its platform model and stakeholders, followed by an analysis of the main functions of the platform; (2) how it channels the money of individuals through saving and payment services; (3) how it relies on donor money and the help of state actors; and (4) how it builds new lucrative markets. At the crossroads of digital studies and economic sociology, this chapter explores the way in which mobile payment services constitute new financial circuits to support development programs and how digital devices reconfigure the politico-economic modalities of governing healthcare coverage in Africa.

## Digital platforms and healthcare

The M-TIBA creators have stated that "[if] you want to give low-income people access to healthcare provisions, somebody has to pay. There is no such thing as free healthcare" (Interview at PharmAccess, Nairobi, 2018). Because the majority of Kenyans pay for healthcare expenses out of pocket, and use mobile money systems like M-PESA to store and transfer funds, mMoney seemed like a perfect way to enable Kenyans to save money for healthcare through incentivized products like M-TIBA. This mobile money-based platform allows users to save for healthcare by depositing money into designated accounts using their phones. It also offers users a wide range of healthcare products and services, including insurance. Piloted in 2015 with 10,000 people in Nairobi, the product allows users to receive money for healthcare savings from multiple sources, such as family, friends, the government, donors and one's own savings. These savings can then be used in health facilities. After completing the testing phase, M-TIBA was officially launched nationwide in September 2016. Modeled on Safaricom's popular M-PESA platform, it was developed in Kenya by PharmAccess[2] and Safaricom.[3] As explained by a PharmAccess agent,

> the M-TIBA app is like a wallet with different pockets. So you have a pocket with your money or money that your auntie gave you, and there is also a pocket that has your insurance cards in it.
>
> *(Interview at PharmAccess, Nairobi, 2018)*

According to PharmAccess, M-TIBA promotes confidence and can be considered, in their words, the Uber of healthcare.

The model proposed by M-TIBA is in fact based on digital platforms like Airbnb or Uber: "While Uber or Airbnb link the supply and demand of transport and housing, M-TIBA can play a central role in linking the international supply and demand for health payments" (Interview at PharmAccess, Nairobi, 2018). The platform manages healthcare payments between donors, patients and healthcare providers; it directs funding from donors to healthcare providers when services are provided to patients. M-TIBA is also part of a growing wave of partnerships involving philanthropic foundations that invest in digital technologies to meet essential healthcare needs. M-TIBA was developed thanks to philanthropic money administered by the PharmAccess and Safaricom foundations. In 2016, these foundations funded a for-profit company, CarePay Limited, to shelter the commercial activities they could not host due to their non-profit status. CarePay administers M-TIBA, collects medical data, manages transactions between donors, beneficiaries and providers, and reports to donors on how their contributions are spent.

Increasingly, however, digital entrepreneurs see their business as socially driven and, as a Safaricom employee explained, "if you solve a social problem, the money will follow" (Interview at Safaricom, Nairobi, 2018) Through projects like M-TIBA, they are applying a new business model of platformization or uberization to social sectors such as health or education in an attempt to solve social problems while also generating income in the countries of the Global South, a promise relayed by several international reports (World Bank, 2016). The digital platform is at the heart of this process, which is overturning traditional structures and mindsets. In rich countries, uberization is massively affecting the transport or hotel sectors; in Africa, it is affecting essential services such as healthcare and education, but remains less studied.

While most of these programs in Africa are launched thanks to philanthropic donations from digital actors, they are based on a commercial framework that aims for financial profitability as quickly as possible. Through the construction of an online platform connected to mobile applications, such programs demonstrate how development actors, tech companies, foundations and governments are striving to create a new financial circuit that collects funds from donors, official development aid organizations, states and beneficiaries to cover healthcare expenses that designated healthcare institutions have to make. Essentially, a service like M-TIBA is used to combine funds from individuals' own pockets, from philanthropic sources and from public and private entrepreneurs through a single platform. Although Telcos and other M-TIBA stakeholders are not traditional financial actors, they nevertheless contribute to the financialization of development programs. They participate in connecting households to the formal financial sphere and develop the marketing of financial products to households. They make a profit by charging fees on increasingly significant volumes of money and by taking a share from individual, public and private funds intended for development or healthcare.

In line with social science research on microfinance (Guérin, 2023, this volume), the following sections propose to trace individual and donor money, to highlight how digitalization avails a unique convergence of these very different financial flows, and to analyze whether these flows are geared toward improving access to healthcare and public health services.

## Money to start the service from the Bottom of the Pyramid

The deployment of mobile phones in developing countries at the beginning of 2000 was concomitant to a new international trend to support and encourage consumption by the poor. Based on Prahalad's concept of "The Fortune at the Bottom of the Pyramid" (Prahalad, 2016), several multinational companies, with Telcos among them, cast the poor as a new market niche by offering new products dedicated to low-income consumers. By applying the rules of capitalism to the poor, these companies aim to reach the masses and become profitable businesses. In Kenya, at least 60% of the population are living at the Bottom of the Pyramid (BoP),[4] and Safaricom has been following the BoP philosophy by conveying the idea that profits come with mass markets. In sub-Saharan Africa, this means reaching the poor. Safaricom is the wealthiest company in Kenya, and one of the most profitable companies in the East and Central African regions. By the end of 2019, Safaricom made a net profit of $627.4 million, with M-PESA being the Telco's "biggest money-maker" (Safaricom, 2019). Safaricom's business model is based on its mobile products dedicated to the BoP. The profits generated by people's mobile money and mobile transactions are partly reinvested in the development of new products dedicated to, according to the vocabulary of the field, the public good and social change, such as M-TIBA.

In fact, Safaricom is regularly advocating for the power of capitalism for good or social business, and M-TIBA products were developed and advanced by its philanthropic branches. Safaricom has a Corporate Social Responsibility (CSR) policy that is articulated and implemented by its CSR department, which encompasses Safaricom Foundation, M-PESA Foundation and the so-called Technology for Development service. The Safaricom and M-PESA foundations are public, charitable trusts established under Kenyan law by two Declarations of Trust in 2003 and 2010. They were established along the lines set by the Vodafone Group Foundation, to articulate and implement the foundation's social investment policy in Kenya. Using Safaricom Foundation money to develop M-TIBA is the first, "indirect" way to channel people's money. Thanks to the huge profits of the Telco, both foundations are funded by annual contributions from Safaricom, determined by the company's board and the Vodafone Group Foundation. However, according to the Kenyan law, the company must not benefit directly from them: "Safaricom Foundation can never do anything which benefits Safaricom directly. It is prohibited. It is a thin line" (Interview at Safaricom, Nairobi, 2018). Nevertheless, the company is in fact using its CSR policy to develop new lucrative products in sectors that are considered, in their words, good for society, primarily in healthcare and education:

> Safaricom cannot do anything with the interest they earn on funds in M-PESA, so they channel it into the foundation. From the government's perspective, it is the money of the people so it should flow back into society. This is the money that was used to start M-TIBA.
>
> *(Interview at CarePay, Nairobi, 2018)*

Thus, with a project like M-TIBA, the Telco has completely blurred the already tenuous lines between philanthropy, development, market and capitalism. This echoes the new tendency of philanthrocapitalism or social business – a way to create new markets through a good cause (Bishop and Green, 2008). Philanthrocapitalism has since been taken up by several authors to explain a new way of giving that has become predominant in many PPPs and development programs financed by private actors (Langevin, Brunet-Bélanger and Lefèvre, 2023, this volume). As Safaricom's so-called Technology for development team explains, the CSR department is dedicated to turning social issues into marketable solutions: "We do commercially viable innovations. Sometimes we work with the foundation because it is the entry point for partnerships" (Interview at Safaricom, Nairobi, 2018). The role of CSR departments in Telcos is to develop products, ensure the products are liked in the market and then move them to the commercial department. In this way, development issues become core businesses. In fact, CSR is used as a philanthropic strategy to develop new profitable BoP markets.

Developed thanks to Safaricom's profits made from Kenyans' mobile consumptions and transactions, M-TIBA directly channels people's money through their mMoney savings. Most people at the BoP do not save money for healthcare, partly because of restrictive and formal saving requirements, including minimum opening balances and the obligation to remit regular fixed amounts to insurance providers. According to their promoters, mMoney-based savings products are attractive to people because they are convenient and provide flexibility. They have emerged as an alternative to both formal and informal means of saving money. Indeed, the M-TIBA wallet has been conceptualized to push people to use phone credits and mMoney as a new currency for healthcare expenses. Safaricom and its partners have devised different strategies to encourage adherence to M-TIBA.

First of all, they created incentive programs to encourage consumers to start using the service. During its first year, they launched a bonus scheme whose main purpose was to get people to subscribe to M-TIBA. As explained by an interviewee:

> If you put money in M-TIBA, they'll give you a bonus. For example, if you put in 100 shillings, you'll get a bonus of 50 shillings every month. But if you deposit in M-PESA, they won't give you anything.
>
> *(Interview at Safaricom, Nairobi, 2018)*

The first 100,000 M-TIBA users who registered and deposited 100 KShs or more in their M-TIBA account received a bonus amount of 50 KShs. Subsequently, users received 50 KShs each month if they deposited 100 KShs or more for the following 11 months. When we conducted our last fieldwork session in 2018, the incentives for the first 100,000 users and the one-year period were over. While M-TIBA was advertising for almost 1 million registered users at the beginning of 2018, only 100,000 were saving through M-TIBA by May 2018, the maximum number of clients entitled to the bonus scheme. According to our interviewees, the end of the bonus scheme marked a collapse in the usage of the wallet, as explained by health professionals working in clinics affiliated with M-TIBA:

> When M-TIBA was still new, the clients were many … the problem now is that the saving on their part is low, the rate at which the clients are registering has declined.
>
> *(Interview with a Clinic staff, Nairobi, 2018)*

Most people saving through M-TIBA initially were benefiting from this incentive mechanism. As soon as the bonus scheme ended, people stopped saving through the wallet. Apart from the bonus scheme, the system did not provide the clear-cut benefits to people that were advertised.

In line with the Polanyian analysis of the economy, the success of these products is heavily dependent on other kinds of relationships, rather than just the encounter between a needy consumer and a perfect product (Polanyi, 1944). The market is inevitably integrated with other types of interdependence that rely on social and political institutions. Since Polanyi's pioneering work, the market construct has been much examined to reveal the central role played by interpersonal mediation, norms and conventions (Guérin, 2020). Digital capitalism does not escape this construct, and Telcos are using a wide range of mediation options for its growth and sustainability. As people rely heavily on local solidarities and community ties, M-TIBA stakeholders tried to exploit these relationships through another strategy. Because families and friends frequently contribute to health expenses in developing countries, Safaricom has tried to promote the idea of targeted, collective mobile payment through M-TIBA. They advertised that M-TIBA was a way to ensure that the money given to your relative would be exclusively used for health expenses. As explained by Safaricom:

> If I send money to my mother today (5,000 KShs) and tell her that this is for her medical bills, chances are very high that she'll use it to buy sugar or something else. But if you send it into her health wallet, she can only use it in a hospital facility.
>
> *(Interview at Safaricom, Nairobi, 2018)*

In fact, none of the interviewees were using M-TIBA in this manner. M-TIBA users who transferred or received money from their wife, husband or children did so through M-PESA and not M-TIBA. This means that people use M-PESA to transfer money to their relatives and subsequently transfer their M-PESA money to their M-TIBA wallet if they consider this necessary. Users are not channeling their transfers through M-TIBA directly. So digital entrepreneurs believed that individuals' mistrust would push them toward a closed wallet like M-TIBA, yet clients were in fact using virtual money systems because a trust-based relationship had already been established. Otherwise, users would stick to tangible notes and coins.

In the same vein, healthcare providers used the service as an advance of credit for health expenses. Providers would claim the amount through the digital system either in installments or later, as explained by this health worker:

> They're clients I know. Such clients will tell you to just give them the drugs, charge whatever is on their M-TIBA …and I agree …But there are those clients that I don't see every day, and these are the clients that will now pay in cash.
>
> *(Interview with a Clinic staff, Nairobi, 2018)*

Moreover, M-TIBA does not seem to have a strong influence on the choice of the healthcare provider. Patients already frequented these providers before M-TIBA and the use of M-TIBA is not linked to any particular assurance of quality, as explained by this interviewee: "I used to go there a long time ago. I already delivered there and my kids are big now" (Interview with a M-TIBA user, Nairobi, 2018). Patients were already coming to these facilities; however, they now replace cash payment with M-TIBA if required or if there is an obvious advantage. Contrary to what its implementers were promoting, M-TIBA does not seem to be a trust-enabler. Rather than creating trust, the service is in fact banking on preexisting relationships. As the business-to-consumer model of M-TIBA did not seem to be functioning well during our last fieldwork session, we realized that its implementers' strategy to build new digital markets was not only targeting BoP consumers, but also trying to sustain their service on business-to-business models with the Kenyan government, as well as with private donors and private clinics.

## Donors' money and the state power to sustain M-TIBA

In addition to consumers' payments made via mMoney, international aid funds are contributing to the mMonetization of healthcare. According to their promoters, health wallets offer a unique platform for directing development partners' funds to individual beneficiaries' mobile accounts. This decreases leakage and fraud commonly attributed to the former chains of traditional development intermediaries. Following the recent credo of direct money transfer to the poor (Ferguson, 2015), funders can decide to allocate a precise amount of money to specific patients, funds that they can then use through their health wallets. Donors can transfer their funds to a number of M-TIBA accounts directly. With this method, funders do not have to handle complicated logistical issues on the supply side, but simply pay a fee for the maintenance of the platform. This practice was explained by CarePay as follows:

> Traditionally, big donor organizations would give money to hospitals and then just hope that it would reach the patients. But in our system, if a donor wants to pay for maternity care for 50,000 mothers, they provide the money and get a receipt for everything bought for these mothers. They will then pay us a small project management fee.
>
> *(Interview at Carepay, Nairobi, 2018)*

This business model shows that CarePay is taxing every transaction and taking a share of donors' funds for processing their money through the platform. This also has direct consequences on public health facilities, as donations that would normally be dedicated to public hospitals are diverted toward digital firms to finance digital health products like M-TIBA. In such a model, the public health system, and thereby the state, seems to be completely eclipsed, with a health program functioning outside its control. International private donors provide money directly to people for their health expenses. This money is to be spent through a specific, private, digital platform. While private stakeholders are the main actors in such mMoney services, the participation of public authorities and governments is nevertheless indispensable, primarily in terms of image. In order to limit the risks of being accused of blatant neocolonialism, international private actors are strongly encouraged to develop partnerships with the governments of developing countries where they wish to implement their activities. Therefore, a partnership with the government to build an ambitious health platform was a must for M-TIBA.

Beyond image issues, collaborating with public authorities can be useful for obvious reasons of field knowledge. Even though the implementers of M-TIBA were reluctant to work with the government and public infrastructures at the beginning of the project, they started a new partnership with the National Health Insurance Fund (NHIF) in 2018, making discussions with public institutions and agents a necessary step to the deployment of M-TIBA. This partnership can be seen as a recognition of the weaknesses of a service that focused only on money transfers, and not on the quality of healthcare. Because of coverage, quality control and logistical issues raised by hospital empanelment, M-TIBA needed the government on board. In fact, if private foundations and international companies oversee and manage these projects, local anchorage is essential for effectively deploying the service on the ground. This local expertise is a compelling reason for involving public actors in these projects. In the case of M-TIBA, because the implementers do not want to handle the enrolment of healthcare facilities and the quality issues related to this process, they need the NHIF as a logistical partner. Local public actors facilitate the deployment of programs at the grassroots level, and the state becomes a necessary partner to sustain the service and extend its reach. Nevertheless, the implication of the state goes beyond logistical issues, as it is also a way of ensuring the financial sustainability of the product, as explained in the final part of this chapter.

## The goal of building new data-driven private health markets

In 2018, M-TIBA implementers used donors' money ($10 million) to pay for NHIF coverage of 20,000 women in Nairobi, as a proof of principle. These women, who did not have any health coverage before, used the M-TIBA wallet for their health expenses in one of the 100 facilities selected for the trial phase. Their NHIF annual premiums were paid by donors' money for one full year. This partnership constituted a first phase that could lead to many different avenues. For instance, they could use the same M-TIBA platform to add other insurance schemes sold by private insurers – an option that was already awaiting accreditation from public authorities in May 2018. Another option would be to sell the use of the digital platform to the government, to aid the distribution of their free NHIF programs (e.g. for pregnant women or the elderly). If the government is included in the M-TIBA program, both as a logistical partner and as an expert on local issues, it can also be seen as a powerful client and an additional guarantee of its financial sustainability. The State then becomes a trading partner to which the digital platform can be sold once philanthropic grants have dried up. This commercial dimension, and attempts to sell products to governments in the Global South that were involved in such PPPs, have already been analyzed for partnerships regarding access to medication or vaccines (Ehrenstein, 2023, this volume; McGoey, 2015). The involvement of governments as future buyers is also very prevalent in digital health partnerships. If private donors are paying for NHIF coverage of 20,000 women through M-TIBA today, the idea is to transition this program to the government for the national free pregnancy scheme. Once the philanthropic grants have ended, the program being taken over by the government is seen as a very profitable outcome, as explained by Safaricom:

> We had spent some time with the Minister for Health and he was so keen on us using M-TIBA to help them with the free maternity initiative. I can

see a very big opportunity for M-TIBA, whereby it will start making a lot of money for both CarePay and Safaricom.

*(Interview at Safaricom, Nairobi, 2018)*

The role of the state in mMoney for health programs is thus far from negligible. However, this partnership is not a win-win situation, contrary to what is frequently advertised. First, money paid into the health wallet can only be used in the private healthcare sector, which means that public hospitals will not benefit from this program. In 2018, as a national program, M-TIBA was restricted to 500 healthcare providers listed primarily in Nairobi. All of these providers were small private clinics, as explained by CarePay:

> We now have 500 facilities that we are connected to; all of them are private or religion-oriented facilities because it is very hard to work with government facilities.
>
> *(Interview at Carepay, Nairobi, 2018)*

This then means that both donors' and individuals' money collected through M-TIBA will only contribute to the development of digital services and private clinics in urban areas. If M-TIBA is the chosen path to UHC, health inclusion would imply financial as well as geographical accessibility of healthcare infrastructures. The limited geographic coverage, in terms of affiliated facilities, is in fact a significant problem for the sustainability and accessibility of this type of healthcare program. Due to the low enrolment of facilities, many users of M-TIBA simply dropped out of the system after a few months, as they could not use it in their preferred facilities, as explained by these two interviewees:

> In the village where I come from, the nearest M-TIBA clinic is a 300-shilling fare away. So, you just go to another clinic instead of using M-TIBA.
>
> *(Interview with a M-TIBA user, Nairobi, 2018)*

> I told my parents about it and they registered, but there are no M-TIBA clinics where they live.
>
> *(Interview with a M-TIBA user, Nairobi, 2018)*

The pro-business and pro-private interest dynamic of the program means that the money raised by people and donors alike through M-TIBA only contributes to the development of private clinics and does not strengthen the public health structures and hospitals which are responsible for providing affordable access to healthcare for all Kenyans. Governments are helping to deploy such digital platforms, which are then primarily used to build new private health markets instead of strengthening or funding public health institutions.

A final point regarding the kind of markets that M-TIBA is able to build thanks to government support concerns the availability of health data. The increasing use of digital healthcare has intensified the production and use of health data. Several scholars show that the digitization of personal data in the Global North is producing new forms of quantification and monitoring of life, and that the use of such data commercially is often unknown to users (Lupton, 2016). There is little research on these issues in the Global South, or on the mechanisms for creating value from this data and the benefits generated by data extraction (Taylor and Broeders, 2015). In fact, extracting and selling health data is one of the central, but least publicized goals of M-TIBA. As explained in its terms and conditions, CarePay and Safaricom are allowed

> to record data relating to the use of the Service and to share or divulge any of this data on a strictly anonymous basis with relevant stakeholders.
>
> *(M-TIBA, n.d.)*

This particular condition is fundamental for the M-TIBA creators. The overall concept of the M-TIBA platform is to not only enable money transfers that were already offered through M-PESA, but to also collect and "share" health data with different partners – both governments and big pharma, as stated by one employee at CarePay:

> We are placing 20,000 women on NHIF cover expecting again the same thing, monitoring the information, understanding who the women are, where they are, what type of services they are using, the cost, and providing that feedback to our partners.
>
> *(Interview at Carepay, Nairobi, 2018)*

Apart from the Safaricom and M-PESA foundations, the M-TIBA project received a generous gift from the Pfizer Foundation to finance the first phase of the NHIF partnership. This provided a way to access crucial market penetration data for Pfizer, as explained by PharmAccess:

> You get a lot of interest as you can imagine …from pharmaceutical companies because that is information on potential clients for them, they see market penetration.
>
> *(Interview at Pharmaccess, Nairobi, 2018)*

Far from the initial dream of the free internet, today digital platforms are products that have market value and refer to property rights. The control of digital platforms thus enables the collection of monopoly rents on money as well as data flows. This data capital is the backbone of the platform capitalism from which M-TIBA arises (Srnicek, 2017). The core business of M-TIBA is therefore not only to manage money transfers, but also to acquire health data on which they have a firm grip, and to build new health data markets out of it.

## Conclusion

This chapter analyses how digital platforms shift health coverage from a public service to a commercial good. The boundaries between healthcare as a fundamental right versus a consumer product are entirely redefined. It explains the role of digital companies in national health insurance policies and examines the possible outcomes of a redeployment of health funding from healthcare infrastructures to digital infrastructures. It analyzes the tensions between developmental, philanthropic and commercial issues that underline these types of programs. Even if Telcos and the other stakeholders of M-TIBA are not traditional financial actors, they nevertheless contribute to the financialization of healthcare. They participate in connecting households to the formal financial sphere and in developing a market for digital financial products. They make a profit by taking fees on the handling of increasingly significant volumes of money, and by taking a share from individual, public and philanthropic funds intended for development and health programs.

This chapter invites readers to pay close attention to the fundamental rights of patients, and to verify whether these new mobile services help to ensure patient protection and access to healthcare. Far from simply owning digitized information, digital companies are gradually becoming crucial stakeholders connecting patients with medical services and managing healthcare funds. The fact that a specific company has control over such a central healthcare infrastructure raises multiple questions around its power over the state, citizens and international donors, the risks of monopoly, excessive power and a lack of accountability, not to mention the extraction of value from people's health data. The increasingly strong presence of digital companies in essential sectors such as healthcare, invites us to analyze the turn toward so-called universal market-based health coverage supported by governments and international organizations, which is currently being tested on a full scale in Africa. M-TIBA illustrates a very particular interpretation of what it means to be on the road to Universal Health Coverage (UHC) and offers a privatized and digitalized version of it. From our empirical findings, projects such as M-TIBA are a far cry from the definition of UHC as promoted by WHO. They offer a market-based approach to care and health administration, and they contribute to the commodification of health as well as to the creation of new private health markets geared toward the poor.

## Notes

1 The interviews were aimed at professionals in charge of deploying this application and its users. All individuals interviewed volunteered and agreed to be recorded for the sole purpose of the study. Quotes were anonymized and the location removed to avoid direct identification. M-TIBA users have never been encountered during treatment or at health facilities. Professionals are quoted as "implementers" or by the name of their company in order to respect their anonymity.
2 Pharmaccess is a Dutch Foundation "with a digital agenda dedicated to connecting more people to better healthcare in Africa", financed by donors and clients, such as the World Bank, USAID, Pfizer, or BMGF.

3  The first (and very hegemonic) mobile operator in Kenya, partly owned by the British giant Vodafone.
4  Based on the World Bank's Global Consumption Database, the International Finance Corporation (IFC) describes the Bottom of the Pyramid (BoP) as the population segment living on less than $8.4 per day.

# References

Bishop, M., and Green, M. (2008) *Philanthrocapitalism: How the Rich Can Save the World.* New York: Bloomsbury.

Business Call to Action (2016) *Advancing Bottom of the Pyramid (BoP) Access to Healthcare: A Case Study on Mobile Money Platforms* [online]. Available at: https://www.yumpu. com/en/document/read/55453962/advancing-bottom-of-the-pyramid-bop-access-to-healthcare. (Accessed: 30 June 2022).

Ehrenstein, V. (2023) 'Financial circuits of vaccine procurement in the era of global health,' in *Financializations of Development: Global Games and Local Experiments,* this volume.

Ferguson, J. (2015) *Give a Man a Fish: Reflections on the New Politics of Distribution.* Durham, NC and London: Duke University Press.

GSMA (2010) *Mobile Money Definitions* [online]. Available at: https://www.gsma.com/ mobilefordevelopment/wp-content/uploads/2012/06/mobilemoneydefinitionsno-marks56.pdf. (Accessed: 30 June 2022).

GSMA (2017) *State of the Industry: Mobile Money* [online]. Available at: https://www. gsma.com/mobilefordevelopment/mobile-money/. (Accessed: 30 June 2022).Guérin, I. (2023) 'The financialization of the fight against poverty: from microcredit to social capitalism,' in *Financializations of Development: Global Games and Local Experiments,* this volume.

Guérin, I. (2020) 'Business social et «bas de la pyramide»: la marche forcée du capitalisme social, in: Du social business à l'économie solidaire', in Maïté, J. (ed.), *Du social business à l'économie solidaire. Critique de l'innovation sociale.* Toulouse, Érès, «Sociologie économ-ique», pp. 93–114. DOI: 10.3917/eres.lavil.2020.01.0093.

Jung, R., and Feferman, F. (2014) *The Development of the Kenyan Mobile Ecosystem.* Lewis Henry Morgan lectures. Durham, NC and London: Duke University Press.

Langevin, M., Brunet-Bélanger, A., and Lefèvre, S. A. (2023) 'Financialization through payment infrastructure: the philanthrocapitalism of the Mastercard foundation,' in *Financializations of Development: Global Games and Local Experiments,* this volume.

Lupton, D. (2016) *The Quantified Self: A Sociology of Self-Tracking Cultures.* Cambridge: Polity Press.

McGoey, L. (2015) *No Such Thing as a Free Gift: The Gates Foundation and the Price of Philanthropy.* London and New York: Verso.

M-TIBA (n.d.) *M-TIBA Programs and Bonus Schemes* [online]. Available at: http://m-tiba. co.ke/M-TIBA_Terms_and_Conditions.pdf. (Accessed: 30 June 2022).

Natile, S. (2020) 'Digital Finance Inclusion and the Mobile Money "Social" Enterprise: A Socio-Legal Critique of M-Pesa in Kenya.' *Historical Social Research,* 45(3), pp. 74–94.

PharmAccess Foundation (2017) *M-TIBA Showcased at UHC Conference in Tokyo* [on-line]. Available at: https://www.pharmaccess.org/update/m-tiba-showcased-uhc-conference-tokyo/. (Accessed: 30 June 2022).

Polanyi, K. (1944) *The Great Transformation. The Political and Economic Origins of Our Time.* Boston, MA: Beacon Press.

Prahalad, C.K. (2016) *The Fortune at the Bottom of the Pyramid: Eradicating Poverty through Profits.* Philadelphia, PA: Wharton School Publishing.

Prince, R.J. (2020) A Politics of Numbers? Digital Registration in Kenya's Experiments with Universal Health Coverage, *Somatosphere* [online]. Available at: http://somatosphere.net/2020/digital-registration-kenya-universal-health-coverage.html/. (Accessed: 6 April 2020).

pwc, GSMA (2013) *Socio-Economic Impact of mHealth An Assessment Report for the European Union* [online]. Available at: https://www.gsma.com/iot/wp-content/uploads/2013/06/Socio-economic_impact-of-mHealth_EU_14062013V2.pdf. (Accessed: 6 April 2020).

Safaricom (2019) *Safaricom to Double 4G Sites as Net Profits Grows 14.7% to KES 63.4 Billion* [online]. Available at: https://www.safaricom.co.ke/about/media-center/publications/press-releases/release/585. (Accessed: 30 June 2022).

Srnicek, N. (2017) *Platform Capitalism, Theory Redux.* Cambridge, UK and Malden, MA: Polity.

Taylor, L., and Broeders, D. (2015) 'In the Name of Development: Power, Profit and the Datafication of the Global South.' *Geoforum*, 64, pp. 229–237.

World Bank (2016) *World Development Report 2016: Digital Dividends.* Washington, DC: World Bank.

# 11

# SOCIAL CASH TRANSFERS IN SUB-SAHARAN AFRICA

## Financialization, digitization and financial inclusion

*Lena Gronbach*

## Introduction

The growing influence of finance in the economic, social and political spheres has sparked scholarly interest in this phenomenon. As a result, the study of various aspects of financialization in different institutional and geographic contexts has received growing attention from scholars, policymakers and development practitioners in recent years. While most early studies of financialization focused on its macroeconomic impact in developed economies, recent research has begun to explore the effects of financialization in the developing world and on the everyday lives of people.

This chapter contributes to the growing body of literature on the financialization of development institutions, programs, and policies in the Global South. More specifically, I outline the manifestation of financialization in social cash transfer (SCT) programs in sub-Saharan Africa and illustrate the impact of this process on the beneficiaries of these transfers, using the case of South Africa as an example. Based on a comprehensive review of SCT programs and their respective payment systems in sub-Saharan Africa I show how SCT payments are becoming increasingly digitized, channelled through formal financial structures, and used as a mechanism to draw financially excluded individuals and households into financial circuits.

This review is based on a detailed analysis of over 500 documents and publications, including peer-reviewed academic literature, government documents, SCT program manuals, impact evaluations, funding proposals and media articles from both print and online sources. The review was conducted from mid-2019 to April 2020, and covers the period from 2010 to 2020. The focus of this chapter lies on non-contributory SCT programs that pay benefits directly to poor individuals or households, and which are implemented through national

DOI: 10.4324/9781003039679-14

governments (although in many cases with donor support), either in terms of funding, administration or branding. SCT programs run entirely by humanitarian agencies or Non-Governmental Organizations (NGOs) are not covered in this review as these are typically short-term emergency interventions, aimed at narrowly targeted populations or geographic areas, rather than forming part of a broader and long-term national social protection policy (Gronbach, 2020b). The South African case study is based on a review and analysis of the extensive media coverage of the case, as well as a range of scholarly and non-academic publications on South Africa's SCT payment reforms, covering the period 2015–2019 (Gronbach, 2017). Additional research was conducted from 2017 to 2020.

This chapter is structured as follows: the first part outlines the links between financialization, the rise of social cash transfers, and the use of digital, financially inclusive payment systems implemented through private financial services providers. In addition, it takes a closer look at the business case for private companies and the practice of cross-selling additional financial products to SCT beneficiaries. In the second part, I illustrate how these processes of financialization have played out in South Africa – the country with the largest and most sophisticated SCT payment system in sub-Saharan Africa – and discuss some of the key implications of SCT financialization for beneficiaries and the state.

## Financialization and social cash transfers in sub-Saharan Africa

Since the early 2000s, the rise of financial institutions and new financial elites, as well as the growing influence of finance in the economic, social and political spheres, has spurred a growing scholarly interest in this phenomenon. While most early academic analysis of financialization focused on its macroeconomic impact in developed economies [see van der Zwan (2014) for a categorization of this literature], recent studies have started to include other disciplines, such as geography, sociology, anthropology and development studies. Further, the initial geographical focus on the United States and Europe has been extended to include developing and emerging economies.

A prominent aspect explored by this new strand of financialization literature is what has been termed the "financialization of everyday life" (Langley, 2020). By examining financialization through a socio-cultural lens, recent research analyses the social impact of "the expanded presence of finance in social reproduction, and the ways in which households have become increasingly embroiled in financial markets" (Bayliss, Fine and Robertson, 2017, p. 361). In addition, a closely related strand of literature examines the impact of financialization on various aspects of development, including the emergence of new development actors and financing models, as well as the ways in which processes of financialization affect the lives of the poor (Mader and Duvendack, 2017; Mawdsley, 2018).

This chapter builds on these two clusters of financialization research and examines a relatively new but increasingly common phenomenon at the intersection of development and finance. More specifically, I trace processes of financialization in the design, implementation and impact of SCT programs in sub-Saharan Africa and identify four key characteristics – or inter-related stages – of this process:

1    The adoption and subsequent expansion of national SCT programs;
2    The shift from manual cash payments to digital payment instruments;
3    The contracting of private financial service providers (FSPs);
4    The cross-selling of financial products and services to SCT beneficiaries.

The following sections provide a brief outline of the manifestation of these four stages, thus providing context for the South African case study presented in the second part of this chapter.

## The adoption and expansion of social cash transfers

SCTs have become a key instrument in global efforts to tackle poverty and inequality in the Global South. Impact evidence for SCTs has been overwhelmingly positive, and numerous studies have illustrated their beneficial effects with regard to health, education, consumption, and the reduction of poverty and inequality (Garcia and Moore, 2012). While social assistance is generally defined as including both cash and in-kind transfers, the 2019 *State of Social Assistance in Africa* report found that SCTs were the leading social assistance instrument on the continent. By 2019, all countries in Southern Africa as well as close to 90% of West African countries and 80% of East African countries had at least one type of SCT program in place (United Nations Development Programme, 2019). In terms of their size, these programs ranged from small, regional, or narrowly targeted schemes to large-scale national programs serving several millions of individuals or households. Most commonly, SCTs in sub-Saharan Africa are delivered in the form of social pensions, disability grants, child benefits or poverty-targeted income support payments to households or individuals. Many existing SCT schemes have been expanded to include additional beneficiaries in recent years, and various countries have implemented or announced further scale-ups in response to the Covid-19 pandemic (Gentilini et al., 2020).

Overall, we can observe a clear trend toward the implementation and expansion of SCT programs across the sub-Saharan Africa region, frequently with the support of international donors and development agencies. My previous review of SCT programs (Gronbach, 2020b) shows that most countries in the region – except South Africa, the Seychelles, Namibia, Mauritius, Eswatini, Cape Verde and Botswana – rely predominantly on donor funding for their national SCT programs. This first expansion stage of the financialization process for SCTs is, strictly speaking, not a characteristic of financialization as it is commonly defined in the literature. However, it does represent an important foundation for subsequent financialization processes: it establishes a regular source of income for poor households and individuals, thus introducing them to the formal financial system and connecting them to formal financial institutions.

## From cash to digital payments

Initially, most SCT programs relied on the manual disbursement of cash directly to beneficiaries. However, in light of the recent growth in beneficiary numbers in many countries, this is increasingly deemed too expensive and logistically challenging, particularly for payment delivery to rural areas. Other concerns frequently voiced by digitization advocates include the risks and opportunity costs for beneficiaries when collecting their payments, such as travel expenses, waiting time, and the danger of falling victim to crime. In addition, policymakers have expressed concerns over high levels of fraud, corruption and leakage associated with cash-based transactions. The past ten years have thus seen a growing interest in digital, so-called financially inclusive payment systems, and a shift from cash-based to electronic disbursements through formal financial channels.

My previous review of SCT payment systems (Gronbach, 2020b) reveals an increasing uptake of various digital payment methods, most notably in the form of payment cards, special bank accounts for beneficiaries and mobile phone-based payment methods. While cash continues to be used as a secondary payment instrument by more than half of all programs covered in the review, only 15 programs rely exclusively on manual cash payments. In most cases, cash payments are used in combination with electronic payment instruments, and the majority of programs are in the process of digitizing payments.

In addition to payment cards and bank accounts (used by approximately half of the programs surveyed), mobile money has become an increasingly popular payment instrument for SCTs in sub-Saharan Africa, following the launch of M-Pesa in 2007. Established in 2007 by Vodafone's Kenyan associate Safaricom, M-Pesa is Africa's leading mobile money service with more than 430,000 active agents operating across several countries, and over 42 million registered users (Vodafone, 2020). Sub-Saharan Africa has the highest number of mobile money platforms (144 out of 290 worldwide) and represents close to two-thirds of the global transaction volume and value (GSMA, 2020). Given the rapid growth of the technology on the continent, it is hardly surprising that 22 SCT programs have adopted mobile money as a payment instrument, for instance in Cote d'Ivoire, Madagascar, Tanzania, Senegal, Nigeria and Zimbabwe. With increasing regulatory certainty around the technology, as well as its widespread adoption as a regular means of payment in many African countries, mobile money is likely to play an increasingly central role in the field of digital SCT payments in the future (see Al Dahdah, 2023, this volume).

Overall, while cash continues to play an important role as a (secondary) payment instrument for SCTs, payment digitization in sub-Saharan Africa is advancing. Considering the extent of global digitization efforts, as well as the emergence and spread of new technologies such as mobile money, this trend is likely to continue and gain additional momentum. This second stage of the SCT financialization process is particularly crucial as it creates a need for digital payment systems and technologies, thus creating a platform for private financial companies to enter the sphere of social protection.

## Outsourcing and contracting of private financial service providers

While most governments in sub-Saharan Africa seem eager to adopt digital SCT payment systems, they frequently lack the necessary technology, expertise and experience to implement and manage these systems. Consequently, private financial companies and technology providers have entered the realm of social protection in recent years, forming new alliances and partnerships with governments, humanitarian agencies and NGOs. My review of SCT payment instruments in sub-Saharan Africa indicates that the use of private contractors has been linked to the increasing technological sophistication and complexity of SCT payment systems across the region. Out of the 130 programs surveyed in the study, 50 made payments through commercial banks, either directly into beneficiaries' personal bank accounts or through cash withdrawals from ATMs. Examples include Equity Bank in Kenya, Grindrod Bank and Postbank in South Africa, Standard Bank in Lesotho and Eswatini, and the Commercial Bank of Ethiopia. While used less frequently than commercial banks, microfinance institutions have delivered SCT payments in Malawi, Ethiopia and Niger.

In addition, large retailers, local traders, and mobile money agents are increasingly used as payment agents for SCTs as they represent a flexible and cost-effective alternative to physical bank branches. Last but not least, various non-bank payment providers have specialized in the distribution of SCT payments and have entered into partnerships with governments or implementing agencies. Some of these companies are related to banks, such as ABSA subsidiary AllPay (a former SCT payment provider in South Africa), while others operate as independent companies and only partner with banks where required by law. In the case of cash-based payment systems, the use of private security firms or cash-in-transit companies has been common practice in countries such as Lesotho, Malawi and Namibia (Gronbach, 2020b).

Overall, the use of private FSPs as payment contractors for the delivery of SCTs is not only widespread but can be expected to increase as a result of continuing payment digitization. Consequently, private financial companies increasingly regard SCT payments as an opportunity to access lucrative government contracts by providing much-needed payment technology and infrastructure. This new role of private FSPs illustrates how a social service that was traditionally provided by governments or NGOs has become more and more financialized in recent years. Private companies are given unprecedented access to millions of poor and vulnerable citizens, drawing SCT beneficiaries and their families deeper and deeper into local and global financial circuits and paving the way for the fourth stage of the SCT financialization process.

## Cross-selling credit and additional financial services

The business case for SCT payment providers generally has two components. The first part consists of the fees for setting up the payment infrastructure and disbursing SCTs, paid by the government or implementing agency. However, given the budget constraints faced by most developing countries, the scope for generating profits through these fees is limited. It has therefore been the second component that has come to represent the most lucrative aspect of the business case for SCT payment providers (Porteous, 2012): Once the payment infrastructure has been set up, FSPs can use their powerful position and direct access to beneficiaries to cross-sell additional financial products and services to them. Given that beneficiaries receive regular, guaranteed monthly payments under the digital SCT scheme, fees and interest can be deducted directly from beneficiaries' accounts, making it an almost risk-free endeavor for FSPs.

The innovation inherent in this strategy lies in the use of SCT payments as collateral for payroll-style loans, also commonly referred to as consigned credit or payday loans. Payroll loans are an increasingly popular form of consumer credit for which the principal and interest payments are deducted directly from the borrower's monthly salary payments. Initially restricted to wage-earning individuals and capped to a certain percentage of the borrower's income, the practice has been extended to the recipients of SCTs in various countries, thus transforming social payments into collateral for consumer loans. It is this collateralization of social benefits – with the state acting as the principal guarantor – that represents one of the most powerful and influential manifestations of financialization in the sphere of social protection and in the lives of the poor.

In addition to the South African case (discussed in the next section), evidence from Brazil's *Bolsa Familia* program (Lavinas, 2018) and Mexico's *Prospera* scheme (see Villarreal, 2023, this volume) illustrates the use of payroll-style lending to the beneficiaries of large-scale SCT programs. On the African continent, where most countries are still in the early stages of the SCT financialization process, evidence of cross-selling payroll loans and other financial products is still relatively scarce. However, as more and more countries contract private FSPs to disburse digital SCT payments – including in response to the Covid-19 pandemic – we can expect to see a rise in this phenomenon on the African continent. As the South African case study presented in the following section illustrates, this fourth stage of the SCT financialization process represents a cause for concern, potentially resulting in the exploitation of the poorest and most and vulnerable people by profit-seeking financial companies.

## Case Study: SCT payments in South Africa

While most countries in sub-Saharan Africa still find themselves in the relatively early stages of the SCT financialization process, South Africa's extensive social grant program represents an advanced and thus particularly insightful example of the manifestation and potential implications of financialization. In the South African context, the term *social grants* – rather than *social cash transfers* – is generally used to refer to the country's cash transfer program. The two terms will be used synonymously in the remainder of this chapter. This section illustrates how the country's social grant system was expanded, digitized, outsourced and collateralized, and how the manifestation of the four stages of financialization affected the lives of millions of South Africa's poorest and most vulnerable citizens. As a prominent example of financialization on the African continent, the case of South Africa holds important lessons for other SCT programs in the region and highlights the potential implications of financialization in the spheres of social protection, financial inclusion and development.

## SCT payment reforms in post-apartheid South Africa

Contrary to most other developing countries, South Africa has a long tradition of social welfare, introducing the first social security schemes for workers and maintenance payments for children in 1910. However, the country's social assistance system remained heavily skewed along racial lines throughout most of the 20th century and it was not until the end of apartheid that racial divisions within the system were abolished (Visser, 2004). The end of apartheid brought significant changes in terms of the coverage of social grants. The existing program was reformed and expanded, eligibility criteria were relaxed, and the number of grant recipients increased from 2.5 million in 1998 to over 18 million in 2020 (South African Social Security Agency, 2020).

At the same time, various provincial governments – which, at the time, were responsible for administering and paying social grants – contracted private service providers and pioneered the use of electronic payments in the 1990s and early 2000s. To streamline the highly fragmented payment system and to address concerns over corruption, inefficiencies and sub-standard service delivery (Reddy and Sokomani, 2008), South Africa's new Social Security Agency (SASSA) consolidated the payment function at the national level in 2012 and awarded a five-year contract to Cash Paymaster Services (CPS), a subsidiary of FinTech corporation Net1 UEPS Technologies, Ltd. (Net1). Net1, a financial services and payment technology provider founded in 1989, offers payment solutions for institutions and individuals who lack easy access to banking services. The company is listed on the NASDAQ stock exchange in the United States, as well as on the Johannesburg Stock Exchange, and operates mostly in developing and emerging economies. The company had won its first provincial grant distribution contract in South Africa in 1992 and had started to engage in microlending and the sale of additional financial services to grant beneficiaries at a provincial level in the early 2000s (Breckenridge, 2005).

Under the new national grant payment system, each beneficiary received a free bank account with Grindrod Bank (CPS' banking partner), a SASSA-branded biometric smart card, and access to a suite of free basic banking services. Rather than opting for a so-called multi-channel choice system that would allow beneficiaries to choose their preferred payment channel, or partnering with South Africa's existing commercial banks, SASSA opted for a closed-loop system based on proprietary technology offered by a specialized payment provider. The main reason for this decision was reportedly the fact that only CPS was able to provide a biometric verification feature (North Gauteng High Court, 2012) which was deemed essential in rooting out fraud and leakage in the system. The implementation of this new payment system resulted in an unprecedented increase in the number of banked individuals, and by 2017 grant recipients made up almost a quarter of South Africa's banked population (Centre of Excellence in Financial Services, 2017). Yet the new payment infrastructure also provides Net1 and its subsidiaries access to millions of potential customers to whom – in the company's own words – they could sell "a wide array of financial products and services for which we can charge fees" (Net1, 2013). In less than 15 years, South Africa's social grant program had thus passed through the four stages of financialization, making it the first sub-Saharan African country to fully digitize and outsource the SCT payment process to a private, profit-seeking entity.

## The implications of SCT financialization in South Africa

Shortly after the appointment of CPS, the Black Sash Trust (a veteran human rights organization) discovered the existence and rapid increase of "irregular, unauthorised and undocumented third party debit deductions from social grants beneficiaries' bank accounts" (The Black Sash, 2017). Most of these deductions could be traced back to companies in Net1's network of subsidiaries, which were selling loans, prepaid airtime and electricity, as well as funeral and life cover to grant beneficiaries. These services were advertised to beneficiaries on their monthly grant payout receipts, as well as by company representatives approaching beneficiaries at grant pay points. Fees and interest for these services were then deducted directly from beneficiaries' new bank accounts, in many cases without their explicit consent or knowledge. Reportedly, only the SASSA card number was required to access the financial products sold by Net1's subsidiaries, causing trade union Cosatu to warn that this was "leaving the system open to fraudsters" which could "potentially result in unauthorized deductions on a large scale" (Cosatu, 2013).

Thousands of grant recipients complained that they had never authorized the monthly deductions made from their grant accounts and that they were unable to stop them. Mbomvu (2015), for instance, reports that beneficiaries who complained to SASSA were told that the agency was "not involved in the matter"; disputes lodged with banks or service providers took "months to resolve" and complaints about deductions for loans were "in most instances disputed by CPS officials" (Dlamini, 2014). As a result, grant beneficiaries who experienced deductions were often left with little or no grant income to cover their monthly expenses, thus exacerbating their already precarious financial situation.

A 2016 report by the government's Standing Committee on Community Development (tasked with investigating the deductions), illustrates the magnitude of the problem: 18,807 disputes related to unauthorized deductions were lodged by grant beneficiaries during the 2015/2016 financial year, which increased to 95,429 in 2016/2017. Moreover, the report cautioned that these figures did not reflect the true extent of the problem as there was a significant under-reporting of cases (Standing Committee on Community Development, 2016). The Black Sash estimates that approximately 2.3 million out of the 10 million grant accounts were affected by deductions (Vally, 2016). Although SASSA introduced a dispute resolution mechanism to deal with these deductions, only one-third of the disputes lodged in 2016/2017 had been resolved by October 2017 (Maregele, 2017). The Committee's report further states that the total monetary loss due to unlawful deductions was close to R800 million, of which only R1.5 million had been recovered. As Foley and Swilling (2018, p. 65) accurately observe,

> this is not a loss to the state or the tax payer. This is money which has in effect been stolen from the country's most vulnerable citizens – children, the elderly, and people with disabilities.

In response to the deduction scandal, as well as a series of legal issues concerning the validity of the contract with CPS, SASSA was forced to end its relationship with the company in 2017. While Net1 continues to provide various types of financial services through subsidiaries in other countries (predominantly in developing and emerging economies), CPS eventually went into liquidation in 2020. The company continues to face various legal challenges, including a court case over accusations that CPS understated the profits made from the SASSA grant payment contract (Ferreira, 2021).

Following calls for stronger state supervision – as well as SASSA's refusal to engage with South Africa's private banks – the agency appointed the state-owned South African Post Office (SAPO) as the country's new grant paymaster. While this was perceived as the only way to address the on-going issue of debit deductions and the growing distrust in CPS, the transition to SAPO's new payment system was far from smooth sailing. It was marred by technical glitches, payment delays, confusion over the new payment arrangements, and rising concerns over the cost of the new system (Gronbach, 2020a). Moreover, a closer look at SAPO's business model suggests that its banking branch Postbank might be pursuing a strategy similar to that of its predecessor Net1. In early 2020, the Postbank expressed its commitment to offering credit and life insurance to its clients – including grant beneficiaries – calling it "a critical element of Postbank's mandate and strategy" (Department of Telecommunications and Postal Services, 2020). Further, a security breach at SAPO/Postbank in 2019 exposed the personal details of millions of beneficiaries which – once again – created an opportunity for the misuse of beneficiary data, as well as fraudulent deductions from grant accounts (Masondo, 2020). This suggests that even state-owned institutions, mandated with the provision of an essential service for the country's most vulnerable citizens, are not immune to the effects of financialization. While it remains to be seen whether the South African scenario will repeat itself in other countries in the region, the case highlights the potentially devastating consequences of the increasing financialization of SCT programs and calls for stronger supervision of the activities of private companies in the realm of social protection.

## Conclusion

The SCT payment landscape in sub-Saharan Africa is evolving rapidly. More and more countries are adopting or expanding SCT programs and replacing cash payments with digital transfers administered by private financial companies. As a result of growing beneficiary numbers and rising levels of financial inclusion, SCTs have come to represent not only a lifeline for the poor, but a lucrative profit-making opportunity for financial institutions. Based on a review of SCT payment systems across sub-Saharan Africa, this chapter illustrates that these processes represent a new and increasingly common feature of financialization, development and social welfare in the Global South. And although global development institutions and private financial companies have played a leading role in promoting payment digitization, outsourcing, and additional financial inclusion interventions on the back of SCTs, this approach has also been adopted in government-funded programs and by state-owned payment providers (as illustrated by the case of South Africa).

Processes of financialization are transforming the ways in which SCTs are delivered, as well as the lives of those who receive them. On the one hand, the combination of access to the formal economy and the provision of financial services to the poor have the potential to deliver positive developmental outcomes. Financial inclusion and access to formal financial products can improve the daily lives of millions of poor households and protect them from exploitation by unscrupulous informal lenders [see James (2015) for a discussion of lending practices in South Africa]. On the other hand, however, the South African case illustrates that the extension of credit and other financial services to SCT recipients can also strengthen the reach and influence of financial actors, thus amplifying the adverse impact of financialization on the poorest and most vulnerable citizens. The South African experience thus provides an important counter-narrative to the 'win-win' scenario that is frequently evoked by the advocates of a business strategy that promotes the privatization of development and social services. It highlights the importance of regulating the use of beneficiaries' personal information, adopting appropriate legislation to limit the activities of private contractors, ensuring adequate oversight of payment providers, implementing functioning recourse and complaints mechanisms, and weighing the benefits of financially inclusive payment systems against their potential drawbacks and the risk of financial exploitation.

Although the South African case represents a particularly advanced example of the negative impact of financialization on SCT beneficiaries, it is unlikely to remain an isolated case. Similar developments have already taken place in Latin America (Lavinas, 2018) and reports of unwanted deductions for financial services from beneficiary accounts in Uganda (Parliament of Uganda, 2018) and Kenya (Owino, 2020) have emerged. Unless we re-think the current narrative about financial inclusion, social protection, and the role of private financial players in this process, the increasing financialization of social cash transfer payments is unlikely to deliver desirable development outcomes.

# References

Al Dahdah, M. (2023) '"Top up your healthcare access": mobile money to finance healthcare in sub-Saharan Africa,' in *Financializations of development: Global games and local experiments*, this volume.

Bayliss, K., Fine, B. and Robertson, M. (2017) 'Introduction to Special Issue on the Material Culture of Financialisation,' *New Political Economy*, 22(4), pp. 355–370. DOI: 10.4324/9781351002103-1.

Breckenridge, K. (2005) 'The Biometric State: The Promise and Peril of Digital Government in the New South Africa,' *Journal of Southern African Studies*, 31(2), pp. 267–282. DOI: 10.1080/03057070500109458.

Centre of Excellence in Financial Services (2017) *The Impact of the 4th Industrial Revolution on the South African Financial Services Market* [online]. Available at: https://www.genesis-analytics.com/uploads/downloads/COEFS-TheimpactofthefourthindustrialrevolutiononfinancialservicesinSouthAfrica-final-1-FR.pdf. (Accessed: 13 April 2021).

Cosatu (2013) *COSATU Condemns Grant Distribution Scams* [online]. Available at: https://www.politicsweb.co.za/politics/cosatu-shares-bathabile-dlaminis-anger-against-cas. (Accessed: 18 December 2022).

Department of Telecommunications and Postal Services (2020) *Postbank Responds to Recent Media Articles on SASSA Grants* [online]. Available at: https://www.polity.org.za/article/postbank-responds-to-recent-media-articles-on-sassa-grants-2020-03-06. (Accessed: 31 August 2020).

Dlamini, B. (2014). Media Statement by the Minister of Social Development, Ms Bathabile Dlamini, MP, on the Occasion of the Media Briefing on Unauthorized Deductions. Pretoria [online]. Available at: http://www.dsd.gov.za/index.php?option=com_content&task=view&id=625&Itemid=106. (Accessed: 15 January 2019).

Ferreira, E. (2021) 'ConCourt Orders CPS to File All Records Relating to Its Illicit Profits,' *Mail & Guardian*, 1 April [online]. Available at: https://mg.co.za/news/2021-04-01-concourt-orders-cps-to-file-all-records-relating-to-its-illicit-profits/. (Accessed: 12 April 2021).

Foley, R. and Swilling, M. (2018) *How One Word Can Change the Game: Case Study of State Capture and the South African Social Security Agency*. Stellenbosch: Centre for Complex Systems in Transition, Stellenbosch University.

Garcia, M. and Moore, C.M.T. (2012) *The Cash Dividend: The Rise of Cash Transfer Programs in Sub-Saharan Africa*. Washington, DC: The World Bank Group. DOI: 10.1596/9780821388976_ch02.

Gentilini, U., Almenfi, M., Dale, P., Lopez, A.V. and Zafar, U. (2020) *Social Protection and Jobs Responses to COVID-19: A Real-Time Review of Country Measures*, "Living paper" version 12 [online]. Available at: http://documents1.worldbank.org/curated/

en/454671594649637530/pdf/Social-Protection-and-Jobs-Responses-to-COID-19-A-Real-Time-Review-of-Country-Measures.pdf. (Accessed: 11 August 2020).

Gronbach, L. (2017) *Outsourcing the Disbursement of Social Grants and Banking the Unbanked: The Case of Net1 UEPS Technologies, Ltd. in South Africa.* Thesis submitted for the Master of Social Sciences in Development Studies. University of Pretoria, Pretoria.

Gronbach, L. (2020a) 'Postbank Security Breach Highlights SASSA's Failures,' *GroundUp*, 17 June [online]. Available at: https://www.groundup.org.za/article/postbank-security-breach-highlights-sassas-failures/. (Accessed: 31 August 2020).

Gronbach, L. (2020b) *Social Cash Transfer Payment Systems in Sub-Saharan Africa*, CSSR Working Paper No. 452, May 2020. Cape Town: Centre for Social Science Research, University of Cape Town.

GSMA (2020) *State of the Industry Report on Mobile Money 2019.* London: GSM Association.

James, D. (2015) *Money from Nothing. Indebtedness and Aspiration in South Africa.* Stanford, CA: Stanford University Press. DOI: 10.1515/9780804793155.

Langley, P. (2020) 'The Financialization of Life,' in Mader, P., Mertens, D. and Van der Zwan, N. (eds.), *The Routledge International Handbook of Financialization.* New York: Routledge. DOI: 10.4324/9781315142876-6.

Lavinas, L. (2018) 'The Collateralization of Social Policy under Financialized Capitalism,' *Development and Change*, 49(2), pp. 502–517. DOI: 10.1111/dech.12370.

Mader, P. and Duvendack, M. (2017) 'Poverty Reduction or the Financialization of Poverty?,' in Bateman, M. and Maclean, K. (eds.), *Seduced and Betrayed: Exposing the contemporary microfinance phenomenon* (pp. 33–48). Albuquerque: University of New Mexico Press.

Maregele, B. (2017) 'Only one third of SASSA disputed deductions resolved,' *GroundUp*, 10 June [online]. Available at: https://www.groundup.org.za/article/only-one-third-sassa-disputed-deductions-resolved/. (Accessed: 22 November 2018).

Masondo, S. (2020) 'Postbank Forced to Replace 12-million Bank Cards after Employees Steal "Master Key,"' *Sunday Times*, 14 June [online]. Available at: https://www.timeslive.co.za/sunday-times/news/2020-06-14-postbank-forced-to-replace-12-million-bank-cards-after-employees-steal-master-key/. (Accessed: 31 August 2020).

Mawdsley, E. (2018) 'Development Geography II: Financialization,' *Progress in Human Geography*, 42(2), pp. 264–274. DOI: 10.1177/0309132516678747.

Mbomvu, N. (2015) 'Social Grants - Pensioners Complain About Deductions for Airtime,' *AllAfrica*, 4 November [online]. Available at: http://allafrica.com/stories/201511051029.html. (Accessed: 21 February 2021).

Net1 (2013) *Annual Report Pursuant to Section 13 or 15(d) of the Securities Exchange Act of 1934 for the Fiscal Year Ended June 30, 2013.* Washington, DC: Securities and Exchange Commission [online]. Available at: https://www.sec.gov/Archives/edgar/data/1041514/000106299313004373/form10k.htm. (Accessed: 12 April 2021).

North Gauteng High Court (2012) *CASE NO: 7447/2012 Judgement.* Pretoria: North Gauteng High Court [online]. Available at: http://www.saflii.org/za/cases/ZAGPPHC/2012/185.html. (Accessed: 13 April 2021).

Owino, S. (2020) 'Outstanding Fuliza Loans Now Haunt Kazi Mtaani Recruits,' *Nation*, 20 August [online]. Available at: https://nation.africa/kenya/news/mobile-loans-trap-kazi-mtaani-recruits-1921378. (Accessed: 28 August 2020).

Parliament of Uganda (2018) *Report of the Committee on Gender, Labour and Social Development on the Social Assistance Grant for Empowerment (SAGE) Scheme* [online]. Available at: https://www.parliament.go.ug/cmis/views/549876de-58d3-48c9-b01b-1571476d81fe%253B1.0. (Accessed: 12 November 2019).

Porteous, D. (2012) *Is There a Business Case for Offering Services to G2P Recipients?* [online]. Available at: http://www.cgap.org/blog/there-business-case-offering-services-g2p-recipients. (Accessed: 18 April 2018).

Reddy, T. and Sokomani, A. (2008) *Corruption and Social Grants in South Africa*, Monograph 154. Cape Town: Institute for Security Studies.

South African Social Security Agency (2020) *2019/20 Annual Report* [online]. Available at: https://www.sassa.gov.za/annual%20reports/Documents/SASSA%20Annual%20 Report%202020.PDF. (Accessed: 13 April 2021).

Standing Committee on Community Development (2016) *Report of the Standing Committee on Community Development on the Briefing Meeting by the South African Social Security Agency (SASSA) on Tuesday 31 May 2016.*

The Black Sash (2017) *Hands Off Our Grants Campaign*, Cape Town: The Black Sash [online]. Available at: https://www.blacksash.org.za/index.php/sash-in-action/advocacy-in-partnership/hands-off-our-grants. (Accessed: 18 December 2022).

United Nations Development Programme (2019) *The State of Social Assistance in Africa.* New York: United Nations.

Vally, N.T. (2016) 'Insecurity in South African Social Security: An Examination of Social Grant Deductions, Cancellations, and Waiting,' *Journal of Southern African Studies*, 42(5), pp. 965–982. DOI: 10.1080/03057070.2016.1223748.

Van der Zwan, N. (2014) 'Making Sense of Financialization,' *Socio-Economic Review*, 12, pp. 99–129. DOI: 10.1093/ser/mwt020.

Villarreal, M. (2023) 'Conditional cash transfer programs in Mexico,' in *Financializations of Development: Global Games and Local Experiments*, this volume.

Visser, W. (2004) *'Shifting RDP into GEAR'. The ANC Government's Dilemma in Providing an Equitable System of Social Security for the 'New' South Africa.* Paper presented at the 40th ITH Linzer Konferenz, Linz, Austria, on 17 September 2004 [online]. Available at: http://academic.sun.ac.za/history/downloads/visser/rdp_into_gear.pdf. (Accessed: 13 April 2021).

Vodafone (2020) *M-Pesa* [online]. Available at: https://www.vodafone.com/what-we-do/ services/m-pesa. (Accessed: 8 May 2020).

# 12

# CONDITIONAL CASH TRANSFER PROGRAMS IN MEXICO

## Financial inclusion policies and the involvement of private finance actors

*Magdalena Villarreal*

Private businesses have been involved in Mexican policy for many years. The question is in what guise and to what degree they join efforts toward what has been identified as the so-called common good. For a long period, Mexico's social policy entailed subsidies to education, staples, credit, promotion of low-income housing programs, and services including health and food baskets for the poorest. Here, private businesses, such as powdered-milk providers, construction industry and other enterprises were brought in. Such practices continue to this day, but there tends to be skepticism from the general public concerning the profit-oriented agenda of private-sector businesses.

In this chapter, I discuss PROIIF, a financial-inclusion program in Mexico, to address the kinds of dilemmas that present themselves at the interface between different actors involved in the implementation of social policy, particularly regarding the participation of the private sector. In the case I study, the private actors involved include banks and other financial intermediaries who are tasked with the distribution of cash transfers, as well as some credit services. In focusing on this interface, my aim is to reveal the ways in which social development policy dovetails with financialization processes. First, these programs contribute to the growing monetization and bankarization of poor households, connecting them to formal financial circuits. Second, this new circuit is intertwined with the regional and communitarian circulation of money and resources that further its progressive transformation.

I base my analysis on an anthropological study carried out in 2016–2017, in which, after an extensive review of relevant information, our team selected 52 random households of PROIIF participants at five locations. Each location was situated in a different socioeconomic and geographic region in Mexico. We carried out in-depth interviews with different members of each household and participated to the degree possible in everyday life events that would provide

DOI: 10.4324/9781003039679-15

us with clues as to their financial practices, their social and economic concerns, and their relationship to government officials. We registered community inter- action in field diaries and carried out five focal groups with beneficiaries. We also held two dozen interviews with the field officers, a few with the financial intermediaries involved, and many with selected executives from central offices managing the program, in an effort to come to grips with the differential ways in which they conceived the program and their diverse undertakings. Guided by an actor-oriented approach (Long, 2001; Long and Villarreal, 2004), we explored the participants' perspectives, their understandings of the program, and the ways in which their financial practices intertwined with other concerns and responsibilities in their everyday lives. We paid particular attention to spaces of interaction that could reveal their underlying conceptions of the program and expectations concerning financial possibilities.

The chapter is structured in two sections. In the first one, I provide a general background of the program and its main features. The second section portrays the beneficiaries, delving into the circuits in which their resources flow and the ways in which they used the program. Here I also discuss some of the problems entailed in the intervention of private businesses in social policy and, in the final section, I briefly describe the dissolution of the program and the new road map as presented by the recently installed government.

## Cash-transfer programs and their contribution to financialization

This section introduces the Conditional Cash Transfer Program (CCT) I have studied and situates it in the discussion on financialization.

### *The pecuniary turn of Mexico's poverty-reduction programs*

An important change in Mexico's social development guidelines took place in 1997, when a new government program awarded cash transfers to those classified as extremely poor. Social policy thus took an explicit pecuniary turn. Transfers to households were made conditional upon carrying out certain responsibilities pertaining to medium- and long-term investment in human capital for household members (Boltvinik et al., 2019), including the procurement of health, education and nutrition, acknowledged as indispensable elements for economic growth. The first program of this kind, PROGRESA (i.e. to progress), was followed by two others, namely Oportunidades (i.e. opportunities) and PROSPERA (i.e. to prosper), altogether extending over a period of 20 years (see also Valencia Lomelí et al., 2019). The conditions included regular visits for medical check-ups for the whole family, participation at health-related talks, school attendance by children, and mothers' involvement in community activities which varied by region, but could include preparing food for young students' breakfasts at school, sweeping streets, etc. The explicit reasoning was that this would ensure health, nutrition and education, which in turn would help match social policy to the general market orientation of the economy, investing in human capital. It would, the main promotors argued, allow the beneficiaries the freedom to decide how they wanted to use their money (previously, beneficiaries received resources mostly in the way of food and subsidies) (Levy, 1991, pp. 53–54).

Table 12.1 depicts these programs and some of the main sub-programs of PROSPERA (the most recent one) in a simplified form, to help the reader

**TABLE 12.1** Cash transfer programs in Mexico

| Year | Program | Sub program | Beneficiaries in 2017 | Main elements | Main problems |
|---|---|---|---|---|---|
| 1997 | PROGRESA | | | | |
| 2002 | Oportunidades | | | | |
| 2014–2018 | PROSPERA | Health | Almost 7 million families registered | Provide health services | Services provided by already existing institutions. Problems of access and lack of infrastructure and doctors. Often had shortages of medicine. Only covered some ailments. A large percentage of beneficiaries did not use it. |
| | | Education | Almost 7 million families registered | Ensure that all children attend school | Existing educational services could not cater for all students appropriately. Insufficient infrastructure. More teacher training needed. |
| | | Nutrition | 5.5 million families receive milk, but many also receive food baskets | Provide access to nutritious food, including milk and other staples | Depended on pre-existing programs that did not cover current needs |
| | | Elderly | 705,247 elders | Provide cash transference for elderly | Small stipend but welcomed by elderly |
| | | PROIIF | 1,030,000 families | Access to formal financial services | Deficiencies in the bank's operation, lack of infrastructure, did not diminish over-indebtedness |

understand the status of PROIIF, which is the main focus of this chapter. Many more sub-programs were implemented with different degrees of success. Some of the problems were related to the incapacities to adequately deliver the services that beneficiaries were supposed to use as a condition to receive the cash transfer.

PROSPERA grew exponentially, starting with 300,000 beneficiary families in 1997 to almost 7,000,000 in 2018, when it had become an indispensable income for numerous families. The aim to alleviate poverty and thus reduce dependency on aid was not met (Boltvinik et al., 2019). Although formal rhetoric stated that cash would be used as a means for the advancement of household economy, in practice, beneficiaries spent a large percentage on health and to pay off debts – mostly acquired for everyday consumption (Villarreal, 2009; Villarreal et al., 2017).

In 2014, a sub-program of PROSPERA was created: PROIIF (Programa Integral de Inclusión Financiera/Integral Program for Financial Inclusion).[1] It was designed to promote financial inclusion, encouraging beneficiaries to save part of their small stipend and receive credit, as well as offer insurance, financial education and funeral services. PROIIF was designed as one of the tools of the 2013–2018 National Development Plan that established financial inclusion as one of its important objectives (Gobierno de la República, 2013). This plan corresponds to the presidential period of Enrique Peña Nieto, a right-wing president who was in favor of privatization in all government policies. The underlying argument was that, through household savings, poverty and inequality would be reduced. Financial inclusion would also provide protection vis-à-vis diverse contingencies and would help deliver loans that facilitate the development of productive projects. Mexico, here, was following the international consensus. Financial inclusion is indeed promoted by G20, Financial Inclusion Experts Group (FIEG), the Better than Cash Alliance and foundations such as The Bill and Melinda Gates Foundation, Mastercard, Visa and Credit Suisse, and is considered important for economic policy. Social policy can thus be a good way to develop bankarization and to include beneficiaries into the formal financial system.

The financial inclusion policy was linked to Mexican financial reform, ratified in 2014. Among other measures, it mandated the development bank, BANSEFI (Banco del Ahorro Nacional y Servicios Financieros/National Savings and Financial Services Bank), to design and implement a financial inclusion program for the population that was excluded, in particular vulnerable groups such as those linked to conditional transfer programs (Cue, 2014). These legal frameworks and national plans involving financial inclusion promoted the creation of PROIIF, to be operated by BANSEFI. Although it is a public bank largely subsidized by the state, BANSEFI followed the same kind of rules as private banks and tended to prioritize profit in its operations. It was assigned the distribution of government cash transfers to recipients.

## Cash-transfer programs as contributors to financialization

By facilitating access to consumer credit, the program opened the door for private financial institutions, as well as national and transnational companies, to tap into the bottom of the pyramid. The addressees of these programs generally welcomed the prospect of having access to different spaces for consumption and formal financial services, particularly credit. Most of them were already in debt and had been obliged to sell assets in order to cover their increasing monetary needs. The trail to financialization was thus taking shape.

Converting assets into cash is one of the main features of monetization. And monetization, as Servet and Saiag (2014, p. 27) explain, is the first level of financialization. It takes shape in the increasing commodification of everyday conditions of domestic reproduction. Speculative financial and other markets are, they say, indispensable to the very existence of monetization. This gives way to an increasing gap between needs and cash incomes, thereby fostering a second level of financialization. The authors contend that cash-transfer programs implemented in developing countries are really part of the process of financialization (Servet and Saiag, 2014, p. 30). Indeed, such programs pull poor people into formal financial circuits that are themselves connected to national and even global finance. As Pellandini-Simányi (2021, p. 290) explains, these processes tend to "responsibilize households and compel them to make individual arrangements for their future financial welfare," wherein they adopt "investorial-entrepreneurial subjectivities, such as entrepreneurial, risk-tolerant, self-responsible attitudes" and "use investment and insurance products." This, the author argues, "makes households worse off, forcing them to take on credit to maintain their living standard" (Pellandini-Simányi, 2021, p. 290). The fact is that these programs facilitate credit by providing the poor regular revenues which formal finance can count on in order to cover other debts. As such, they tend to boost indebtedness and the financialization of everyday life.

With these considerations in mind, I explore the PROIIF program to delve into the flows of pecuniary circuits that made their way into local economic practices. I follow Marois (2012), Cushen (2013), and Chiapello and Knoll (2020) to show how such circuits are shaped, driven and diverted through the interaction of diverse actors whose aims may clash, but tend to find points of convergence. This is because financial circuits are not composed only of monetary resources and transactions, but also involve social, cultural, political and symbolic elements. In the process, power relations play a critical role.

At least three key critical effects of financialization present themselves at the bottom of the pyramid. The first addresses the relevance of the role that cash transfer programs took on in the development of bankarization and financial inclusion. Financial practices (including saving, credit and other transactions) carried out via banks and other formal financial institutions began to take hold in the poorer households.

The second involves how these new formal circuits performed into a preexisting long-standing process of indebtedness, wherein people had to convert different types of resources, such as social relations, physical assets (including homes, vehicles, appliances, jewelery) and environmental resources (e.g. future access to water) into financial instruments, particularly debt. This led to over-indebtedness, which in turn increasingly led people to engage with any available financial institutions, including banks, micro-financial businesses, credit institutions and government programs. The new circuits promoted by the Mexican social policy were then added to existing ones and tended to change local circuits based on social networks in an important way. Friends and relatives found it almost impossible to support each other's liabilities, and debt service fees from local moneylenders piled up.

Third, this shift also entailed transformations of the local economy, which increasingly depended on the speculative dynamics of powerful external institutions, and thus tended to fall out of control of households and communities. Extra-regional financial circuits made their way into these spheres, transforming local monetary and social-currency flows. Private financial actors and formal banking systems were used to implement the poverty-alleviation program. This exemplifies the intricate processes involving financialization, privatization and development.

The next section exemplifies how these processes are present in the case studied. This program was not very far-reaching, but it did contribute to transform local financial circuits.

## The Mexican cash-transfer program and the financialization of the bottom of the pyramid

The process of bankarization in the context of Mexican social policy triggered change in regional and local circuits. The public debates following these processes concerned, among other issues, the appropriate divide between public and private financial-service providers in the context of poverty alleviation, which we now turn to.

### Bankarization in Mexican social policy

For some time, the Mexican State had been declaring its interest in procuring financial inclusion at the bottom of the pyramid (Cue, 2014). The representatives of the Ministry of Treasury and Public Credit stated in 2014 that national policies on social inclusion should favor the substitution of cash for electronic money, using the new technologies that allowed the population access to financial services (SHCP, 2014). They decreed the bankarization of all social programs and governmental salaries. Their justification was that financial access for people who normally did not have access to credit should be encouraged, in such a way that they could generate credit histories. For this, they said, it was necessary to work hand-in-hand with the private sector to install financial infrastructure, including ATMs and bank headquarters in all the municipalities of the poorer South and Southeast of the country.

The substitution of cash for electronic money was quickly implemented for government cash transfers. Former cash-transfer programs used to rely on cash distribution, but in 2014, it was decided that the transfer should be done exclusively by electronic transaction. This allowed the government a degree of control, particularly with respect to the political use of such disbursements, which no longer had to be intermediated by different offices, as well as for taxation purposes, since it allowed transactions to be traced. In order to access their money, beneficiaries opened an account and could go to a BANSEFI teller or use bank cards to pay in certain stores or receive cash directly from an ATM. The goal was to use social programs to disperse pecuniary benefits by bank transfer, thus training the population to use cards and manage their money via banks.

At the time, collaboration with BANSEFI was critical because, as a government program, PROIIFF lacked the capacity to provide financial services, and BANSEFI was a development bank, operating 536 offices in different states all over the country. It only had 37 ATMs (as compared with the 11,130 ATMs for one of the private banks, with ATMs only in urban areas), but could link up with other banks (particularly the Military Bank, which had 65 offices and 351 ATMs, a number of which were in small cities around the country) and department stores to extend payment services. However, such a partnership was not very successful, as we shall discuss below.

In addition to BANSEFI, private institutions, such as insurance companies, MasterCard (which provided the software and plastic for the cards), and a few private banks were involved in the program. Other commercial banks lobbied to be allowed in as part of the distribution network, but BANSEFI kept a tight hold. Yet, other private influencers, such as consultants and lobbyists, also made their voice heard. As one of the consultants put it:

> The government is privileging a very inefficient bank to disburse the funds. The door should be opened to all those interested in participating. Private financial institutions would be much more efficient, knowledgeable as they are of finances and markets... PROIIFF is not a large program, but repayment is secure and it can open up to other financial devices.
> *(Interview with consultant, Mexico City, 3/28/2017).*

PROIIF was created to address financial inclusion directly. Financial services offered by this sub-program were dependent on the cash transfer received by the beneficiaries of PROSPERA. Beneficiaries could save part of their bi-monthly stipend, (allowance that, roughly speaking, could range from Mex$500 to Mex$3,000: approximately $75–$150, depending on how many of the household's children attended school and whether it included an elderly person) and borrow a certain amount that would be deducted from their future transfers. At the time of the study, the program had only been introduced in a few regions and managed to incorporate about 7% of total PROSPERA beneficiaries, although many beneficiaries from different regions expressed their interest to join PROIIFF.

It was actually a favorable lending scenario from the perspective of the bank: there were hundreds of micro-borrowers that could not default. The amount of cash each family received via PROSPERA was quite low, but beneficiaries could enroll in PROIIF to save a percentage of this money and also acquire a limited amount of credit (ranging from $25 to $100). Money was automatically taken from their account before the beneficiaries received their stipend. This was also expected to fuel the economy at the bottom of the pyramid by boosting consumption. In addition, it would encourage people's inclusion in a system with credit histories and scores. They could be trusted to access different kinds of loans and consumer credit. Formalized financial devices were thus established as part of government aid. According to a beneficiary of the program, who used those financial devices:

> I asked for the loan [from the moneylender] because I knew I would receive the loan from PROIIF soon. I knew that I would be able to pay at least part of my debt to the moneylender. And PROIIF is not difficult… it is money that I have not seen, it is not in my hands, so I do not feel the loss.
>
> *(Beneficiary from Jalisco State)*

Financial education was compulsory, but it only consisted of a massive session with several dozen participants lasting up to two hours, in which the program was explained to all the beneficiaries who attended, providing them with information on the use of the account and the card (which most of them had not used before). Women could almost never remember what was said during those two hours under the hot sun in an open space, where loudspeakers rarely managed to overcome the hustle and bustle of passers-by and crowds.

> They said we should save, not waste electricity (giggles) or spend on soft drinks… We should keep our accounts in order… I don't remember what else they said, there was a lot of noise, it was hot… They gave me some papers… I must have them somewhere.
>
> *(Beneficiary from Baja California State)*

Insurance (from private, mostly transnational, insurance companies cooperating with the program)[2] was supposed to offer protection vis-à-vis accidental death, paralysis or dismemberment. It covered $750 in case of death, and funeral assistance for Mex$7,500 ($375). Yet very few of our interviewees knew of this benefit and none had used it, although it was discounted from their account.

Additional benefit packages could include, depending on where beneficiaries were located, additional life insurance for the husband and/or children, free calls to other Mexican states or to the United States and Canada for an extra cost or another package that included funeral services for the family, ambulance service, discounts for construction materials, medicine, electronic appliances, clothes, preventive dental and eyecare services. But again, few of our interviewees knew of these packages and they were rarely, if ever, used. Bureaucracy was too cumbersome and/or officers denied them the service.

> I never paid for that service. I need every penny I have. But my cousin, his wife died, and he tried to get funeral benefits and maybe some money, but he had to call Mexico City. He tried and tried, and they did not answer. When they did answer, it turned out to be a call center. The young girl on the other side of the phone was not able to help him. After more calls, he finally gave up.
>
> *(Beneficiary from Zapotlanejo)*

I now turn to the pre-existing local financial circuits in order to understand how this new circuit would fit into pre-existing practices.

## *Changing local and regional financial circuits*

PROSPERA beneficiaries that signed up for PROIIF had to have a small amount of savings in their program account in order to ask for a loan. All beneficiaries had been selected from the population classified as suffering extreme poverty. Women were generally chosen instead of men, under the consideration that women are in charge of the children and that they are generally more responsible. An important percentage had only studied up to third grade or did not have any formal education at all. Their husbands, if they had one, tended to hold precarious jobs or were unemployed. Few of the women had a stable job. Stable jobs were difficult for them to get or to hold on to, because their children were young (one of the conditions to receive the PROSPERA allowance was that they have children in school or elderly to take care for at home), but also because another condition to receive the allowance was to attend meetings, do community work (such as sweeping streets or helping give out meals to school children), and take their family to the local clinic. This was difficult to do if you had a job. Yet almost all of the women engaged in different additional economic activities: domestic helper, selling clothes or selling prepared food, fruit, sweets or plastic trinkets. Cash circulated among friends, neighbors and family.

Seventy-two percent of our interviewees had never used formal services from banks, department stores or other institutions. Financial circuits in these scenarios involved money, but a large percentage of exchanges were made in-kind and as social currencies, including services and favors. Loan sharks could charge as much as 30% interest per month, yet the borrower would often classify it as a favor, since the need for cash was compelling. "They are lenders," explained one of the beneficiaries, "it is their business. They charge interests in order to generate money and help other people."

The unsteady situation of household economies required a great deal of indebtedness here and there. Usury prevailed in different forms. Local moneylenders began to give way to more established – and mostly external – lending establishments. This impacted the social and economic scaffolding of communities. In Cozumel, a touristic island on the Caribbean, television sets and motorcycles – bought out of need for daily transport and for entertainment – became, as one woman put it, "life-saving boards," since they could be pawned at nearby shops. Although only cities have pawn shops, such exchanges are very common all over the country. People who owned a car or a piece of jewelery could exchange it for some greatly needed cash, always less than what the good was worth on the marketplace. And people could use trust based on high status to acquire loans or goods on deferred payment (Villarreal, 2007; Villarreal et al., 2017). Such financial practices entailed social relations, networking and moral sanctions. There were procedures, commitments, obligations, as well as other social and cultural concerns. Financial circuits were thus shaped and redirected by local social dynamics.

However, increasing need for money was matched by the speedy introduction of micro-financial institutions, present in the financial practices of a fifth of the households considered in the study. These mostly worked with social-guarantee models, organizing groups in each community where all the members back each loan. This reduced risk for micro-financial institutions and passed it on to the users. Increasingly, women learned to borrow from one institution to pay their debts to another. Families juggled[3] between different financial-service establishments in order to stay afloat. Over-indebtedness was rampant and different, generally external and financial circuits made headway. PROIIF dovetailed very well with this context, covering a portion of the financial needs of beneficiaries, particularly with regard to the need to engage in debt in order to pay off other debts. By 2018, PROSPERA, the umbrella conditional cash-transfer program, had become an indispensable part of a poor family's economy. According to our sample, it represented 24% of the income obtained by the poorest families, whose need for cash was increasing.

## The debate on private-public management of poor people's cash

A problematic notion, particularly for those involved with private-sector interests, involved the idea that cash transfers were gifts enabling so-called free rides for opportunistic beneficiaries that did not make an effort to work. This concern was addressed to a degree with the conditionality of the transfers. They were not free gifts. People had to contribute in the form of strengthening human capital.

The question that followed was how the disbursement of poor people's cash should be managed. Some officers considered that a private bank should be brought in, since BANSEFI was inefficient in this regard. But the question entailed a whole conception of development and financial issues, as well as of social policy and its targets. Underlying it were notions concerning the addressees of the program: the, sometimes implicit, dilemma was whether addressees should be conceived of as recipients of cash transfers, beneficiaries, clients or – more in line with market orientations – entrepreneurs. As *recipients*, they would have no obligation toward government. It was their right to receive a stipend. A similar association was linked to the label of *beneficiaries*, but here, there was a recognition of the state as provider for a specific target group with certain characteristics that, from their point of view, made them deserving of benefits. *Clients*, on the other hand, had to give something in exchange, entailing some negotiations, while *entrepreneurs* should acknowledge the value of the cash transfer, cultivate it and capitalize. This notion was favored by most government officials, particularly those who believed in the role of the market to further progress and development, which tended to coincide with private-sector interests.

We did not interview any representative of the private sector directly, but, from our interviews with government officials, it was clear that they often wore both hats. They worked for the state and had responsibilities in the implementation of the program, but also had private investments in commercial banks and other institutions (Villarreal et al., 2017). Officers sometimes made known they had close links to consultancy firms and other private interest groups. Although they did not say so explicitly, more than a few found the program quite convenient, both for their political interests and for the possibility of establishing alliances with key actors within the private sector.

Yet, the invitation to work hand-in-hand with private institutions (including other commercial banks and private investors), as stated in the National Development Plan, was easier said than done. In Mexico, banks and other private institutions were constrained by their own models of what development entailed. Some private banks were interested in participating in the disbursement of government money to the poor, but their stated interests were clearly profit-oriented. Although BANSEFI was a bank supported by the state and, in theory, was not predominantly profit-oriented, it was wired to provide financial services to customers. Its development goals were calculated in monetary terms. Customers were mostly viewed as numbers. Their aims, their estimates, and their results tended to be quantitatively measured and projected according to criteria linked to the world of finance and entrepreneurship. More than a few bank tellers, for example, did not understand the logic of poverty-alleviation programs. They complained that program beneficiaries were lazy and ignorant, that they only "stretched out their hand to receive money and were not able to manage their accounts in a civilized way" (Interview with BANSEFI Bank officers. November 20–23, 2016). They loathed long queues of indigenous people waiting to be attended at the bank. The need to reach out to people in remote areas entails a great deal of bureaucracy in the everyday operation of the program, and it was not cost-effective for the bank to provide precise and timely information to PROIIF beneficiaries, so they did not do so.

Other important problems concerned the limited resources available to the beneficiaries and the time that elapsed between the application for a loan and the moment they received the money. A department within PROSPERA checked out each of the hundreds of applications for PROIIF loans and made sure the accounts were in order. This took some time, because this information was then sent to the corresponding departments at the bank. Since transfers were bimonthly, beneficiaries normally had to wait two months before they received a loan. However, urgent household needs had to be resolved immediately. Thus, the program did not substitute informal finance for a formal one. Rather, women took on loans from local usurers and their networks, calculating that they would be able to cover at least part of it once they received their PROIIF loan. Under these circumstances, PROSPERA's aim to destine such allowances for educational and other basic needs was quite impossible to achieve. Beneficiaries mostly used it to cover their debts.

On the other hand, high-level government officials involved in the program had explicit ideas concerning the need or not to involve private institutions in addition to (or instead of) BANSEFI in implementing the program. It was clear that BANSEFI was operating with a great deal of inefficiency, and some claimed that the solution was to bring in other private, commercial banks. A lively debate took place between stakeholders, including officials whose alliances with the private sector were strong (Cue, 2014; Villarreal et al., 2017), as well as consultants and private-interest holders. The contention was that, because the aim of banks was to make a profit, they had to be competent. This, they claimed, would take the beneficiaries into a so-called normal scenario in which private banks would compete to take part in the disbursement of funds to the poor and the, in their words, most efficient would win. It was argued that modernization and entrepreneurship were what pushed economies forward. The government, represented by PROIIF officials, was implicitly accused of following backward policies. As mentioned above, private institutions (such as insurance companies, private banks allowing access to their ATMs, as well as consultancy firms, lobbyists, etc.) were already participating as subcontractors to the program, but handing over a key operation to private banks and institutions was quite another issue.

Many stakeholders stated that a private bank's mission is to make profit and they would certainly exploit beneficiaries one way or another. Some of them suggested resorting to non-governmental organizations (NGOs). BANSEFI already had working links to *La Red de la Gente,* which comprised a number of cooperatives, NGOs and credit unions. These were mostly not-for-profit organizations and had access to remote areas. The problem was that inclusion of many small organizations would entail loss of control for the program's central offices. Too many actors with different interests were involved, and leadership and power relations were an issue for a government institution that lives on politics.

The tension that grew in the partnership between PROIIF and BANSEFI has everything to do with strains intrinsic to the intertwining of efforts in development and financialization. As mentioned above, considerations as to the role of the state in promoting financial inclusion were the object of differences, as well as the degree to which development endeavors could be left in the hands of private institutions whose aim it was to make money regardless of social processes. Government officials' discussions entailed different points of view as to whether recipients of cash transfers were to be considered clients, beneficiaries or entrepreneurs. Also implicit were different conceptions as to where the dividing line was between the responsibility of the state and that of the individual. Numerous stakeholders considered that community and other social matters were not relevant to financial inclusion.

The issue had not been resolved yet when the program came to an end. However, development policy had left strong traces in its contribution to processes of financialization at the bottom of the pyramid.

## The end of the program. New beginnings?

In 2019, the new, center-left government of Mexico headed by Andrés Manuel López Obrador, closed PROSPERA and its sub-programs, including PROIIF. This represented the end of 20 years of conditional cash-transfer programs. Instead of reforming PROSPERA, the government instituted a new program based on cash transfers to targeted populations, including children attending school and older adults, but mostly young teenagers who were studying or training for jobs. So-called co-responsibility was transformed into direct support for beneficiaries, limiting aid to ten-month periods, after which new evaluations had to be made in order to continue the transfers. Numerous prior intermediary institutions were slashed, and BANSEFI was transformed into the so-called Bank of Wellbeing, which disbursed some of the government transfers to beneficiaries of different programs. Although government rhetoric strongly campaigned against privatization, new financial institutions, such as Banco Azteca, were included in the disbursement of government funds to the poor. This particular bank has a long experience with low-income clients all over the country, but it has been highly criticized for practicing usury with the poor. Another bank with similar experience was also seeking to engage in the program. Both banks operate within large department stores wherein clients can receive transfers (and remittances from the United States) and acquire refrigerators, washing machines and clothes on credit.

Following European and North American practices, government cash transfers are deposited directly into the beneficiaries' accounts. Education and health are dealt with under different programs, no longer linked to cash transfers. New spaces have been opened up for other development models over which old and new interest groups compete. The question remains as to the degree to which over-indebtedness, the weakening of social support from local networks, and the loss of community and household control over their finances is diminishing. These processes will not only be pushed forward by private institutions and government, but by the local people themselves, many of whom have made it their goal to achieve what they view as progressing and prospering under circumstances made more difficult by a quite financialized milieu.

## Notes

1 PROSPERA (to prosper), and with it PROIIF, was dissolved in 2018 by the new center-left government, in an effort, according to President López Obrador, to overcome the processes of corruption that had found their way into these programs.

2 Private insurance companies had found their way into a number of small savings co-operatives, as well as into government programs oriented to the poor [see Chiapello and Knoll (2020), who discuss this kind of impact investment].
3 See Villarreal et al. (2015); and Guérin et al. (2014) for a discussion on the concept of juggling.

# References

Boltvinik, Julio, Araceli Damián, Jaramillo Molina, and Máximo Ernesto (2019) 'Crónica de un fracaso anunciado. Ha llegado la hora de remplazar el Progresa-Oportunidades-Prospera (POP),' in Gonzalo Hernández Licona, Thania Paola de la Garza Navarrete, Janet Zamudio Chávez, and Iliana Yaschine Arroyo (eds.), *El Progresa-Oportunidades-Prospera, a 20 años de su creación*. Mexico City: CONEVAL, pp. 147–191.

Chiapello, Eve, and Lisa Knoll (eds.) (2020) 'Social Finance, Impact Investing, and the Financialization of the Public Interest,' *Special issue of Historical Social Research*, 45(173), p. 3.

Cue, Yolanda (2014) *Distribución de programas gubernamentales y la inclusión financiera*. Mexico: Bansefi, SHCP.

Cushen, J. (2013) 'Financialization in the Workplace: Hegemonic Narratives, Performative Interventions and the Angry Knowledge Worker,' *Accounting, Organization and Society*, 38(4), pp. 314–331.

Gobierno de la República (2013) *Plan Nacional de Desarrollo 2013–2018*. Estados Unidos Mexicanos: Secretaría de Gobernación (SEGOB).

Guérin, Isabelle, Solene Morvant-Roux, and Magdalena Villarreal (2014) *Microfinance, Debt and Overindebtedness: Juggling with Money*. London: Routledge.

Levy, Santiago (1991) 'Poverty Alleviation in Mexico,' *World Bank Policy Research Working Paper*, WPS 679 [online]. Available at: https://documents1.worldbank.org/curated/en/306571468774696697/pdf/multi0page.pdf. (Accessed: 30 June 2022).

Long, Norman (2001) *Development Sociology. Actor Perspectives*. London: Routledge.

Long, Norman, and Villarreal, Magdalena (2004) 'Redes de deudas y compromisos. La relevancia del dinero y otras divisas en las cadenas comerciales,' in Villarreal, M. (ed.), *Antropología de la Deuda: Crédito, Ahorro, Fiado y Prestado en las finanzas cotidianas*. Mexico: CIESAS, Porrúa and Cámara de Diputados, pp. 27–55.

Marois, Thomas (2012) *States, Banks and Crisis: Emerging finance Capitalism in Mexico and Turkey*. Cheltenham: Edward Elgar Publishing.

Pellandini-Simányi, Léna (2021) 'The Financialization of Everyday life,' in Christian Borch and Robert Wosnitzer (eds.), *The Routledge Handbook of Critical Finance Studies*. New York and London: Routledge, pp. 278–299.

Secretaría de Gobernación (2013) 'Plan Nacional de Desarrollo 2013–2018', in the *Official Gazette of the Federation. Diario de la Federación*. DOF: 20/05/ 2013.

Servet, Jean Michel., and Hadrian. Saiag (2014) 'Household Over-Indebtedness in Northern and Southern Countries,' in Isabelle Guérin, Solène Morvant-Roux, and Magdalena Villarreal (eds.), *Microfinance, Debt and Over-Indebtedness: Juggling with Money*. New York: Routledge.

SHCP [Secretaría de Hacienda y Crédito Público: Ministry of Treasury and Public Credit] (2014) *Impulsar la inclusión financiera es impulsar la equidad social, Nota informativa, Informe semanal del Vocero*, June 23–27. Mexico: SHCP.

Valencia Lomelí, Enrique, Jaramillo Molina, and Máximo Ernesto (2019). 'El Programa Progresa-Oportunidades-Prospera en el régimen de bienestar dual mexicano,' in Gonzalo Hernández Licona, Thania Paola de la Garza Navarrete, Janet Zamudio

Chávez, and Iliana Yaschine Arroyo (eds.), *El Progresa-Oportunidades-Prospera, a 20 años de su creación*. Mexico City: CONEVAL, pp. 114–146.

Villarreal, Magdalena (2007) 'La economía desde una perspectiva de género: de omisiones, inexactitudes y preguntas sin responder en el análisis de la pobreza,' *Revista de estudios de género La Ventana*, 25(3), pp. 7–42.

Villarreal, Magdalena (2009) *Mujeres, Finanzas Sociales y Violencia Económica en Zonas Marginadas de Guadalajara*. Guadalajara: IMMG, IJM, SEDESOL, INDESOL.

Villarreal, Magdalena, Isabelle Guérin, and Santosh Kumar (2015) 'La richesse en jongant: Saraswathi et Carola,' *Critique Internationale*, 69(4), pp. 39–58.

Villarreal, Magdalena et al., (2017) *El Programa Integral de Inclusión Financiera* (PROIFF). Mexico: Coneval.

# 13

# FROM SOCIAL WORKERS TO PROXY-CREDITORS TO BANK TELLERS

## Financialization in the work of microcredit field staff in a South Indian town

*Rajalaxmi Kamath and Nithya Joseph*

The advent of for-profit microfinance institutions (MFIs) has resulted in the replacement of existing local microcredit provisioning by a more financialized, global model in many countries (Aitken, 2013; Bylander et al., 2019). In India, MFIs were preceded by the self-help group (SHG) model, under which non-governmental organizations (NGOs) and state workers supported women who were savings group members in their efforts to pool funds and lend to each other. Nationalized banks granted loans to groups at interest rates comparable to those offered to mainstream clients, based on savings and transaction records (Kumar and Golait, 2008). When MFIs started to operate, they drew capital from across the globe and lent it to women from low-income households; interest rates were higher, and profits went to those remote from the local context in which loans were issued. MFIs boasted high numbers of loans issued and impeccable repayment records (Sriram, 2010). However, these were only possible because they were able to draw on the existing SHG networks. There have been a number of visible crises in the microfinance sector since 2010, with cases of contestation and resistance, clients refusing to repay loans and accusations that MFIs were doing more harm than good (Guérin, Labie and Servet, 2015). The aftermath of the crises has seen changes in state regulation and self-regulation across the microfinance sector (Malegam, 2011). In recent years, a new approach to providing finance-for-development has emerged. Some MFIs have been converted to small finance banks (SFBs), thus permitting them to become sites where customers can save and earn interest (Sriram, 2019).

This chapter pursues a very specific research question: What are the repercussions of the change in circuits of finance-for-development, from local and context-specific ones to global and universalized ones? In order to answer this question, we identify two processes of financialization that have defined changes in micro-lending in India: the shift from NGO and state-supported SHGs to

DOI: 10.4324/9781003039679-16

for-profit MFIs and the shift from MFIs to SFBs. In order to understand these shifts, we rely on the accounts of a group of microcredit field staff[1] in a South Indian town who have experience working in all three types of institutions. The staff moved together from an NGO involved in establishing and managing SHGs to the newly opened branch of an MFI in 2006, after which they became bank employees when the MFI was granted an SFB license in 2017. They offer unique insights, having been involved in implementing various forms of micro-lending over the last three decades, in each of the three stages observable in the evolution of finance-for-development in India.

A small number of insightful granular studies have examined financial inclusion from the perspective of those who are intermediaries (usually referred to as loan officers) between the clients and the institutions that lend to them (see Kar, 2013; Maîtrot, 2019; Sarker, 2013; Siwale and Ritchie, 2012). The everyday work context of MFI field staff is important in examining the work of development finance, which fundamentally "depends on labor of loan officers to actively produce and sustain debt relationships" (Kar, 2013, p. 482). The field staff of MFIs functionally serve as proxy creditors, charged with the task of bringing the poor into global financial networks, so that they end up facing the pressure and responsibility for the repayment of debt, without any ownership of capital (Kar, 2013). Additionally, the field staff often see themselves as development workers and value the respect of those for whom they provide financial services (Sarker, 2013). As a result, they are constantly negotiating an unresolved tension between capitalist expansion and ethical concerns centered on client relationships (Kar, 2013).

The field staff whose careers we trace worked to provide microcredit to women in the same town from the early 1990s–2018. They engaged in tasks such as managing groups, filling out loan applications and handling cash through out. However, the essence of their work and relationships with these women changed dramatically as the institutions they worked in changed. Field staff descriptions of their everyday work clearly reveal differences in the management objectives of the institutions and other stakeholders, including state bodies, nationalized and private banks, international aid agencies and private investors, all of whom shaped the form that micro-lending took in each phase. The field staff also highlighted their own roles in provision of products and services to clients, as well as in negotiations and contestations with clients and with the broader community.

This chapter argues that changes in the work of the field staff are illustrative of changes in the financial circuits in which they were embedded, as well as differences in institutional functions relative to flows of capital and interest.

## Context and methodology

This chapter draws on interviews with stakeholders across the microfinance sector in the town of Ramanagaram in Karnataka. The state of Karnataka in South India was a pioneer of the local SHG model, beginning in the late 1980s. It is therefore not surprising that it also attracted MFIs when they began to operate in India in the late 1990s. The authors have been working in Ramanagaram since 2007, trying to understand the financial lives of MFI clients (Dattasharma, Kamath and Ramanathan, 2016; Joseph, 2013). In March and April of 2018, we conducted a series of semi-structured interviews with the field staff of an MFI called Sudharan, which was working in Ramanagaram. In 2006, the field staff had moved together from NGO Kalyani (which was promoting SHG formation and facilitating linkages of SHGs to banks in that region) to the MFI Sudharan. In 2017, Sudharan was granted a banking license from the Central Bank of India and the former field staff were absorbed into the new bank as formal employees. The interviews asked in detail about (1) their work before joining the MFI; (2) the transition from NGO to MFI; (3) the crisis that erupted in Ramanagaram at the same time as similar crises were occurring at other sites in India; (4) the period that followed this crisis and (5) their current role as bank employees. The interviews reflected interactions with this group of field staff over a ten-year period – watching them at work, as well as carrying out interviews and focus group discussions (see Joseph, 2013) – and extensive fieldwork concerning the financial practices of MFI clients (see Dattasharma, Kamath and Ramanathan, 2016).

Ramesh, who joined the NGO in 1989, soon after completing a Bachelor's degree in Social Work, headed the Urban Lending team; three other field workers reported to him. He went on to become the head of the Ramanagaram branch of the MFI, serving as the Customer Relations Manager. A few years later, he was made the Area Manager of the MFI, responsible for multiple districts across the state of Karnataka. He then became the bank's Regional Manager for South India and now holds one of the highest positions in the bank.

Madhu and Lakshmi were women in their early twenties when they were recruited as field staff by the NGO in the late 1990s. They became Customer Relations Staff in the MFI, serving through the period of expansion, crisis and recovery and have now become bank employees, staffing the teller booths in the town branch of the bank.

## The SHG bank linkage model

As in other parts of Karnataka, NGOs that formed SHGs began working in Ramanagaram in the late 1980s; the association of these SHGs with banks began in 1991. As employees of the NGO Kalyani, the field staff worked with women's SHGs to facilitate savings, internal lending and applications for bank loans. They remained autonomous from both the SHG and the bank and were thus not considered to have any financial or other interest in the lending that went on in the SHGs. Interest on internal loans went to group members themselves and interest on other loans went to the bank. The NGO trained, managed and paid the staff using funds from three general sources: (1) international aid agencies; (2) state bodies such as NABARD and the Karnataka Department of Women and Child Development and (3) nominal contributions made by savings groups.

When Ramesh joined Kalyani in 1989, the idea of SHG formation had captured the attention of civil society actors in India. NGOs were coming together to learn and share their methods and funders were keen to support them. Ramesh noted that his early work involved convincing male household members and religious leaders that women should be allowed to leave their homes to participate in SHG activity. He was then involved in forming groups and facilitating savings, as well as internal lending.

When Madhu and Lakshmi joined almost a decade later, Ramesh trained them so they could join the Urban Lending team. Each of the field staff emphasized that the focus in the SHG model was on decision-making and control by the loan beneficiaries and other local actors. The women involved in SHGs were saving and sharing their profits, so the money stayed within the group. Staff incomes were low and uncertain and were funded in part by payments from SHG members to the NGO, in the form of fees for assistance provided and commissions on bank loans that staff helped SHG members' access. Staff work schedules depended on SHG preferences; as Madhu noted, "We would hold meetings when it was convenient for members; if it was in the evening we would go then" (Interview with Madhu; March 2018; Sudharan Office, Ramanagaram).

Lakshmi explained that they worked with groups to help them decide the interest rates for their internal loans, typically settling on 2% per month, which was much lower than informal lenders, who charged 5% or even as much as 10% per month; the interest collected from these internal loans was shared by all group members. In addition to such loans being less expensive, repayments were also flexible; if an SHG member could not repay an internal loan on time, they could pay the amount due with additional interest the following month. The interest on bank loans was 12% per annum, whereas informal loan interest was higher: 3%–10% per month, which translates to 36%–120% per annum. Lakshmi said SHG members were grateful to the staff for helping them access credit that freed them from dependence on bank loans were desirable and made possible by the SHG membership informal loans.

The staff appreciated the careful instruction they received on topics that were of use to the community, as well as how they approached those with whom they worked. According to Madhu:

> It was not just for our work but also for our own lives. We learned patience and soft skills. All these things are also helping us now in our present work. We had training in gender, understanding emotions, listening and eye contact. They had a training session on each word.
>
> *(Interview with Madhu; March 2018; Sudharan Office, Ramanagaram)*

The staff in turn held sessions for the SHGs on issues such as gender awareness and health practices. Madhu said, "We were speaking to them about healthy food, illnesses, things that were useful for the group members." Women often stayed after meetings to discuss domestic and health-related problems with the staff.

In 1999, the first major changes began to take place in SHGs. The national Swarnajayanti Gram Swarozgar Yojana (SGSY) program was established, with the aim of banks making microloans available to SHGs across the country. This central government program envisioned a nationwide scaling up of SHG lending and set targets for state governments and banks, both for SHG formation and bank lending to SHGs. The government recruited the staff of the NGO Kalyani to work as trainers for the state workers who were to manage the SHGs that were formed as part of the SGSY program. As Ramesh noted, the emphasis for those implementing the SGSY program was on fulfilling the targets set. Training and capacity building for the SHG members was severely compromised. State SHGs were formed en masse with the promise of government benefits and subsidies. The members of SGSY groups often did not know each other or understand the basic procedures involved in saving, lending to each other, accessing bank loans or repaying them. Following the the implementation of the SGSY program, banks had to tackle high NPAs (Non-Performing Assets) in their SHG lending portfolio as a result of members of state-formed groups beginning to default on loans.

Even though the processes followed by the NGO Kalyani had not changed, the NGO staff found that interactions with savings group members and bank managers, many of whom they had been working with for several years, did begin to change. At first, since state SHGs received subsidies, they were considered more beneficial than NGO-run groups. The NGO staff found themselves struggling to prove the legitimacy of the groups to their members. Then, as defaults on SGSY loans began to increase, the staff found that defaults on loans they had facilitated through the NGO were also on the rise. This was because women were now servicing multiple loans (obtained through different groups), along with a general deterioration in repayment discipline. The NGO staff found themselves needing to assist bank managers, with whom they had worked to get loans sanctioned, in order to negotiate loan repayment with the savings groups.

The NGO staff realized that they had little power to address systemic issues, even if they were called upon to liaise between different parties, to conduct training sessions and to share insights. This was because they belonged to a third party, which was only providing support to the savings groups and not to the institutions that were funding the SGSY or to the banks issuing loans.

The NGO staff were also of the opinion that the SGSY made it easier for MFIs to enter this region; the pace at which groups had been formed through the program meant there was an extensive network of potential clients that could be easily targeted. At the same time, since the groups did not have strong saving and internal lending practices or credibility with banks, they were more willing to take MFI loans, despite the high interest rates. As in other parts of the state (Pattenden, 2010) and country (Guérin et al., 2021), it was SHGs comprising of women from upper caste and class households which continued – and did not take the more expensive MFI loans.

In 2005, the funding for Kalyani was discontinued, due in part to the shift in discourse and policy in favor of for-profit MFIs, a phenomenon that was widely observed at the time (see Augsburg and Fouillet, 2013). Additionally, with the change in the central government, regulations around international aid were tightened, making it tougher for NGOs to get foreign donations. Jennifer, the head of Kalyani, heard that an MFI was planning to set up a branch in Raman-agaram and hire staff, so she arranged for her team to be interviewed by them. When they were selected, she told them, "You need to be competitive now; you're entering the corporate world" (Interview with Jennifer, April 2018, Kaly-ani NGO office, Bangalore).

## The for-profit MFI model

The turn of the century saw the entry of MFI lending in India, first with a change in the way existing NGOs operated, and then with the establishment of for-profit entities. This model was appealing, due to its ability to reach a large number of clients, to increase in scale rapidly and to easily count the impact in terms of the number of clients reached, portfolio quality, amount loaned and loan recovery (Sriram, 2010).

### Early days of work in the MFI

The field staff of Kalyani joined the MFI Sudharan in 2006, along with six other colleagues from the NGO. Ramesh was appointed as the Customer Relations Manager and the others as Customer Relations Staff at the newly formed branch. At the time, Sudharan was the third MFI in Ramanagaram; two others had begun lending in 2003 and 2005, respectively. This was the first semi-urban branch of Sudharan and so top management from the MFI spent time with the staff conducting surveys to evaluate the market. The team felt that these early interactions meant that they were recognized and listened to at the head office of the institution, even several years after the fact.

When Sudharan first started operations in Ramanagaram, the management encouraged the staff to continue to support functioning SHGs that they had been involved with, at the same time as recruiting clients through networks established through their earlier NGO work. Madhu said, "Some of the SHG groups that we set up as part of Kalyani were still working. They maintained the linkages, rotated everything" (Interview with Madhu; March 2018; Sudharan Office, Ramanagaram). Madhu was referring to the rotation of the pooled funds within the SHGs for intra-lending among members. The management recog-nized that it was good for their clients to continue being involved in intra-group saving and borrowing and thus having access to lower cost credit while taking MFI loans from them at 30% interest.

Lakshmi described the early work after they moved to the MFI as follows: "We distributed pamphlets and brochures and would share the information we learnt during training. Then we would tell people to form groups and come to us" (Interview with Lakshmi; March 2018; Sudharan Office, Ramanagaram). They explained that groups of ten women would be required to function as

guarantors for each other and to ensure all loans were repaid; this was emphasized in the training sessions. She added:

> We told them that while earlier we had to help them get loans from the
> bank, now the loan came directly from the organization. Once a group was
> formed, we would spend one week in training and setting up [processes for
> applying for MFI loans]. Then, after the loan was issued, we would visit
> weekly for repayments.

## The establishment of groups and routines

MFI Joint Liability Groups (JLGs) were established and each staff member was in
charge of organizing between 20 and 30 group meetings each week. As a large
proportion of clients were daily wage workers, they held most meetings between
6 and 8 a.m. each morning. As Madhu noted, unlike the SHG, where meetings
were based on group convenience, "at the MFI, there was a fixed time; you had
to come and you had to pay" (Interview with Madhu; March 2018; Sudharan
Office, Ramanagaram). The staff moved quickly between groups, which convened to quickly say the MFI prayer, following the custom of Grameen Bank for
clients to recite oaths at the start of a meeting; they then signed the attendance
register and made their cash repayments. Madhu noted that their earlier experience helped them with repayment collection; "We had learned cash handling,
so we were familiar with that when we moved to the MFI" (Interview with
Madhu; March 2018; Sudharan Office, Ramanagaram).

In the MFI, they had to maintain log books, fill out forms (loan applications,
insurance forms, loan utilization forms, etc.) and complete a large volume of
paperwork (about 7–8 pages per borrower, multiplied by around 40 clients in a
center).

The field staff all agreed that the relationship with the group members had
changed, having become more transactional. According to Lakshmi:

> Even now there is a difference between the old SHG members and the new
> MFI clients, in their respect, in their responses. We had a different rela-
> tionship in Kalyani and that continued with those who joined Sudharan
> from there.
>
> *(Interview with Lakshmi; March 2018; Sudharan Office, Ramanagaram)*

Lakshmi also felt that even if they were handling cash in the NGO, it was different with the MFI: "We were freer before; in Sudharan we always had money
tension."

## The beginning of the MFI crisis

There were more than ten for-profit MFIs lending in the town of Ramanagaram
by early 2009. Each sought to expand their client base and used incentives to

motivate staff to form new groups and reach high repayment targets. This incentivization reduced the resolve of the MFI workers to perform sound background checks which would disqualify potential clients. They often did not ensure that the women forming a group knew each other well and did not explain the group guarantee clause to them or collect sufficient documentation. Madhu recounted that the burden of multiple loans on clients with uncertain incomes resulted in defaults; clients either came to meetings and could not pay or ran away from Ramanagaram and could not be traced. Clients who were making regular payments were suddenly faced with unexpected increases in the cost of their loans because they had to pay the share of those who had defaulted, in addition to making their own repayment. Once repayment problems began, the staff of all MFIs started strictly enforcing the group guarantee clauses, with some using both coercive and persuasive tactics to ensure compliance. Madhu explained that their counterparts in other MFIs devised ad-hoc rules to ensure repayments, such as locking clients in the room where the meeting was being held until all payments had been collected. This created resentment toward both the MFIs and their staff.

### The repayment standoff

One morning in March of 2009, almost all of the Muslim clients in Ramanagaram refused to make their weekly repayments, on the grounds that they had received orders from the local mosques which forbade them from paying and from interacting with MFI staff. Religious leaders had issued a statement saying that disobeying them would result in being forced to leave the area and being denied entry to the mosque as well as burial rites; this was being done to protect people from exploitative lending practices. As the staff saw it, the religious leaders were partly justified in protesting certain practices that MFIs had been following. However, they argued that the leaders, as employers in the local economy, had felt threatened by MFIs, which offered credit to workers (whom these same leaders had been holding in debt for decades); in other words, the Muslim ban on MFIs was partly motivated by personal interest. As Madhu recalled the incident:

> People were paying so well … and then suddenly they just stopped paying. They came with three sacks full of loan cards and threw it at the District Commissioner's office. It was so hard to see that, cards from so many organizations just dumped there. We used to give Rupees 2,000 loans for festivals; we had just issued hundreds of such loans. Then so quickly people changed.
>
> *(Interview with Madhu; March 2018; Sudharan Office, Ramanagaram)*

In the early days, some customers had said "Madhu-madam, don't come to our house, we will collect the money and come give it to you in the evenings." But the religious leaders heard about this and forced them to stop. As Madhu said, "Because I was from Kalyani, my customers paid for some time and even after that they always talked to me nicely," but added that once the stand-off was established on the issue of repayment, they just would not change, citing community rules. Madhu noted:

> We were so stressed at that time. We thought if we kept going to their homes in a little while people would pay, but it never happened. Even if we said, "Just give us 50 or 100," they wouldn't pay.
> *(Interview with Madhu; March 2018; Sudharan Office, Ramanagaram)*

While the staff had previously returned to the office with almost all payments due to them by 9 a.m., now they spent the whole day going door-to-door trying to coax individuals to repay, returning with no more than a few notes. Madhu said that one of their colleagues had fainted in the field after hours of house visits, while another became ill and had to be hospitalized as a result of the stress faced at the time.

## Recovery and regulation

In the period following the repayment crisis, the staff began finding ways to engage in dialog with other MFI staff and religious leaders, to follow new systems and to learn to handle different loan products. Later they enforced new rules and regulations. They had to work closely with their counterparts in other MFIs, whom they had earlier regarded as competitors, in deciding who should receive loans and in re-scheduling existing loans. They also interacted more with the staff of other MFIs in a formal setting, thanks to the Association for Karnataka Microfinance (AKMi), which put in place a system for dialog between MFIs across the state.

The standoff resulted in the introduction of individual loans (both with and without collateral requirements), which constituted the beginning of a shift away from the celebrated group-based lending which had been at the center of the Grameen model. This shift was not easy on the loan officers; identifying individual clients, disbursing loans and collecting repayments all took longer. Sudharan added further checks and audits and aligned staff pay with financial incentives, based on ratings of the savings groups.

The Reserve Bank of India (RBI) brought the MFI sector under the national credit rating agency, allowing lenders to check outstanding loans and the repayment history of potential borrowers before sanctioning loans. Ramesh felt that this move saved the MFI sector.

## The small finance bank

The 2015 issuing of small finance bank licenses in India led to the expansion and transformation of key MFI players, who received a majority of the licenses. This spearheaded the move toward mainstreaming the finance-for-development sector in India, such that funds for all, including low-income households, would flow from banks and bank-like entities. The motivation behind pushing this change was to provide an opportunity for MFIs to deepen client relationships (Sriram, 2019). With a mandate to continue working in the same locations, SFBs were permitted to accept savings, as well as to make loans to small business units, small and marginal farmers, micro and small industries and unorganized sector entities. They were also authorized to distribute mutual fund units, insurance products and pension products. While their MFI operations continued, SFBs worked as a parallel entity, reaching higher income groups in addition to their former clientele. They had to rethink the ways in which they structured and administered products in order to serve liability accounts. SFBs made their own investments with deposits in order to offer customers returns on savings.

The MFI staff at Sudharan moved to the new SFB, where they worked with banking customers, whose deposits were crucial in order to make the transition, and facilitated the disbursal of secured loans. Ramesh (who now held a senior position in the SFB) said, "Our banking work is overlaying our original network; we still have a team as an MFI who recommend people to us" (Interview with Ramesh; March 2018, Sudharan office Ramanagaram). He added:

> People were apprehensive to save because they thought if someone in the group doesn't repay, then maybe our savings will be taken away. We told them that wouldn't happen, but still the doubt is there.

The staff at the bank had to learn how to convince and reassure potential clients identified by their colleagues in the MFI division. Ramesh said:

> Now that we're becoming a bank, we have to change our mindset and training. You can't treat your customers like asset customers, now they are liability customers.

The staff had to learn more about secured loans and working with men as well as women customers; for the first time, the work of the institution that employed them was not gender-specific.

Ramesh was in charge of identifying branches across South India. He was required to find a balance between urban and rural locations, between brick-and-mortar branches and regions served by banking correspondents, as per the stipulations of the RBI. He interacted with the institutions in which the bank now invested, which included other MFIs. Regarding his own trajectory from NGO worker to a senior role in the bank, he noted:

> We knew the community and we learnt the procedures. Sudharan recognized this and encouraged us; they recognized hard work and gave a lot of opportunity for growth.

Ramesh also appreciated that other field staff that had joined the MFI with him had also grown in their roles. He said:

> The MFI staff have been taken on in the bank; some of them only have a 10th or 12th standard pass but they've had so much training they are using international banking software now. Even bankers with MBAs have problems with some of the software that our field staff is using.

Madhu echoed this, saying that she would help the new bank staff learn the software used by the MFI, while learning from them about banking software. Describing the banking work that she and Lakshmi do, she said, "We collect individual loan repayments, customer deposits and close the ATM every day" (Interview with Madhu; March 2018; Sudharan Office, Ramanagaram), adding that:

> In the MFI we used to put all the cash in bundles and put it in the vault, but now we have to do the flap and signature; there are more operations. It takes time even if everything goes well; then if the accounts don't tally it's a different thing!

The group of staff felt that having been promoted to their present position is an indication that the institution employing them appreciates the knowledge and relationships they brought from the SHG, the hardships they endured during the crisis and their persistence through the recovery period. According to Madhu:

> When they were becoming a bank, my family asked, "What will happen now? Will they hire you if you don't have qualifications to be a bank employee?" But the head of the bank said, "We will take all our old staff and we will train them." Our families appreciate this.

In terms of their personal journeys as bank employees, the staff felt that they had regained the respectability that they had lost during the crisis. At the same time, they were also nostalgic about certain aspects of their earlier roles in the NGO and were very aware of how changes in their position as MFF and bank staff were perceived in the community. As Madhu said, "In Kalyani we were really close to the people with whom we worked, whereas in Sudharan the relationship is only financial."

In Table 13.1 we summarize our findings comparing the three institutional contexts:

## Conclusion

The experiences of this group of field staff across three institutions reveal the distinct and complex financial circuits in which different forms of micro-lending in Ramanagaram have been embedded over a period of 30 years. The changes in the everyday work of the staff, as well as in their social and financial status,

**TABLE 13.1** Comparison of the three models

| Circuits of finance | NGO SHG (1990–2005) | MFI (2006–2017) | SFB (2018–Present) |
|---|---|---|---|
| Source of capital | Savings of the SHG members | International or national private investors | Deposits from the clients<br>Bank refinancing |
| Destination of interests earned | After 1999, loan could be granted by national banks<br>Stay in the SHG for internal loans<br>They go to nationalized banks for external loans | Return to investors | Paid to deposit account holders by the bank |
| Financing of staff salaries | Subsidies and gifts from international aid agencies, and donors | Self-financed by the profit made | Self-financed by the profit made |
| Formal financial institutions involved | Nationalized banks | International investors | Public or Private banks |
| Financial services delivered | Opening of bank accounts<br>Assistance in applying for bank loans | Issuing microfinance loans to joint liability groups | Savings accounts<br>Bank loans to any eligible customer<br>Investment products |
| Staff members role toward the beneficiaries | Facilitators of group saving and lending<br>Providing life skills training<br>Advisers on many aspects of their life | Customer relations<br>Disbursement of loans<br>Repayment collectors | Customer relations<br>Bank teller operators<br>Convincing liability customers to make deposits in the bank |
| Target groups | Low-income women | Low-income women | Women and men with the ability to save and make deposits |
| Accomplishments of the model | Allows women with the ability to save money, the opportunity to earn interest and access to lower cost credit | Provides larger scale access, including those unable to save | Extends mainstream formal financial services to rural and low-income households |
| Challenges encountered | The breakdown of SHGs: inability to repay large bank loans, manipulation by group leaders and bank staff, disruption by the large-scale SGSY program<br>Funding cuts to NGOs following a shift in global discourse in favor of for-profit microfinance | Excessive competition between MFI, lending without discretion drives over-indebtedness<br>Repayment standoff and crisis | Microfinance customers wary of making bank deposits |

reflect the non-linear and multidimensional changes in the relationships between these institutions and profits from lending. Their accounts offer a unique view of the conceptualization and implementation of finance-for-development in India.

In the SHG Bank Linkage model, where the initial emphasis was on the internal lending of savings, all the interest earned went back to group members. When the association with nationalized banks began, the role of the staff was to facilitate access to low-cost credit. They were not employed by the institutions that issued the loans or earned the interest on them. Even if there were problems with the functioning of the SHGs, the staff did not face the burden of loan defaults or losses to their own income. Their relationships with the people they worked with were also unaffected. In the private microfinance model, where capital from wealthy investors is lent to low-income clients at high interest rates, there was a one-directional flow of profits to the institution that employed the staff. Conflict with clients arose because the staff had to demand repayment. In addition, they had to negotiate accusations that they had changed because of the personal financial gains at the MFI, in the form of higher wages and incentives, even if they were not directly collecting the interest on the loans. In the universal banking model, their focus was on convincing customers to make savings deposits with them, as the ones eliciting capital, rather than disbursing credit and demanding repayments. Their clients held secured loans linked to credit scores and concern about collateral and ratings-mediated repayments, unlike unsecured group MFI loans, where the collateral had been the tenuous relationships between clients who were guarantors for each other.

The case of this group of staff is an exemplar for understanding the ways in which national and international flows of finance have shaped micro-credit provisioning in India. The relationship of the staff in question to flows of finance determined the specifics of their work: procedures, targets, incentives, reporting, interactions with management and behavior toward clients. Their accounts illuminate the work of the organizations and individual actors involved in the different models of micro-lending implemented over time. Since the staff served as conduits of credit to the same set of clients, their narratives offer a unique opportunity to understand how transformations in financial circuits from the local and context-specific to the more global and universal have changed the delivery and impact of small loans designed to lift households out of poverty.

## Note

[1] This chapter uses the term field staff instead of loan officers to account for the different roles held prior to, and after, working as MFI employees.

## References

Aitken, R. (2013) 'The Financialization of Micro-credit,' *Development and Change*, 44(3), pp. 473–499. DOI: 10.1111/dech.12027.

Augsburg, B. and Fouillet, C. (2013) 'Profit Empowerment: The Microfinance Institution's Mission Drift,' in Haase, D. (ed.), *The Credibility of Microcredit*. Leiden: Brill, pp. 199–226. DOI: 10.1163/9789004252189_010.

Bylander, M., Res, P., Jacoby, L., Bradley, P. and Pérez, A.B. (2019) 'Over-indebtedness and Microcredit in Cambodia: Moving beyond Borrower-Centric Frames,' *Development Policy Review*, 37, pp. 140–160. DOI: 10.1111/dpr.12399.

Dattasharma, A., Kamath, R. and Ramanathan, S. (2016) 'The Burden of Microfinance Debt: Lessons from the Ramanagaram Financial Diaries,' *Development and Change*, 47(1), pp. 130–156. DOI: 10.1111/dech.12218.

Guérin, I., Guermond, V., Joseph, N., Natarajan, N. and Venkatasubramanian, G. (2021) 'COVID-19 and the Unequalizing Infrastructures of Financial Inclusion in Tamil Nadu,' *Development and Change*, 52(4), pp. 927–951.

Guérin, I., Labie, M. and Servet, J.-M. (eds.) (2015) *The Crises of Microcredit*. London: Zedbooks. DOI: 10.5040/9781350250932.0006.Joseph, N. (2013) 'Mortgaging Used Sari-Skirts, Spear-Heading Resistance,' in Guérin, I., Morvant-Roux, S. and Villarreal, M. (eds.), *Microfinance, Debt and Over-Indebtedness: Juggling with Money*. Routledge Studies in Development Economics, 104, pp. 272–295. DOI: 10.4324/9780203508817.

Kar, S. (2013) 'Recovering Debts: Microfinance Loan Officers and the Work of 'Proxy-Creditors' in India,' *American Ethnologist*, 40(3), pp. 480–493. DOI: 10.1111/amet.12034.

Kumar, P. and Golait, R. (2008) *Bank Penetration and SHG-Bank Linkage Programme: A Critique*. New Delhi: Reserve Bank of India.

Maîtrot, M. (2019) 'Understanding Social Performance: A "Practice Drift" at the Frontline of Microfinance Institutions in Bangladesh,' *Development and Change*, 50(3), pp. 623–654. DOI: 10.1111/dech.12398.

Malegam, Y.H. (2011) *Report of the Sub-committee of the Central Board of Directors of Reserve Bank of India to Study Issues and Concerns in the MFI Sector*. Committee Report, RBI.

Pattenden, J. (2010) 'A Neoliberalisation of Civil Society? Self-help Groups and the Labouring Class Poor in Rural South India,' *The Journal of Peasant Studies*, 37(3), pp. 485–512. DOI: 10.1080/03066150.2010.494372.

Sarker, D. (2013) 'Pressure on Loan Officers in Microfinance Institutions: An Ethical Perspective,' *Journal of Economics and Sustainable Development*, 4(12), pp. 84–88. DOI: 10.7176/JESD/4-12-84.

Siwale, J.N. and Ritchie, J. (2012) 'Disclosing the Loan Officer's Role in Microfinance Development,' *International Small Business Journal*, 30(4), pp. 432–450. DOI: 10.1177/0266242610373687.

Sriram, M.S. (2010) 'Commercialisation of Microfinance in India: A Discussion of the Emperor's Apparel,' *Economic and Political Weekly*, pp. 65–73 [Online]. Available at: http://www.jstor.org/stable/40738497. (Accessed: July 31, 2021).

Sriram, M.S. (2019) 'Financial Inclusion: Agenda for Policy Intervention,' *Vikalpa*, 44(4), pp. 163–166. DOI: 10.1177/0256090919900395.

# 14

# FINANCIAL LITERACY TRAINING IN CAMBODIA AS A TOOL TO FORM BORROWERS' SUBJECTIVITIES

*Phasy Res*

## Introduction

> The subjects of our study struggle with the possibilities and dangers of economic globalization, the threat of endless violence and insecurity, and the new infrastructures and forms of political domination and resistance that lie in the shadows of grand claims of democratization and reform. Once the door to the study of subjectivity is open, anthropology and its practitioners must find new ways to engage particularities of affect, cognition, and moral responsibility, and action.
>
> *(Biehl, Good and Kleinman, 2007, p. 1)*

Inspired by the empirical and theoretical studies of subjectivities (see Biehl, Good and Kleinman, 2007; Ortner, 2005), this case study attempts to understand the processes of subjectivities formation regarding investment-related risk and debt responsibility. The study attempts to do so through the analysis of financial literacy training in Cambodia. In this analysis, the subjectivities of borrowers are formed through the financial lens that reflects a set of values, moralities, logics and possibilities, which are fashioned to serve the needs of finance and to legitimize the financial epistemology (e.g. Guérin, 2012; Swidler and Watkins, 2008; Young, 2010). The financial epistemology regards the interpretation of the world through the lens of the financial investors (see also Chiapello, 2020).

Such attempts to construct the realities, possibilities or moral values to serve the financial needs have been observed in Bangladesh, in India as well as in France (see Karim, 2011; Lazarus, 2020; Young, 2010). For example, Karim (2011) conducted an ethnographic investigation which found that the NGOs (which were

DOI: 10.4324/9781003039679-17

also microfinance providers) appeal to the honor of Bangladeshi women through a shaming technique to achieve full loan recoveries. When Young (2010, p. 618) conducted a study on loan officers, he observed that the officers required their clients to recite an oath to ensure that the use of the money was for the benefit of their family and that debt would be repaid on time. In France, financial education workshops were used as a way to familiarize the population with privatized pension schemes (Lazarus, 2020).

In Cambodia, financial literacy training emerged in response to the widespread household over-indebtedness. An unpublished survey sponsored by microfinance funders ($N = 802$) conducted in Cambodia in 2017 of borrowing households in 12 provinces and Phnom Penh (the capital city),[1] suggested that 28% of households borrowing through microfinance institutions (MFIs) were insolvent, and another 22% were critical or at risk (MFC and Good Return, 2017). In the same year, the National Bank of Cambodia (NBC) and their international partners launched a national campaign on financial education called *Let's Talk Money*. The campaign mainly stressed individual responsibilities for over-indebtedness; it was aired and broadcast by the national radio and television. The campaign was also included in the national educational curriculum. Simultaneously, financial literacy training programs have been implemented by major MFIs and non-governmental organizations (mainly local ones). The funders of these financial literacy programs included the Asian Development Bank (ADB), Australian Aid, the International Fund for Agricultural Development (IFAD), the Food and Agriculture Organization of the United Nations (FAO), the International Labour Organization (ILO), Agence Française de Développement (AFD), the United States Agency for International Development (USAID) as well as a host of smaller international and local organizations.

In light of the rise of financial literacy training programs in Cambodia two main questions arise: First, how is financial literacy training implemented on the ground? Second, how do the local communities respond to the training? Scholars argue that the current financial literacy training is merely a tool to serve the financial institutions, rather than providing technical skills such as the assessment of different forms of risk (e.g., financial, economic, political, environmental, and personal) in doing business (see Bylander and Res, 2020; Guérin, 2012; Lazarus, 2020; Res, 2021b). Additionally, this chapter argues that the current financial literacy program also serves to deepen the financialization of development in Cambodia through the formation of borrowers' subjectivities. Financialization of development refers to a configuration of new kinds of financial markets for development problems, in this case: microfinance as a financial market-based solution for poverty alleviation. I will support my argument by scrutinizing the narrative of embracing an entrepreneurial mindset. The mindset that dictates the willingness to take on risk and to embrace over-indebtedness as an individual responsibility.

It is important to note that, risk is a key form of financial subjectivity, and opening up to risk is crucial for financial expansion. According to Aitken

(2020, p. 371), the key forms of financial subjectivity are neoliberal commitments. The author defines neoliberal commitments as:

> a self that is governed in the name of its own choice and security, an entrepreneurial practice of 'investment' as long-term work on the self, and an ongoing openness to risk as a key to active citizenship.
>
> *(Aitken, 2020, p. 371)*

In line with this understanding, risk is a central theme of this chapter. The ability to shift risk on to borrowers allows MFIs to generate its profit even at the times of COVID-19 crisis in which some borrowers should be granted debt forgiveness.

All the analysis in this chapter is drawn from 18 observations and 15 interviews. In detail, I observed 17 financial literacy workshops led by two major MFIs, called CASH and LOY,[2] and one financial literacy training run by a local NGO. The 18 observed financial literacy workshops were run by three different trainers (two women and one man). In addition, I conducted 15 semi-structured interviews with female participants who attended the CASH MFI financial literacy training. Note that all interviewees were selected by the CASH trainer, which may have shaped the degree of open contestation to MFIs' logic. Despite this limitation, the research was still able to capture how some local community members in this interview openly contested the MFIs' narrative of over-indebted households. The data were collected between July and December 2017.[3] All the trainers were university graduates, from middle-class backgrounds. Two of the three trainers had extensive experience working with development organizations, while participants were mostly women with only primary formal education. Almost all of the participants were from low-income households who engage in farming activities (mung bean and rice). Participating in the observed training was not compulsory, but participants received $2.50 in cash, or a small package of daily products per participation. The CASH training workshop was held over a period of 20 weeks with one hour of class each week (a total of 20 hours). The rest of the training sessions observed were provided on a one-time basis, lasting approximately two to three hours. Due to the familiarity with the trainer, the atmosphere of the CASH workshop was livelier.

The chapter starts by providing a brief background on the microfinance sector in Cambodia, and its relation to development. The following section discusses subjectivities as a framework of analysis. Using this framework, I focus on how (primarily) MFIs shift all the responsibility of household investment-related risk and debt repayment onto borrowers to ensure that debt is repaid at any cost. This chapter also examines how local communities contest the concept of individual household risk and the portrayal of over-indebted households as according to the trainers' vocabulary – reckless and irresponsible. This chapter thus builds on the argument made by Bylander and Res (2020) on the neoliberal logics of financial literacy training. The chapter concludes by raising concerns regarding the reorientation of development policies as a lack of financial resources. It suggests two possibilities for a potential reversal of the public understanding of household investment-related risk and the portrayal of over-indebted households as allegedly reckless and irresponsible.

## Background: the evolution of the microfinance sector in Cambodia

Promoting finance as the central solution to alleviate poverty creates a microfinance sector where the poor are celebrated as champions who can lift themselves out of poverty with their entrepreneurial skills through the allegedly successful use of micro-loan (Bateman, 2010; Kar, 2018; Mader, 2015).[4] In Cambodia, the microfinance sector has undergone rapid transformation over the past three decades. Cambodia opened up as a free market economy in the early 1990s and, at that time, microcredit was provided to the rural poor as part of development programs. These programs were led by international organizations whose main mission was to eradicate poverty. The most well-known and pioneering MFI was the Association of Cambodian Local Economic Development Agencies (ACLEDA), an MFI that sprouted out of a development project originally spearheaded by the United Nations Development Program (UNDP). The majority of Cambodia's large MFIs have their roots in the development sector. A few years after ACLEDA was formed, other international non-governmental organizations (INGOs) in the development field joined the microfinance sector. For example, in 1994, the humanitarian NGO Catholic Relief Services founded a village bank, Theaneakea Phum, which was later bought by an international corporation and renamed LOLC (Cambodia). In 1995, Prasac was started as a development project funded by the European Union (EU), aiming to rehabilitate and support the agricultural sector. AMRET was the result of GRET, a French NGO, experimenting with a project to deliver microcredit to the rural population in Cambodia, and around the same time Irish NGO Concern Worldwide established Angkor Mikroheranhvatho Kampuchea (AMK), OCSD/OXFAM Quebec established Hattha Kaksekar and Kredit was established by World Relief US (Res, 2021a; information extracted from MFIs/bank's annual reports and websites).

By the early 2000s, most of these organizations had transformed and received licenses to operate as MFIs from the National Bank of Cambodia. A decade after the sector's transformation, some scholars began raising concerns that Cambodia had one of the most saturated microfinance sectors in the world (Bylander, 2017; Gonzalez, 2010; Gonzalez and Javoy, 2011; Krauss et al., 2012). At the end of 2009, the microfinance system in Cambodia consisted of 20 licensed MFIs, 26 registered rural credit operators and around 60 NGOs, all of which provided informal financial services throughout the country (NBC, 2009). By 2018, there were 353 MFIs, comprised of seven microfinance deposit-taking institutions, 73 MFIs and 273 rural credit operators (NBC, 2018).

How did this transformation affect the MFIs' commitment to lift low-income households out of poverty? Most of them abandoned their social missions with time, and the pressure is mounting for the few who still maintain a social mission. Similar transformations, where MFIs distanced themselves from their social missions to maximize profits, were also documented in Bangladesh (Karim, 2011) and India (Mader, 2015; see also Kamath and Joseph, 2023, this volume).

As Cambodia's market has further opened to attract international capital and global ventures, there is cause for concern. In 2018, according to a survey of international investors, Cambodia received 8.4% of all microfinance-specific investments in the world (Symbiotics, 2018, cited in Green, 2020a, p. 5). The sector's loan portfolio is ranked second globally after India, a country with a population size almost 85 times larger than Cambodia's (Symbiotics, 2018, cited in Green, 2020a, p. 5). This financing can encourage risky lending (such examples can be seen worldwide, such as the subprime housing mortgage crisis in the late 2000s in the United States), and it can increase the risk of household over-indebtedness.

To date, microfinance in Cambodia is being used to replace a number of development programs including: building decent houses and latrines, paying healthcare costs (Ir Por et al., 2019), funding education, and providing access to clean water (Pimhidzai et al., 2019). During the COVID-19 crisis, microfinance was being promoted and used as a market-based relief and recovery strategy for affected households (see also Brickell et al., 2020). For example, financial institutions have responded by supplying social emergency loans and internal refinancing, where new loans are given to already indebted household (Res, 2021a). An increasing trend of reorienting development policies as a lack of financial resources raises questions regarding what it means to be indebted, and what it means to be a citizen. This reorientation also allows MFIs to actively engage in development policies, in forming the meaning of indebtedness and citizenship. These formations are vital for laying the safe groundwork for microfinance expansion. This leads to the following section, discussing subjectivities as a framework of analysis.

## Subjectivities as a framework of analysis

Subjectivity as a concept allows researchers to unravel the inner mechanisms that shape the ways individuals relate to the world. Subjectivity also provides space for analyzing local contestations or some scholars refer to this as subjective countercurrents (see Ortner, 2005), or the capacity of subjects to reflect. Identifying what is being projected upon the self and the agency to reflect on this, makes the subjectivity of selves a complex concept. As Ortner (2005, p. 45) asserts,

> subjectivities are complex because they are culturally and emotionally complex, but also because of the ongoing work of reflexivity, [and] monitoring the relationship of the self to the world.

Similarly, Biehl, Good and Kleinman (2007, p. 14) state,

> subjectivity is not just the outcome of social control or the unconscious; it also provides the ground for subjects to think through their circumstances and to feel through their contradictions.

Based on this understanding of subjectivity formation – being acted upon and the capacity to reflect – together with a concept of financial subjectivity discussed in Aitken (2020), I attempted to unfold the financial ontology of risk-responsibility and of over-indebtedness: how the reality of risk and over-indebtedness are constructed.

The term *financial ontology* refers to how MFIs and their staff understand the realities of the issues they deal with and, in this specific case, how they understand household investment-related risk-responsibility and over-indebtedness. One needs to understand that over-indebtedness is a potential financial risk for MFIs, so it is in the MFIs' interest to construct different understandings of risk-responsibility, of household over-indebtedness, and of how they are connected. The construction of new realities pertaining to risk-responsibility and over-indebtedness allows MFIs to profit at any cost. This is demonstrated by empirical examples in the following section.

## The construction of risk reality

In the training sessions, MFIs trainers enthusiastically encouraged participants to take out a loan to invest in income-generating activities. For example, Thida, one of the LOY trainers, said "borrowing is not a bad thing, it depends on how you use it" (Observation 3, 24 August 2017, Battambang). Then she went on to define, "a good loan is to increase income while [a] bad loan is to increase expenses." This binary definition illustrates a lack of complex understanding of or an unwillingness to acknowledge the external risk when it comes to household investment. Additionally, being willing to take risks and fail was embraced and highlighted as an entrepreneurial mindset that is a prerequisite for a successful business venture. This was reflected in the CASH MFI training moto: "If you fall, stand up." In the LOY MFI training, Thida asserts, in order to use a loan successfully one needs to possess an entrepreneurial spirit. This was described as being fearless, eager to learn, having the ability to listen, to work hard, being a doer and not letting oneself be put off by criticism.

Across the observed training sessions, the entrepreneurial mindset of investment was taught. All trainers introduced the word *investment* to local communities. As one LOY MFI trainer defined, "investment means [to] use money to create more money," (Observation 3, 24 August 2017, Battambang) while overall in CASH trainings *investment* and *debt repayment* were demonstrated as equally admirable goals. An NGO trainer explained, one needs to be smart in order to make a profit from an investment. As Socheata, an NGO trainer, said, "if you are smart in the business, you will earn some money back, and if you are not smart you might not get any profits" (Observation 10, 30 September 2017, Siem Reap). *Smart* was defined as the ability to make a distinction between investment and expenses. The NGO trainer asserted that the capacity of households to make this distinction will allow them to identify business opportunities in their communities. In terms of microfinance borrowers, they are expected to cultivate the ability to identify business opportunities so that they can utilize a loan in trainers' word productively or successfully. Following the trainers' logic, the unsuccessful use of a loan results in over-indebtedness and this consequence can be understood as a lack of entrepreneurial mindset, spirit and skill.

These examples show how local communities are strongly encouraged to be risk-takers by taking out a loan to invest. At the same time, they are responsible for the risk as they were told repeatedly to repay debt at any cost (this point is further elaborated below). Placing all responsibility of investment-related risk onto indebted households illustrates how MFIs are making profits at any cost. Thus, the repeated failures of business ventures result in accumulated debt for households, while the MFIs accumulate profits. Drawing on my experience in researching the microfinance sector since 2017, no form of systemic debt forgiveness (e.g. personal bankruptcy law) is practiced even during a crisis such as the COVID-19 pandemic (see more details on this in Res, 2021a, 2021b).

## The construction of an over-indebted reality

During the training workshops, instead of directing individuals to, or raising awareness of, the few supporting mechanisms for debt-distressed households, the MFI trainers depict over-indebted households as being reckless and irresponsible. In the CASH MFI sessions, participants were asked to come up with Khmer proverbs that reflect wasteful spending habits. A woman shouted, "just because the elephant shits so much, doesn't mean you should shit as much as an elephant!" Another offered: "The size of the pot matches the size of the stove." Yet another shared, "the sail should be the right size for its boat." In the microfinance world, borrowers must spend proportionally to their income, spending otherwise is considered wasteful. This wasteful spending habit is portrayed as one of the causes of household over-indebtedness. Apart from framing over-indebtedness as spending more than one's ability to earn, the responsibility of over-indebtedness is passed onto borrowers through the discourse of unplanned expenses. The habit of unplanned expense is compared to a leaky pipeline. A leaky pipeline does not know where the water goes, just as unplanned spenders do not know where the money goes.

The most common depiction of recklessness across the MFIs' and NGOs' financial literacy training is the dichotomy of wants versus needs. Despite the reality that the difference between a want and a need expense can be very small for these households, the three trainers made a clear distinction between these two types of expenses. Socheata, an NGO trainer, defined a need expense as something that is essential for survival, such as water, food and shelter, whereas the list of want expenses included cigarettes, alcohol, lotions and makeup. This list of the supposedly want expenses is problematic as it places the sole responsibility on the individual, while disregarding the role of addiction, and societal pressures placed on young women in the Southeast Asian region to achieve fair skin.

The term *recklessness* was also used to describe borrowers who become co-signers to help their neighbors or communities.[5] A scenario was given by Thida, LOY MFI trainer:

> I saw a case where people [were] making a career as a co-signer. Suppose I [was] a borrower and you were a co-signer. I borrow $20,000, and I don't have a co-signer yet, so I ask you to be one. I tell you that I will give you $1,000 or $2,000 if you decide to be my co-signer. Since you want the money, you decide to be one. Then I run away with $20,000 and you get only $1,000 or $2,000. This is an example, but I have seen such cases many times.
>
> *(Observation 18, 19 December 2017, Battambang)*

Drawing on observation 18, one participant protested, "sometimes they are our relatives." Thida sarcastically responded, "well, as you listen to news nowadays relatives are killing each other for money." Thida continued, "if you decide to be a co-signer, please try to memorize this mantra, if they do not repay, it is my…" Participants completed the sentence: "my responsibility." Similarly, a CASH participant raised a question as to what happens if the borrower defaults when they are a co-signer. The CASH MFI trainer asked participants to carefully evaluate their neighbors' ability to repay before deciding to be a loan guarantor. One participant protested: "They are our neighbors who come to us for help, so we have to" (Observation 11, 10 October 2017, Kompong Chhnang). The trainer remarked: "Well, being a helpful and understanding person brings you trouble in this case" (Observation 11, 10 October 2017, Kompong Chhnang). The above dialogues can provoke distrust in the community. This provocation of distrust among community members has been documented in Karim's (2011) book *Microfinance and Its Discontents: Women in Debt in Bangladesh*. The dialogue also illustrates an enforcement of individualized risk and debt responsibilities (see also Bylander and Res, 2020; Guérin, 2012).

### Shifting responsibilities of risk and over-indebtedness

Financial risk and over-indebtedness are identical for MFIs. Thus, to continue the microfinance expansion and to mitigate the financial loss resulting from borrowers' defaults, the responsibilities of risk and over-indebtedness must be shifted onto borrowers. Once these responsibilities are transferred to the individual, MFIs demand that debt must be repaid at any cost. This is strongly emphasized throughout the observed training sessions led by MFIs, but less strongly in the training led by the local NGO. Drawing on an observation 17 made in the morning on 19 December 2017 in Battambang, Thida, the LOY MFI trainer, asked "what is debt?" A village chief responded, "debt, we must repay." A LOY female participant added, "we need to save to repay the debt." Whereas Seiha, a CASH MFI trainer, emphasized, "you should keep money aside every day to repay the debt... Don't forget to add that into an expense, otherwise at the end of the month you will need to borrow in order to repay." (Observation 8, 27 September 2017, Kompong Chhnang). Seiha continued: "Don't worry if your income is less than your expenses because you use it to repay the debt, it is not a bad thing." Seiha's sentence implies that debt forgiveness is unlikely, and that borrowers must prioritize debt repayment over household well-being.

Drawing from the interviews with indebted households, the concept of debt repayment at any cost has become the norm. The existing literature has shown that the debt repayment at any cost has coerced households especially the most vulnerable ones to resorting to risky coping strategies, such as land sale (Green, 2019, 2020b; Green and Bylander, 2021; LICADHO and Sahmakum Teang Tnaut, 2019), distress migration (Bylander, 2014; Green and Estes, 2018; IOM, 2019; LI-CADHO, 2020; Ovesen and Trankell, 2014), withdrawal of children from school or children dropping out of school (LICADHO and Sahmakum Teang Tnaut, 2019) and declining household nutrition through a reduction in food consumption (Seng, 2018). Engaging in such strategies makes debt-distressed households more vulnerable (see more details on this in Res, 2021a). It is important to note that the practice of debt repayment through any means was common even before the existence of the financial literacy training programs. However, what this chapter aims to emphasize that, instead of identifying such practices as problematic, the financial literacy training led by CASH and LOY MFI legitimize them. They are able to do so by drawing on the financial ontology of risk and over-indebtedness as individuals' responsibilities instead of a shared one.

### The contestation of financial subjectivities by local communities

Local communities often contest and resist development projects that bring negative effects and destruction to their communities. For example, the contestation and resistance to city beautification, road construction, hydropower dams, irrigation schemes, timber and mineral extractions and economic land concession in Cambodia as well as in Southeast Asian regions, are well documented (see Bourdier, 2019; Li, 2007; Scott, 1985; Springer, 2015; Tsing, 2005). The contestation and resistance can be passive or provocative, well organized or disorganized. It occurs through language, body language, signs (Hall and Jefferson, 1989; Hebdige, 1979) as well as through a host of provocative actions. For example, Scott (1985, p. 29) documents less visible forms of resistance, which were expressed through daily practices such as "foot-dragging, dissimulation, false compliance, pilfering, feigned ignorance, slander, arson, sabotage and so forth." While in Li's (2007) book, central Sulawesi (Indonesia) highlanders rejected the irrigation and settlement schemes by retreating deeper into the jungle.

Similar to Scott (1985) and Li (2007), this case study attempts to illustrate a contestation of financial subjectivities by local communities. In the following paragraphs, I illustrate two main forms of contestation by the local communities. The first form of the contestation is participants stopped coming to the workshops. The second form is participants offered an alternative understanding of household-related risk and over-indebtedness.

Throughout the 13 consecutive observations of CASH workshops, the number of participants gradually decreased. At one point, the CASH MFIs trainer needed to go from house to house to collect participants. The gradual decrease in participation can be interpreted as individuals not finding the workshop relevant to their daily issues of dealing with a lack of income and indebtedness. The irrelevance of the workshop content to the daily struggles faced by participants is well expressed by a CASH participant who said,

> I don't think the class is effective for debt-distressed households. They are sitting in the class while their mind is wandering off, thinking about how to repay the debt.
>
> *(Interview 15, 11 October 2017, Kompong Chhnang)*

This corroborates with the findings of Guérin (2012, p. 20) who asserts, "financial education programs' frameworks of reference are highly disconnected from ground realities." Non-participation is probably one of the most common and effective forms of how local communities reject the financial subjectivities that are being imposed upon them.

Moreover, in CASH and LOY training sessions, participants challenged the trainers who insisted that participants needed to save in order to meet the debt repayment obligations. In both training sessions, participants were encouraged to set an amount aside before spending any income. However, participants repeatedly raised concerns that they could not save any money because they did not have any income in the first place. The MFI trainers dismissed the concerns of income irregularity raised by the local communities and saw it as an excuse not to save. According to the author's observations, participants disagreed silently with such logic.

In the LOY training, participants questioned the merit of an entrepreneurial mindset as a way to determine the degree of success of a productive loan usage. As a LOY participant voiced, "well, it depends on your fate, good fate and bad fate" (Observation 18, 19 December 2017, Battambang). Since almost all participants were farmers, the fate described here refers to whether the fields receive sufficient rain and other uncontrollable risks that farmers encounter when borrowing to invest in their farms (see also Res, 2021a). Scholars have raised concerns over the environmental risks and livelihood risks that indebted households are facing (see Bylander, 2015; Res, 2021a). This contestation indicates that investment-related risk can be external and thereby it is sometimes beyond an individual's ability to control such risks.

Similarly, during the 15 in-depth interviews with CASH participants, they indicated that investment-related risks that are beyond the control of individuals were also contributing factors to over-indebtedness. Systematically, all participants who personally knew over-indebted households identified structural drivers of over-indebtedness. This challenges the MFIs' discourse of over-indebtedness (see also Bylander et al., 2019). For example, one interviewee stated: "When the mung beans farm does not yield as expected, they don't have enough money to repay" (Interview 2, 26 September 2017, Kompong Chhnang). Another participant added that her neighbor became over-indebted because the household took out a loan to invest in a pig farm. However, the pigs caught a disease and died. Since then, her neighbor has been over-indebted. These two examples show that local communities identify external factors as drivers of over-indebtedness. This offers an alternative understanding of household-investment-related risk and of over-indebtedness than the ones that MFIs construct.

## Conclusion

Drawing on the empirical data, this chapter concludes that financial literacy training workshops conducted in Cambodia are merely a tool to form the financial subjectivities of borrowers. This subjectivities formation is crucial for preparing a safe and stable foundation for the continuation of microfinance expansion. Since the MFI sector is increasingly saturated and facing a growing risk of default, there is an urgent need for a strong foundation to allow the sector to continue its expansion.

As this chapter shows, MFIs shift the responsibilities of risk and over-indebtedness onto borrowers through the discourse of an entrepreneurial mindset as well as by depicting over-indebted households as reckless and irresponsible. By doing so, MFIs demand that debt must be repaid at any cost. Drawing on my research experience in the microfinance sector since 2017, debt forgiveness is not practiced systemically (see also Res, 2021a). Although participants are actively rejecting the formation of such subjectivities, and understand that drivers of over-indebtedness are often external or structural, the practices of debt repayment at any cost have become the norm. This norm has far-reaching implications in the community beyond the financial literacy training (see more on the doctrine of debt obligation in Graeber, 2011; Guérin and Kumar, 2020; Phlong, 2009).

Moreover, this chapter addresses the MFIs' efforts to reorient development policies as a lack of financial resources. This reorientation can impair citizens not be able to imagine alternative possibilities for development (see Bateman, 2010; Escobar, 1995; Mader, 2015). For example, Mader (2015, p. 37) asserts, "the microfinance system is increasingly making diverse problems of poverty into problems of finance and no longer problems of politics, redistribution or social action." Therefore, in order to address this concern, this chapter suggests two possibilities. Critical financial literacy scholarship suggests that instead of focusing on individual behavior, financial literacy should empower citizens by increasing their understanding of "the role of finance in society and to fight for financial regulation" (Hutten et al., 2018, cited in Lazarus, 2020, p. 397). In line with this demand, a reverse narration regarding financial literacy training is needed. First, this would imply that local communities are encouraged to critically question the legitimacy and effectiveness of microfinance as a development strategy. Second, it would be important to re-narrate that household investment-related risks can be external, that risk can be the result of weather extremes, global financial crises, a pandemic, etc. Through such countercurrent efforts, it is hoped that an increasing number of communities will stand in solidarity with debt-distressed households in demanding national mechanisms that allow systematic debt forgiveness.

## Acknowledgment

I would like to thank Dr. Maryann Bylander who has guided me throughout this research. Dr. Ève Chiapello, Dr. Anita Engels and anonymous reviewers who have provided critical and effective comments for the improvement of this chapter. Special thanks to Dr. Eduardo Gonçalves Gresse who worked with me closely to incorporate feedback. My appreciation goes to the financial literacy training providers, and all participants in this research, without whom this research would not have been possible.

## Notes

1 The reason that this survey findings are not published probably due to the lobby made by Cambodia Microfinance Association (CMA).
2 Both names are pseudonyms. Loy is the Khmer word for money.
3 The data was collected through a collaborative project between Dr. Maryann Bylander and the author.
4 This chapter uses microfinance instead of microcredit to emphasize its formal nature.
5 Apart from mortgaging land or housing certificate of ownership as a collateral, having a co-signer is a compulsory element for microfinance loan.

## References

Aitken, R. (2020) '"A Machine for Living" The Cultural Economy of Financial Subjectivity,' in Mertens, D. and Van der Zwan, N. (eds.), *International Handbook of Financialization*. London: Routledge, pp. 369–379.

Bateman, M. (2010) *Why Doesn't Microfinance Work? The Destructive Rise of Local Neoliberalism*. London: Zed Books.

Biehl, J., Good, B.J. and Kleinman, A. (eds.) (2007) *Subjectivity: Ethnographic Investigations*. Berkeley: University of California Press, pp. 1–17.

Bourdier, F. (2019) 'From Confrontation to Mediation: Cambodian Farmers Expelled by a Vietnamese Company,' *Journal of Current Southeast Asian Affairs*, pp. 1–22. DOI: 10.1177/1868103419845537.

Brickell, K., et al. (2020) 'Compounding Crises of Social Reproduction: Microfinance, Over-indebtedness and the COVID-19 Pandemic,' *World Development*, 136, pp. 1–4. DOI: 10.1016/j.worlddev.2020.105087.

Bylander, M. (2014) 'Borrowing across Borders: Migration and Microcredit in Rural Cambodia,' *Development and Change*, 45, pp. 284–307. DOI: 10.1111/dech.12080.

Bylander, M. (2015) 'Depending on the Sky: Environmental Distress, Migration and Coping in Rural CAMBODIA,' *International Migration*, 53(5), pp. 135–147. DOI: 10.1111/imig.12087.

Bylander, M. (2017) 'Micro Saturated: The Promises and Pitfalls of Microcredit as a Development Solution,' in Brickell, K. and Springer, S. (eds.), *The Handbook of Contemporary Cambodia*. Abingdon: Routledge, pp. 64–75.

Bylander, M. and Res, P. (2020) '"If You Fall, Stand Up Again": The Moral Nature of Financial Literacy in the Global South,' *Development & Change*, pp. 1–28. DOI: 10.1111/dech.12627.

Bylander, M., Res, P., Jacoby, L., Bradley, P. and Blobel Pérez, A. (2019) 'Over-indebtedness and Microcredit in Cambodia: Moving beyond Borrower-Centric Frames,' *Development Policy Review*, 37(S2), pp. O140–O160. DOI: 10.1111/dpr.12399.

Chiapello, È. (2020) 'Financialization as a Socio-Technical Process,' in Mader, P., Mertens, D. and Van der Zwan, N. (eds.), *International Handbook of Financialization*. London: Routledge, pp. 81–91.

Escobar, A. (1995). *Encountering Development: The Making and Unmaking of the Third Word*. Princeton, NJ: Princeton University Press.

Gonzalez, A. (2010). *Is Microfinance Growing Too Fast?* Washington, DC: Microfinance Information Exchange.

Gonzalez, A. and Javoy, E. (2011) *Microfinance and the Role of Policies and Procedures in Saturated Markets and during Periods of Fast Growth* [Online]. Available at: https://www.findevgateway.org/paper/2011/09/microfinance-and-role-policies-and-procedures-saturated-markets-and-during-periods. (Accessed: 26 March 2021).

Graeber, D. (2011) *Debt: The First 5,000 Years*. Brooklyn, NY: Melville House.

Green, W.N. (2019) 'From Rice Fields to Financial Assets: Valuing Land for Microfinance in Cambodia,' *Royal Geographical Society*, 44(4), pp. 749–762. DOI: 10.1111/tran.12310.

Green, W.N. (2020a) 'Financial Landscapes of Agrarian Change in Cambodia,' *Geoforum*. Article in Press. DOI: 10.1016/j.geoforum.2020.02.001.

Green, W.N. (2020b) 'Regulating Over-indebtedness: Local State Power in Cambodia's Microfinance Market,' *Development and Change*, 51(6), pp. 1429–1453. DOI: 10.1111/dech.12620.

Green, W.N. and Bylander, M. (2021) 'The Exclusionary Power of Microfinance: Over-indebtedness and Land Dispossession in Cambodia,' *Sociology of Development*, 7(2), pp. 202–229. DOI: 10.1525/sod.2021.7.2.202.

Green, W.N. and Estes, J. (2018) 'Precarious Debt: Microfinance Subjects and Inter-generational Dependency in Cambodia,' *Antipode*, 51(1), pp. 129–147. DOI: 10.1111/anti.12413.

Guérin, I. (2012) *Households' Over-indebtedness and the Fallacy of Financial Education: Insights from Economic Anthropology*. Microfinance in Crisis Working Papers Serie, 1. Paris: Paris I Sorbonne University and IRD.

Guérin, I. and Kumar, S. (2020) 'Unpayable Debt: Debt, Gender, and Sex in Financialized India,' *American Ethnologist*, pp. 1–15.

Hall, S. and Jefferson, T. (1989) *Resistance through Rituals: Youth Subcultures in Post-war Britain*. London: Routledge.

Hebdige, D. (1979) *Subculture: The Meaning of Styles*. London and New York: Routledge.

IOM (2019) *Debt and the Migrant Experience: Insights from Southeast Asia*. Bangkok: International Organization for Migration.

Ir Por, B.J., Asante, A.D., Liverani, M., Jan, S., Chhim, S. and Wiseman, V. (2019) 'Exploring the Determinants of Distress Health Financing in Cambodia,' *Health Policy and Planning*, 34, pi26–pi37. DOI: 10.1093/heapol/czz006.

Kamath, R. and Joseph, N. (2023) 'From social workers to proxy-creditors to bank tellers: financialization in the work of microcredit field staff in a South Indian town,' in *Financializations of Development: Global Games and Local Experiments*, this volume.

Kar, S. (2018) *Financializing Poverty: Labor and Risk in Indian Microfinance*. Stanford, CA: Stanford University Press.

Karim, L. (2011) *Microfinance and Its Discontents: Women and Debt in Bangladesh*. Minneapolis: University of Minnesota Press.

Krauss, A., Lontzek, L., Meyer, J. and Frommelt, M. (2012). *Lack of Access or Crowded Markets? Toward a Better Understanding of Microfinance Market Penetration* [online]. Available at: https://www.findevgateway.org/paper/2012/08/lack-access-or-crowded-markets-towards-better-understanding-microfinance-market. (Accessed: 26 March 2021).

Lazarus, J. (2020) 'Financial Literacy Education: A Questionable Answer to the Financialization of Everyday Life,' in Mader, P., Mertens, D. and Van der Zwan, N. (eds.), *International Handbook of Financialization*. London: Routledge, pp. 390–399.

LICADHO (2020) *Driven Out: One Village's Experience with MFIs and Cross-border Migration* [online]. Available at: https://www.licadho-cambodia.org/reports.php?perm=229. (Accessed: 26 March 2021).

LICADHO and Sahmakum Teang Tnaut (2019) *Collateral Damage: Land Loss and Abuses in Cambodia's Microfinance Sector* [online]. Available at: https://www.licadho-cambodia.org/reports.php?perm=228. (Accessed: 26 March 2021).

Li, T.M. (2007) *The Will to Improve: The Governmentality, Development, and the Practices of Politics*. Durham: Duke University Press.

Mader, P. (2015) *The Political Economy of Microfinance: Financializing Poverty*. Hampshire: Palgrave Macmillan.

MFC and Good Return (2017) *Over-indebtedness Study Cambodia II: Final Report*. Phnom Penh: Microfinance Center and Good Return (unpublished).

NBC (2009) *2009 Annual Report* [online]. Available at: https://www.nbc.org.kh/download_files/publication/annual_rep_eng/Annual%20Report%202009%20Eng.pdf. (Accessed: 26 March 2021).

NBC (2018) *2018 Annual Report* [online]. Available at: https://www.nbc.org.kh/download_files/publication/annual_rep_kh/annual_report_2018_kh.pdf. (Accessed: 26 March 2021).

Ortner, S.B. (2005) 'Subjectivity and Cultural Critique,' *Anthropological Theory*, 5(1), pp. 31–52. DOI: 10.1177/1463499605050867.

Ovesen, J. and Trankell, I.-B. (2014) 'Symbiosis of Microcredit and Private Money-lending in Cambodia,' *The Asia Pacific Journal of Anthropology*, 15, pp. 178–196. DOI: 10.1080/14442213.2014.894116.

Phlong, P. (2009). *Informal Credit Systems in Cambodia*. MA Thesis, Northern Illinois University.

Pimhidzai, O., Tong, K., Anantavrasilpa, R., Popovic, A., Mel, S., Sanchez, M. and Miguel, E. (2019) *Microfinance and Household Welfare. Cambodia Policy Note*. Washington, DC: World Bank Group.

Res, P. (2021a) 'Microfinance in Times of COVID-19: Consumer Protection and the Loan Restructuring Process in Cambodia,' released by *The Center for Khmer Studies* [online]. Available at: https://khmerstudies.org/covid-19-impacts-on-microfinance-and-vulnerable-households/. (Accessed: 26 March 2021).

Res, P. (2021b) 'Policy Brief: Personal Bankruptcy Law as an Entry Point for Credit Consumer Protection Dialogue,' *The Asia Foundation*, pp. 70–80 [online]. Available at: https://policypulse.org/wp-content/uploads/2021/11/NPF-Booklet-Final%E2%80 %8B%E2%80%8B%E2%80%8B%E2%80%8B-small.pdf. (Accessed: 26 March 2021).

Scott, J.C. (1985) *Weapons of the Weak Everyday Forms of Peasant Resistance.* New Haven, CT: Yale University Press.

Seng, K. (2018) 'Revisiting Microcredit's Poverty-Reducing Promise: Evidence from Cambodia: Microcredit's Poverty-Reducing Promise,' *Journal of International Development*, 30(4), pp. 615–642. DOI: 10.1002/jid.3336.

Springer, S. (2015) *Violent Neoliberalism: Development, Discourses, and Dispossession in Cambodia.* New York: St. Martin's Press.

Swidler, A. and Watkins, S. (2008) '"Teach a Man to Fish": The Sustainability Doctrine and Its Social Consequences,' *World Development*, 37(7), pp. 1182–1196. DOI: 10.1016/j. worlddev.2008.11.002.

Tsing, A.L. (2005) *Friction: An Ethnography of Global Connection.* Princeton, NJ and Woodstock: Princeton University Press.

Young, S. (2010) 'Gender, Mobility and the Financialisation of Development,' *Geopolitics*, 15(3), pp. 606–627. DOI: 10.1080/14650040903501104.

# 15

# THE FINANCIALIZATION OF THE FIGHT AGAINST POVERTY

## From microcredit to social capitalism[1]

*Isabelle Guérin*

Financialization is a process of converting something – a good, service, entity or situation – into a source of financial value and financial profit. This is particularly true of the fight against poverty, one of the key components of development policies since the 1990s (Roy, 2010). Microcredit had paved the way, creating an unprecedented business model promising to combine social progress and financial profitability. While this so-called double bottom line rhetoric persists among some microcredit promoters, ground realities highlight significant trade-offs. Today we know that promises of financial profitability have been kept (at least for some of the microcredit providers) but that they hardly combine with the achievement of social progress and improvement of clients' well-being.[2] We also know that the double bottom-line rhetoric has mainly had the effect of financializing microcredit and its clients, converting them into financial assets and creating a complex financial architecture enabling this conversion (Aitken, 2013; Mader, 2015; Servet, 2015).

Yet the rhetoric of the double bottom line continues to infuse the world of development. Drawing on lessons from microcredit, this chapter explores the contradictions of the double bottom-line rhetoric. The apparent success of microcredit has inspired the creation of a wide range of pro-poor markets in various sectors such as sanitation, health, food and energy, expected to promote both financial gains and social goods and build what can be called social capitalism. On the investor side, microcredit has also contributed to the expansion of so-called impact investing. Building on the same rhetoric – promising social and financial gains to investors – impact investing developed after the 2008 crisis (Chiapello, 2020; Chiapello and Knoll, 2020). Largely driven by microcredit, impact investing in developing countries is now seeking to diversify. The drifts of microcredit allow us to question the promises of this advent form of financialization of development.

DOI: 10.4324/9781003039679-18

The first section describes how microcredit has actively contributed to the financialization of anti-poverty policies by "problematizing" poverty as a problem of "under-investment" (Chiapello, 2020). This problematization is based on several hypotheses and promises: the existence of a latent and large demand, the automatic improvement of welfare and the share of value. The next sections examine these three assumptions in light of field observations. They suggest that, in many cases, social capitalism imposes demands more than it meets demands, privatizes poverty and public goods more than it improves welfare, and hoards wealth more than it shares it since most risks are subcontracted to local populations. The chapter draws on two types of data: a wide range of secondary data, and my own fieldwork, conducted over the last 20 years in South India and various parts of the world. In addition to in-depth surveys of microcredit users, I rely on numerous discussions and debates with managers of microcredit organizations and social investment funds, engineers working on the design of social capitalism goods, staff of bilateral and multilateral development organizations, and staff of large companies now involved in social capitalism. For reasons of space, I focus on general trends, without going into the diversity and complexity of situations, motivations and rationales underlying financialization processes.

## From microcredit to social capitalism: the extension of the financialization of anti-poverty policies

The initial goal of microcredit was to allegedly "democratize" finance. By allowing assetless people to access small unsecured loans, the objective of microcredit was to help the poor to start or consolidate a business, better manage their household cash flows and thus improve their well-being and escape poverty. In the 1970s, the first promoters of microcredit were non-profit organizations such as non-governmental organizations (NGOs), cooperatives or development banks. Over time, microcredit has gradually evolved into a vast financial industry with strict profitability criteria. Microcredit has been financialized, in the sense that it is now considered a financial asset, which in turn required the invention of new valuation methods and rating agencies, the creation of complex financial circuits and specific forms of intermediation and the use of sophisticated risk management and securitization methods (Aitken, 2013). Subsidies still exist, but they are so-called "smart subsidies" supposed to help providers achieve financial sustainability.

This process of financialization has entailed an intense work of legitimization and "problematization" (Chiapello, 2020). This implied first of all conceptualizing poverty as a financial problem (Mader, 2015). This consisted then of considering that the financial profitability of microcredit providers was both possible and necessary in order to scale up and ensure the sustainability of the supply (Servet, 2015). This transformation has been a chaotic process in the last two decades, leading to serious crises of over-indebtedness, generating much criticism and disillusionment (Hudon, Labie and Szafarz, 2019), sometimes leading to reversals (see Kamath and Joseph, this volume). Even today, the question of the trade-off between financial gains and social goods continues to be the subject of thorough inquiries (Morduch and Ogden, 2019).

However, despite strong criticisms and very mixed evidence regarding its real social impacts, microcredit has paved the way for a new conception of poverty: one of the great successes of microcredit is certainly to have convinced the investment world that the double bottom line is a realistic objective (Morduch and Ogden, 2019). Muhammad Yunus, the founder of the famous Grameen Bank, played a decisive role in this area. After winning the Nobel Peace Prize in 2006, Yunus took advantage of his success to transform his microcredit business model into a "social business" model applied to a wide range of private goods and services (cell phone, agricultural inputs, textile crafts, fish farming) and to public goods and services such as health, education or energy (Yunus, 2009). Here too, the legitimization discourse is twofold: access to essential goods is seen above all as a problem of under-investment; and the market is seen as the only way to ensure a large-scale and sustainable response over time.

Yunus' social business model prohibits the payment of dividends to shareholders and considers that social value can be a sufficient reason to attract investors (Yunus, 2009, p. 25). By contrast, the Bottom of the pyramid (BoP) approach, another popular pro-poor market ideology, relies on financial profitability to attract investors. For BoP promoters, paying dividends to investors is the only way to attract the maximum amount of financing, and this in turn will allow scaling up and massive impact. Initiated in the 1990s by the economist C. K. Prahalad, the BoP approach went through successive stages and really developed in the 2000s. It is likely that Vikram Akula, founder of one of the first microcredit organizations listed on the stock exchange [Swayam Krishi Sangham (SKS), now Bharat Financial Inclusion Limited (BFIL)], and active promoter of the BoP approach, has greatly contributed to its dissemination.

Today, a wide range of actors and entities in the world of development, and now in the corporate and financial sector, have taken up the idea of expanding pro-poor markets as a source of both social value and financial profits. In 2007, the financial arm of the World Bank took up the subject by calculating the size and amount of potential pro-poor markets, by continent and by sector (Hammond, 2007). The largest bilateral development organizations have followed. A new actor appears on the development scene: the corporate sector, now seen as a major stakeholder in the fight against poverty, both in terms of its financial strength and its ability to innovate. NGOs remain a major player, but need to reconsider their business model since subsidies have lost their legitimacy or are conditioned by the search for financial sustainability. Last but not least, pro-poor markets are also driven by social investors. In the early days of impact investing, microcredit accounted for most of it in developing countries (CGAP, 2013), and it still accounts for a significant part of it today, albeit unevenly across countries.[3] Impact investing keeps on growing in volume, especially in developing countries.[4] Social investors are constantly looking for new opportunities, and new pro-poor markets appear as a promising option.

New partnerships involving social investment funds, corporations, NGOs, consultants, sometimes researchers and public entities are thus emerging to give birth to social capitalism, and this in various sectors. Let us give a few examples, which are by no means exhaustive. In the field of insurance, social capitalism offers products similar to those of traditional markets such as health insurance, life insurance or, specifically for farmers, agricultural insurance against climatic risks. In the field of energy, social capitalism offers solar lamps and low-burning stoves designed to reduce wood consumption and alleviate the toxic effects of burning wood. In the field of food, social capitalism offers nutrition supplements and yoghurts with added vitamins to fight malnutrition. In the field of sanitation, social capitalism offers different types of latrines. The use of new technologies (mobile phones and smart cards) is giving birth to all kinds of "e-services" from mobile phone banking to "e-health" (see Al Dahdah, this volume) and "digital brokers", who sell support services for the use of new technologies to illiterate people (Schwittay, 2011). Durable consumer goods (solar lamps, latrines, ovens), but also connections to water and gas networks are sometimes sold on credit, thanks to partnerships with microcredit providers (Mader, 2015).

It is difficult to really measure the extent of these pro-poor markets and their degree of financialization. We are certainly in a "weak form of financialization" (Chiapello, 2020), in the sense that a multitude of stakeholders are designing and experimenting with new models, but the number of projects and financial volumes are still low (Laville, Juan and Subirats, 2020).

At this stage, it is certainly useful to draw lessons from microcredit since its false promises are equally valid. The first promise is the existence of a latent and large demand, which would simply have to be met and which thus offers prospects of financial gains. The automatic improvement of well-being is the second assumption. This would be achieved through the creation of small businesses, improved financial management of household budgets or the access to various basic and public goods such as health care, sanitation, lighting or pollution reduction. So-called value sharing is the third assumption. The design of specific methods of production and distribution that create "local value" is a leitmotif, which is expected to create wealth, reduce distribution costs and "fairly" share the value in question (Santos, 2012). Examined in light of ground realities, these assumptions prove to be very fragile.

## Meeting or imposing demands?

The promoters of social capitalism believe that poverty emanates first and foremost from wants and unsatisfied demands that only need to be filled. In the mid-2000s, the financial arm of the World Bank, the International Finance Corporation, estimated that the potential market was 4 billion customers, with a total purchasing power of $4.7 trillion (Hammond, 2007). "The solutions are ultimately market oriented and demand driven", write the authors of the report (Hammond, 2007, p. 7) and the idea of a so-called demand-driven approach is a recurring argument of social capitalism promoters [see, for instance, Benioff and

Southwick (2003); CARE and ENEA (2011); Cormack and Gudeman (2009); Faber and Naidoo (2014)].

The analysis of actual demands, however, calls for more caution, both in terms of quantity and quality. The problems that social capitalism claims to solve are very real, but the solutions do not correspond to the economic, social, and cultural complexity of ground realities. For potential customers, social capitalism goods and services raise many questions and uncertainties, and therefore resistance. Uncertainties are first technical: do the product characteristics meet local constraints? Uncertainties are then social: how do goods and services affect status and position in the local hierarchies? Uncertainties are also moral: how do goods and services comply with local values and norms?

Let us look first at microcredit. Microcredit supply has grown steadily over the last 15 years, and the scale of banking exclusion (estimated at approximately 2 billion adults) implies tremendous expansion prospects (IFC, 2017). There is no doubt that there is a demand: in many contexts, real incomes are falling or stagnating, expenses are increasing and therefore people need cash. A first deviation from the official objective can be noted here: where demand exists, it is much more often for consumption and making ends meet than for entrepreneurship (Bateman, 2010; Cull and Morduch, 2017).

The scale of demand also needs to be questioned. Among those who are regarded as so-called financially excluded, not all need credit. The features of market credit are the first restriction. Although local populations are often accustomed to the nuts and bolts of debt, they are not very familiar with formal procedures with their set repayment schedules for a predetermined price and period, which are so different from the negotiability and flexibility of "informal" arrangements (Johnson, 2013). Furthermore, people have their own "fiduciary culture" (Shipton, 2010). Microcredit is supposed to replace expensive informal sources of credit. However, informal sources of credit can play an important role in providing a sense of identity and belonging to a group (Guérin, Morvant-Roux and Villarreal, 2013). Barriers may also be moral with respect to credit itself, sometimes considered as a source of dishonour and disgrace, as observed among slum dwellers in West-Bengal (Kar, 2018) or in rural Morocco (Morvant-Roux et al., 2014). In some rural contexts, mortgage-type loans can be considered a real offence because they threaten to separate people "from home, from kith and kin, and from ancestral graves", as observed in rural Kenya (Shipton, 2009, p. ix).

Insurance is another financial service in vogue, but its uptake is much more improbable. The very principle of insurance – payment in anticipation of a risk that, by definition, is not sure to happen – sits uncomfortably with the local systems of representations based on the principles of reciprocity ("I help you, you'll help me in the future") (Churchill, 2002, pp. 384–385; Gautier et al., 2016). Insurance is both a prediction of the future, and in some cases, an estimate of the price of life (life insurance), and of nature (agricultural or climatic insurance). This may contradict local views of life and nature as sacred and priceless, as observed in various places and periods of history (Fourcade, 2011; Zelizer, 1978).

It explains in great part contemporary forms of resistance observed in China (Chan, 2009), rural India (Fouillet, 2007; Kar, 2018) and Mexico (Gautier et al., 2016). Today, most microinsurance is sold as a package with a microcredit, restricted to covering the repayment of the loan and therefore mainly intended to secure the lender (Kar, 2018).

There is less hindsight for other forms of advent pro-poor markets, but the lack of attention to ground realities seems to be valid as well. We shall take the example of low-combustion stoves. Although their advantages are crystal clear in theory, their use is more uncertain. Resistances vary according to context, social groups and type of oven. They may stem from different cooking techniques, unsuitability for cooking quickly or large quantities, loss of the social space that traditional ovens allow, as observed in various parts of rural Mexico (Catalán-Vázquez et al., 2018; Sesan, 2012). In environments where food preparation and cooking methods form an integral part of often-female family know-how, and hence identities and modes of recognition, it is easy to imagine how hard it is to change habits whatever the arguments in terms of savings, environmental protection, and individual and family health.

Similar observations can be made for latrines. The benefits seem obvious in terms of public health and women's safety (open defecation puts them at risk of rape, finding a suitable place can be very time-consuming and stressful). But here again, the real demand for latrines is sometimes far from that expected. We know that the perceptions of clean and dirty, defilement and disgust, purity and impurity vary a surprising amount from one society and social group to the next (Douglas and Isherwood, 1980). This is most often ignored by latrine designers, especially in India (Desai, McFarlane and Graham, 2015).

One may wonder whether the objective of social capitalism is to respond to a demand, as its promoters suggest, or to impose a demand. In the pioneering field of microcredit, it is clear that supply often exceeds demand. Constrained by profitability and therefore growth objectives, credit providers often deploy multiples techniques to push clients into debt, regardless of their real needs. These include door-to-door promotion campaigns (and now, increasingly, by mobile phone), moral pressure and exploitation of the specific profile of customers through techniques inspired by psychology and marketing, alliances with consumer goods companies, allocation of a new loan before the previous one has been repaid (Fouillet et al., 2016; Guérin, Labie and Servet, 2015; Guérin, Morvant-Roux and Villarreal, 2013).

## Fighting poverty or individualizing and privatizing poverty eradication?

In many cases, local people have very good reasons to resist. In theory, the products of social capitalism are supposed to improve welfare. This is their *raison d'être*. In practice, this is far from being the case, simply because of the poor quality of the products. The lack of quality reflects first a flawed vision of poverty

eradication and public goods. Both are confined to a private and individual problem, whereas they involve a systemic and structural approach. The lack of quality
also reflects profitability constraints. Too often, the qualities of the product are
less thought out in relation to the specificities and constraints of the end-users but
more to attract financiers and ensure the financial sustainability of the provider.

Here again, microcredit has led the way. Services are often of poor quality for
two main reasons: a high cost, often higher than the return on the investment
financed by the credit (and the gap is even higher when the microcredits are actually used for consumption, which is often the case) and standardized features,
both in terms of amounts and repayment terms. These standard terms are small
loans, repayable on a regular basis (weekly or monthly). This standardization
does not fit well with seasonal (such as agriculture) or irregular activities, and
with investment applications, which would require higher amounts considered
too risky by microcredit providers. High cost and product standardization are
the only way to meet the profitability requirements of promoters and investors.

More fundamentally, claiming to combat poverty through the creation of
microenterprises and financial management presupposes a purely individual conception of poverty. The poor are held responsible for their own situation and capable of coping on their own. Not only is credit only one constraint among many
in the barriers to enterprise creation, but local markets have a systemic feature
that social capitalism ignores: entrepreneurs struggle to grow simply because they
lack customers and if a poor starts a business, a neighbouring business is likely
to close down (Bateman, 2010; Guérin, Labie and Servet, 2015). By enabling
borrowers to make ends meet, microcredit serves primarily to offset irregular
and low wages and the absence or inadequacy of social protection (Guérin,
Morvant-Roux and Villarreal, 2013).

These two problems – poor quality and individualization of the problem to
be solved – seem to be equally true for many other social capitalism products.
Some goods break down quickly and are designed in such a way that users cannot
repair them themselves (Cross, 2013). Regarding latrines, bad quality includes for
instance a poor ventilation due to lack of adequate construction or materials, poor
cleanliness maintenance due to lack of water, which is even more troublesome
when toilets are adjacent to a kitchen (Desai, McFarlane and Graham, 2015).

Where the products of social capitalism are collective or public goods, the
lack of concern for the infrastructure of these collective or public goods is highly
problematic. Social capitalism promoters are often only concerned with end-user
access to the service and barely give any thought to the infrastructure so vital
to its quality (Baron et al., 2019). Such is the case with individual water and gas
connection services when the general supply system suffers from multiple dys-
functions, as observed in Argentina (Isaurralde, 2017) and south-India (Mader,
2015). Such is also the case with latrines devoid of any sanitation systems, as
observed in Vietnam (Reis and Mollinga, 2012), agricultural insurance sold in
situations where there is a total lack of any policy to mitigate agricultural and climate risks (price volatility, drought, land degradation, etc.), as observed in rural

India (Da Costa, 2013). Such is also the case for health insurance and healthcare information measures when the healthcare is defective in its health centres, doctors or medication, as observed in various parts of the world (Gautier et al., 2016). In many cases, social capitalism does no more than distribute products that could be called "humanitarian" (Redfield, 2012) in the sense that they are designed to temporarily and often inadequately offset the failings of the state in providing public goods.

## Sharing wealth and risks or hoarding wealth and subcontracting risks?

Among social capitalism advocates, the development of methods of production and distribution that create local value is a leitmotif said to create wealth, reduce distribution costs and fairly share value. The raison d'être of microcredit is to help the poor get wealthier. With the extension of pro-poor markets to a wide range of products, the idea is also to regenerate local economies capable of creating wealth for a wide range of stakeholders, from local populations to social investors. The report from the IFC, the World Bank's financial branch, takes up the idea of "localizing value creation" based on an array of forms of "ecosystems of vendors or suppliers" ranging from franchises to independent sellers and user communities (Hammond, 2007, p. 10). The creation of a market, however, and whatever it may be, implies taking risks. Given the multiple resistances described above, the risks are very high. And yet, pressed by financial constraints, the promoters of social capitalism refuse to take risks that are in fact often largely and invisibly sub-contracted to local populations (Elyachar, 2012).

Here again, the case of microcredit is emblematic, as has been amply demonstrated. Due to financial profitability constraints, many microcredit organizations have adopted a minimum tolerance for default, delegating financial risk management to clients. This zero tolerance toward repayment is the culmination of the financialization of microcredit and translates into worrying problems of clients' over-indebtedness (Guérin, Labie and Servet, 2015). The same applies to investors, most of whom, for example, refuse to lend in local currency, which means that local microcredit providers are those that bear the foreign exchange risks (Sinclair, 2012).

The delegation of risks is observed at another level: the sale. Microcredit promoters rely on credit agents who often have precise portfolio objectives and incentives, both in terms of the number of clients, volume lent and quality of repayments. Given the degree of social and moral resistance they face, these loan officers have to work hard to legitimize the presence of new lenders in the local political arena. They may have to build alliances with various sorts of local power structures, as observed in south-India (Guérin and Kumar, 2017), to build trust with customers, as observed in Paraguay (Schuster, 2015), to overcome moral reticence, whether it is the negative image of the moneylender; as observed in West Bengal (Kar, 2018) or the negative image of the debt itself, as observed in

Morocco (Morvant-Roux and Roesch, 2015). Beyond the paid staff, microcredit group leaders often do part of this hard work for free (Guérin and Kumar, 2017).

The case of microcredit is emblematic because by definition, like any financial relationship, it involves taking risks. However, the question arises for other goods and services: when they sell poorly or not at all, when the effects do not live up to expectations and cause more harm than good, who bears the risks?

The case of Yogurt for Power, in Bangladesh, is instructive in this regard. Yogurt for Power is a partnership between the Grameen foundation and the foundation of the multinational Danone, the world's third-largest dairy products company. The initiative is presented by Yunus himself as the pioneering example of successful social business after microcredit (Yunus, 2009). The initial objective was to support an entire agro-food chain, from the rearing of dairy cows to the distribution of vitamin-rich yogurts. Detailed field analyses describe the failures of successive experiments, linked to the scepticism of local populations toward these female street vendors daring to challenge the dominant patriarchal order because of their presence in the public space, offering yoghurts with an inconclusive consistency or taste, and what is more, at prohibitive prices (Faivre-Tavignot, Lehmann-Ortega and Moingeon, 2010; Servet, 2013). Obviously, the question of risk-taking has been overlooked. It can be assumed that the cost paid by the company is minor due to tax exemptions (Servet, 2013), while the high price has certainly been paid by female yoghurt sellers, many of whom went into debt to sell perishable products that the population did not want.

Risk transfer through subcontracting of sales has also been observed for highly nutritious baby food in Madagascar (Pleuvret et al., 2010) or e-services in Bangladesh (Huang, 2017) and Costa Rica (Schwittay, 2011). Subcontracting is either done directly to individuals, often poorly paid, or first to NGOs, which then subcontract to individuals. To date, there are few detailed analyses of the genealogy of the products of social capitalism. There is reason to fear, however, that the case of Yogurt for Power is not unique. In South India, for nearly two decades, I have observed various attempts to create production chains in the fields of handicrafts and food processing inspired by social capitalism. They emerge and decline with a scenario that repeats itself over and over again: products that are poorly designed or even at odds with local habits (mushrooms, paper glasses, candles), or products intended for an urban market but of insufficient quality and uncompetitive in relation to manufactured products (textiles, handicrafts, cosmetics or cleaning products).

## Conclusion

Social capitalism is an attempt to financialize the fight against poverty by creating new markets that are both capable of serving the poor and attracting social investors. Inspired by the apparent success of microcredit and its double bottom-line rhetoric, these pro-poor markets claim to be demand-driven, improve welfare and share value. Yet, the same microcredit drifts seem to be on the horizon. Local demand is very different from what is imagined by social capitalism promoters, and sometimes does not exist. The products offered are of poor quality, they do not fit well with local constraints, social norms and cultural practices. Moreover, many of these products do not bring the expected welfare since they require much deeper structural measures, investments and policies that are hardly compatible with the short-term financial gains expected by investors. Such measures include the creation of local markets for micro-entrepreneurs, social protection for informal workers and infrastructures for collective and public goods. Last but not least, value sharing hardly takes place since an important part of the risks are subcontracted to local populations. Ultimately, many social capitalism initiatives look like risky experiments for which local populations pay a large part of the price.

The financialization of microcredit, one of the flagship anti-poverty measures of the last decades, has had three major consequences on the structure of microcredit markets. For providers, it has meant the creation of solid entities, operating in stable environments and capable of attracting investors. Yet these providers are few in numbers. For clients, it has meant selecting the most profitable, willing to borrow regularly and able to pay on time. There are also few of them. This has had a third consequence, which is very damaging for the whole sector: an excessive concentration of investments and therefore of supply in a few fields only. This can be observed at different scales: in economically and politically stable regions of the world, in few providers capable of absorbing large investments, and finally in a narrow segment of clients (Fouillet et al., 2016; Sinclair, 2012). With the expansion of social capitalism into many other products, the same process can be feared: an excessive concentration on the few profitable products, to the detriment of the whole range of goods, services and infrastructures that are unprofitable but desperately needed by the poor.

## Notes

1  I sincerely thank the three editors for their very constructive comments and patience.
2  For a recent overview, see for example (Hudon, Labie and Szafarz, 2019).
3  Precise data are hard to get given the diversity of definitions of "impact investing", "financial services", "development financial institutions". One may however refer to GIIN data (GIIN, 2019).
4  According to GIIN data, impact investing assets worldwide grew by 17% per year between 2014 and 2018 (compound annual growth rate). Middle-East-North-Africa and South Asia experienced the highest rates (43 et 24%, respectively (GIIN, 2019, p. 2)).

## References

Aitken, Rob (2013) 'The Financialization of Micro-Credit,' *Development and Change* 44(3), pp. 473–499. DOI: 10.1111/dech.12027.

Al Dahdah, Marine. (2023) '"Top up your healthcare access": mobile money to finance healthcare in sub-Saharan Africa,' in *Financializations of Development: Global Games and Local Experiments*, this volume.

Baron, Catherine, Joshua Greene, Philip Mader and Solène Morvant-Roux (2019) *Water-Microcredit Models and Market Inclusion: Shifting Debts and Responsibility*, IDS Working Paper 522. Brighton: IDS.

Bateman, Milford (2010) *Why Doesn't Microfinance Work? The Destructive Rise of Local Neoliberalism*. London: Zed Books.

Benioff, Marc, and Karen Southwick (2003) *Compassionate Capitalism, How Corporations Can Make Doing Good an Integral Part of Doing Well*. New York: Career Press.

CARE, and ENEA (2011) *Les Grandes Entreprises et Le BoP (Bas de La Pyramide)*. Paris: CARE/ENEA [Online]. Available at: https://www.carefrance.org/ressources/docume nts/1/246,2011-20-20CARE-ENEA-20Consulting-20-.pdf. (Accessed: 30 June 2022).

Catalán-Vázquez, Minerva, Rosario Fernández-Plata, David Martínez-Briseño, Blanca Pelcastre-Villafuerte, Horacio Riojas-Rodríguez, Laura Suárez-González, Rogelio Pérez-Padilla and Astrid Schilmann (2018) 'Factors that Enable or Limit the Sustained Use of Improved Firewood Cookstoves: Qualitative Findings Eight Years after an Intervention in Rural Mexico,' *PLoS ONE* 13(2). DOI: 10.1371/journal.pone.0193238.

CGAP. 2013. "Where Do Impact Investing and Microfinance Meet?" CGAP Brief [Online]. Available at: https://www.cgap.org/research/publication/where-do-impact-investing-and-microfinance-meet. (Accessed: 30 June 2022).

Chan, Cheris Shun-ching (2009) 'Creating a Market in the Presence of Cultural Resistance: The Case of Life Insurance in China,' *Theory and Society* 38(3), pp. 271–305. DOI: 10.1007/s11186-008-9081-1.

Chiapello, Eve (2020) 'Financialization as a Socio-Technical Process,' in Mader, P., Mertens, D. and van der Zwan, N. (eds.), *The Routledge International Handbook of Financialization*, pp. 81–91. London and New York: Routledge.

Chiapello, Eve and Lisa Knoll (2020) 'Social Finance and Impact Investing. Governing Welfare in the Era of Financialization,' *Historical Social Research/Historische Sozialforschung* 45(3), pp. 7–30. DOI: 10.12759/hsr.45.2020.3.7-30.

Churchill, Craig (2002) 'Trying to Understand the Demand for Microinsurance,' *Journal of International Development* 14(3), pp. 381–387. DOI: 10.1002/jid.882.

Cormack, P. and R. Gudeman (2009) *Responsible Capitalism. Essays on Morality, Ethics and Business*. London: Publisher first.

Cross, Jamie (2013) 'The 100th Object: Solar Lighting Technology and Humanitarian Goods,' *Journal of Material Culture* 18(4), pp. 367–387. DOI: 10.1177/1359183513498959.

Cull, Robert and Jonathan Morduch (2017) *Microfinance and Economic Development*. Policy Research Working Paper 8252. Washington: World Bank.

Da Costa, Dia (2013) 'The "Rule of Experts" in Making a Dynamic Micro-Insurance Industry in India,' *Journal of Peasant Studies* 40(5), pp. 845–865. DOI: 10.1080/03066150.2013.857659.

Desai, Renu, Colin McFarlane and Stephen Graham (2015) 'The Politics of Open Defecation: Informality, Body, and Infrastructure in Mumbai,' *Antipode* 47(1), pp. 98–120. DOI: 10.1111/anti.12117.

Douglas, Mary and Baron Isherwood (1980) *The World of Goods*. Harmondsworth: Penguin Books.

Elyachar, Julia (2012) 'Next Practices: Knowledge, Infrastructure, and Public Goods at the Bottom of the Pyramid,' *Public Culture* 24(1 [66]), pp. 109–129. DOI: 10.1215/08992363-1443583.

Faber, Emmanuel and Jay Naidoo (2014) 'Innover Par La Mobilisation Des Acteurs: 10 Propositions Pour Une Nouvelle Approche de l'aide Au Développement.' Paris: Ministère des Affaires étrangères et du Développement international. [Online]. Available at: https://

www.vie-publique.fr/rapport/36718-innover-par-la-mobilisation-des-acteurs-10-propositions-pour-une-nouve. (Accessed: 30 June 2022).

Faivre-Tavignot, B., B. Lehmann-Ortega and B. Moingeon (2010) 'Le Social Business, Laboratoire d'apprentissage Des Stratégies de Rupture,' *Revue Française de Gestion* 208–209(9), pp. 175–189. DOI: 10.3166/RFG.208-209.175-189.

Fouillet, Cyril (2007) 'La Gestion Des Risques Climatiques: Quel Rôle Pour La Microassurance?,' *Autrepart* 4, pp. 199–212.

Fouillet, Cyril, Isabelle Guérin, Solène Morvant-Roux and Jean-Michel Servet (2016) 'De Gré Ou de Force: Le Microcrédit Comme Dispositif Néolibéral,' *Revue Tiers Monde* 1, pp. 21–48. DOI: 10.3917/rtm.225.0021.

Fourcade, Marion (2011) "Cents and Sensibility: Economic Valuation and the Nature of 'Nature,'" *American Journal of Sociology* 116(6), pp. 1721–77.

Gautier, Lara, Isabelle Guérin, Albino Kalolo and Annabelle Sulmont (2016) 'Micro-Health Insurance: The User Perspective,' *Private Sector Development* 25, pp. 36–38.

GIIN (2019) *Annual Impact Investor Survey 2019*, Global Impact Investing Network [Online]. Available at: https://thegiin.org/research/publication/impinv-survey-2019. (Accessed: 30 June 2022).

Guérin, Isabelle, Marc Labie and Jean-Michel Servet (eds.) (2015) *The Crises of Microcredit*. London: Zed Book.

Guérin, Isabelle and Santosh Kumar (2017) 'Market, Freedom and the Illusions of Microcredit. Patronage, Caste, Class and Patriarchy in Rural South India,' *The Journal of Development Studies* 53(5), pp. 741–754. DOI: 0.1080/00220388.2016.1205735.

Guérin, Isabelle, Solène Morvant-Roux and Magdalena Villarreal (eds.) (2013) *Microfinance, Debt and over-Indebtedness: Juggling with Money*. London and New York: Routledge.

Hammond, Allen L. (2007) *The Next 4 Billion: Market Size and Business Strategy at the Base of the Pyramid*. Washington: International Finance Corporation/World Bank Institute [Online]. Available at: https://www.wri.org/publication/next-4-billion. (Accessed: 30 June 2022).

Huang, Julia Qermezi (2017) 'The Ambiguous Figures of Social Enterprise: Gendered Flexibility and Relational Work among the IAgents of Bangladesh,' *American Ethnologist* 44(4), pp. 603–616. DOI: 10.1111/amet.12560.

Hudon, Marek, Marc Labie and Ariane Szafarz (eds.) (2019) *A Research Agenda for Financial Inclusion and Microfinance*. Cheltenham: Edward Elgar Publishing.

IFC (2017) *Strategy and Business Outlook FY18-FY20. Creating Markets and Mobilising Private Capital*. Washington, DC: International Finance Corporation.

Isaurralde, Magdalena (2017) 'L'accès Aux Services En Réseau Par Le Microcrédit: Un Palliatif Au Retrait de l'État et Du Service Public?,' *Revue Internationale Des Etudes Du Developpement* 2, pp. 193–214. DOI: 10.3917/ried.230.0193.

Johnson, Susan (2013) 'Debt, over- Indebtedness and Wellbeing: An Exploration,' in Guérin, I., Morvant-Roux, S. and Villarreal, M. (eds.), *Microfinance, Debt and Over-Indebtedness*, pp. 64–85. London: Routledge.

Kamath, Rajalaxmi, and Joseph, Nithya. (2023) 'From social workers to proxy-creditors to bank tellers: financialization in the work of microcredit field staff in a South Indian town,' in *Financializations of Development: Global Games and Local Experiments*, this volume.

Kar, Sohini (2018) *Financializing Poverty: Labor and Risk in Indian Microfinance*. Stanford: Stanford University Press.

Laville, Jean-Louis, Maïte Juan and Juan Subirats (eds.) (2020) *Du Social Business à l'économie Solidaire: Critique de l'innovation Sociale*. Toulouse: Erès.

Mader, Philip (2015) *The Political Economy of Microfinance: Financializing Poverty*. Basingstoke: Palgrave Macmillan.

Morduch, Jonathan and Timothy N. Ogden (2019) 'The Challenges of Social Investment through the Lens of Microfinance,' in Hudon, M., Labie, M. and Szafarz, A. (eds.), *A Research Agenda for Financial Inclusion and Microfinance*, pp. 12–26. Cheltenham: Edward Elgar Publishing.

Morvant-Roux, Solène, Isabelle Guérin, Marc Roesch and Jean-Yves Moisseron (2014) 'Adding Value to Randomization with Qualitative Analysis: The Case of Microcredit in Rural Morocco,' *World Development* 56, pp. 302–312. DOI: 10.1016/j.worlddev.2013.03.002.

Morvant-Roux, Solène and Marc Roesch (2015) 'The Social Credibility of Microcredit in Morocco after the Default Crisis,' in Guérin, I., Labie, M. and Servet, J.M. (eds.), *The Crises of Microcredit*, pp. 113–130. London: Zed Book.

Pleuvret, E., O. Bruyeron, L. Arnaud and S. Trèche (2010) 'Le Business Social Pour Lutter Contre La Malnutrition Infantile: L'élaboration d'un Service de Vente d'aliments Pour Jeunes Enfants à Madagascar (1997–2008),' *Coopérer Aujourd'hui*, 69, Paris: GRET [Online]. Available at: https://horizon.documentation.ird.fr/exl-doc/pleins_textes/divers12-08/010051117.pdf. (Accessed: 30 June 2022).

Redfield, Peter (2012) 'Bioexpectations: Life Technologies as Humanitarian Goods,' *Public Culture* 24(1 [66]), pp. 157–184. DOI: 10.1215/08992363-1443592.

Reis, Nadine and Peter Mollinga (2012) 'Water Supply or "Beautiful Latrines"? Microcredit for Rural Water Supply and Sanitation in the Mekong Delta, Vietnam,' *ASEAS–Austrian Journal of South-East Asian Studies* 5(1), pp. 10–29. DOI: 10.4232/10.ASEAS-5.1-2.

Roy, Ananya (2010) *Poverty Capital. Microfinance and the Making of Development*. London and New York: Routledge.

Santos, Filipe M. (2012) 'A Positive Theory of Social Entrepreneurship,' *Journal of Business Ethics* 111(3), pp. 335–351. DOI: 10.1007/s10551-012-1413-4.

Schuster, Caroline (2015) *Social Collateral Women and Microfinance in Paraguay's Smuggling Economy*. Stanford: Stanford University Press.

Schwittay, Anke (2011) 'The Marketization of Poverty,' *Current Anthropology* 52(S3), pp. S71–S82. DOI: 10.1086/656472.

Servet, Jean-Michel (2013), 'Le Social Business et La Société de Consommation Pour Les Pauvres. Comment Une Nouvelle Philanthropie Prétend Solvabiliser Le Bas de La Pyramide,' in Guérin, I. and Selim, M. (eds.), *A Quoi et Comment Dépenser Son Argent? Hommes et Femmes Face Aux Mutations Globales de La Consommation*, pp. 15–40. Paris: L'Harmattan.

Servet, Jean-Michel (2015) *La Vraie Révolution Du Microcrédit*. Paris: Odile Jacob.

Sesan, Temilade (2012) 'Navigating the Limitations of Energy Poverty: Lessons from the Promotion of Improved Cooking Technologies in Kenya,' *Energy Policy* 47, pp. 202–210. DOI: 10.1016/j.enpol.2012.04.058.

Shipton, Parker MacDonald (2009) *Mortgaging the Ancestors: Ideologies of Attachment in Africa*. Yale: Yale University Press.

Shipton, Parker MacDonald (2010) *Credit between Cultures: Credit between Cultures: Farmers, Financiers, and Misunderstanding in Africa*. New Haven: Yale University Press.

Sinclair, Hugues (2012) *Confessions of a Microfinance Heretic. How Microlending Lost Its Way and Betrayed the Poor*. San Francisco: Berret-Kohler publications.

Yunus, Muhammad (2009) *Creating a World without Poverty: Social Business and the Future of Capitalism*. New York: Public Affairs.

Zelizer, Viviana A. (1978) 'Human Values and the Market: The Case of Life Insurance and Death in 19th-Century America,' *American Journal of Sociology* 84(3), pp. 591–610.

# 16

# FINANCIALIZING DEVELOPMENT

## Processes and implications

*Anita Engels, Eduardo Gonçalves Gresse and Ève Chiapello*

## Financializations of development around the world

This book aims to contribute to the understanding of interactions between financialization and development by focusing on a number of initiatives and policies
carried out in the name of development. The collection of case studies gathered for this purpose shows a multifaceted picture of how the financialization of
economies and societies is produced by development efforts. This approach leads
us to consider multiple intertwined processes of financialization, and therefore to
use *financializations* in plural for the title of the book. We classified the financializations of development into two different categories that organize the two parts
of the book, the presentation of the cases and the situations studied.

In the first part (*financing development*), we looked at some of these financialization processes that are orchestrated in institutions of the Global North,
where banks, investors, foundations and other powerful and globally operating
actors create discourses and financial instruments to attract financial flows for
the implementation of development goals in the Global South. Through the
dissemination of a financial gap narrative, these influential actors weave local
development issues into a global discourse on development as a funding problem. With such a narrative framing, tackling poverty and other development
problems requires financialized solutions. The case studies dealing with Development Finance Institutions (DFIs), private mega-foundations, banks, national
and supranational development agencies provide ample insights into the complex
processes through which the circuits for financing development policies become
increasingly financialized by relying on concepts, practices and techniques of
private finance, as well as on private financial institutions.

In the second part (*finance as development*), we explored financialization processes that started even earlier, with the aim to improve the monetary and financial

DOI: 10.4324/9781003039679-19

inclusion of people. The case studies assembled in this second part include initiatives in the Global South pressing for the insertion of recipients into new formal financial circuits. We discussed experiments of building financial infrastructures in developing countries, providing financial literacy and bankability, and actively creating cash and mobile money demands, together with new channels of access to meet these demands.

A cursory overview has already demonstrated that financialization does little to improve the living conditions of vulnerable people in the Global South. On the contrary, financialized development policies often deepen existing dependencies or create new ones. The financial gap is not closed, yet power shifts take place that reinforce financial actors as development agents and leave them with substantial capacity to attain financial goals through their engagement in development issues. Financialization processes create favorable regulation and conditions for financial actors, so that the financial risks are lowered or taken over by public institutions, while a constant or even expanding flow of profits is secured by investors. Many case studies have shown that this comes at the expense of development goals, such as poverty eradication, health, education and food security.

This chapter summarizes the key findings of the case studies presented in this book. We first revisit the different studies to identify the different financializing operations described in the chapters (Tables 16.1 and 16.2). Financialization is not an abstract process that occurs inexorably for functional reasons. Instead, it is a process driven by individuals and organizations working to change how things are done, with whom and how the money is handled and channeled (Chiapello, 2019). It is due to the work of a diverse group of actors that the sphere of influence of private financial and banking actors is gradually expanding, as well as their ability to extract value from other businesses, non-profit organizations, governments and households. This extended influence and profit-making by financial actors is a central element of financialization (Epstein, 2005). The case studies collected in this book help us understand these processes, with a particular focus on development issues.

## The work of financializing development

Despite the diversity of the situations described, it is possible to find common elements in the financialization processes described in the chapters. To explore these processes, we draw on the framework proposed by Chiapello (2020), which analyzes financialization work through the identification of three interconnected operations that are also regarded as logically ordered stages of financialization.

First, *problematization* refers to the processes of redefining things and activities through the lens of finance. This operation involves categorizing and interpreting specific problems and appropriate solutions using the narratives and perspectives of investors. In the case of development policies, this amounts to reformulating development problems in terms that establish the reliance on private financial actors, or their tools and techniques, as a solution. This first financialization stage presupposes a significant amount of discursive work, installing specific cognitive schemes, using a vocabulary derived from finance and framing the questions in such a way that the financialized answer is self-evident.

The second operation, *tangibilization*, relates to the ways in which ideas, expectations or promises are translated into explicit tools and devices aimed at enabling financial actors to address development issues through the establishment of figures and benchmarks. It therefore involves the production of knowledge and expertise to make potential objects of investment, their qualities and associated risks, tangible. Tangibilization thus gives embodiment to the investors' visions by identifying and quantifying what is worth investing, assigning value and including it in reports, as well as in optimization calculations and investment decisions. It is a matter of making visible, for investors in particular, the existence of development projects or initiatives ready to welcome their commitment. Significant "investments in form" (Thévenot, 1984) are required to convert the general narratives of the first stage into quantified arguments. Tools shaping the world, producing a financialized view of it, and offering affordances to financial actors, are put in place. Once, at this stage, the work of financialization is well advanced, there are financialized narratives and data sets, calculations and technical innovations opening the way toward the actual involvement of private finance in development policies and programs.

Nevertheless, it is only with the third and last stage, *financial structuring*, that the financialization process is complete. This operation builds financial links between private finance and development policies. Financial structuring consists of organizing monetary flows to create financial circuits and products aimed at attracting investments. This stage requires the mobilization of specific competences, (principally legal and financial) to bring about change in the legal and regulatory frameworks, and to elaborate cleverly structured financial operations. Creating a financial circuit largely proceeds from the work of law writing; defining the entities that receive funds managed under certain criteria by specific people and signing contracts with other entities that organize monetary exchanges and lay down the terms for such transactions. Financial structuring, therefore, requires the mobilization of profit-seeking professionals and specific competences, in particular legal and financial, to enable change in regulatory frameworks and elaborate strategic financial operations.

As Chiapello (2020, p. 85) explains,

> problematization, tangibilization and financial structuring are generic operations that are not exclusively related to financialization. These operations become part of a financialization process when they are embedded in financialized valuation.

In this book, we identified two main types of problematization of development issues, which inform the two parts of the book.

The cases in the first part (*financing development*) problematize the issue of development in terms of a financial gap; that is, a lack of money. It is because there is not enough money to meet investment needs, for example to finance the UN Sustainable Development Goals (SDGs), that it is important to imagine new financing methods that could attract private finance. This type of problematization leads to the reduction of all development problems to the question of finding the necessary funds.

The cases gathered in the second part (*finance as development*) present a different problematization of development. Here, the focus centers on the capacity of individuals to participate in a modern monetary economy. Once included in the monetary economy, they would be able to develop themselves economically and ensure their own income. The development of market exchanges and monetary transactions is seen as both a sign of development and one of its conditions (GDP is typically a measure of the monetized economic sphere).

The following tables (Tables 16.1 and 16.2) summarize how each of the cases in the book exemplifies the three types of operations. A final column highlights the consequences of these financialization processes, as discussed in the respective chapters.

The 15 case studies summarized in Tables 16.1 and 16.2 unearth the concrete operations of financializing development, along with the substantial work and effort involved in those processes. The case studies also shed light on the consequences of the financializations of development.

With regard to the first financialization operation (*problematization*), the case studies show a wide range of narrative shifts through which key concepts are reframed. With the first type of problematization, which emphasizes a financing gap as the main problem for development, all doors are opened to the ecology of financial actors, such as banks and other financial institutions, private investors, private service providers and private foundations. Financial gap narratives serve to embed financial instruments in development policies and programs. Development problems are increasingly assessed through the eyes of finance (self-assessment, project planning, evaluation processes, etc.) and reframed in a convenient way for financial actors. Market-based solutions are imagined, and social problems are transformed into investment opportunities. With the second type of problematization, which considers financialization as an end in itself, the subjects of development are turned into loan recipients. They become objects of financial inclusion, bancarization, financial literacy and cash transfer programs. This process highlights their roles as consumers or entrepreneurs, instead of citizens. Moreover, the target objects of development policies (e.g. infrastructure, poverty reduction, health and education) are all reframed according to financialized perspectives.

While the tables above summarize *problematization* in two simple common operations, the columns show a rich collection of concrete steps toward *tangibilization* and *financial structuring*.

As mentioned above, *tangibilization* relates to the translation of ideas into management tools, devices and quantifications. It comprises the construction of

**TABLE 16.1** Analysis of the "financing development" cases (part 1)

| Problematization: | Innovative financing systems and instruments are required to attract money from private actors and to close the development financing gap | | |
|---|---|---|---|
| Author(s): Case Study | Tangibilization (metrics, tools, "investment in forms") | Financial Structuring (special types of financial channeling) | Consequences |
| Ducastel, Bourblanc and Adelle: *DFIs investment in agriculture* | Standard financial risk management (not adapted to specific agriculture requirements). Environmental and social guidelines. | Opening the capital of DFIs to private finance. Investment through private financial intermediaries. Blending finance facilities. | Lack of investment in agriculture. Strong selectivity: prioritization of capital-intensive investment (e.g. sugar or palm oil) in agricultural production. No increase in funds. |
| Ronal: *Private equity (PE) investment of DFIs* | Financialized expertise. Impact assessment tools de-coupled from financial decisions. | Creation of a sovereign PE fund. Blended finance structuring (use of tax money to guarantee or de-risk private finance investment). | Development understood as a financial market opportunity. Hybridization of public intervention logic with financial investment logic. |
| Mah: *EU blended finance policy* | New rules for calculating ODA. | Blended finance facilities. | The instrumentalizing of development aid by the new EU foreign policy. Development aid increasingly oriented toward helping private actors to invest in the Global South. |
| Grubbauer and Hilbrandt: *City Credit worthiness initiative* | Training academies to turn cities into credible lenders on capital markets. Online self-assessment tool. | Technical assistance facilities targeted toward subnational authorities, to help them attract private finance. | Move development finance from national to local scale. Potential conflicts between national and local governments. Vulnerability of cities that are not regular players in financial markets. |
| Bayliss and Van Waeyenberge: *Public Private Partnerships (PPP) in infrastructure* | Standardized project preparation and platform development for advertising potential investees. Building of PPP units. Regulation changes. | Public Private Partnerships. Provision of public money for de-risking and securing private profits (numerous financial facilities). | State conceived as a commissioner rather than a provider of services. Infrastructure policy captured by finance. |

*(Continued)*

| Problematization: | Innovative financing systems and instruments are required to attract money from private actors and to close the development financing gap | | |
|---|---|---|---|
| *Author(s): Case Study* | *Tangibilization (metrics, tools, "investment in forms")* | *Financial Structuring (special types of financial channeling)* | *Consequences* |
| Gresse and Preusser de Mattos: *Financialization of SDGs* | Asset-allocation guidelines. Stock-exchange sustainability index. Valuation methods to assign monetary value to SDGs. | Creation of SDG-related funds. | Increasing communication around sustainable investment, without concrete action toward sustainable development. No binding regulation, only private initiative. |
| Ehrenstein: *Global Health partnership Gavi* | Independent expert recommendations (epidemiology statistics and cost-benefit calculations). Pricing system. | Shaping of markets via Advanced Market Commitments. Aid used to incentivize vaccine producers. Governments still buy the vaccines. | Under-procurement of vaccines that are not included. Private intellectual property over public goods (vaccine) not challenged. Overprized production. |
| Alenda-Demoutiez: *Development Impact Bonds (DIBs)* | Working group to prepare the financial device. Contracting the terms of impact. Defining the metrics. | Invention of DIBs (private finance repaid with interest). Complex structuring involving philanthropic, governmental and venture (impact investing) capital. | Governance of social projects oriented toward financial interests. Negation of conflicts between actors of development projects. Development money is used to provide interests to private foundations. Tackling poverty converted into an investable issue. |

**TABLE 16.2** Analysis of the "finance as development" cases (part 2)

| Problematization | To solve development problems, it is crucial to increase the capacity of individuals to participate in a modern monetary economy and to support private entrepreneurship | | |
|---|---|---|---|
| Author(s): Case Study | Tangibilization (metrics, tools, "investment in forms") | Financial Structuring (special types of financial channeling) | Consequences |
| Langevin, Brunet-Bélanger and Lefèvre: *Philanthrocapitalism of Mastercard Foundation* | Scaling competition for financial service startups, mentoring and digital platform technologies. | Financial support to Fintech start-ups and entrepreneurs. Technical agreement and co-development with Mastercard. | The company's foundation helps develop digital payments, which are the source of the company's profits. Money and data flow from developing economies to the centers of accumulation. |
| Al Dahdah: *Mobile money and health access* | Digital platform connecting healthcare centers to health wallets (mobile money). Incentive programs. | The private platform attracts development money. Subsidized incentive program to convince the population to use the platform. Telecommunication companies as financial intermediaries. | Aid to the health sector is diverted from public institutions to private digital service providers. Individual health data for sale. Privatization of the payment infrastructures channeling public money. |
| Gronbach: *Social Cash Transfer (SCT) in South Africa* | Design of cash transfer scheme. | Public scheme of SCT. Digitalization of cash distribution and use of a private financial intermediary. Use of SCT as collateral for loans. | Authoritarian deduction and extortion of money by the service provider. Collateralization of social benefits. Rising household debt and financial exploitation of the poor. |
| Villarreal: *Conditional Cash Transfer (CCT) programs* | Design of cash transfer scheme. Conditionalities (such as financial education). | Public scheme of cash transfers. Private banks as an intermediary for CCT. Connection with a micro-credit scheme. | Forced bancarization. Inclusion of local financial circuits into global circuits. |

(Continued)

| Problematization | | To solve development problems, it is crucial to increase the capacity of individuals to participate in a modern monetary economy and to support private entrepreneurship | | |
|---|---|---|---|---|
| Author(s): Case Study | Tangibilization (metrics, tools, "investment in forms") | Financial Structuring (special types of financial channeling) | Consequences |
| Kamath and Joseph: Evolution of micro-finance organizations in South India | Establishment of various, increasingly financialized institutional and organizational settings. Employee training. | Creation of for-profit entities invested by national or foreign capital. | Social workers independent from financial institutions are converted into financial employees in charge of financial discipline. Drawing micro-borrowers into global financial circuits. Bancarization. |
| Res: Financial literacy trainings | Content and methods of the financial training. | Prioritize debt repayment. | Shift responsibilities of over-indebtedness onto the borrowers. Formation of subjectivities around risk and debt responsibilities. |
| Guérin: Pro-poor markets and social investors | Design of specific production methods supposedly able to combine financial gains with social goods. | Entrepreneurship. Creation of businesses in sanitation, health, food and energy. Attraction of private (social) investors. | Risks borne by local population. Prioritize profitable goods, services and infrastructure over needed ones. Often poor services. |

digital platforms, financial risk management tools, asset-allocation guidelines, sustainability indices, impact assessment tools and self-assessment tools. This is accompanied by the metering and valuation of work at different levels. For example, the calculation of Official Development Assistance (ODA) by the underlying OECD Committee (DAC-OECD) is changed and complemented by new indicators. Financialization work also requires staff with specific capabilities and mindsets, namely those able to shape and manipulate the new tools. Some development institutions explicitly hire staff with a financial background. In other case studies, much effort is invested in training and educating the recipients of aid to turn them into financially literate, bancarized consumers.

The operation of *financial structuring* usually supports the injection of capital from private investors into development policies and initiatives. New types of financial products can be invented, as in the case of Development Impact Bonds (DIBs). New financial vehicles with sustainable promises are advertised, such as SDG-related funds. However, what is striking is that substantial public funds must be committed prior to private investments in development goals. Without such commitment of public money, private investors are not interested. Public funds and development finance are used to leverage private finance. Blended finance arrangements aim to de-risk private investors and guarantee a certain rate of return (Gabor, 2021). The public sector is also very often the end payer, such as with public-private partnerships (PPP). Building an investable world also requires the construction of new markets (e.g. for certain vaccines) or at least the reshaping of social providers (such as NGOs) that need to become investable, private companies (see the case of microfinance, Kamath and Joseph, 2023, this volume, and Mader, 2015). Philanthrocapitalist foundations prefer providing seed capital to new ventures rather than making grants. Social programs and social policies are transformed to meet the interests of financial actors, which ultimately supersede the needs of the recipients. Local and context-specific financial circuits are connected to global circuits through international IT, financial companies or foreign capital investment. These financial links change the social quality of local networks and communities. Overall, the case studies reveal that public resources have been channeled to private actors, and there is a flow of resources from local communities in developing economies to the centers of capital accumulation.

In sum, the case studies show many examples of how the financializations of development transform development goals, the processes of giving and receiving aid, and even the subjectivities of the recipients as they are gradually turned into financialized consumers and invested entrepreneurs. In the next section, we discuss in more detail some consequences of these processes for development.

## Consequences of financializing development

The ways in which the financializations of development operate worldwide reveal a series of consequences for development on the ground. We shall mention four that are closely connected.

First, financial actors have become powerful development agents over the last three decades. With the commodification of development issues (e.g. health care) and the reframing of welfare states by financialization since the 1990s, the influence of financial actors, such as DFIs, public and private banks, along with large telecommunication and payment service companies in development governance, has substantially increased. This reconfiguration of actors and roles in development governance has led to a significant power shift. Public policies and donors have become less influential than the decisions and policies of private investors when implementing development programs. In turn, this shift often results in tensions with other development agents, such as NGOs, which face new challenges in the selection of service providers and project partners. Interestingly, powerful financial actors do not seek to undermine the role of the state as a development provider. Instead, they aim to work with the state as a development agent, advocating for regulations that meet their own goals (i.e. profit-making, risk reduction, business expansion). Indeed, the changing role and growing influence of financial actors as development agents are very much connected to private sector development strategies (e.g. financialized solutions for poverty reduction, financial inclusion or health care provision).

Second, the so-called financial gap narrative works as both a justification and an instrument of financialization. Widely disseminated by a broad array of state and non-state development agents, this narrative essentially claims that the implementation of development programs and the realization of development goals are not possible without leveraging financial resources, especially from private investors. Consequently, development policies and programs are more welcoming to private sector investors and provide, for example, financial resources or other supportive and de-risking tools and services to private sector actors.

Third, financializing development involves the redefinition of development as a normative concept and objective. Instead of a systemic, structural problem, development is conceived through the lens of investors, and development initiatives, programs and policies are designed to fit the norms and practices of financial actors. Examples range from defining poverty as a problem related to individual decision-making (e.g. in financial literacy programs), to the understanding of financial inclusion as a precondition of development, if not a development goal in itself. According to this logic, vulnerable people are perceived as consumers or investees, instead of citizens. We argue that the redefinition of development according to investors' perspectives serves mainly the goals of the investors rather than the needs of the recipients. Indeed, the needs of the people that are addressed are mainly those that can be met through marketized and private solutions, and what financial actors propose is often not the most effective way to treat the pressing social problems in education, health, etc.

Finally, the ways in which the financializations of development operate worldwide reveal that the main outcome is the attainment of financial goals (e.g. favorable regulations, increased profits, lower risks) at the expense of development goals (e.g. improved income, health care, and education). In other words, while financialization changes the meaning of development, and thereby the design and implementation of development programs and policies according to the rules of finance, people on the ground hardly benefit from this. Through financialization, social capitalism imposes new demands on vulnerable people rather than meeting their demands. That is, instead of meeting local development demands (e.g. food security, access to public services), financialization prioritizes the perspectives of wealthy social actors (e.g. global finance actors, large corporations, agribusiness). In fact, those who should benefit from financialized development programs often neither participate in their design, nor benefit from the solutions proposed by foreign, developed actors. Quite the contrary, with no development on the ground and the transfer of risks from global, powerful stakeholders to vulnerable local actors, persistent structural problems remain (e.g. poverty, poor public services) while others arise (e.g. over-indebtedness, deterioration of public systems).

## Alternatives to financializations of development

Billions of people in the Global South still suffer from poor living conditions, insufficient access to housing, health care, education and other basic infrastructure and services. The case studies assembled in this book demonstrate that simply trying to channel private funds into the field of development does not improve this situation. Considering the numerous negative, or at least ambivalent, consequences of financialized development policies addressed above, the question arises: What are the alternative ways of dealing with the existing and growing development needs worldwide?

Different ideas come to mind. We briefly mention some of them, not necessarily because they could easily replace financialized development policies, but because these options let us clearly see the complexities of development problems in an unequal and unjust world. As we have shown, financialization eventually takes place due to the prevalence of certain forms of *problematization* that frame what is conceivable. As a result, many alternative reflections and solutions are disregarded from the outset. Of course, many actors in development projects are not unaware of these issues, but the dominant ideological frameworks make it difficult to tackle them.

The first point concerns the role played by the states of the Global South. Many of our case studies have shown reconfigurations of their role. They are asked to reorient their efforts toward guarantees and favorable regulatory settings for the financialized engagement of actors from the Global North; de-risking investments and creating the conditions for a widely bancarized, monetarized and financialized population of prospective recipients. We do not see passive or incapable states here, but states that go through a lot of effort to attract investors for development projects. In many of the discussed case studies, one wonders why the states are not involved in a more direct way that would make unnecessary the involvement of a huge ecology of actors from the world of finance. Financialization involves the privatization of profits and the socialization of risks and costs.

An alternative to financialization would probably start by bringing the state back as a prominent development agent (Calvert, 2005; Mazzucato, 2018; Williams, 2014) and the promotion of welfare states committed to the redistribution of wealth and provision of basic public services.

However, the adoption of non-financialized types of policies by states pre-supposes that the states are even able to do so and thus, reveals a whole new set of questions. If the local political staff has a strong responsibility in the choice of the policies conducted, the actors of the Global North who organize the development policies, or who own and manage the big companies operating in these countries, also bear an important part of it. This book focuses on the financialization of development policies and initiatives and has left aside the study of other financial circuits that should be brought back into the picture as alternatives.

First, we reason that the foreign currency indebtedness of the states of the South imposes on them the development of export agriculture and the exploitation of their natural resources to obtain foreign currency. But this debt is also a product of development finance; a consequence that we have left out of the picture until now. The yoke of debt prevents these countries from developing a public strategic autonomy (just as in the countries of the North, whose currencies are nevertheless more solid) (Lemoine, 2022; Pénet and Flores Zendejas, 2021; Streeck, 2014). Another way of dealing with financing development could therefore be to work, not on the additional indebtedness of countries, but on the cancellation of their debt (Hickel, 2017, Laskaridis et al., 2020; Toussaint, 2019).

The other essential financial flows for states that we have not yet mentioned is that of taxes (Morel and Palme, 2019; Obinger, 2021; Prasad and Deng, 2009). Here again, it would be important to question the portion of the profits made by the industrial and commercial multinationals of the North from their activities in the South that remains in these countries. The Corporate Social Responsibility (CSR) activities of the companies that they publicize widely, or the infrastructures that they build locally, essentially for their own activities, cannot compensate for deficient taxation (Durst, 2019). Increasing the capacity of states to raise taxes should therefore be a strategic priority. Constrained by both high levels of public debt and downward pressure from taxes, states are rendered impotent. Seen from this angle, many of the initiatives we have highlighted in this book act, at best, as patches that allow an oppressive system to continue and to be prolonged, especially since these patches are also often based on the same diptych of debt and exploitation.

Other non-directly financial issues must be brought into the equation. Indeed, some non-monetary and non-financial elements alter the conditions under which economies of the Global South try to survive. For example, trade regulations that define the access to or the blockage from markets reflect an age-long debate about negative and even deteriorating terms of trade for developing countries wishing to enter markets in the Global North (Hadass and Williamson, 2003). Another crucial set of regulations defines the terms of international mobility; the freedom to cross borders and to stay, temporarily or longer, in other countries (Casey, 2010). A more accessible policy of immigration could open more development options.

Finally, the concept of development itself might be open for reconsideration. While the UN Sustainable Development Goals envision a world in which the global human population thrives at a level of well-being that can be sustained for future generations, this concept is based on a growth-focused model. In the past, scholarly positions suggesting de-growth models of development (e.g. Meadows et al., 1972) have been ridiculed and marginalized. However, quite recently, the academic and political debates on alternatives to growth-based development models have gained momentum. One example is the Intergovernmental Panel on Climate Change (IPCC) which, for the first time in its long history of providing a global risk assessment on anthropogenic climate change, has indicated that development based on a growth model might not be in line with the globally endorsed goal to keep the world's temperature rise well below 2°C (Schipper et al., 2022). We argue that a de-growth perspective would also reconfigure the basis for non-financialized development solutions (see, for instance, Hickel, 2021; Kallis et al., 2018; Koch, 2020).

As the case studies presented in this book indicate, financializations of development seem to be diffusing worldwide. And what is documented here for Global South countries is also relevant for developed countries (see, for example, Mertens, Thiemann and Volbering, 2021; Chiapello and Knoll, 2020). Exploring alternatives to financialization processes goes obviously well beyond the scope of the book, but it is a way to highlight that financializing development programs and policies are not an unsurpassable horizon. Exploring non-financialized development solutions helps expand the scope of possibilities for a real sustainable development.

## References

Calvert, P. (2005) 'Changing Notions of Development: Bringing the State Back in,' in Haynes, J. (ed.), *Palgrave Advances in Development Studies.* New York: Palgrave Macmillan, pp. 47–64.

Casey, J.P. (2010) 'Open Borders: Absurd Chimera or Inevitable Future Policy?,' *International Migration*, 48(5), pp. 14–62. DOI: 10.1111/j.1468-2435.2009.00514.x

Chiapello, E. (2019) 'The Work of Financialisation,' in Lenglet, M., Chambost, I. and Tadjeddine, Y. (eds.), *The Making of Finance.* London: Routledge, pp. 192–200.

Chiapello, E. (2020) 'Financialization as a Socio-Technical Process,' in Mader, P., Mertens, D. and van der Zwan, N. (eds.), *The Routledge International Handbook of Financialization.* London: Routledge, pp. 81–91.

Chiapello, E. and Knoll, L. (2020) 'Social Finance and Impact Investing. Governing Welfare in the Era of Financialization,' *Historical Social Research/Historische Sozialforschung*, 45(3), pp. 7–30. DOI: 10.12759/hsr.45.2020.3.7-30.

Durst, M.C. (2019) *Taxing Multinational Business in Lower Income Countries: Economics, Politics and Social Responsibility.* Brighton: IDS.

Epstein, G.A. (ed.) (2005) *Financialization and the World Economy.* Cheltenham, UK: Edward Elgar Publishing.

Gabor, D. (2021) 'The Wall Street Consensus,' *Development and Change*, 52, pp. 429–459. DOI: 10.1111/dech.12645.

Hadass, Y.S. and Williamson, J.G. (2003) 'Terms-of-Trade Shocks and Economic Performance, 1870–1940: Prebisch and Singer Revisited,' *Economic Development and Cultural Change*, 51(3), pp. 629–656. DOI:10.1086/375259

Hickel, J. (2017) *The Divide: A Brief Guide to Global Inequality and Its Solutions.* New York: Random House.

Hickel, J. (2021) 'The Anti-Colonial Politics of Degrowth,' *Political Geography*, 88. DOI: 10.1016/j.polgeo.2021.102404.

Kallis, G., Kostakis, V., Lange, S., Muraca, B., Paulson, S. and Schmelzer, M. (2018) 'Research on Degrowth,' *Annual Review of Environment and Resources*, 43, pp. 291–316. DOI: 10.1146/annurev-environ-102017-025941

Kamath, R., and Joseph, N. (2023) 'From social workers to proxy-creditors to bank tellers: financialization in the work of microcredit field staff in a South Indian town' in *Financializations of Development: Global Games and Local Experiments*, this volume.

Koch, M. (2020) 'Structure, Action and Change: A Bourdieusian Perspective on the Pre-conditions for a Degrowth Transition,' *Sustainability: Science, Practice and Policy*, 16(1), pp. 4–14. DOI: 10.1080/15487733.2020.1754693

Laskaridis, C., et al. (2020) 'Historical Perspectives on Current Struggles against Illegitimate Debt,' in Mader, P., et al. (eds.), *The Routledge International Handbook of Financialization*. Abingdon: Routledge, pp. 482–493.

Lemoine, B. (2022) *La démocratie disciplinée par la dette.* Paris: La Découverte.

Mader, P. (2015) *The Political Economy of Microfinance. Financialising Poverty.* London: Palgrave Macmillan.

Mazzucato, M. (2018) 'The Entrepreneurial State: Socializing Both Risks and Rewards,' *Real-World Economics Review*, 84, pp. 201–217.

Meadows, D.H., Meadows, D.L., Randers, J. and Behrens, W.W. (1972) *The Limits to Growth: A Report for the Club of Rome's Project on the Predicament of Mankind.* New York: Universe Books.

Mertens, D., Thiemann, M. and Volberding, P. (eds.) (2021). *The Reinvention of Development Banking in the European Union: Industrial Policy in the Single Market and the Emergence of a Field.* Oxford: Oxford University Press.

Morel, N. and Palme, J. (2019) 'Financing the Welfare State and the Politics of Taxation,' in Greve, B. (ed.), *The Routledge Handbook of the Welfare State*, 2nd ed. London: Routledge, pp. 467–476.

Obinger, H. (2021) 'Social Expenditure and Welfare State Financing,' in Béland, D., Morgan, K.J., Obinger, H. and Pierson, C. (eds.), *The Oxford Handbook of the Welfare State*, 2nd ed. Oxford: Oxford University Press, pp. 453–472.

Pénet, P. and Flores Zendejas, J. (eds.) (2021) *Sovereign Debt Diplomacies: Rethinking Sovereign Debt from Colonial Empires to Hegemony.* Oxford: Oxford University Press.

Prasad, M. and Deng, Y. (2009) 'Taxation and Worlds of Welfare,' *Socio-Economic Revue*, 7, pp. 431–457. DOI: 10.1093/ser/mwp005

Schipper, E.L.F., et al. (2022) 'Climate Resilient Development Pathways,' in Pörtner, H.-O., et al. (eds.), *Climate Change 2022: Impacts, Adaptation, and Vulnerability.* Contribution of Working Group II to the Sixth Assessment Report of the Intergovernmental Panel on Climate Change. Cambridge University Press. [online]. Available at: https://www.ipcc.ch/report/ar6/wg2/.

Streeck, W. (2014) *Buying Time: The Delayed Crisis of Democratic Capitalism.* New York: Verso Books.

Thévenot, L. (1984) 'Rules and Implement: Investment in Forms,' *Social Science Information*, 23(1), pp. 1–45. DOI: 10.1177/053901884023001001

Toussaint, E. (2019) *Le système dette: histoire des dettes souveraines et de leur répudiation.* Paris: Les Liens qui libèrent.

Williams, M. (2014) *The End of Development State?* New York: Routledge.

# INDEX

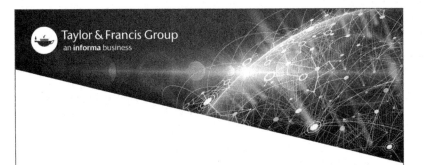

Printed in the United States
by Baker & Taylor Publisher Services